Fourth Workshop on NLP for Similar Languages, Varieties and Dialects (VarDial 2017)

Valencia, Spain
3 April 2017

ISBN: 978-1-5108-3872-7

Preface

VarDial is a well-established series of workshops held annually and co-located with top-tier international NLP conferences. Previous editions of VarDial were VarDial'2014, which was co-located with COLING'2014, LT4VarDial'2015, which was held together with RANLP'2015, and finally VarDial'2016 co-located with COLING'2016. The great interest of the community has made possible the fourth edition of the Workshop on NLP for Similar Languages, Varieties and Dialects (VarDial'2017), co-located with EACL'2017 in Valencia, Spain.

The VarDial series has attracted researchers working on a wide range of topics related to linguistic variation such as building and adapting language resources for language varieties and dialects, creating language technology and applications that make use of language closeness, and exploiting existing resources in a related language or a language variety.

We believe that this is a very timely series of workshops, as research in language variation is much needed in today's multi-lingual world, where several closely-related languages, language varieties, and dialects are in daily use, not only as spoken colloquial language but also in written media, e.g., in SMS, chats, and social networks. Language resources for these varieties and dialects are sparse and extending them could be very labor-intensive. Yet, these efforts can often be reduced by making use of pre-existing resources and tools for related, resource-richer languages.

As part of the workshop, we organized the first VarDial evaluation campaign with four shared tasks: Discriminating between Similar Languages (DSL), Arabic Dialect Identification (ADI), German Dialect Identification (GDI), and Cross-Lingual Parsing (CLP). The campaign received a very positive response from the community. A total of 28 teams subscribed to participate in the four shared tasks, 19 of them submitted official runs, and 15 of the latter also wrote system description papers, which appear in this volume along with a shared task report by the task organizers.

We further received 14 regular VarDial workshop papers, and we selected nine of them to be presented at the workshop. The papers that appear in this volume reflect the wide range of interests related to language variation. We include papers applying NLP tools to perform dialect analysis, to study mutual intelligibility and diatopic variation in historical corpora, as well as core NLP tasks and applications such as dialect and similar language identification, adaptation of POS taggers, and machine translation between similar languages and dialects.

We take the opportunity to thank the VarDial program committee and the additional reviewers for their thorough reviews. We further thank the VarDial Evaluation Campaign participants, as well as the participants with regular research papers, for the valuable feedback and discussions.

The organizers: Preslav Nakov, Marcos Zampieri, Nikola Ljubešić, Jörg Tiedemann, Shervin Malmasi, and Ahmed Ali

Workshop Organisers

Preslav Nakov (Qatar Computing Research Institute, HBKU, Qatar)
Marcos Zampieri (University of Cologne, Germany)
Nikola Ljubešić (Jožef Stefan Institute, Slovenia, and University of Zagreb, Croatia)
Jörg Tiedemann (University of Helsinki, Finland)
Shervin Malmasi (Harvard Medical School, USA)
Ahmed Ali (Qatar Computing Research Institute, HBKU, Qatar)

VarDial Evaluation Campaign - Shared Task Organisers

Marcos Zampieri (University of Cologne, Germany)
Preslav Nakov (Qatar Computing Research Institute, HBKU, Qatar)
Shervin Malmasi (Harvard Medical School, USA)
Nikola Ljubešić (Jožef Stefan Institute, Slovenia, and University of Zagreb, Croatia)
Jörg Tiedemann (University of Helsinki, Finland)
Ahmed Ali (Qatar Computing Research Institute, HBKU, Qatar)
Yves Scherrer (University of Geneva, Switzerland)
Noëmi Aepli (University of Zürich, Switzerland)

Programme Committee

Željko Agić (IT University of Copenhagen, Denmark)
Cesar Aguilar (Pontifical Catholic University of Chile, Chile)
Laura Alonso y Alemany (University of Cordoba, Argentina)
Tim Baldwin (The University of Melbourne, Australia)
Jorge Baptista (University of Algarve and INESC-ID, Portugal)
Eckhard Bick (University of Southern Denmark, Denmark)
Francis Bond (Nanyang Technological University, Singapore)
Aoife Cahill (Educational Testing Service, USA)
David Chiang (University of Notre Dame, USA)
Paul Cook (University of New Brunswick, Canada)
Marta Costa-Jussà (Universitat Politècnica de Catalunya, Spain)
Jon Dehdari (Saarland University and DFKI, Germany)
Liviu Dinu (University of Bucharest, Romania)
Stefanie Dipper (Ruhr University Bochum, Germany)
Sascha Diwersy (University of Montpellier, France)
Mark Dras (Macquarie University, Australia)
Tomaž Erjavec (Jožef Stefan Institute, Slovenia)
Mikel L. Forcada (Universitat d'Alacant, Spain)
Binyam Gebrekidan Gebre (Phillips Research, Holland)
Cyril Goutte (National Research Council, Canada)
Nizar Habash (New York University Abu Dhabi, UAE)
Chu-Ren Huang (Hong Kong Polytechnic University, Hong Kong)
Jeremy Jancsary (Nuance Communications, Austria)
Lung-Hao Lee (National Taiwan Normal University, Taiwan)
Marco Lui (Rome2Rio Ltd., Australia)

Teresa Lynn (Dublin City University, Ireland)
John Nerbonne (University of Groningen, Netherlands and University of Freiburg, Germany)
Graham Neubig (Nara Institute of Science and Technology, Japan)
Kemal Oflazer (Carnegie-Mellon University in Qatar, Qatar)
Maciej Ogrodniczuk (Institute of Computer Science, Polish Academy of Sciences, Poland)
Petya Osenova (Bulgarian Academy of Sciences, Bulgaria)
Santanu Pal (Saarland University, Germany)
Reinhard Rapp (University of Mainz, Germany and University of Aix-Marsaille, France)
Paolo Rosso (Polytechnic University of Valencia, Spain)
Fatiha Sadat (Université du Québec à Montréal, Canada)
Tanja Samardžić (University of Zürich, Switzerland)
Felipe Sánchez Martínez (Universitat d'Alacant, Spain)
Kevin Scannell (Saint Louis University, USA)
Yves Scherrer (University of Geneva, Switzerland)
Serge Sharoff (University of Leeds, UK)
Kiril Simov (Bulgarian Academy of Sciences, Bulgaria)
Milena Slavcheva (Bulgarian Academy of Sciences, Bulgaria)
Marko Tadić (University of Zagreb, Croatia)
Liling Tan (Rakuten Institute of Technology, Singapore)
Elke Teich (Saarland University, Germany)
Joel Tetreault (Grammarly, USA)
Francis Tyers (UiT Norgga árktalaš universitehta, Norway)
Duško Vitas (University of Belgrade, Serbia)
Taro Watanabe (Google Inc., Japan)
Pidong Wang (Machine Zone Inc., USA)

Additional Reviewers

Yves Bestgen (Université Catholique de Louvain, Belgium)
Johannes Bjerva (University of Groningen, Netherlands)
Alina Maria Ciobanu (University of Bucharest, Romania)
Çağrı Çöltekin (University of Tübingen, Germany)
Marcelo Criscuolo (University of São Paulo, Brazil)
Abualsoud Hanani (Birzeit University, Palestine)
Pablo Gamallo (University of Santiago de Compostela, Spain)
Helena Gómez-Adorno (Instituto Politécnico Nacional, Mexico)
Radu Tudor Ionescu (University of Bucharest, Romania)
Tommi Jauhiainen (University of Helsinki, Finland)
Martin Kroon (University of Groningen, Netherlands)
Peter Makavorov (University of Zürich, Switzerland)
David Marecek (Charles University Prague, Czech Republic)
Ilia Markov (Instituto Politecnico Nacional, Mexico)
Maria Medvedeva (Saarland University, Germany)
Sergiu Nisioi (University of Bucharest, Romania)
Stephen Taylor (Fitchburg State University, USA)
Zdeněk Žabokrtský (Charles University Prague, Czech Republic)
Daniel Zeman (Charles University Prague, Czech Republic)

Table of Contents

Conference Program

Monday, April 3, 2017

9:30–9:40   *Opening*

09:40–10:00   *Findings of the VarDial Evaluation Campaign 2017*
Marcos Zampieri, Shervin Malmasi, Nikola Ljubešić, Preslav Nakov, Ahmed Ali, Jörg Tiedemann, Yves Scherrer and Noëmi Aepli

10:00–10:30   *Dialectometric analysis of language variation in Twitter*
Gonzalo Donoso and David Sanchez

10:30–11:00   *Computational analysis of Gondi dialects*
Taraka Rama, Çağrı Çöltekin and Pavel Sofroniev

11.00–11.30   *Coffee break*

11:30–12:00   *Investigating Diatopic Variation in a Historical Corpus*
Stefanie Dipper and Sandra Waldenberger

12.00–13.00   **Invited talk - Paolo Rosso (Polytechnic University of Valencia, Spain)**

    Author Profiling at PAN: from Age and Gender Identification to Language Variety Identification (invited talk)
Paolo Rosso

13.00–14.30   *Lunch*

Tübingen system in VarDial 2017 shared task: experiments with language identification and cross-lingual parsing
Çağrı Çöltekin and Taraka Rama

When Sparse Traditional Models Outperform Dense Neural Networks: the Curious Case of Discriminating between Similar Languages
Maria Medvedeva, Martin Kroon and Barbara Plank

German Dialect Identification in Interview Transcriptions
Shervin Malmasi and Marcos Zampieri

CLUZH at VarDial GDI 2017: Testing a Variety of Machine Learning Tools for the Classification of Swiss German Dialects
Simon Clematide and Peter Makarov

Arabic Dialect Identification Using iVectors and ASR Transcripts
Shervin Malmasi and Marcos Zampieri

Discriminating between Similar Languages using Weighted Subword Features
Adrien Barbaresi

16.00–16.30   ***Coffee break***

16:30–17:00   *Exploring Lexical and Syntactic Features for Language Variety Identification*
Chris van der Lee and Antal van den Bosch

17:00–17:30   *Learning to Identify Arabic and German Dialects using Multiple Kernels*
Radu Tudor Ionescu and Andrei Butnaru

17:30–18:00   *Slavic Forest, Norwegian Wood*
Rudolf Rosa, Daniel Zeman, David Mareček and Zdeněk Žabokrtský

18.00   ***Closing remarks***

Findings of the VarDial Evaluation Campaign 2017

Marcos Zampieri[1], Shervin Malmasi[2,3], Nikola Ljubešić[4,5], Preslav Nakov[6]
Ahmed Ali[6], Jörg Tiedemann[7], Yves Scherrer[8], Noëmi Aepli[9]

[1]University of Cologne, Germany, [2]Harvard Medical School, USA
[3]Macquarie University, Australia, [4]University of Zagreb, Croatia
[5]Jožef Stefan Institute, Slovenia, [6]Qatar Computing Research Institute, HBKU, Qatar
[7]University of Helsinki, Finland, [8]University of Geneva, Switzerland
[9]University of Zurich, Switzerland

Abstract

We present the results of the VarDial Evaluation Campaign on Natural Language Processing (NLP) for Similar Languages, Varieties and Dialects, which we organized as part of the fourth edition of the VarDial workshop at EACL'2017. This year, we included four shared tasks: Discriminating between Similar Languages (DSL), Arabic Dialect Identification (ADI), German Dialect Identification (GDI), and Cross-lingual Dependency Parsing (CLP). A total of 19 teams submitted runs across the four tasks, and 15 of them wrote system description papers.

1 Introduction

The VarDial Evaluation Campaign targets Natural Language Processing (NLP) for similar languages, varieties and dialects, and it was organized within the scope of the VarDial'2017 workshop. The campaign is an evolution of the DSL shared tasks, which were organized as part of the previous editions of the VarDial workshop (Zampieri et al., 2014; Zampieri et al., 2015b; Malmasi et al., 2016), and which have focused on the discrimination of similar languages and language varieties as well as on dialect identification.

Since the first DSL challenge, we have observed a substantial increase in the interest from the community. The 2016 edition of the DSL task, which included a sub-task on Arabic Dialect Identification, attracted a notably larger number of participants compared to the previous two editions. Thus, we decided to further extend the scope of the shared task, turning it into a more comprehensive evaluation campaign with several independent shared tasks, which included but were not limited to dialect and similar language identification.

1.1 Shared Tasks

The VarDial Evaluation Campaign 2017 included four tasks:

Discriminating between Similar Languages (DSL): This was the fourth iteration of the multilingual similar language and language variety identification task. The goal was to recognize the language of short excerpts of texts extracted from newspapers. This included several similar languages and language varieties: Bosnian, Croatian, and Serbian; Malay and Indonesian; Persian and Dari; Canadian and Hexagonal French; Brazilian and European Portuguese; Argentinian, Peninsular, and Peruvian Spanish.

Arabic Dialect Identification (ADI): This was the second iteration of the ADI task, which was organized as a sub-task of the DSL task in 2016 (Malmasi et al., 2016). The goal was to recognize the dialect of speech transcripts along with acoustic features. The following Arabic dialects were included: Egyptian, Gulf, Levantine, North-African, and Modern Standard Arabic (MSA).

German Dialect Identification (GDI): This task included Swiss German dialects from four areas: Basel, Bern, Lucerne, and Zurich. We provided manually annotated speech transcripts for all dialect areas; unlike ADI, we provided no acoustic data for this task.

Cross-lingual Dependency Parsing (CLP): The task is to parse some *target language* (TL) without annotated training data for that language but given annotated data for a closely related-language(s), called *source language* (SL). We included the following language pairs: Croatian (TL) – Slovenian (SL), Slovak (TL) – Czech (SL), Norwegian (TL) – Danish, and Norwegian (TL) – Swedish (SL). Note that the latter two pairs include a triple of related languages.

1

Proceedings of the Fourth Workshop on NLP for Similar Languages, Varieties and Dialects, pages 1–15,
Valencia, Spain, April 3, 2017. ©2017 Association for Computational Linguistics

Team	DSL	ADI	GDI	CLP	System Description Paper
ahaqst		✓	✓		(Hanani et al., 2017)
bayesline	✓				–
CECL	✓		✓		(Bestgen, 2017)
cic_ualg	✓				(Gómez-Adorno et al., 2017)
Citius_Ixa_Imaxin	✓		✓		(Gamallo et al., 2017)
CLUZH			✓		(Clematide and Makarov, 2017)
CUNI				✓	(Rosa et al., 2017)
deepCybErNet	✓	✓	✓		–
gauge	✓				–
Helsinki-CLP				✓	(Tiedemann, 2017)
MAZA (ADI)		✓			(Malmasi and Zampieri, 2017a)
MAZA (GDI)			✓		(Malmasi and Zampieri, 2017b)
mm_lct	✓				(Medvedeva et al., 2017)
qcri_mit		✓	✓		–
SUKI	✓				(Jauhiainen et al., 2017)
timeflow	✓				(Criscuolo and Aluisio, 2017)
tubasfs	✓	✓	✓	✓	(Çöltekin and Rama, 2017)
unibuckernel		✓	✓		(Ionescu and Butnaru, 2017)
XAC_Bayesline	✓		✓		(Barbaresi, 2017)
Total	**11**	**6**	**10**	**3**	**15**

Table 1: The teams that participated in the VarDial'2017 Evaluation Campaign.

1.2 Participating Teams

The VarDial Evaluation Campaign received a positive response from the research community: a total of 26 teams enrolled to participate, 19 teams eventually submitted systems, and 15 of them wrote system description papers. Table 1 lists the participating teams and the shared tasks they took part in.[1] We can see that each task received multiple submissions, ranging from 3 for CLP to 11 for DSL. Below we describe the individual tasks.

2 Discriminating between Similar Languages (DSL)

Discriminating between similar languages is one of the main challenges faced by language identification systems. Since 2014 the DSL shared task has been organized every year providing scholars and developers with an opportunity to evaluate language identification methods using a standard dataset and evaluation methodology. Albeit related to other shared tasks such as the 2014 *Tweet-LID* challenge (Zubiaga et al., 2014) and the 2016 shared task on Geolocation Prediction (Han et al., 2016), the DSL shared task continues to be the only shared task focusing on the discrimination between similar languages and language varieties.

The fourth edition of the DSL shared task was motivated by the success of the previous editions and by the growing interest of the research community in the identification of dialects and similar languages, as evidenced by recent publications (Xu et al., 2016; Radford and Gallé, 2016; Castro et al., 2016). We also saw the number of system submissions to the DSL challenge grow from 8 in 2014 to 10 in 2015 and then to 17 in 2016.[2]

The 2015 and the 2016 editions of the DSL task focused on one under-explored aspect of the task in order to keep it interesting and challenging.

In 2015 (Zampieri et al., 2015b), we investigated the extent to which named entities influenced system performance. Obviously, newspapers from Brazil mention *Rio de Janeiro* more often than those in Portugal do, and Argentinian newspapers talk more about *Buenos Aires* than those in Spain. In order to investigate this aspect, in 2015 we provided participants with two test sets, one containing the original unmodified texts (test set A) and another one containing texts with capitalized named entities substituted by placeholders (test set B). Eventually, we observed that the impact of named entities was not as sizable as we had anticipated.

---

[1] The MAZA team submitted two separate papers: one for each task they participated in.

[2] This number does not include the submissions to the Arabic Dialect Identification subtask of DSL in 2016.

At DSL 2015, the four best systems, MAC (Malmasi and Dras, 2015b), MMS (Zampieri et al., 2015a), NRC (Goutte and Léger, 2015), and SUKI (Jauhiainen et al., 2015) performed similarly on test set B compared to test set A: in the closed training setting, where the systems were trained only using the training data provided by the DSL organizers, their accuracy dropped from 95.54 to 94.01, from 95.24 to 92.78, from 95.24 to 93.01, and from 94.67 to 93.02, respectively.[3]

Finally, inspired by recent work on language identification of user-generated content (Ljubešić and Kranjčić, 2015; Abainia et al., 2016), in the DSL 2016 task (Malmasi et al., 2016), we looked at how systems perform on discriminating between similar languages and language varieties across different domains, an aspect highlighted by Lui and Cook (2013) and Lui (2014). For this purpose, we provided an out-of-domain test set containing manually annotated microblog posts written in Bosnian, Croatian, Serbian, Brazilian and European Portuguese.

2.1 Task Setup

We applied the methodology of Tan et al. (2014) in order to compile version 4.0 of the DSL Corpus Collection (DSLCC), which contains short excerpts of journalistic texts; we describe the corpus in detail in Section 2.2 below.

We first released the training and the development datasets, in which all instances were labeled with the correct language or language variety. One month later, the participants received an unlabeled test set, which they had to annotate with their system's prediction. The participating teams were allowed to use the DSLCC v4.0 corpus or any other dataset, and we had two types of training conditions.

- **Closed Training:** using only the corpora provided by the organizers (DSLCC v4.0);

- **Open Training:** using any additional data including previous versions of the DSLCC corpus.

For each kind of training, we allowed a maximum of three runs per team, i.e., six in total.

2.2 Dataset

The DSLCC v4.0[4] contains 22,000 short excerpts of news texts for each language or language variety divided into 20,000 texts for training (18,000 texts) and development (2,000 texts), and 2,000 texts for testing. It contains a total of 8.6 million tokens for training and over half a million tokens for testing. The fourteen languages included in the v4.0 grouped by similarity are Bosnian, Croatian, and Serbian; Malay and Indonesian; Persian and Dari; Canadian and Hexagonal French; Brazilian and European Portuguese; Argentinian, Peninsular, and Peruvian Spanish. In Table 2, we present the number of instances and the total number of documents and tokens we released for each language or language variety.

As indicated in Table 2, some languages were available in all previous versions of the DSLCC corpus (e.g., Bosnian, Croatian, and Serbian) or only in some of them (e.g., Canadian and Hexagonal French). As v4.0 is comparable to the previous versions of the DSLCC, this provided teams with more training data to use in the open training track.

Note that Peruvian Spanish, Persian, and Dari appear for the first time in the DSL task. However, they were previously included in language identification experiments: Peruvian Spanish was used in four-way classification together with texts from Argentina, Mexico, and Spain, for which an F1 of 0.876 was reported (Zampieri et al.,), and there were previous experiments in discriminating between Persian and Dari, which achieved 0.96 accuracy (Malmasi and Dras, 2015a).

2.3 Participants and Approaches

Twenty teams enrolled to participate in this edition of the DSL shared task and eleven of them submitted results. This represents a slight decrease in participation compared to the 2016 edition, which followed an uphill trend in participation since the first DSL organized in 2014. In our opinion, this slight decrease in participation does not represent less interest of the scientific community in the topic. Discriminating between similar languages and language varieties continues to be a vibrant research topic and the interest of the community is confirmed by the recent aforementioned publications (Xu et al., 2016; Radford and Gallé, 2016).

---

[3]For a comprehensive evaluation of the 2014 and 2015 editions of the DSL shared task see (Goutte et al., 2016).

[4]All versions of the DSLCC dataset are available at `http://ttg.uni-saarland.de/resources/DSLCC`

Language/Variety	Class	Train & Dev.		Test		Previous DSLCC		
		Instances	Tokens	Instances	Tokens	v1.0	v2.0/2.1	v3.0
Bosnian	bs	20,000	716,537	1,000	35,756	✓	✓	✓
Croatian	hr	20,000	845,639	1,000	42,774	✓	✓	✓
Serbian	sr	20,000	777,363	1,000	39,003	✓	✓	✓
Indonesian	id	20,000	800,639	1,000	39,954	✓	✓	✓
Malay	my	20,000	591,246	1,000	29,028	✓	✓	✓
Brazilian Portuguese	pt-BR	20,000	907,657	1,000	45,715	✓	✓	✓
European Portuguese	pt-PT	20,000	832,664	1,000	41,689	✓	✓	✓
Argentine Spanish	es-AR	20,000	939,425	1,000	42,392	✓	✓	✓
Castilian Spanish	es-ES	20,000	1,000,235	1,000	50,134	✓	✓	✓
Peruvian Spanish	es-PE	20,000	569,587	1,000	28,097			
Canadian French	fr-CA	20,000	712,467	1,000	36,121			✓
Hexagonal French	fr-FR	20,000	871,026	1,000	44,076			✓
Persian	fa-IR	20,000	824,640	1,000	41,900			
Dari	fa-AF	20,000	601,025	1,000	30,121			
Total		280,000	8,639,459	14,000	546,790			

Table 2: DSLCC v4.0: the languages included in the corpus grouped by similarity.

The slight decrease in participation is largely due to bad timing. Because of EACL-related deadlines, DSL 2017 was organized only a few months after the 2016 edition had finished, and the training data was released between Christmas and New Year's Eve. Moreover, this year the DSL was not a standalone task,[5] and it was part of a larger evaluation campaign. This has resulted in participants splitting between the four tasks we were running as part of the VarDial Evaluation Campaign. Yet, the DSL task attracted the highest number of participants, both new and returning.

We find a variety of computational approaches and features used by the participating systems. Below, we present a brief overview of each submission, ordered by the weighted F1 score. The interested reader can find more information about an individual system in the respective system description paper, which is referred to in the last column of Table 1.

- **CECL:** The system uses a two-step approach as in (Goutte et al., 2014). The first step identifies the language group using an SVM classifier with a linear kernel trained on character n-grams (1-4) that occur at least 100 times in the dataset weighted by Okapi BM25 (Robertson et al., 1995). The second step discriminates between each language within the group using a set of SVM classifiers trained on a variety of features such as character n-grams of various orders, global statistics such as proportion of capitalized letters, punctuation marks, and spaces, and finally POS tags modeled as n-grams (1-5) for French, Portuguese, and Spanish obtained by annotating the corpus using TreeTagger (Schmid, 1994).

- **mm_lct:** This team submitted three runs. Run 1 (their best) used seven SVM classifiers in two steps. First, one SVM classifier finds the language group, and then six individual SVM classifiers distinguish between the languages in each group. Run 2 used a linear-kernel SVM trained using word n-grams (1–2) and character n-grams (up to 6). Run 3 used a recurrent neural network (RNN).

- **XAC_Bayesline:** This system is a refined version of the Bayesline system (Tan et al., 2014), which was based on character n-grams and a Na"ive Bayes classifier. The system followed the work of the system submitted to the DSL 2016 by Barbaresi (2016).

- **tubasfs:** Following the success of tubasfs at DSL 2016 (Çöltekin and Rama, 2016), which was ranked first in the closed training track, this year's tubasfs submission used a linear SVM classifier. The system used both characters and words as features, and carefully optimized hyperparameters: n-gram size and margin/regularization parameter for SVM.

---

[5]In 2016 ADI and DSL were organized under the name *DSL shared task*, and ADI was run as a sub-task.

- **gauge:** This team submitted a total of three runs. Run 1 used an SVM classifier with character n-grams (2–6), run 2 (their best run) used logistic regression trained using character n-grams (1–6), and run 3 used hard voting of three systems: SVM, Logistic Regression, and Na"ive Bayes and character n-grams (2–6) as features.

- **cic_ualg:** This team submitted three runs. Runs 1 and 2 first predict the language group, and then discriminate between the languages within that group. The first step uses an SVM classifier with a combination of character 3–5-grams, typed character 3-grams, applying the character n-gram categories introduced by Sapkota et al. (2015), and word unigrams using TF-weighting. The second step uses the same features and different classifiers: SVMs + Multinominal Naïve Bayes (MNB) in run 1, and MNB in run 2 (which works best). Run 3 uses a single MNB classifier to discriminate between all fourteen languages.

- **SUKI:** This team's submission was based on the token-based backoff method used in SUKI's DSL submission in 2015 (Jauhiainen et al., 2015) and in 2016 (Jauhiainen et al., 2016). Run 1 used character 1–8-grams, and run 2 (their best) used loglike mapping (Brown, 2014) instead of relative frequencies, together with character 1–7-grams.

- **timeflow:** This system used a two-step classifier, as introduced by Goutte et al. (2014); a similar approach was used by some other teams. First, they used a Na"ive Bayes classifier trained on character n-grams to detect the language group. Then, they distinguished the language or language variety within the detected group using Convolutional Neural Networks (CNNs) with learned word embeddings and Multi-Layer Perceptron (MLP) with TF.IDF vectors.

- **Citius_Ixa_Imaxin:** This team was the only one to participate in both the open and the closed tracks. Their system was based on language model perplexity. The best performance in the closed training condition was obtained in run 1, which applied a voting scheme over 1–3 word n-gram and 5–7 characters n-grams.

- **bayesline:** This team participated with a Multinomial Naïve Bayes (MNB) classifier similar to that of Tan et al. (2014), with no special parameter tuning, as this system was initially intended to serve as an intelligent baseline for the task (but now it has matured into a competitive system). In their best-performing run 1, they relied primarily on character 4-grams as features. The feature sets they used were selected by a search strategy as proposed in (Scarton et al., 2015).

- **deepCybErNet:** This team approached the task using a neural network based on Long Short-Term Memory (LSTM). Neural networks have been successfully applied to several NLP tasks in recent years, but the results of the deepCybErNet team in the DSL and the GDI tasks in 2017, as well as in DSL 2016 (Malmasi et al., 2016), suggest that using neural networks is of limited use in our limited training data scenario: neural networks have many parameters to optimize, which takes a lot of training data, much more than what we provide here.

2.4 Results

Only one team, *Citius_Ixa_Imaxin*, submitted results to the open training track, achieving 0.9 accuracy. As there were no other submissions to compare against, in this section we report and discuss the results obtained by participants in the closed training track only.

Table 3 presents the best results obtained by the participating teams. We rank them based on their weighted F1 score (weighted by the number of examples in each class).

Rank	Team	F1 (weighted)
1	CECL	0.927
2	mm_lct	0.925
3	XAC_Bayesline	0.925
4	tubasfs	0.925
5	gauge	0.916
6	cic_ualg	0.915
7	SUKI	0.910
8	timeflow	0.907
9	Citius_Ixa_Imaxin	0.902
10	bayesline	0.889
11	deepCybErNet	0.202

Table 3: DSL task: closed submission results.

The *CECL* team achieved best performance: F1=0.927. It is followed by three teams, all tied with an F1 score of 0.925: namely *mm_lct*, *XAC_Bayesline*, and *tubasfs*.

The system description paper of *CECL* (Bestgen, 2017) provides some interesting insights about the DSL task. First, they found out that BM25 weighting, which was previously applied to native language identification (NLI) (Wang et al., 2016), worked better than using TF.IDF. They further highlighted the similarity between similar language identification and NLI as evidenced by a number of entries in the DSL task that are adaptations of systems used for NLI (Goutte et al., 2013; Gebre et al., 2013; Jarvis et al., 2013).

We observe that the variation in performance among the top ten teams is less than four percentage points. The team ranked last (eleventh) approached the task using LSTM and achieved an F1 score of 0.202. Unfortunately, they did not submit a system description paper, and thus we do not have much detail about their system. However, in the DSL 2016 task (Malmasi et al., 2016), neural network-based approaches already proved not to be very competitive for the task. See (Medvedeva et al., 2017) for a comparison between the performance of an SVM and an RNN approach for the DSL task.

2.5 Summary

The fourth edition of the DSL shared task allowed us once again to compare a variety of approaches for the task of discriminating between similar languages and language varieties using the same dataset: DSLCC v4.0. Even though previous versions of the DSLCC were available for use in an open track condition, all teams with the exception of *Citius_Ixa_Imaxin* chose to compete in the closed training track only.

The participants took advantage of the experience acquired in the previous editions of the DSL task, and in absolute terms achieved the highest scores among all four editions of the DSL challenge. *CECL* achieved 0.927 F1-score and *mm_lct*, *XAC_Bayesline*, and *tubasfs* achieved 0.925.

For the reasons discussed in Section 2.3, the participation in the DSL 2017 was slightly lower than in the 2016 edition, but it was still higher than in 2014 and 2015.

3 Arabic Dialect Identification (ADI)

The ADI task was introduced in 2016 (Malmasi et al., 2016), where it was run as a subtask of the DSL task. Unlike the DSL task, which is about text, the ADI task is based on speech transcripts, as Arabic dialects are mostly used in conversation. The ADI task asks to discriminate at the utterance level between five Arabic varieties, namely Modern Standard Arabic (MSA) and four Arabic dialects: Egyptian (EGY), Gulf (GLF), Levantine (LAV), and North African (NOR).

This year's edition of the task was motivated by the success of the 2016 edition and by the growing interest in dialectal Arabic in general. In 2016, we provided task participants with input speech transcripts generated using Arabic Large Vocabulary Speech Recognition (LVCSR) following the approach in (Ali et al., 2014a), from which we further extracted and provided lexical features. This year, we added a multi-model aspect to the task by further providing acoustic features.

3.1 Dataset

As we said above, this year we used both speech transcripts and acoustic features. The speech transcription was generated by a multi-dialect LVCSR system trained on 1,200+ speech hours for acoustic modeling and on 110+ million words for language modeling; more detail about the system, which is the winning system of the Arabic Multi-Genre Broadcast (MGB-2) challenge, can be found in (Khurana and Ali, 2016).

For the acoustic features, we released a 400-dimensional i-vector for each utterance. We extracted these i-vectors using Bottle Neck Features (BNF) trained on 60 hours of speech data; see (Ali et al., 2016) for detail.

The data for the ADI task comes from a multi-dialectal speech corpus created from high-quality broadcast, debate and discussion programs from Al Jazeera, and as such contains a combination of spontaneous and scripted speech (Wray and Ali, 2015). We collected the training dataset from the Broadcast News domain in four Arabic dialects (EGY, LAV, GLF, and NOR) as well as in MSA. The audio recordings were carried out at 16Khz. The recordings were then segmented in order to avoid speaker overlap, also removing any non-speech parts such as music and background noise; more detail about the training data can be found in (Bahari et al., 2014).

Dialect	Dialect	Training			Development			Testing		
		Ex.	Dur.	Words	Ex.	Dur.	Words	Ex.	Dur.	Words
Egyptian	EGY	3,093	12.4	76	298	2	11.0	302	2.0	11.6
Gulf	GLF	2,744	10.0	56	264	2	11.9	250	2.1	12.3
Levantine	LAV	2,851	10.3	53	330	2	10.3	334	2.0	10.9
MSA	MSA	2183	10.4	69	281	2	13.4	262	1.9	13.0
North African	NOR	2,954	10.5	38	351	2	9.9	344	2.1	10.3
Total		13,825	53.6	292	1524	10	56.5	1492	10.1	58.1

Table 4: The ADI data: examples (Ex.) in utterances, duration (Dur.) in hours, and words in 1000s.

Although the test and the development datasets came from the same broadcast domain, the recording setup was different from the training data. We downloaded the test and the development data directly from the high-quality video server for Al Jazeera (brightcove) over a period between July 2104 and January 2015, as part of QCRI's Advanced Transcription Service (QATS) (Ali et al., 2014b). In addition to the lexical and the acoustic features, we also released the audio files.[6] Table 4 shows some statistics about the ADI training, development and testing datasets.

3.2 Participants and Approaches

We received six submissions for the ADI task, all for the closed training condition. The teams below are sorted according to their performance on the test dataset.

- **unibuckernel:** This team submitted two runs. Run 1 was a Kernel Ridge Regression (KRR) classifier trained on the sum of a blended presence bits kernel based on 3–5-grams, a blended intersection kernel based on 3–7-grams, a kernel based on Local Rank Distance (LRD) with n-grams of 3 to 7 characters, and a quadratic RBF kernel based on i-vectors. This setup achieved an F1 of 0.642 on the development set, and 0.763 on the test set. Run 2 was a Kernel Discriminant Analysis (KDA) classifier trained on the sum of a blended presence bits kernel using 3–5-grams, a blended intersection kernel based on 3–7-grams, a kernel based on LRD with 3 to 7 characters, and a quadratic RBF kernel based on i-vectors. This setup achieved an F1 of 0.75 on the test set. More detail can be found in (Ionescu and Butnaru, 2017).

- **MAZA:** This team submitted three runs. Run 1 was a voting ensemble (F1=0.72), run 2 was a mean probability ensemble (F1=0.67), and run 3 was a meta classifier (F1=0.61). They used character 1–8-grams, word unigrams, and i-vectors. More detail about the system can be found in (Malmasi and Zampieri, 2017a).

- **tubasfs:** This team submitted two runs. Run 1 used a linear SVM with words and i-vectors, achieving an F1 of 0.70. Run 2 only used word features, which yielded an F1 of 0.57. More detail about the system can be found in (Çöltekin and Rama, 2017).

- **ahaqst:** This team submitted three runs. Run 1 used a focal multiclass model to combine the outputs of a word-based SVM multiclass model, and an i-vector-based SVM multiclass model, achieving an F1 of 0.63. Run 2 combined Na"ive Bayes with multinomial distribution, SVM with a Radial Basis Function (RBF) kernel, logistic regression, and Random Forests with 300 trees, achieving an F1 of 0.31. Run 3 combined five systems, which used WAV files only for recognizing Arabic dialects, i-Vectors plus Gaussian Mixture Model-Universal Background Model (GMM-UBM) plus phonotactic plus GMM tokenization (256 bigrams and 20,148 unigrams), achieving an F1 of 0.59. More detail about their system can be found in (Hanani et al., 2017).

- **qcri_mit:** This team submitted three runs. Run 1 combined (*i*) normalized scores from an SVM model trained on Latent Dirichlet Allocation (LDA) i-vectors (down to a 4-dimensional vector) with (*ii*) an SVM classifier trained on character 1–4-grams, achieving an F1 score of 0.616. Run 2 combined (*i*) an SVM using LDA with Within-Class Covariance Normalization (WCCN) i-vector with (*ii*) an SVM trained on count-based bag of character 2–6-grams, achieving an F1 of 0.615. Run 3 combined (*i*) an SVM model using LDA with WCCN i-vector (as in Run 2) with (*ii*) an SVM model trained on count bag of characters 2–4-grams, which yielded an F1 of 0.612.

- **deepCybErNet:** This team submitted two runs. Run 1 adopted a Bi-LSTM architecture using the lexical features, and achieved an F1 score of 0.208, while run 2 used the i-vector features and achieved an F1 of 0.574.

3.3 Results

Table 5 shows the evaluation results for the ADI task. Note that those participants who had used the development data for training their models obtained substantial gains, e.g., the winning system *unibuckernel* achieved an F1 of 0.763. However, this same system would have scored only 0.611, had they trained on the training data only. We attribute this to both the development and the testing data coming from the recording setup, and that is why using the i-vectors particularity has helped to model the channel, not only the dialect.

Rank	Team	F1 (weighted)
1	unibuckernel	0.763
2	MAZA	0.717
3	tubasfs	0.697
4	ahaqst	0.628
5	qcrimit	0.616
6	deepCybErNet	0.574

Table 5: ADI task: closed submission results.

3.4 Summary

This year's ADI task was very successful, as for the first time in VarDial the participants were provided with acoustic features. Indeed, as we have seen above, the i-vectors were widely used by the participating teams. Most participants took advantage of the fact that the development data came from the same recording setup as the testing data, which has boosted their results. Moreover, one team used the raw audio files. In the future, we plan another iteration of the task, where we would add phonotactic features and phoneme duration.

4 German Dialect Identification (GDI)

This year, we introduced a new dialectal area, which focused on German dialects of Switzerland. Indeed, the German-speaking part of Switzerland is characterized by the widespread use of dialects in everyday communication, and by a large number of different dialects and dialectal areas.

There have been two major approaches to Swiss German dialect identification in the literature. The *corpus-based approach* predicts the dialect of any text fragment extracted from a corpus (Scherrer and Rambow, 2010; Hollenstein and Aepli, 2015). The *dialectological approach* tries to identify a small set of distinguishing dialectal features, which are then elicited interactively from the user in order to identify his or her dialect (Leemann et al., 2016). In this task, we adopt a corpus-based approach, and we develop a new dataset for this.

4.1 Dataset

We extracted the training and the test datasets from the ArchiMob corpus of Spoken Swiss German (Samardžić et al., 2016). The current release of the corpus contains transcriptions of 34 oral history interviews with informants speaking different Swiss German dialects.

Each interview was transcribed by one of four transcribers, using the writing system "Schwyzertütschi Dialäktschrift" proposed by Dieth (1986). The transcription is expected to show the phonetic properties of the variety, but in a way that is legible for everybody who is familiar with the standard German orthography. Although its objective is to keep track of the pronunciation, Dieth's transcription method is orthographic and partially adapted to the spelling habits in standard German. Therefore, it does not provide the same precision and explicitness as phonetic transcription methods do. Moreover, the transcription choices are dependent on the dialect, the accentuation of the syllables and – to a substantial degree – also the dialectal background of the transcriber. Also, the practice of using Dieth's system changed over time, so that some transcribers (e.g., transcriber P in Table 6) made more distinctions concerning the openness of vowels than others. The transcriptions exclusively used lowercase. Note that Dieth's system is hardly known by laymen, so that Swiss German data extracted from social media would look fairly different from our transcripts.

Dialect	Doc.	Utter.	Trans.	Dist.
BE	1142	794	P	<5
	1170	872	P	45
	1215	2,223	M	13
	1121*	906	M	<5
BS	1044	952	A	<5
	1073	1,407	P	23
	1075	1,052	P	<5
	1263*	939	A	<5
LU	1007	815	P	11
	1195	1,070	P	13
	1261	1,329	P	<5
	1008*	916	A	5
ZH	1082	842	M	<5
	1087	933	M	<5
	1143	759	P	6
	1244	728	M	19
	1270	702	P	6
	1225*	877	M	<5

Table 6: ArchiMob interviews used for the GDI task. *Doc.* = document identifier (starred identifiers refer to the test set), *Utter.* = number of utterances included in the GDI dataset, *Trans.* = identifier of the transcriber, *Dist.* = distance (in kilometers) from the core city of the dialect area.

We have been able to identify four dialectal areas for which sufficient amounts of data were available and which were known to be distinct enough. The selected dialect areas correspond to four large agglomerations in the German-speaking part of Switzerland: Zurich (ZH), Basel (BS), Bern (BE), and Lucerne (LU).

The training set contains utterances from at least 3 interviews per dialect, and the test set contains utterances from another interview (see Table 6). The data were sampled such that at least one of the training interviews was transcribed by the same transcriber as the corresponding test interview, except for LU. For LU and BS, we included additional transcripts (i.e., those transcribed by A) not available in the current ArchiMob release.

The training set contains about 14,000 instances (between 3,000 and 4,000 instances per dialect) with a total of 114,000 tokens (28,000 per dialect). The test set contains about 3,600 instances (900 per dialect) with a total of 29,500 tokens (7,000–8,000 per dialect). We did not provide a development set. The acoustic data were not released in this edition, but they are in principle available.

4.2 Task Setup

The task setup of the German Dialect Identification (GDI) task was analogous to the DSL task, except that we did not allow open training, because the test sets for the Zurich and the Bern dialects were already made publicly available through the ArchiMob release.

4.3 Participants and Approaches

A total of ten teams participated in the GDI task, which is very close to the participation in this year's DSL task (11 teams), but somewhat lower than the first edition of ADI (18 teams). All teams except one (*CLUZH*) also participated in the DSL or the ADI tasks. Below, we provide a short description of the approach taken by each team, where the teams are ordered by their performance on the test data in descending order:

- **MAZA** This team submitted three runs, all of which are based on a combination of probabilistic classifiers. Their best run (run 3) is a meta-classifier based on individual SVM classifiers using character 1–8-grams and word unigrams (Malmasi and Zampieri, 2017b).

- **CECL** This team submitted three runs, all based on SVM classifiers using character 1–5-grams, weighted by BM25. The different runs used different decision rules, with run 3 performing best (Bestgen, 2017).

- **CLUZH** This team submitted three runs. Run 1 used a Multinomial Na"ive Bayes classifier with character n-grams. Run 2, which performed best, used a Conditional Random Fields (CRF) classifier, where each word of the sentence is represented by character n-gram features, prefix and suffix n-gram combinations, and word shapes. Run 3 used majority voting of runs 1 and 2, and an SVM classifier (Clematide and Makarov, 2017).

- **qcri_mit** This team submitted three runs based on different combinations of SVM classifiers and Stochastic Gradient classifiers with different loss functions. Their best-performing run (run 3) consisted of an SVM classifier with 1–5-grams, another SVM with 1–8-grams, and an SGD with Modified Huber Loss and L2 regularization and 1–5-gram features.

- **unibuckernel** This team submitted three runs, all of which are based on multiple string kernels combined with either Kernel Ridge Regression (KRR) or Kernel Discriminant Analysis. Their best run (run 1) used a KRR classifier trained on the sum of the blended presence bits kernel based on 3–6-grams, the blended intersection kernel based on 3–6-grams, and the kernel based on LRD with 3–5-grams (Ionescu and Butnaru, 2017).

- **tubasfs** This team submitted a single system, based on a linear SVM classifier. Their system used both characters and words as features, and optimized hyperparameters (the n-gram size and margin/regularization parameter for SVM) (Çöltekin and Rama, 2017).

- **ahaqst** This team submitted two runs, both based on cross-entropy. Run 2, which performed better, approximated cross-entropy using strings of up to 25 bytes (Hanani et al., 2017).

- **Citius_Ixa_Imaxin** This team submitted three runs, all of which are based on language model perplexity. Run 2 was based on word unigram features, and it was their best (Gamallo et al., 2017).

- **XAC_Bayesline** This team submitted one run. As for DSL, it is an adaptation of the system submitted to the DSL 2016 by Barbaresi (2016).

- **deepCybErNet** This team submitted two runs based on LSTM neural networks. Run 1 uses character features, whereas run 2 uses word features.

4.4 Results

Table 7 shows the results of the GDI task, reporting the best run of each team. Like in the DSL task, all teams except *deepCybErNet* obtained similar scores.

The per-dialect results look rather similar across the teams. For BE and BS, precision and recall were fairly balanced around 0.7. LU is characterized by very low recall (around 0.3), whereas ZH features higher than average recall values of around 0.9. An exception to this trend is the *CECL* submission, which shows more balanced figures for LU, with a recall of 0.52, but at the expense of precision: 0.55 instead of around 0.7.

Rank	Team	F1 (weighted)
1	MAZA	0.662
2	CECL	0.661
3	CLUZH	0.653
4	qcri_mit	0.639
5	unibuckernel	0.637
6	tubasfs	0.626
7	ahaqst	0.614
8	Citius_Ixa_Imaxin	0.612
9	XAC_Bayesline	0.605
10	deepCybErNet	0.263

Table 7: GDI task: closed submission results.

The bad performance of LU can be explained by transcriber effects. As shown in Table 6, it is the only dialect for which no utterances from the test transcriber (A) are included in the training set. This hypothesis is supported by the fact that LU is most often confused with BS (which contains training data by A, but is dialectologically rather distant from LU), and by the fact that the participants have not observed such low recall in their cross-validation experiments on the training data. The exact nature of these transcriber effects remains to be investigated and should be better controlled in future iterations of this shared task.

We see two reasons for the high recall of ZH. On the one hand, the training set is dialectally more homogeneous (all documents except for one stem from the city of Zurich and its suburbs) but more heterogeneous in terms of document and transcriber distributions. This probably allows the models to focus on dialectal specificities and to disregard spurious transcriber particularities. On the other hand, Scherrer and Rambow (2010) as well as Hollenstein and Aepli (2015) found ZH to be one of the most easily identifiable dialects, suggesting that it acts as a sort of default dialect with few characteristic traits. Dialectometrical studies (Scherrer and Stoeckle, 2016) have partially confirmed this role of the Zurich dialect.

4.5 Summary

This first edition of the GDI task was a success, given the short time between the 2016 and 2017 editions. In the future, we would like to better control transcriber effects, either by a more thorough selection of training and test data, or by adding transcriber-independent features such as acoustic features, as has been done in the ADI task this year. Further dialectal areas could also be added.

5 Cross-lingual Dependency Parsing (CLP)

VarDial 2017 featured for the first time a cross-lingual parsing task for closely related languages.[7] Transfer learning and annotation projection are popular approaches in this field and various techniques and models have been proposed in the literature in particular in connection with dependency parsing (Hwa et al., 2005; McDonald et al., 2013; Täckström et al., 2012; Tiedemann, 2014). The motivation for cross-lingual models is the attempt to bootstrap tools for languages that do not have annotated resources, which are typically necessary for supervised data-driven techniques, using data and resources from other languages. This is especially successful for closely related languages with similar syntactic structures and strong lexical overlap (Agić et al., 2012). With this background, it is a natural extension for our shared task to consider cross-lingual parsing as well. We do so by simulating the resource-poor situation by selecting language pairs from the Universal Dependencies (UD) project (Nivre et al., 2016) that match the setup and come close to a realistic case for the approach (using UD release 1.4). The UD datasets are especially useful as they try to harmonize the annotation across languages as much as possible, which facilitates the cross-lingual scenario.

Language	Sentences	Words
Czech	68,495	1.3M
Danish	4,868	89k
Swedish	4,303	67k
Slovenian	6,471	119k

Table 8: CLP task: source language training data.

We selected Croatian, Norwegian and Slovak as the target languages and pre-defined source languages that may be used for the cross-lingual parsing. For Norwegian, we have two possible source languages: Danish and Swedish. For Croatian, the source is Slovenian, and for Slovak it is Czech. We provided training data for each source language (a copy of the original UD data), pre-trained part-of-speech (PoS) and morphological taggers for the target languages, and development data with predicted PoS labels and predicted morphology (based on the provided taggers).

Avoiding gold labels is important here in order to avoid exaggerated results that blur the picture of a more realistic setup (Tiedemann, 2015). The tagger models are trained on the original target language treebanks using UDpipe (Straka et al., 2016) with standard settings and without any optimization of the hyper parameters. The size of the source language data is given in Table 5. We can see that for Czech we have by far the largest corpus, which will also be reflected in the results we obtain.

Language-pair	Sentences	Words
Czech-Slovak	5.7M	77M
Danish-Norwegian	4.9M	69M
Swedish-Norwegian	4.2M	60M
Slovenian-Croatian	12.8M	172M

Table 9: CLP task: parallel training data.

Participants were asked not to use the development data with their gold standard annotation of dependency relations for any training purposes. The purpose of the development datasets is entirely for testing model performance during system development. All the knowledge used for parsing should origin in the provided source language data. Other sources (except for target language sources) could also be used in unconstrained submissions, but none of the participants chose that option. For the constrained setup, we also provided parallel datasets coming from OPUS (Tiedemann, 2012) that could be used for training cross-lingual parsers in any way. The datasets included translated movie subtitles and contained quite a bit of noise in terms of alignment, encoding, and translation quality. They were also from a very different domain, which made the setup quite realistic considering that one would used whatever could be found for the task. The sizes of the parallel datasets are given in Table 8.

In the setup of the shared task, we also provided simple baselines and an "upper bound" of a model trained on annotated target language data. The cross-lingual baselines included delexicalized models (based on universal PoS tags only) and a straightforward application of lexicalized source language parsers to the target language without any kind of adaptation. All these models were trained using UDPipe without any parameter optimization and should be seen as lazy baselines for rapid tool development.

---

[7]For data and other information see `https://bitbucket.org/hy-crossNLP/vardial2017`

Supervised Models		LAS	UAS
Croatian	Croatian	68.51	75.61
Norwegian	Norwegian	78.23	82.28
Slovak	Slovak	69.14	76.57
Delexicalized Models		LAS	UAS
Croatian	Slovenian	50.81	62.64
Norwegian	Danish	55.17	65.23
Norwegian	Swedish	57.54	66.96
Norwegian	Danish+Swedish	58.80	68.58
Slovak	Czech	48.91	60.68
Non-adapted Source Models		LAS	UAS
Croatian	Slovenian	53.35	63.94
Norwegian	Danish	54.91	64.53
Norwegian	Swedish	56.63	66.24
Norwegian	Danish+Swedish	59.95	69.02
Slovak	Czech	53.72	65.70

Table 10: CLP task: baseline models in terms of labeled attachment scores (LAS) and unlabeled attachment scores (UAS).

We received three submissions (denoted by *tubasfs*, *CUNI* and *Helsinki-CLP*) for the CLP task and all of them submitted results for all language pairs. All three submissions used some kind of annotation projection instead of model transfer. Two of them applied word-by-word translation (Çöltekin and Rama, 2017; Rosa et al., 2017) based on lexical translations learned from the parallel corpora. The third one (Tiedemann, 2017) applied a mix of annotation projection (Tiedemann, 2014) and treebank translation (Tiedemann et al., 2014). The overall results are shown in Table 11.

LAS	Croatian	Norwegian	Slovak
CUNI	60.70	70.21	78.12
Helsinki-CLP	57.98	68.60	73.14
tubasfs	55.20	65.62	64.05

UAS	Croatian	Norwegian	Slovak
CUNI	69.73	77.13	84.92
Helsinki-CLP	69.57	76.77	82.87
tubasfs	75.61	74.61	73.16

Table 11: CLP task: closed submission results.

From the results, we can see that *CUNI* is the clear winner especially in terms of labeled attachment scores. The difference to the second-best submission is large in particular on the Slovak data. The picture is not that clear in terms of unlabeled attachment scores.

The difference in LAS between the two top submissions is most likely due to the label normalization that the winning system applied besides the direct annotation projection. They also applied a more selective projection of morphological features and used the extensive parallel data provided for the task in order to train reliable word embeddings for the target language. Another improvement was obtained by relabeling the test sets with morpho-syntactic information learned from the projected datasets. This is especially useful for Slovak, which gains a lot from the tagger that is trained on large amounts of projected Czech data instead of applying the information provided by the supervised tagger trained on smaller amounts of target language data. Their system also applied a joint model for tagging and parsing, which improved the overall performance.

We can also see striking differences between the results for the three target languages. Overall, Croatian is the least successful case with improvements of 2-7 points in LAS over the non-adapted baseline. For Norwegian, the two top-scoring teams achieve over 10 LAS points of improvement for the winning submission. However, for both Croatian and Norwegian, the cross-lingual models are still far behind the fully-supervised upper bound that scores 8 LAS points above them. For Slovak, the picture is different. The two top submissions both score above the "upper bound" of fully-supervised parsing, which is quite an impressive result. This is certainly due to the large amounts of training data that we have for the source language (Czech) and the close relation between the two languages supports the success as well. Nevertheless, the results demonstrate the real-world use of the techniques tested in our shared task.

6 Conclusion and Future Work

We have presented the methods, the data, the evaluation setup, and the results for four shared tasks taht we organized as part of the VarDial 2017 evaluation campaign. To the best of our knowledge, this is the first comprehensive evaluation campaign on NLP for Similar Languages, Varieties and Dialects. Three tasks (ADI, GDI, and DSL) dealt with dialect and language variety identification, focusing on Arabic, German and several groups of similar languages, respectively, whereas the CLP task dealt with parsing.

Along with the results of each shared task, we also included short descriptions of each participating system in order to provide readers with an overview of all approaches proposed for each task. For a complete description of each system, we included references to the fifteen system description papers that were accepted for presentation at the VarDial workshop at EACL'2017.

Given the success of the VarDial evaluation campaign, we believe that there is room for another edition with more shared tasks. Possible topics of interest for future shared tasks include machine translation between similar languages and POS tagging of dialects, among others.

Acknowledgments

We would like to thank the participants of the previous editions of the DSL shared task for their participation, support, and feedback, which have motivated us to turn the task into a more comprehensive evaluation campaign as of this year.

We further thank all participants in this year's VarDial evaluation campaign for their valuable comments and suggestions.

References

Kheireddine Abainia, Siham Ouamour, and Halim Sayoud. 2016. Effective Language Identification of Forum Texts Based on Statistical Approaches. *Information Processing & Management*, 52(4):491–512.

Željko Agić, Danijela Merkler, and Daša Berović. 2012. Slovene-Croatian treebank transfer using bilingual lexicon improves Croatian dependency parsing. In *Proceedings of IS-LTC*.

Ahmed Ali, Yifan Zhang, Patrick Cardinal, Najim Dahak, Stephan Vogel, and Jim Glass. 2014a. A complete Kaldi recipe for building Arabic speech recognition systems. In *Proceedings of SLT*.

Ahmed Ali, Yifan Zhang, and Stephan Vogel. 2014b. QCRI Advanced Transcription System (QATS). In *Proceedings of SLT*.

Ahmed Ali, Najim Dehak, Patrick Cardinal, Sameer Khurana, Sree Harsha Yella, James Glass, Peter Bell, and Steve Renals. 2016. Automatic dialect detection in Arabic broadcast speech. In *Proceedings of INTERSPEECH*.

Mohamad Hasan Bahari, Najim Dehak, Lukas Burget, Ahmed Ali, Jim Glass, et al. 2014. Non-negative factor analysis for GMM weight adaptation. *IEEE Transactions on Audio Speech and Language Processing*.

Adrien Barbaresi. 2016. An unsupervised morphological criterion for discriminating similar languages. In *Proceedings of the VarDial Workshop*.

Adrien Barbaresi. 2017. Discriminating between similar languages using weighted subword features. In *Proceedings of the VarDial Workshop*.

Yves Bestgen. 2017. Improving the character ngram model for the DSL task with BM25 weighting and less frequently used feature sets. In *Proceedings of the VarDial Workshop*.

Ralf Brown. 2014. Non-linear mapping for improved identification of 1300+ languages. In *Proceedings of EMNLP*.

Dayvid Castro, Ellen Souza, and Adriano LI de Oliveira. 2016. Discriminating between Brazilian and European Portuguese national varieties on Twitter texts. In *Proceedings of BRACIS*.

Çağrı Çöltekin and Taraka Rama. 2016. Discriminating similar languages with linear SVMs and neural networks. In *Proceedings of the VarDial Workshop*.

Çağrı Çöltekin and Taraka Rama. 2017. Tübingen system in VarDial 2017 shared task: Experiments with language identification and cross-lingual parsing. In *Proceedings of the VarDial Workshop*.

Simon Clematide and Peter Makarov. 2017. CLUZH at VarDial GDI 2017: Testing a variety of machine learning tools for the classification of Swiss German dialects. In *Proceedings of the VarDial Workshop*.

Marcelo Criscuolo and Sandra Aluisio. 2017. Discriminating between similar languages with word-level convolutional neural networks. In *Proceedings of the VarDial Workshop*.

Eugen Dieth. 1986. *Schwyzertütschi Dialäktschrift*. Sauerländer, Aarau, 2 edition.

Pablo Gamallo, Jose Ramon Pichel, and Iñaki Alegria. 2017. A method based on perplexity for similar languages discrimination. In *Proceedings of the VarDial Workshop*.

Binyam Gebrekidan Gebre, Marcos Zampieri, Peter Wittenburg, and Tom Heskes. 2013. Improving native language identification with TF-IDF weighting. In *Proceedings of the BEA workshop*.

Helena Gómez-Adorno, Ilia Markov, Jorge Baptista, Grigori Sidorov, and David Pinto. 2017. Discriminating between similar languages using a combination of typed and untyped character n-grams and words. In *Proceedings of the VarDial Workshop*.

Cyril Goutte and Serge Léger. 2015. Experiments in discriminating similar languages. In *Proceedings of the LT4VarDial Workshop*.

Cyril Goutte, Serge Léger, and Marine Carpuat. 2013. Feature space selection and combination for native language identification. In *Proceedings of the BEA Workshop*.

Cyril Goutte, Serge Léger, and Marine Carpuat. 2014. The NRC system for discriminating similar languages. In *Proceedings of the VarDial Workshop*.

Cyril Goutte, Serge Léger, Shervin Malmasi, and Marcos Zampieri. 2016. Discriminating similar languages: Evaluations and explorations. In *Proceedings of LREC*.

Bo Han, Afshin Rahimi, Leon Derczynski, and Timothy Baldwin. 2016. Twitter geolocation prediction shared task of the 2016 workshop on noisy user-generated text. In *Proceedings of the W-NUT Workshop*.

Abualsoud Hanani, Aziz Qaroush, and Stephen Taylor. 2017. Identifying dialects with textual and acoustic cues. In *Proceedings of the VarDial Workshop*.

Nora Hollenstein and Noëmi Aepli. 2015. A resource for natural language processing of Swiss German dialects. In *Proceedings of GSCL*.

Rebecca Hwa, Philip Resnik, Amy Weinberg, Clara Cabezas, and Okan Kolak. 2005. Bootstrapping parsers via syntactic projection across parallel texts. *Natural Language Engineering*, 11(3):311–325.

Radu Tudor Ionescu and Andrei Butnaru. 2017. Learning to identify Arabic and German dialects using multiple kernels. In *Proceedings of the VarDial Workshop*.

Scott Jarvis, Yves Bestgen, and Steve Pepper. 2013. Maximizing classification accuracy in native language identification. In *Proceedings of the BEA Workshop*.

Tommi Jauhiainen, Heidi Jauhiainen, and Krister Lindén. 2015. Discriminating Similar Languages with Token-based Backoff. In *Proceedings of the LT4VarDial Workshop*.

Tommi Jauhiainen, Krister Lindén, and Heidi Jauhiainen. 2016. HeLI, a word-based backoff method for language identification. In *Proceedings of the VarDial Workshop*.

Tommi Jauhiainen, Krister Lindén, and Heidi Jauhiainen. 2017. Evaluating HeLI with non-linear mappings. In *Proceedings of the VarDial Workshop*.

Sameer Khurana and Ahmed Ali. 2016. QCRI advanced transcription system (QATS) for the Arabic Multi-Dialect Broadcast Media Recognition: MGB-2 Challenge. In *Proceedings of SLT*.

Adrian Leemann, Marie-José Kolly, Ross Purves, David Britain, and Elvira Glaser. 2016. Crowdsourcing language change with smartphone applications. *PLOS ONE*, 11(1):1–25.

Nikola Ljubešić and Denis Kranjčić. 2015. Discriminating between closely related languages on Twitter. *Informatica*, 39(1).

Marco Lui and Paul Cook. 2013. Classifying English documents by national dialect. In *Proceedings of ALTA*.

Marco Lui. 2014. *Generalized language identification*. Ph.D. thesis, University of Melbourne.

Shervin Malmasi and Mark Dras. 2015a. Automatic language identification for Persian and Dari texts. In *Proceedings of PACLING*.

Shervin Malmasi and Mark Dras. 2015b. Language identification using classifier ensembles. In *Proceedings of the VarDial Workshop*.

Shervin Malmasi and Marcos Zampieri. 2017a. Arabic dialect identification using iVectors and ASR transcripts. In *Proceedings of the VarDial Workshop*.

Shervin Malmasi and Marcos Zampieri. 2017b. German dialect identification in interview transcriptions. In *Proceedings of the VarDial Workshop*.

Shervin Malmasi, Marcos Zampieri, Nikola Ljubešić, Preslav Nakov, Ahmed Ali, and Jörg Tiedemann. 2016. Discriminating between similar languages and Arabic dialect identification: A report on the third DSL shared task. In *Proceedings of the VarDial Workshop*.

Ryan McDonald, Joakim Nivre, Yvonne Quirmbach-Brundage, Yoav Goldberg, Dipanjan Das, Kuzman Ganchev, Keith Hall, Slav Petrov, Hao Zhang, Oscar Täckström, Claudia Bedini, Núria Bertomeu Castelló, and Jungmee Lee. 2013. Universal dependency annotation for multilingual parsing. In *Proceedings of ACL*.

Maria Medvedeva, Martin Kroon, and Barbara Plank. 2017. When sparse traditional models outperform dense neural networks: the curious case of discriminating between similar languages. In *Proceedings of the VarDial Workshop*.

Joakim Nivre, Marie-Catherine de Marneffe, Filip Ginter, Yoav Goldberg, Jan Hajic, Christopher D Manning, Ryan McDonald, Slav Petrov, Sampo Pyysalo, Natalia Silveira, et al. 2016. Universal dependencies v1: A multilingual treebank collection. In *Proceedings of LREC*.

Will Radford and Matthias Gallé. 2016. Discriminating between similar languages in Twitter using label propagation. *arXiv preprint arXiv:1607.05408*.

Stephen E. Robertson, Steve Walker, Susan Jones, Micheline M Hancock-Beaulieu, Mike Gatford, et al. 1995. Okapi at TREC-3. In *Proceedings of TREC*.

Rudolf Rosa, Daniel Zeman, David Mareček, and Zdeněk Žabokrtský. 2017. Slavic forest, Norwegian wood. In *Proceedings of the VarDial Workshop*.

Tanja Samardžić, Yves Scherrer, and Elvira Glaser. 2016. ArchiMob – a corpus of spoken Swiss German. In *Proceedings of LREC*.

Upendra Sapkota, Steven Bethard, Manuel Montes-y Gómez, and Thamar Solorio. 2015. Not all character n-grams are created equal: A study in authorship attribution. In *Proceedings of NAACL*.

Carolina Scarton, Liling Tan, and Lucia Specia. 2015. USHEF and USAAR-USHEF participation in the WMT15 quality estimation shared task. In *Proceedings of WMT*.

Yves Scherrer and Owen Rambow. 2010. Word-based dialect identification with georeferenced rules. In *Proceedings of EMNLP*.

Yves Scherrer and Philipp Stoeckle. 2016. A quantitative approach to Swiss German – dialectometric analyses and comparisons of linguistic levels. *Dialectologia et Geolinguistica*, 24(1):92–125.

Helmut Schmid. 1994. Probabilistic part-of-speech tagging using decision trees. In *Proceedings of NeMLaP*.

Milan Straka, Jan Hajič, and Straková. 2016. UD-Pipe: Trainable pipeline for processing CoNLL-U files performing tokenization, morphological analysis, POS tagging and parsing. In *Proceedings of LREC*.

Oscar Täckström, Ryan McDonald, and Jakob Uszkoreit. 2012. Cross-lingual word clusters for direct transfer of linguistic structure. In *Proceedings of NAACL*.

Liling Tan, Marcos Zampieri, Nikola Ljubešić, and Jörg Tiedemann. 2014. Merging comparable data sources for the discrimination of similar languages: The DSL corpus collection. In *Proceedings of the BUCC Workshop*.

Jörg Tiedemann, Željko Agić, and Joakim Nivre. 2014. Treebank translation for cross-lingual parser induction. In *Proceedings of CoNLL*.

Jörg Tiedemann. 2012. Parallel Data, Tools and Interfaces in OPUS. In *Proceedings of LREC*.

Jörg Tiedemann. 2014. Rediscovering annotation projection for cross-lingual parser induction. In *Proceedings of COLING*.

Jörg Tiedemann. 2015. Cross-lingual dependency parsing with universal dependencies and predicted PoS labels. In *Proceedings of Depling*.

Jörg Tiedemann. 2017. Cross-lingual dependency parsing for closely related languages - Helsinki's submission to VarDial 2017. In *Proceedings of the VarDial Workshop*.

Lan Wang, Masahiro Tanaka, and Hayato Yamana. 2016. What is your Mother Tongue?: Improving Chinese native language identification by cleaning noisy data and adopting BM25. In *Proceedings of ICBDA*.

Samantha Wray and Ahmed Ali. 2015. Crowdsource a little to label a lot: Labeling a speech corpus of dialectal Arabic. In *Proceedings of INTERSPEECH*.

Fan Xu, Mingwen Wang, and Maoxi Li. 2016. Sentence-level dialects identification in the Greater China region. *International Journal on Natural Language Computing (IJNLC)*, 5(6).

Marcos Zampieri, Binyam Gebrekidan Gebre, and Sascha Diwersy. N-gram language models and POS distribution for the identification of Spanish varieties.

Marcos Zampieri, Liling Tan, Nikola Ljubešić, and Jörg Tiedemann. 2014. A report on the DSL shared task 2014. In *Proceedings of the VarDial Workshop*.

Marcos Zampieri, Binyam Gebrekidan Gebre, Hernani Costa, and Josef van Genabith. 2015a. Comparing approaches to the identification of similar languages. In *Proceedings of the VarDial Workshop*.

Marcos Zampieri, Liling Tan, Nikola Ljubešić, Jörg Tiedemann, and Preslav Nakov. 2015b. Overview of the DSL shared task 2015. In *Proceedings of the LT4VarDial Workshop*.

Arkaitz Zubiaga, Inaki San Vicente, Pablo Gamallo, José Ramom Pichel, Inaki Alegria, Nora Aranberri, Aitzol Ezeiza, and Victor Fresno. 2014. Overview of TweetLID: Tweet language identification at SE-PLN 2014. In *Proceedings of the TweetLID Workshop*.

Dialectometric analysis of language variation in Twitter

Gonzalo Donoso
IFISC (UIB-CSIC)
Palma de Mallorca, Spain
gdonoso94@hotmail.com

David Sánchez
IFISC (UIB-CSIC)
Palma de Mallorca, Spain
david.sanchez@uib.es

Abstract

In the last few years, microblogging platforms such as Twitter have given rise to a deluge of textual data that can be used for the analysis of informal communication between millions of individuals. In this work, we propose an information-theoretic approach to geographic language variation using a corpus based on Twitter. We test our models with tens of concepts and their associated keywords detected in Spanish tweets geolocated in Spain. We employ dialectometric measures (cosine similarity and Jensen-Shannon divergence) to quantify the linguistic distance on the lexical level between cells created in a uniform grid over the map. This can be done for a single concept or in the general case taking into account an average of the considered variants. The latter permits an analysis of the dialects that naturally emerge from the data. Interestingly, our results reveal the existence of two dialect macrovarieties. The first group includes a region-specific speech spoken in small towns and rural areas whereas the second cluster encompasses cities that tend to use a more uniform variety. Since the results obtained with the two different metrics qualitatively agree, our work suggests that social media corpora can be efficiently used for dialectometric analyses.

1 Introduction

Dialects are language varieties defined across space. These varieties can differ in distinct linguistic levels (phonetic, morphosyntactic, lexical), which determine a particular regional speech (Chambers and Trudgill, 1998). The extension and boundaries (always diffuse) of a dialect area are obtained from the variation of one or many features such as, e.g., the different word alternations for a given concept. Typically, the dialect forms plotted on a map appear as a geographical continuum that gradually connects places with slightly different diatopic characteristics. A dialectometric analysis aims at a computational approach to dialect distribution, providing quantitative linguistic distances between locations (Séguy, 1971; Goebl, 2006; Wieling and Nerbonne, 2015).

Dialectometric data is based upon a corpus that contains the linguistic information needed for the statistical analysis. The traditional approach is to generate these data from surveys and questionnaires that address variable types used by a few informants. Upon appropriate weighting, the distance metric can thus be mapped on an atlas. In the last few years, however, the impressive upswing of microblogging platforms has led to a scenario in which human communication features can be studied without the effort that traditional studies usually require. Platforms such as Twitter, Flickr, Instagram or Facebook bring us the possibility of investigating massive amounts of data in an automatic fashion. Furthermore, microblogging services provide us with real-time communication among users that, importantly, tend to employ an oral speech. Another difference with traditional approaches is that while the latter focus on male, rural informants, users of social platforms are likely to be young, urban people (Smith and Rainie, 2010), which opens the route to novel investigations on today's usage of language. Thanks to advances in geolocation, it is now possible to directly examine the diatopic properties of specific regions. Examples of computational linguistic works that investigate regional variation with Twitter or Facebook corpora thus far comprise English (Eisenstein et al., 2014; Doyle, 2014; Kulka-

Proceedings of the Fourth Workshop on NLP for Similar Languages, Varieties and Dialects, pages 16–25,
Valencia, Spain, April 3, 2017. ©2017 Association for Computational Linguistics

rni et al., 2016; Huang et al., 2016; Blodgett et al., 2016), Spanish (Gonçalves and Sánchez, 2014; Gonçalves and Sánchez, 2016; Malmasi et al., 2016), German (Scheffler et al., 2014), Arabic (Lin et al., 2014) and Dutch (Tulkens et al., 2016). It is noticeable that many of these works combine big data techniques with probabilistic tools or machine learning strategies to unveil linguistic phenomena that are absent or hard to obtain from conventional methods (interviews, hand-crafted corpora, etc.).

The subject of this paper is the language variation in a microblogging platform using dialectrometric measures. In contrast to previous works, here we precisely determine the linguistic distance between different places by means of two metrics. Our analysis shows that the results obtained with both metrics are compatible, which encourages future developments in the field. We illustrate our main findings with a careful analysis of the dialect division of Spanish. For definiteness, we restrict ourselves to Spain but the method can be straightforwardly applied to larger areas. We find that, due to language diversity, cities and main towns have similar linguistic distances unlike rural areas, which differ in their homogeneous forms. but obtained with a completely different method

2 Methods

Our corpus consists of approximately 11 million geotagged tweets produced in Europe in Spanish language between October 2014 and June 2016. (Although we will focus on Spain, we will not consider in this work the speech of the Canary Islands due to difficulties with the data extraction). The classification of tweets is accomplished by applying the Compact Language Detector (CLD) (McCandless, 2012) to our dataset. CLD exhibits accurate benchmarks and is thus good for our purposes, although a different detector might be used (Lui and Baldwin, 2012). We have empirically checked that when CLD determines the language with a probability of at least 60% the results are extremely reliable. Therefore, we only take into account those tweets for which the probability of being written in Spanish is greater than 0.6. Further, we remove unwanted characters, such as hashtags or at-mentions, using Twokenize (O'Connor et al., 2010), a tokenizer designed for Twitter text in English, adapted to our goals.

We present the spatial coordinates of all tweets

Figure 1: Heatmap of Spanish tweets geolocated in Europe. There exist 11208831 tweets arising from a language detection and tokenization procedure. We have zoomed in those arising in Spain, Portugal and the south of France.

in figure 1 (only the south-western part of Europe is shown for clarity). As expected, most of the tweets are localized in Spain, mainly around major cities and along main roads.

Next, we select a word list from *Varilex* (Ueda et al., 2015), a lexical database that contains Spanish variation across the world. We consider 89 concepts expressed in different forms. Our selection eliminates possible semantic ambiguities. The complete list of keywords is included in the supplementary material below. For each concept, we determine the coordinates of the tweets in which the different keywords appear. From our corpus, we find that 219362 tweets include at least one form corresponding to any of the selected concepts.

The pictorial representation of these concepts is made using a shapefile of both the Iberian Peninsula and the Balearic Islands. Then, we construct a polygon grid over the shapefile. The size of the cells ($0.35° \times 0.35°$) roughly corresponds to $1200 \, \text{km}^2$. We locate the cell in which a given keyword matches and assign a different color to each keyword. We follow a majority criterion, i.e., we depict the cell with the keyword color whose absolute frequency is maximum. This procedure nicely yields a useful geographical representation of how the different variants for a concept are distributed over the space.

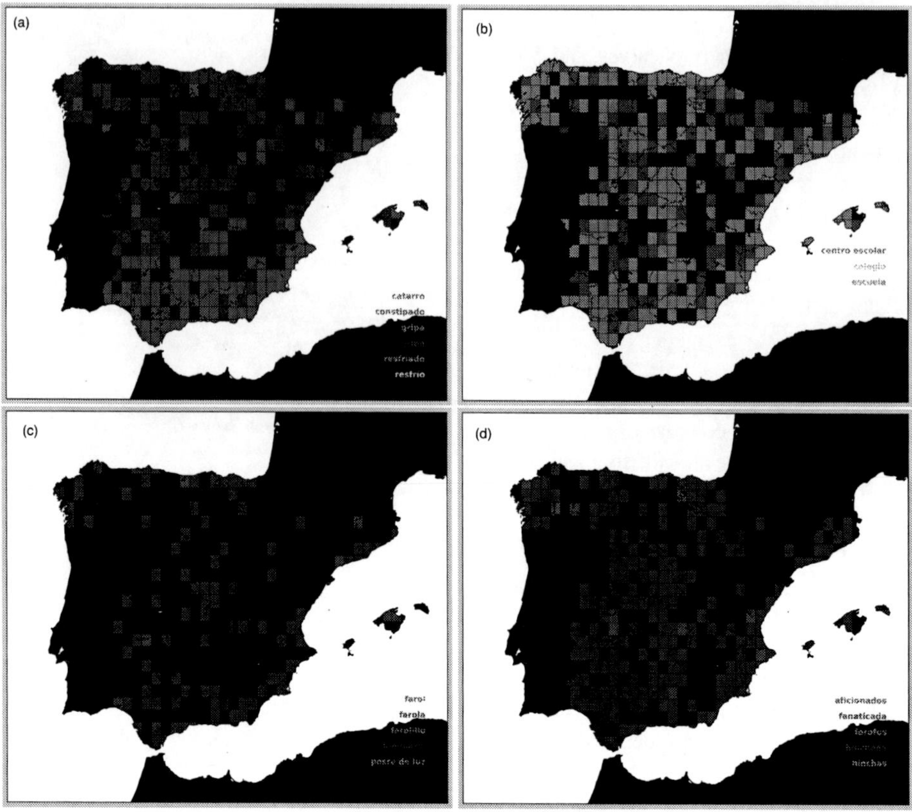

Figure 2: Spatial distribution of a few representative concepts based on the maximum absolute frequency criterion. Each concept has a lexical variation as indicated in the figure. The concepts are: (a) *cold*, (b) *school*, (c) *streetlight*, (d) *fans*.

2.1 Language distance

The dialectometric differences are quantified between regions defined with the aid of our cells. For this purpose we take into account two metrics, which we now briefly discuss.

2.1.1 Cosine similarity

This metric is a vector comparison measure. It is widely used in text classification, information retrieval and data mining (Murphy, 2012). Let u and v be two vectors whose components are given by the relative frequencies of the lexical variations for a concept within a cell. Quite generally, u and v represent points in a high-dimensional space. The similarity measure $d(u, v)$ between these two vectors is related to their inner product conveniently normalized to the product of their lengths,

$$d(u, v) = 1 - \frac{u \cdot v}{|u||v|}. \tag{1}$$

This expression has an easy interpretation. If both vectors lie parallel, the direction cosine is 1 and thus the distance becomes $d = 0$. Since all vector components in our approach are positive, the upper bound of d is 1, which is attained when the two vectors are maximally dissimilar.

2.1.2 Jensen-Shannon metric

This distance is a similarity measure between probability density functions (Lin, 1991). It is a symmetrized version of a more general metric, the Kullback-Leibler divergence. Let P and Q be two probability distributions. In our case, these functions are built from the relative frequencies of each concept variation. Our frequentist approach differs from previous dialectometric works, which prefer to measure distances using the Dice similarity coefficient or the Jaccard index (Manning and Schütze, 1999).

The Kullback-Leibler divergence is defined as

$$D_{KL}(P||Q) = \sum_i P(i) \log \frac{P(i)}{Q(i)} \,. \qquad (2)$$

We now symmetrize this expression and take the square root,

$$JSD(P||Q) = \sqrt{\frac{D_{KL}(P||M) + D_{KL}(Q||M)]}{2}} \,, \qquad (3)$$

where $M = (P + Q)/2$. The Jensen-Shannon distance $JSD(P||Q)$ is indeed a metric, i.e., it satisfies the triangle inequality. Additionally, $JSD(P||Q)$ fulfills the metric requirements of non-negativity, $d(x,y) = 0$ if and only if $x = y$ (identity of indiscernibles) and symmetry (by construction). This distance has been employed in bioinformatics and genome comparison (Sims et al., 2009; Itzkovitz et al., 2010), social sciences (DeDeo et al., 2013) and machine learning (Goodfellow et al., 2014). To the best of our knowledge, it has not been used in studies of language variation. An exception is the work of Sanders (2010), where JSD is calculated for an analysis of syntactic variation of Swedish. Here, we propose to apply the Jensen-Shannon metric to *lexical* variation. Below, we demonstrate that this idea leads to quite promising results.

2.1.3 Average distance

Equations 1 and 3 give the distance between cells A and B for a certain concept. We assign the global linguistic distance in terms of lexical variability between two cells to the mean value

$$D(A, B) = \frac{\sum_i d_i(A, B)}{N} \,, \qquad (4)$$

where d_i is the distance between cells A and B for the i-th concept and N is the total number of concepts used to compute the distance. In the cosine similarity model, we replace d_i in equation 4 with equation 1 whereas in the Jensen-Shannon metric d_i is given by equation 3.

3 Results and discussion

We first check the quality of our corpus with a few selected concepts. Examples of their spatial distributions can be seen in figure 2. The lexical variation depends on the particular concept and on the keyword frequency. We recall that the majority rule demands that we depict the cell with the color

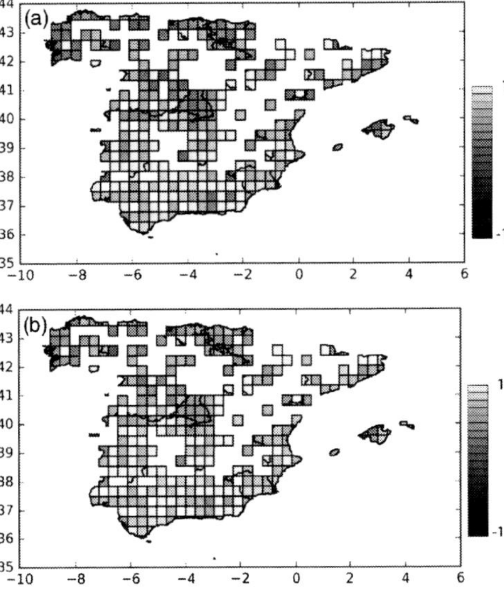

Figure 3: Linguistic distances for the concept *cold* using (a) cosine similarity and (b) Jensen-Shannon divergence metrics. The horizontal (vertical) axis is expressed in longitude (latitude) coordinates.

corresponding to the most popular word. Despite a few cells appearing to be blank, we have instances in most of the map. Importantly, our results agree with the distribution for the concept *cold* reported by Gonçalves and Sánchez (2014) with a different corpus. The north-south bipartition of the variation suggested in figure 2(a) also agrees with more traditional studies (Ordóñez, 2011). As a consequence, these consistencies support the validity of our data. The novelty of our approach is to further analyze this dialect distribution with a quantitative measure as discussed below.

3.1 Single-concept case

Let us quantify the lexical difference between regions using the concept *cold* as an illustration. First, we generate a symmetric matrix of linguistic distances $m_{ij}(d)$ between pairs of cells i and j with d calculated using equation (1) or equation (3). Then, we find the maximum possible d value in the matrix (d_{max}) and select either its corresponding i_{max} or j_{max} index as the reference cell. Since both metrics are symmetric, the choice between i_{max} and j_{max} should not affect the results much (see below for a detailed analysis). Next, we normalize all values to d_{max} and plot the distances to the reference cell using a color

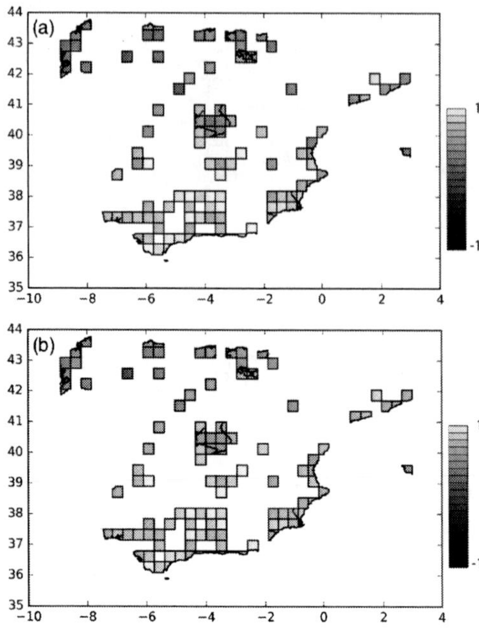

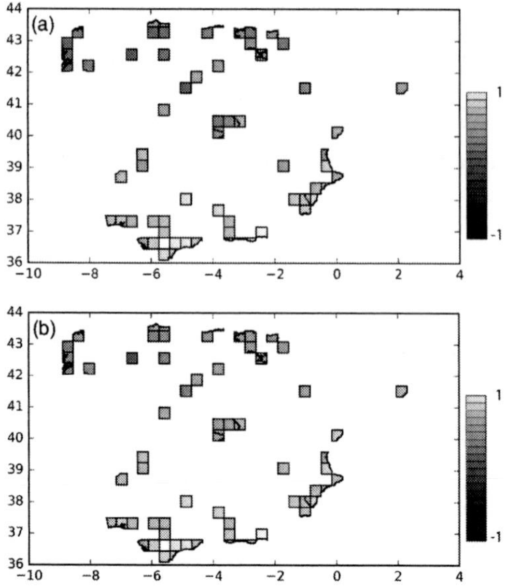

Figure 4: Linguistic distances as in figure 3 but with a minimum threshold of 5 tweets in each cell using (a) cosine similarity and (b) Jensen-Shannon metric.

Figure 5: Linguistic distances as in figure 3 but with a minimum threshold of 10 tweets in each cell using (a) cosine similarity and (b) Jensen-Shannon metric.

scale within the range $[-1, 1]$, whose lowest and highest values are set for convenience due to the normalization procedure. The results are shown in figure 3. Panel (a) [(b)] is obtained with the cosine similarity (Jensen-Shannon metric). Crucially, we observe that both metrics give similar results, which confirm the robustness of our dialectometric method.

Clearly, cells with a low number of tweets will largely contribute to fluctuations in the maps. To avoid this noise-related effect, we impose in figure 4 a minimum threshold of 5 tweets in every cell. Obviously, the number of colored cells decreases but fluctuations become quenched at the same time. If the threshold is increased up to 10 tweets, we obtain the results plotted in figure 5, where the north-south bipartition is now better seen. We stress that there exist minimal differences between the cosine similarity and the Jensen-Shannon metric models.

3.2 Global distance

Our previous analysis assessed the lexical distance for a single concept (*cold*). Let us now take into account all concepts and calculate the averaged distances using equation (4). To do so, we proceed as above and measure the distance from any of the two cells that presents the maximal value of d, where d is now calculated from equation 4. As aforementioned, d_{max} connects two cells, which denote as C_1 and C_2. Any of these can be selected as the reference cell from which the remaining linguistic distances are plotted in the map. To ensure that we obtain the same results, we plot the distance distribution in both directions. The results with the cosine similarity model are shown in figure 6. It is worth noting that qualitatively the overall picture is only slightly modified when the reference cell is changed from C_1 [figure 6(a)] to C_2 [figure 6(b)]. The same conclusion is reached when the distance is calculated with the Jensen-Shannon metric model, see figures 7(a) and (b).

After averaging over all concepts, we lose information on the lexical variation that each concept presents but on the other hand one can now investigate which regions show similar geolectal variation, yielding well defined linguistic varieties. Those cells that have similar colors in either figure 6 or figure 7 are expected to be ascribed to the same dialect zone. Thus, we can distinguish two main regions or clusters in the maps. The purple

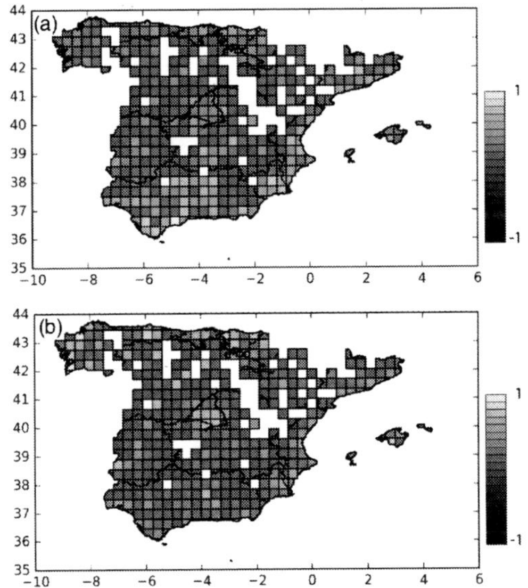
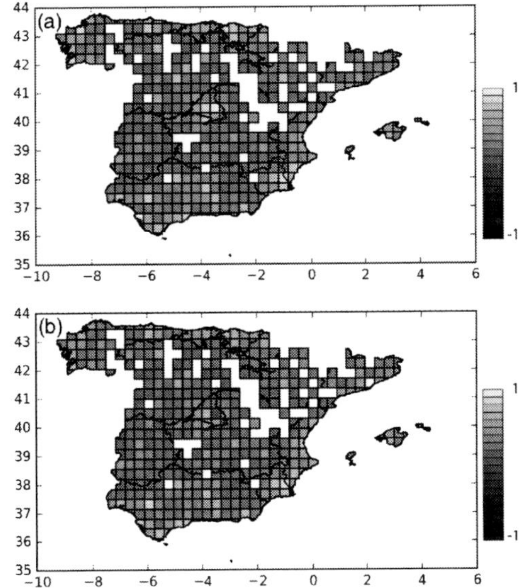

Figure 6: Global distances averaged over all concepts. Here, we use the cosine similarity measure to calculate the distance. The color distribution displays a small variation from (a) to (b) due to the change of the reference cell.

Figure 7: Global distances averaged over all concepts. Here, we use the Jensen-Shannon metric to calculate the distance. The color distribution displays a small variation from (a) to (b) due to the change of the reference cell.

background covers most of the map and represents rural regions with small, scattered population. Our analysis shows that this group of cells possesses more specific words in their lexicon. In contrast, the green and yellow cells form a second cluster that is largely concentrated on the center and along the coastline, which correspond to big cities and industrialized areas. In these cells, the use of standard Spanish language is widespread due probably to school education, media, travelers, etc. The character of its vocabulary is more uniform as compared with the purple group. While the purple cluster prefer particular utterances, the lexicon of the urban group includes most of the keywords. Importantly, we emphasize that both distance measures (cosine similarity and Jensen-Shanon) give rise to the same result, with little discrepancies on the numerical values that are not significant. The presence of two Twitter superdialects (urban and rural) has been recently suggested (Gonçalves and Sánchez, 2014) based on a machine learning approach. Here, we arrive at the same conclusion but with a totally distinct model and corpus. The advantage of our proposal is that it may serve as a useful tool for dialectometric purposes.

4 Conclusions

To sum up, we have presented a dialectrometric analysis of lexical variation in social media posts employing information-theoretic measures of language distances. We have considered a grid of cells in Spain and have calculated the linguistic distances in terms of dialects between the different regions. Using a Twitter corpus, we have found that the synchronic variation of Spanish can be grouped into two types of clusters. The first region shows more lexical items and is present in big cities. The second cluster corresponds to rural regions, i.e., mostly villages and less industrialized regions. Furthermore, we have checked that the different metrics used here lead to similar results in the analysis of the lexical variation for a representative concept and provide a reasonable description to language variation in Twitter.

We remark that the small amount of tweets generated after matching the lexical variations of concepts within our automatic corpus puts a limit to the quantitative analysis, making the differences between regions small. Our work might be improved by similarly examining Spanish tweets worldwide, specially in Latin America and the

United States. This approach should give more information on the lexical variation on the global scale and would help linguists in their dialectal classification work of micro- and macro-varieties. Our work hence represents a first step into the ambitious task of a thorough characterization of language variation using big data resources and information-theoretic methods.

Acknowledgments

We thank both F. Lamanna and Y. Kawasaki for useful discussions and the anonymous reviewers for nice suggestions. GD acknowledges support from the SURF@IFISC program.

References

Su Lin Blodgett, Lisa Green, and Brendan O'Connor. 2016. Demographic dialectal variation in social media: A case study of African-American English. *EMNLP 2016*.

Jack K. Chambers and Peter Trudgill. 1998. *Dialectology*. Cambridge University Press.

Simon DeDeo, Robert X. D. Hawkins, Sara Klingenstein, and Tim Hitchcock. 2013. Bootstrap methods for the empirical study of decision-making and information flows in social systems. *Entropy*, 15:2246–2276.

Gabriel Doyle. 2014. Mapping dialectal variation by querying social media. *EACL*.

Jacob Eisenstein, Brendan O'Connor, Noah A. Smith, and Eric P. Xing. 2014. Diffusion of lexical change in social media. *PLoS ONE*, 9:E113114.

Hans Goebl. 2006. Recent advances in Salzburg dialectometry. *Lit. Linguist. Computing*, 21:411–435.

Bruno Gonçalves and David Sánchez. 2014. Crowdsourcing dialect characterization through Twitter. *PLoS One*, 9:E112074.

Bruno Gonçalves and David Sánchez. 2016. Learning about Spanish dialects through Twitter. *RILI*, XVI 2:65–75.

Ian J. Goodfellow, Jean Pouget-Abadie, Mehdi Mirza, Bing Xu, David Warde-Farley, Sherjil Ozair, Aaron Courville, and Yoshua Bengio. 2014. Generative adversarial networks. *arXiv:1406.2661*.

Yuan Huang, Diansheng Guo, Alice Kasakoff, and Jack Grieve. 2016. Understanding U.S. regional linguistic variation with Twitter data analysis. *Computers, Environment and Urban Systems*, 54.

Shalev Itzkovitz, Eran Hodis, and Eran Segal. 2010. Overlapping codes within protein-coding sequences. *Genome Res.*, 20:1582–9.

Vivek Kulkarni, Bryan Perozzi, and Steven Skiena. 2016. Freshman or fresher? Quantifying the geographic variation of language in online social media. *Proceedings of the Tenth International AAAI Conference on Web and Social Media*.

Chu-Cheng Lin, Waleed Ammar, Lori Levin, and Chris Dyer. 2014. The CMU submission for the shared task on language identification in code-switched data. *EMNLP 2014*.

Jinhua Lin. 1991. Divergence measures based on Shannon entropy. *IEEE Trans. Inf. Theory*, 37:145–151.

Marco Lui and Timothy Baldwin. 2012. langid.py: an off-the-shelf language identification tool. In *PProceedings of the ACL 2012 System Demonstrations (ACL'12)*, pages 25–30, Stroudsbourg, PA, USA. Association for Computational Linguistics.

Shervin Malmasi, Marcos Zampieri, Nikola Ljubešić, Preslav Nakov, Ahmed Ali, and Jörg Tiedemann. 2016. Discriminating between similar languages and Arabic dialect identification: A report on the Third DSL Shared Task. In *Proceedings of the Third Workshop on NLP for Similar Languages, Varieties and Dialects (VarDial3)*, pages 1–14, Osaka, Japan, December. The COLING 2016 Organizing Committee.

Christopher Manning and Hinrich Schütze. 1999. *Foundations of statistican natural language*. Massachusetts Institute of Technology.

Michael McCandless. 2012. http://code.google.com/p/chromium-compact-language-detector.

Kevin P. Murphy. 2012. *Machine learning. A probabilistic perspective*. Massachussetts Institute of Technology.

Brendan O'Connor, Michel Krieger, and David Ahn. 2010. Tweetmotif: Exploratory search and topic summarization for twitter. *ICWSM-2010*.

Inés Fernández Ordóñez, 2011. *El norte peninsular y su papel en la historia de la lengua española*. Cilengua.

Nathan C. Sanders. 2010. *A statistical method for syntactic dialectometry*. PhD dissertation. Indiana University.

Tatjana Scheffler, Johannes Gontrum, Matthias Wegel, and Steve Wendler. 2014. Mapping German tweets to geographic regions. *Proceedings of the NLP4CMC Workshop at Konvens*.

Jean Séguy. 1971. La relation entre la distance spatiale et la distance lexicale. *Rev. Linguist. Rom.*, 35:335–57.

Gregory E. Sims, Se-Ran Jun, Guohong A. Wu, and Sung-Hou Kim. 2009. Alignment-free genome comparison with feature frequency profiles (FFP) and optimal resolutions. *Proc. Natl. Acad. Sci. U. S. A.*, 106:2677–82.

Aaron Smith and Lee Rainie. 2010. 8% of online Americans use Twitter. *http://www.pewinternet.org/2010/12/09/8-of-online-americans-use-twitter/*.

Stéphan Tulkens, Chris Emmery, and Walter Daelemans. 2016. Evaluating unsupervised Dutch word embeddings as a linguistic resource. *LREC 2016, Tenth International Conference on Language Resources and Evaluation*.

Hiroto Ueda, Toshihiro Takagaki, and Antonio Ruiz Tinoco. 2015. Varilex: Variación léxica del español del mundo. *University of Tokyo*.

Martijn Wieling and John Nerbonne. 2015. Advances in dialectometry. *Annu. Rev. Linguist.*, 1:243–64.

Supplementary material

Here we provide a list of our employed concepts and their lexical variants.

Concept	Keywords
stapler	abrochador, abrochadora, clipiador, clipiadora, clipsadera, corchetera, cosedora, engrampador, engrampadora, engrapador, engrapadora, grapadora, ponchadora, presilladora
sidewalk	acera, andén, badén, calzada, contén, escarpa, vereda
bedspread	acolchado, colcha, colchón, cubrecama, cubrecamas, cubrelecho, edredón, sobrecama
flight attendant	aeromoza, azafata, hostess, stewardess
poster	afiche, anuncio, cartel, cartelón, letrero, póster, propaganda, rótulo, tablón de anuncio
pencil sharpner	afilalápices, afilalápiz, afilaminas, maquineta, sacapunta, sacapuntas, tajador, tajalápices, tajalápiz
bra	ajustador, ajustadores, brasiel, brassiere, corpiño, portaseno, sostén, soutien, sutién, sujetador, tallador
swimming pool	alberca, pileta, piscina

Concept	Keywords
elevator	ascensor, elevador
glasses	anteojos, espejuelos, gafas, gafotas, lentes
popcorn	alepa, cabritas de maíz, canchita, canguil, cocaleca, cotufas, crispetas, crispetos, maíz pira, palomitas, pipocas, pochocle, pochoclo, pocorn, popcorn, poporopo, pororó, rosita de maíz, tostones
sandals	alpargata, chanclas, chancletas, chinelas, cholas, cutalas, cutaras, pantuflas, sandalias, zapatillas
aluminum paper	alusa-foil, foil, papel albal, albal, papel reinolds, papel aluminio, papel de aluminio, papel de estaño, papel de plata, papel encerado, papel estañado, papel para cocinar, papel platina
store window	aparador, escaparate, mostrador, vidriera, vitrina
coat hanger	armador, cercha, colgador, gancho de ropa, percha, perchero
headphones	audífonos, auriculares, cascos, casquitos, headphones, hédfons, talquis
car	auto, automóvil, carro, coche, concho, movi
bus	autobús, autocar, bus, camioneta, guagua, microbús, ómnibus, taxibús
jeans	azulón, azulones, blue jean, bluyín, blue jeans, bluyíns, jeans, yíns, lois, mahón, mahones, pantalón de mezclilla, pantalones de mezclilla, pantalón vaquero, pantalones vaqueros, pantalones tejanos, vaqueros, tejanos, pitusa, pitusas
backpack	backpack, bolsón, macuto, mochila, morral, salveque
boat	barca, bote, canoa, cayuco, chalana, lancha, patera, yola
miss	echar de menos, extrañar, añorar

Concept	Keywords	Concept	Keywords
fender	barrero, cubrebarro, cubrerruedas, guardabarro, guardafango, guardalodo, guardalodos, guardapolvo, lodera, polvera, quitalodo, salpicadera, salpicadero, tapabarro	matchstick	cerilla, cerillo, fósforo
		headlight	cristal de frente, cristal delantero, luna delantera, lunas delanteras, luneta, parabrisa, parabrisas, vidrio delantero, windshield
sandwich	bocadillo, bocadito, bocata, emparedado, sandwich, sangüis, sangüich, sanwich	skirt	enagua, falda, pollera, saya
		blackboard	encerado, pizarra, pizarrón, tablero
suitcase	bolso de viaje, maleta, valija, veliz	dish drainer	escurreplatos, escurridero, escurridor, platera, secaplatos, secavajilla
boxers	bombacho, bóxers, calzón, calzoncillo, calzoncillos, pantaloncillos, ropa interior, slip, trusa, taparrabos, jokey	poncho	estola, jorongo, mañanera, poncho, ruana
		street light	farol, farola, farolillo, luminaria, poste de luz, poste eléctrico
lighter	bricke, brík, chispero, encendedor, fosforera, lighter, láiter, mechero, yesquero, zippo	dishwasher	friegaplatos, lavadora de platos, lavaloza, lavaplatos, lavatrastos, lavavajilla, lavavajillas, máquina de lavar platos
backhoe	buldózer, buldócer, caterpillar, caterpílar, excavadora, máquina excavadora, maquina topadora, motopala, pala excavadora, pala mecánica, retroexcavadora, topadora	refrigerator	frigorífico, heladera, hielera, nevera, refrigerador, refrigeradora
pot/pan	cacerola, cacico, cacillo, caldero, cazo, cazuela, olla, paila, pota, tartera, cazuela, sartén, freidera, freidero, fridera, paila	toilet paper	papel confórt, papel confor, papel de baño, papel de inodoro, papel de water, papel de váter, papel higiénico, papel sanitario, papel toalet, rollo de papel
socks	calcetas, calcetines, medias, soquetes	record player	wurlitzer, burlítser, chancha, compactera, gramola, juke box, máquina de música, pianola, rocola, tragamonedas, roconola, sinfonola, tocadiscos, traganíquel, vellonera, vitrola
reclining chair	cheilón, butaca, camastro, catre, cheslón, gandula, hamaca, perezosa, repo, reposera, silla de extensión, silla de playa, silla de sol, silla plegable, silla plegadiza, silla reclinable, tumbona	slice of cheese	lámina de queso, lasca de queso, loncha de queso, lonja de queso, rebanada de queso, rodaja de queso, slice de queso, tajada de queso, queso de sandwich, queso en lonchas, queso en rebanadas, queso en slice, queso americano, tranchetes
living room	comedor, cuarto de estar, estancia, líving, livin, recibidor, sala de estar, salita de estar, salón	demijohn	bidón, bombona, botella grande, garrafa, garrafón, tambuche, candungo, pomo plástico
computer	computador, computadora, microcomputador, microcomputadora, ordenador, PC		
washer	lavadora, lavarropa, lavarropas, máquina de lavar		

Concept	Keywords
plaster	banda adhesiva, curita, esparadrapo, tirita
attic	ático, altillo, azotea, buhardilla, guardilla, penthouse, mansarda, tabanco
wardrobe	armario, closet, placard, ropero, guardarropas
bracers	breteles, bruteles, suspensores, tiradores, tirantes
ring	anillo, argolla, aro, sortija, cintillo
tape recorder	cassette, casete, grabador, grabadora, magnetofón, tocacintas, magnetófono
merry-go-round	caballitos, calesita, carrusel, tiovivo, machina
loudspeaker	altavoz, altoparlante, altovoz, amplificador, megáfono, parlante, magnavoz
flower pot	maceta, macetero, matera, matero, tiesto, macetera, plantera
fans	afición, aficionados, fanáticos, fanaticada, forofos, hinchada, hinchas, seguidores
waiter	camarero, barman, mesero, mesonero, mozo, camarera
school	colegio, escuela, centro escolar, scuela
amusement	distracciones, diversión, entretención, entretenimiento, pasatiempo
stay	estada, estadía, estancia
miss	equivocación, error, falencia, fallo
cheek	cachetes, carrillos, galtas, mejillas, mofletes, pómulo
monkey	chango, chimpancé, macaco, mono, mico, simio, chongo
mosquito	cínife, mosco, mosquito, zancudo
chance	bicoca, chance, ocasión, oportunidad
sponsor	auspiciador, auspiciante, espónsor, patrocinador, patrocinante, propiciador, sponsor
park	aparcar, estacionar, parquear

Concept	Keywords
parcel	encomienda, paquete postal
banana	banana, banano, cambur, guineo, plátano, tombo
dust	nube de polvo, polvadera, polvareda, polvazal, polvero, polvoreda, polvorín, terral, terregal, tierral, tolvanera
bar	bar, boliche, cantina, cervecería, pulpería, taberna, tasca, expendio, piquera
earthquake	movimiento telúrico, movimiento sísmico, remezón, seísmo, sismo, temblor de tierra, terremoto
shooting	abaleo, balacera, baleada, tiroteo
glance	ojeada, miradita, vistazo
greasy	engrasado, grasiento, grasoso, mantecoso, seboso
beautiful	bella, bonita, hermosa, linda, preciosa
cold	catarro, constipado, coriza, gripa, gripe, resfrío, resfriado, trancazo
cellophane tape	celo, celofán, cinta adhesiva, cinta scotch, cintex, scotch, teip, dúrex, diurex, cinta pegante
crane	grúa, guinche, tecle
fruit cup	ensalada de frutas, macedonia, clericó, cóctel de frutas, tuttifruti, tutifruti
gas station	bomba de gasolina, bomba de nafta, estación de servicio, gasolinera, bencinera, bomba de bencina, gasolinería, surtidor de gasolina
interview	entrevistar, reportear, interviuvar
obstinate	cabezón, cabezudo, cabeza dura, cabezota, obstinado, porfiado, terco, testarudo, tozudo
peanut	cacahuate, cacahuete, maní, cacahué, cacaomani
scratch	arañazo, arañón, aruñetazo, aruñón, rajuño, rayón, rasguño, rasguñón
sweetener	edulcorante, endulzante, endulcina, endulzador, sacarina
thaw	descongelar, deshielar

Computational analysis of Gondi dialects

Taraka Rama and **Çağrı Çöltekin** and **Pavel Sofroniev**
Department of Linguistics
University of Tübingen, Germany
taraka-rama.kasicheyanula@uni-tuebingen.de
cagri.coeltekin@sfs.uni-tuebingen.de
pavel.sofroniev@student.uni-tuebingen.de

Abstract

This paper presents a computational analysis of Gondi dialects spoken in central India. We present a digitized data set of the dialect area, and analyze the data using different techniques from dialectometry, deep learning, and computational biology. We show that the methods largely agree with each other and with the earlier non-computational analyses of the language group.

1 Introduction

Gondi languages are spoken across a large region in the central part of India (cf. figure 1). The languages belong to the Dravidian language family and are closely related to Telugu, a major literary language spoken in South India. The Gondi languages received wide attention in comparative linguistics (Burrow and Bhattacharya, 1960; Garapati, 1991; Smith, 1991) due to their dialectal variation. On the one hand, the languages look like a dialect chain while, on the other hand, some of the dialects are shown to exhibit high levels of mutual unintelligibility (Beine, 1994).

Smith (1991) and Garapati (1991) perform classical comparative analyses of the dialects and classify the Gondi dialects into two subgroups: Northwest and Southeast. Garapati (1991) compares Gondi dialects where most of the dialects belong to Northwest subgroup and only three dialects belong to Southeast subgroup. In a different study, Beine (1994) collected lexical word lists transcribed in International Phonetic Alphabet (IPA) for 210 concepts belonging to 46 sites and attempted to perform a classification based on word similarity. Beine (1994) determines two words to be cognate (having descended from the same common ancestor) if they are identical in form and meaning. The average similarity between two sites is determined as the average number of identical words between the two sites. The author describes the experiments of the results qualitatively and does not perform any quantitative analysis. Until now, there has been no computational analysis of the lexical word lists to determine the exact relationship between these languages. We digitize the dataset and then perform a computational analysis.

Recent years have seen an increase in the number of computational methods applied to the study of both dialect and language classification. For instance, Nerbonne (2009) applied Levenshtein distance for the classification of Dutch and German dialects. Nerbonne finds that the classification offered by Levenshtein distance largely agrees with the traditional dialectological knowledge of Dutch and German areas. In this paper, we apply the dialectometric analysis to the Gondi language word lists.

In the related field of computational historical linguistics, Gray and Atkinson (2003) applied Bayesian phylogenetic methods from computational biology to date the age of Proto-Indo-European language tree. The authors use cognate judgments given by historical linguists to infer both the topology and the root age of the Indo-European family. In parallel to this work, Kondrak (2009) applied phonetically motivated string similarity measures and word alignment inspired methods for the purpose of determining if two words are cognates or not. This work was followed by List (2012) and Rama (2015) who employed statistical and string kernel methods for determining cognates in multilingual word lists.

In typical dialectometric studies (Nerbonne, 2009), the assumption that all the pronunciations of a particular word are cognates is often justified by the data. However, we cannot assume that this is the case in Gondi dialects since there are sig-

Proceedings of the Fourth Workshop on NLP for Similar Languages, Varieties and Dialects, pages 26–35,
Valencia, Spain, April 3, 2017. ©2017 Association for Computational Linguistics

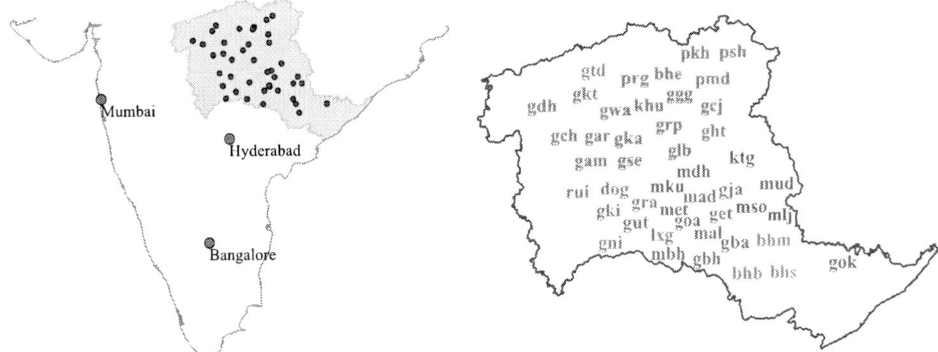

Figure 1: The Gondi language area with major cities in focus. The dialect/site codes and the geographical distribution of the codes are based on Beine (1994).

nificant amount of lexical replacement due to borrowing (from contact) and internal lexical innovations. Moreover, the previous comparative linguistic studies classify the Gondi dialects using sound correspondences and lexical cognates. In this paper, we will use the Pointwise Mutual Information (Wieling et al., 2009) method for obtaining sound change matrices and use the matrix to automatically identify cognates.

The comparative linguistic research classified the Gondi dialects into five different genetic groups (cf. table 1). However, the exact branching of the Gondi dialects is yet a open question. In this paper, we apply both dialectometric and phylogenetic approaches to determine the exact branching structure of the dialects.

The paper is organized as followed. In section 2, we describe the dataset and the gold standard dialect classification used in our experiments. In section 3, we describe the various techniques for computing and visualizing the dialectal differences. In section 4, we describe the results of the different analyses. We conclude the paper in section 5.

2 Datasets

The word lists for our experiments are derived from the fieldwork of Beine (1994). Beine (1994) provides multilingual word lists for 210 meanings in 46 sites in central India which is shown in figure 1. In the following sections, we use the Glottolog classification (Nordhoff and Hammarström, 2011) as gold standard to evaluate the various analyses. Glottolog is a openly available resource that summarizes the genetic relationships of the world's dialects and languages from published scholarly linguistic articles. For reference, we provide the Glottolog classification[1] of the Gondi dialects in table 1. The Glottolog classification is derived from comparative linguistics (Garapati, 1991; Smith, 1991) and dialect mutual intelligibility tests (Beine, 1994).

Dialect codes	Classification
gdh, gam, gar. gse. glb, gtd, gkt, gch, prg, gka, gwa, grp, khu, ggg, gcj, bhe, pmd, psh, pkh, ght	Northwest Gondi, Northern Gondi
rui, gki, gni, dog, gut, gra, lxg	Northwest Gondi, Southern Gondi
met, get, mad, gba, goa, mal, gja, gbh, mbh	Southeast Gondi, General Southeast Gondi, Hill Maria-Koya. Hill Maria
mku, mdh, ktg, mud, mso, mlj, gok	Southeast Gondi, General Southeast Gondi, Muria
bhm. bhb. bhs	Southeast Gondi, General Southeast Gondi, Bison Horn Maria

Table 1: Classification of the 46 sites according to Glottolog (Nordhoff and Hammarström, 2011).

The whole dialect region is divided into two major groups: Northwest Gondi and Southeast Gondi which are divided into five major subgroups: Northern Gondi, Southern Gondi, Hill Maria, Bison Horn Maria, Muria where Northern Gondi and Southern Gondi belong to the Northwest Gondi branch whereas the rest of the subgroups belong to Southeast Gondi branch. It has

---

[1]http://glottolog.org/resource/languoid/id/gond1265

27

to be noted that there is no gold standard about the internal structure of dialects belonging to each dialect group.

3 Methods for comparing and visualizing dialectal differences

We use the IPA transcribed data to compute both unweighted and weighted string similarity/distance between two words. We use the same IPA data to train LSTM autoencoders introduced by Rama and Çöltekin (2016) and project the autoencoder based distances onto a map.

As mentioned earlier, the dialectometric analyses typically assume that all words that share the same meaning are cognates. However, as shown by Garapati (1991), some Gondi dialects exhibit a clear tree structure. Both dialectometric and autoencoder methods only provide an aggregate amount of similarity between dialects and do not work with cognates directly. The methods are sensitive to lexical differences only through high dissimilarity of phonetic strings. Since lexical and phonetic differences are likely to indicate different processes of linguistic change, we also analyze the categorical differences due to lexical borrowings/changes. For this purpose, we perform automatic cognate identification and then use the inferred cognates to perform both Bayesian phylogenetic analysis and dialectometric analysis.

3.1 Dialectometry

3.1.1 Computing aggregate distances

In this subsection, we describe how Levenshtein distance and autoencoder based methods are employed for computing site-site distances.

Levenshtein distance: Levenshtein distance is defined as the minimum number of edit operations (insertion, deletion, and substitution) that are required to transform one string to another. We use the Gabmap (Nerbonne et al., 2011) implementation of Levenshtein distance to compute site-site differences.

Autoencoders: Rama and Çöltekin (2016) introduced LSTM autoencoders for the purpose of dialect classification. Autoencoders were employed by Hinton and Salakhutdinov (2006) for reducing the dimensionality of images and documents. Autoencoders learn a dense representation that can be used for clustering the documents and images.

An autoencoder network consists of two parts:
encoder and *decoder*. The encoder network takes a word as an input and transforms the word to a fixed dimension representation. The fixed dimension representation is then supplied as an input to a decoder network that attempts to reconstruct the input word. In our paper, both the encoder and decoder networks are Long-Short Term Memory networks (Hochreiter and Schmidhuber, 1997).

In this paper, each word is represented as a sequence $(x_1, \ldots x_T)$ of one-hot vectors of dimension $|P|$ where P is the total number (58) of IPA symbols across the dialects. The encoder is a LSTM network that transforms each word into $h \in \mathbb{R}^k$ where k is predetermined beforehand (in this paper, k is assigned a value of 32). The decoder consists of another LSTM network that takes h as input at each timestep to predict an output representation. Each output representation is then supplied to a softmax function to yield $\hat{x}_t \in \mathbb{R}^{|P|}$. The autoencoder network is trained using the binary cross-entropy function $(-\sum_t x_t log(\hat{x}_t) + (1 - x_t)log(1 - \hat{x}_t))$ where, x_t is a 1-hot vector and $\hat{x}_t$ is the output of the softmax function at timestep t to learn both the encoder and decoder LSTM's parameters. Following Rama and Çöltekin (2016), we use a bidirectional LSTM as the encoder network and a unidirectional LSTM as the decoder network. Our autoencoder model was implemented using Keras (Chollet, 2015) with Tensorflow (Abadi et al., 2016) as the backend.

3.1.2 Visualization

We use Gabmap, a web-based application for dialectometric analysis for visualizing the site-site distances (Nerbonne et al., 2011; Leinonen et al., 2016).[2] Gabmap provides a number of methods for analyzing and visualizing dialect data. Below, we present maps and graphics that are results of *multi-dimensional scaling* (MDS) *clustering*.

For all analyses, Gabmap aggregates the differences calculated over individual items (concepts) to a site-site distance matrix. With phonetic data, it uses site-site differences based on string edit distance with a higher penalty for vowel–consonant alignments and a lower penalty for the alignments of sound pairs that differ only in IPA diacritics. With binary data, Gabmap uses Hamming distances to compute the site-site differences. The cognate clusters obtained from the automatic iden-

---

[2]Available at `http://gabmap.nl/`.

tification procedure (section 2.2) forms categories (cognate clusters) which are analyzed using binary distances. Finally, we also visualize the distances from the autoencoders (section 2.1) using Gabmap.

Gabmap provides various agglomerative hierarchical clustering methods for clustering analyses. In all the results below, we use Ward's method for calculating cluster differences. For our analyses, we present the clustering results on (color) maps and dendrograms. Since the clustering is known to be relatively unstable, we also present probabilistic dendrograms that are produced by noisy clustering (Nerbonne et al., 2008). In noisy clustering, a single cluster analysis is performed a large number of times ($\sim$ 100) by adding a small noise to the distance matrix that is proportional to the standard deviation of the original distance matrix. The combined analysis then provides statistical support for the branches in a dendrogram.

The multi-dimensional scaling (MDS) is a useful analysis/visualization technique for verifying the clustering results and visualizing the dialect continuum. A site-site (linguistic) distance matrix represents each site on a multi-dimensional space. MDS 'projects' these distances to a smaller dimensional space that can be visualized easily. In dialect data, the distances in few most-important MDS dimensions correlate highly with the original distances, and these dimensions often correspond to linguistically meaningful dimensions. Below, we also present maps where areas around the linguistic similar locations are plotted using similar colors.

3.2 Phylogenetic approaches

3.2.1 Automatic cognate detection

Given a multilingual word list for a concept, the automatic cognate detection procedure (Hauer and Kondrak, 2011) can be broken into two parts:

1. Compute a pairwise similarity score for all word pairs in the concept.
2. Supply the pairwise similarity matrix to a clustering algorithm to output clusters that show high similarity with one another.

Needleman-Wunsch algorithm (NW, Needleman and Wunsch (1970); the similarity counterpart of Levenshtein distance) is a possible choice for computing the similarity between two words. The NW algorithm maximizes similarity whereas Levenshtein distance minimizes the distance between two words. The NW algorithm assigns a score of 1 for character match and a score -1 for character mismatch. Unlike Levenshtein distance, NW algorithm assigns a penalty score for opening a gap (deletion operation) and a penalty for gap extension which models the fact that deletion operations occur in chunks (Jäger, 2013).

The NW algorithm is not sensitive to different sound segment pairs, but a realistic algorithm should assign higher similarity score to sound correspondences such as /l/ $\sim$ /r/ than the sound correspondences /p/ $\sim$ /r/. The weighted Needleman-Wunsch algorithm takes a segment-segment similarity matrix as input and then aligns the two strings to maximize the similarity between the two words.

In dialectometry (Wieling et al., 2009), the segment-segment similarity matrix is estimated using *pointwise mutual information* (PMI). The PMI score for two sounds x and y is defined as followed:

$$pmi(x, y) = log \frac{p(x, y)}{p(x)p(y)} \tag{1}$$

where, $p(x, y)$ is the probability of x, y being matched in a pair of cognate words, whereas, $p(x)$ is the probability of x. A positive PMI value between x and y indicates that the probability of x being aligned with y in a pair of cognates is higher than what would be expected by chance. Conversely, a negative PMI value indicates that an alignment of x with y is more likely the result of chance than of shared inheritance.

The PMI based computation requires a prior list of plausible cognates for computing a weighted similarity matrix between sound segments. In the initial step, we extract cross-lingual word pairs that have a Levenshtein distance less than 0.5 and treat them as a list of plausible cognates. The PMI estimation procedure is described as followed:

1. Compute alignments between the word pairs using a vanilla Needleman-Wunsch algorithm.[3]
2. The computed alignments from step 1 are then used to compute similarity between segments x, y according to the following formula:

---

[3] We set the gap-opening penalty to -2.5 and gap extension penalty to -1.75.

3. The PMI matrix obtained from step 2 is used to realign the word pairs and generate a new list of segment alignments. The new list of alignments is employed to compute a new PMI matrix.

4. Steps 2 and 3 are repeated until the difference between PMI matrices reach zero.

In our experience, five iterations were sufficient to reach convergence. At this stage, we use the PMI matrix to compute a word similarity matrix between the words belonging to a single meaning. The word similarity matrix was converted into a word distance matrix using the following transformation: $(1 + exp(x))^{-1}$ where, x is the PMI score between two words. We use the InfoMap clustering algorithm (List et al., 2016) for the purpose of identifying cognate clusters.

3.2.2 Bayesian phylogenetic inference

The Bayesian phylogenetics originated in evolutionary biology and works by inferring the evolutionary relationship (trees) between DNA sequences of species. The same method is applied to binary traits of species (Yang, 2014). A binary trait is typically a presence or absence of a evolutionary character in an biological organism. Computational biologists employ a probabilistic substitution model θ that models the transition probabilities from $0 \rightarrow 1$ and $1 \rightarrow 0$. The substitution matrix would be a 2×2 matrix in the case of a binary data matrix.

A evolutionary tree that explains the relationship between languages consist of topology (τ) and branch lengths ($\mathbf{T}$). The likelihood of the binary data to a tree is computed using the pruning algorithm (Felsenstein, 1981). Ideally, identifying the best tree would involve exhaustive enumeration of the trees and calculating the likelihood of the binary matrix for each tree. However, the number of possible binary tree topologies grows factorially $((2n - 3)!!$ where, n is the number of languages) and, hence intractable even for a small number (20) of languages. The inference problem would be to estimate the joint posterior density of $\tau, \theta, \mathbf{T}$.

The Bayesian phylogenetic inference program (*MrBayes*;[4] Ronquist and Huelsenbeck (2003)) requires a binary matrix (languages $\times$ number of clusters) of 0s and 1s, where, each column shows if a language is present in a cluster or not. The

---

[4] http://mrbayes.sourceforge.net/

German	*Hund*	1	0
Swedish	*hund*	1	0
Hindi	*kutta*	0	1

Table 2: Binary matrix for meaning "dog".

cognate clusters are converted into a binary matrix of 0s and 1s in the following manner. A word for a meaning would belong to one or more cognate sets. For example, in the case of German, Swedish, and Hindi, the word for *dog* in German 'Hund' and Swedish 'hund' would belong to the same cognate set, while Hindi 'kutta' would belong to a different category. The binary trait matrix for these languages for a single meaning, *dog*, would be as in table 2. A Bayesian phylogenetic analysis employs a Markov-Chain Monte-Carlo procedure to navigate across the tree space. In this paper, we ran two independent runs until the trees inferred by the two runs do not differ beyond a threshold of 0.01. In summary, we ran both the chains for 4 million states and sampled trees at every 500 states to avoid auto-correlation. Then, we threw away the initial one million states as burn-in and generated a summary tree of the post burn-in runs (Felsenstein, 2004). The summary tree consists of only those branches which have occurred more than 50% of the time in the posterior sample, consisting of 25000 trees.

4 Results

In this section, we present visualizations of differences in the language area using MDS and noisy clustering.

4.1 String edit distance

In the left map in Figure 2, the first three MDS dimensions are mapped to RGB color space, visualizing the differences between the locations. Note that the major dialectal differences outlined in table 1 are visible in this visualization. For example, the magenta and yellow-green regions separate the Bison Horn Maria and the Hill Maria groups from the surrounding areas with sharp contrasts. The original linguistic distances and the distances based on first three MDS dimensions correlate with $r = 0.90$, hence, retaining about 81% of the variation in the original distances. The middle map in figure 2 displays only the first dimension, which seems to represent a difference between north and south. On the other hand, the

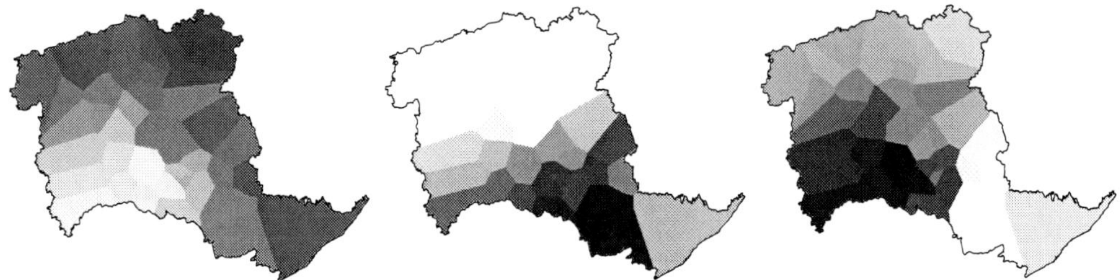

Figure 2: MDS analysis performed by Gabmap with string edit distance. The left map shows first three MDS dimensions mapped to RGB color space. The middle map shows only the first dimension, and the right map shows the second MDS dimension. The first three dimensions correlate with the original distances with $r = 0.73$, $r = 0.55$ and $r = 0.41$, respectively, and first three dimensions with $r = 0.90$.

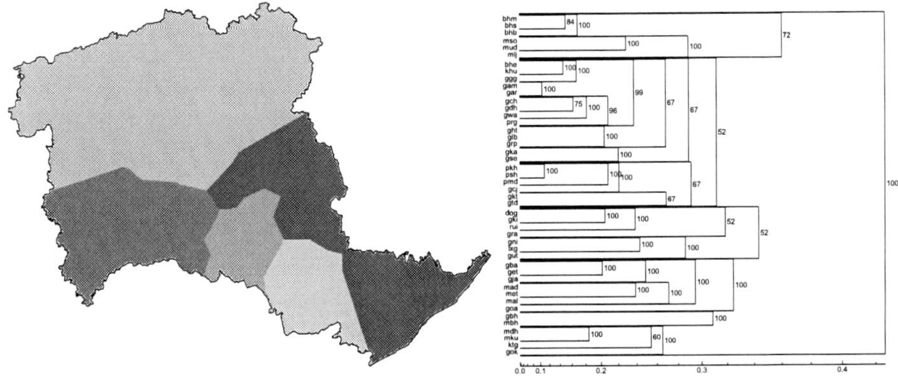

Figure 3: Clustering analysis performed by Gabmap with string edit distance using Ward's method and the color in the map indicate 5 dialect groups. Probabilistic dendrogram from the default Gabmap analysis (string edit distance).

right map (second MDS dimension) seems to indicate a difference between Bison Horn Maria (and to some extent Muria) and the rest.

The clustering results are also complementary to the MDS analysis. The 5-way cluster map presented in figure 3 indicates the expected dialect groups described in table 1. Despite some unexpected results in the detailed clustering, the probabilistic dendrogram presented in figure 3 also shows that the main dialect groups are stable across noisy clustering experiments. For instance, the Bison Horn Maria group (bhm, bhs, bhb) presented on the top part of the dendrogram indicates a very stable group: these locations are clustered together in all the noisy clustering experiments. Similarly, the next three locations (mco, mud, mlj, belonging to Muria area) also show a very strong internal consistency, and combine with the Bison Horn Maria group in 72% of the noisy clustering

experiments. However, other members of Muria group (mdh, mku, ktg, gok at the bottom of the probabilistic dendrogram) seem to be placed often apart from the rest of the group.

4.2 Binary distances

Next, we present the MDS analysis based on lexical distances in figure 4. For this analysis, we identify cognates for each meaning (cf. section 2.2), and treat the cognate clusters found in each location as the only (categorical) features for analysis. The overall picture seems to be similar to the analysis based on the phonetic data, although the north-south differences are more visible in this analysis. Besides the first three dimensions (left map), both first (middle map) and second (right map) dimensions indicate differences between north and south. The left figure shows that there is a gradual transition from the Northern dialects (gtd, gkt, prg, ggg, khu, bhe, gcj, pmd, psh,

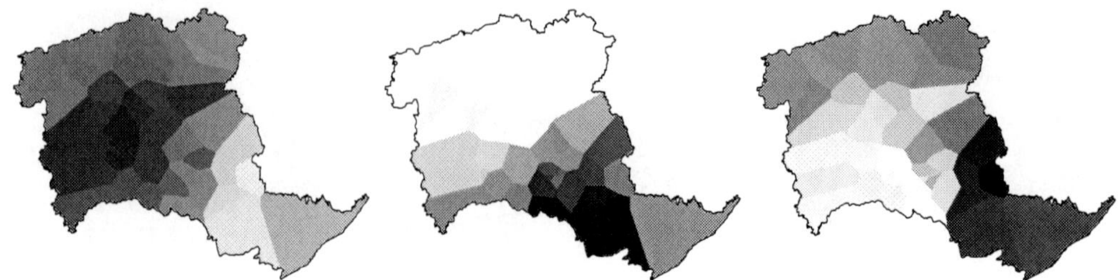

Figure 4: MDS analysis performed by Gabmap with categorical differences. The left map shows first three MDS dimensions mapped to RGB color space. The middle map shows only the first dimension, and the right map shows the second MDS dimension. The first three dimensions correlate with the original distances with $r = 0.77$, $r = 0.53$ and $r = 0.41$, respectively, and first three dimensions with $r = 0.94$.

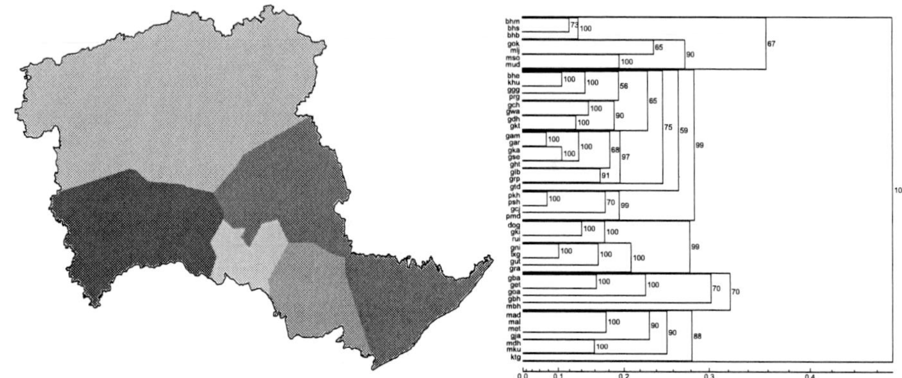

Figure 5: The dendrogram shows the results of the hierarchical clustering (left) based on binary matrix. Probabilistic dendrogram from the Gabmap analysis with Hamming distances.

pkh) to the rest of the northern dialects that share borders with Muria and Southern dialects. There is a transition between Southern dialects to the Hill Maria dialects where, the Hill Maria dialects do not show much variation.

The clustering analysis of the binary matrix from cognate detection step is projected on the geographical map of the region in figure 5. The map retrieves the five clear subgroups listed in table 1. Then, we perform a noisy clustering analysis of the Hamming distance matrix which is shown in the same figure. The dendrogram places Bison-Horn Maria dialects (bhm, bhs, bhb) along with the eastern dialects of Muria subgroup. It also places all the Northern Gondi dialects into a single cluster with high confidence. The dendrogram also places all the southern dialects into a single cluster. On the other hand, the dendrogram incorrectly places the Hill Maria dialects along with the western dialects of Muria subgroup. With slight

variation in the detail, the cluster analysis and the probabilistic dendrogram presented in figure 5 are similar to the analysis based on phonetic differences.

4.3 Autoencoder distances

The MDS analysis of autoencoder-based distances are shown in figure 6. The RGB color map of the first three dimensions shows the five dialect regions. The figure shows a clear boundary between Northern and Southern Gondi dialects. The map shows the Bison Horn Maria region to be of distinct blue color that does not show much variance. The autoencoder MDS dimensions correlate the highest with the autoencoder distance matrix. The first dimension (middle map in figure 6) clearly distinguishes the Northern dialects from the rest. The second dimension distinguishes Southern Gondi dialects and Muria dialects from the rest of the dialects.

The clustering analysis of the autoencoder dis-

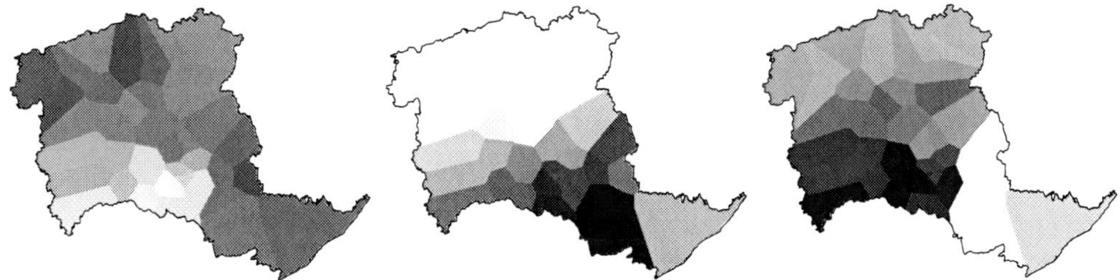

Figure 6: MDS analysis performed by Gabmap with autoencoder differences. The left map shows first three MDS dimensions mapped to RGB color space. The middle map shows only the first dimension, and the right map shows the second MDS dimension. The first three dimensions correlate with the original distances with $r = 0.74$, $r = 0.57$ and $r = 0.49$, respectively, and first three dimensions with $r = 0.92$.

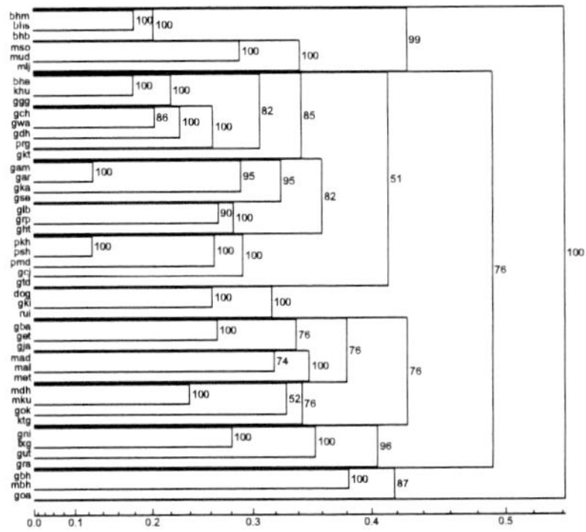

Figure 7: Probabilistic dendrogram from the Gabmap analysis with autoencoder distances. The clustering result is similar to the left map in figure 3.

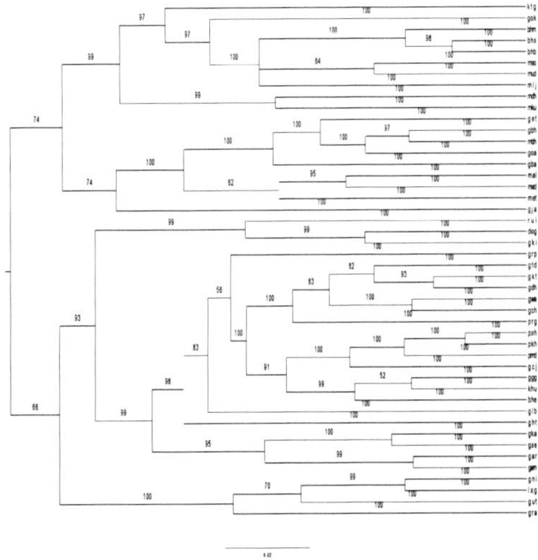

Figure 8: The majority consensus tree of the Bayesian posterior trees.

tances are projected on to the geographical map in figure 7. The map retrieves the five subgroups in table 1. The noisy clustering clearly puts the Bison Horn Maria group into a single cluster. It also places all the northern dialects into a single group with 100% confidence. On the other hand, the dendrogram splits the Southern Gondi dialects into eastern and western parts. The eastern parts are placed along with the Hill Maria dialects. The clustering analysis also splits the Muria dialects into three parts. However, the dendrogram places *gok* (a eastern Muria dialect) incorrectly with Far Western Muria (mku).

4.4 Bayesian analysis

The summary tree of the Bayesian analysis is shown in figure 8. The figure also shows the percentage of times each branch exists in the posterior sample of trees. The tree clearly divided North-

west Gondi from Southeast Gondi groups. The tree places all the Northern Gondi dialects into a single group in 99% of the trees. The southern dialects are split into two different branches with *rui, dog, gki* branching later from the common Northwest Gondi later than the rest of the Southern Gondi dialects. The tree clearly splits the Hill Maria dialects from rest of Southeast Gondi dialects. The tree also places all the Bison Horn Maria dialects into a single group but does not put them into a different group from the rest of the Muria dialects.

5 Conclusion

In this paper, we performed analysis using tools from dialectometry and computational historical linguistics for the analysis of Gondi dialects. The dialectometric analysis rightly retrieves all the subgroups in the region. However, both edit distance and autoencoder distances differ in the noisy clustering analysis. On the other hand, the noisy clustering analysis on the binary cognate matrix yields the best results. The Bayesian tree based on cognate analysis also retrieves the top level subgroups right but does not clearly distinguish Bison Horn Maria group from Muria dialects. As a matter of fact, the Bayesian tree agrees the highest with the gold standard classification from Glottolog.

The contributions of the paper is as followed. We digitized a multilingual lexical wordlist for 46 dialects and applied both dialectometric and phylogenetic methods for the classification of dialects and find that phylogenetic methods perform the best when compared to the gold standard classification.

Acknowledgments

The authors thank the five reviewers for the comments which helped improve the paper. The first and third authors are supported by the ERC Advanced Grant 324246 EVOLAEMP, which is gratefully acknowledged.
The code and the data for the experiments is available at https://github.com/ PhyloStar/Gondi-Dialect-Analysis

References

Martın Abadi, Ashish Agarwal, Paul Barham, Eugene Brevdo, Zhifeng Chen, Craig Citro, Greg S Corrado, Andy Davis, Jeffrey Dean, Matthieu Devin, et al. 2016. Tensorflow: Large-scale machine learning on heterogeneous distributed systems. *arXiv preprint arXiv:1603.04467*.

David K. Beine. 1994. A sociolinguistic survey of the Gondi-speaking communities of central india. Master's thesis, San Diego State University, San Diego.

Thomas Burrow and S. Bhattacharya. 1960. A comparative vocabulary of the Gondi dialects. *Journal of the Asiatic Society*, 2:73–251.

François Chollet. 2015. Keras. *GitHub repository: https://github. com/fchollet/keras*.

Joseph Felsenstein. 1981. Evolutionary trees from DNA sequences: A maximum likelihood approach. *Journal of Molecular Evolution*, 17(6):368–376.

Joseph Felsenstein. 2004. *Inferring phylogenies*. Sinauer Associates, Sunderland, Massachusetts.

Umamaheshwar Rao Garapati. 1991. Subgrouping of the Gondi dialects. In B. Lakshmi Bai and B. Ramakrishna Reddy, editors, *Studies in Dravidian and general linguistics: a festschrift for Bh. Krishnamurti*, pages 73–90. Centre of Advanced Study in Linguistics, Osmania University.

Russell D. Gray and Quentin D. Atkinson. 2003. Language-tree divergence times support the Anatolian theory of Indo-European origin. *Nature*, 426(6965):435–439.

Bradley Hauer and Grzegorz Kondrak. 2011. Clustering semantically equivalent words into cognate sets in multilingual lists. In *Proceedings of 5th International Joint Conference on Natural Language Processing*, pages 865–873, Chiang Mai, Thailand, November. Asian Federation of Natural Language Processing.

Geoffrey E Hinton and Ruslan R Salakhutdinov. 2006. Reducing the dimensionality of data with neural networks. *Science*, 313(5786):504–507.

Sepp Hochreiter and Jürgen Schmidhuber. 1997. Long short-term memory. *Neural computation*, 9(8):1735–1780.

Gerhard Jäger. 2013. Phylogenetic inference from word lists using weighted alignment with empirically determined weights. *Language Dynamics and Change*, 3(2):245–291.

Grzegorz Kondrak. 2009. Identification of cognates and recurrent sound correspondences in word lists. *Traitement Automatique des Langues et Langues Anciennes*, 50(2):201–235, October.

Therese Leinonen, Çağrı Çöltekin, and John Nerbonne. 2016. Using Gabmap. *Lingua*, 178:71–83.

Johann-Mattis List, Philippe Lopez, and Eric Bapteste. 2016. Using sequence similarity networks to identify partial cognates in multilingual wordlists. In *Proceedings of the 54th Annual Meeting of the Association for Computational Linguistics (Volume 2: Short Papers)*, pages 599–605, Berlin, Germany, August. Association for Computational Linguistics.

Johann-Mattis List. 2012. LexStat: Automatic detection of cognates in multilingual wordlists. In *Proceedings of the EACL 2012 Joint Workshop of LINGVIS & UNCLH*, pages 117–125, Avignon, France, April. Association for Computational Linguistics.

Saul B. Needleman and Christian D. Wunsch. 1970. A general method applicable to the search for similarities in the amino acid sequence of two proteins. *Journal of Molecular Biology*, 48(3):443–453.

John Nerbonne, Peter Kleiweg, Wilbert Heeringa, and Franz Manni. 2008. Projecting dialect differences to geography: Bootstrap clustering vs. noisy clustering. In Christine Preisach, Lars Schmidt-Thieme, Hans Burkhardt, and Reinhold Decker, editors, *Data Analysis, Machine Learning, and Applications. Proc. of the 31st Annual Meeting of the German Classification Society*, pages 647–654, Berlin. Springer.

John Nerbonne, Rinke Colen, Charlotte Gooskens, Peter Kleiweg, and Therese Leinonen. 2011. Gabmap – a web application for dialectology. *Dialectologia*, Special Issue II:65–89.

John Nerbonne. 2009. Data-driven dialectology. *Language and Linguistics Compass*, 3(1):175–198.

Sebastian Nordhoff and Harald Hammarström. 2011. Glottolog/Langdoc: Defining dialects, languages, and language families as collections of resources. In *Proceedings of the First International Workshop on Linked Science*, volume 783, pages 53–58.

Taraka Rama and Çağri Çöltekin. 2016. LSTM autoencoders for dialect analysis. In *Proceedings of the Third Workshop on NLP for Similar Languages, Varieties and Dialects (VarDial3)*, pages 25–32, Osaka, Japan, December. The COLING 2016 Organizing Committee.

Taraka Rama. 2015. Automatic cognate identification with gap-weighted string subsequences. In *Proceedings of the 2015 Conference of the North American Chapter of the Association for Computational Linguistics: Human Language Technologies.*, pages 1227–1231.

Fredrik Ronquist and John P Huelsenbeck. 2003. Mrbayes 3: Bayesian phylogenetic inference under mixed models. *Bioinformatics*, 19(12):1572–1574.

Ian Smith. 1991. Interpreting conflicting isoglosses: Historical relationships among the Gondi dialects. In B. Lakshmi Bai and B. Ramakrishna Reddy, editors, *Studies in Dravidian and general linguistics: a festschrift for Bh. Krishnamurti*, pages 27–48. Centre of Advanced Study in Linguistics, Osmania University.

Martijn Wieling, Jelena Prokić, and John Nerbonne. 2009. Evaluating the pairwise string alignment of pronunciations. In *Proceedings of the EACL 2009 Workshop on Language Technology and Resources for Cultural Heritage, Social Sciences, Humanities, and Education*, pages 26–34. Association for Computational Linguistics.

Ziheng Yang. 2014. *Molecular evolution: A statistical approach*. Oxford University Press, Oxford.

Investigating Diatopic Variation in a Historical Corpus

Stefanie Dipper
Department of Linguistics
Ruhr-Universität Bochum
44780 Bochum, Germany
`dipper@linguistics.rub.de`

Sandra Waldenberger
German Department
Ruhr-Universität Bochum
44780 Bochum, Germany
`sandra.waldenberger@rub.de`

Abstract

This paper investigates diatopic variation in a historical corpus of German. Based on equivalent word forms from different language areas, replacement rules and mappings are derived which describe the relations between these word forms. These rules and mappings are then interpreted as reflections of morphological, phonological or graphemic variation. Based on sample rules and mappings, we show that our approach can replicate results from historical linguistics. While previous studies were restricted to predefined word lists, or confined to single authors or texts, our approach uses a much wider range of data available in historical corpora.

1 Introduction

In this paper we give an outline of our joint endeavor—combining computational and German historical linguistics—to develop a set of methods with the goal of uncovering and investigating the whole range of variation on the word level in a large scale corpus of historical texts. This is in contrast to traditional approaches in historical linguistics, who often use a predefined list of carefully-selected words for comparing linguistic variation.

In recent years, an increasing number of corpora of historical German has been built and published, including reference corpora of historical German, some still under construction (Donhauser, 2015; Klein et al., 2016; Schmitz et al., 2013; Peters and Nagel, 2014). Data from texts of historical and thus non-standard German is always strongly characterized by variation on every level of the language system. Hence, designing methods to gather and analyze the scope and scale of variation present in these corpora is a hot topic as well as a methodological challenge. Purely manual analysis is ruled out by the large amount of data provided by these corpora, necessitating the application of automatic methods.

We address the challenge of dealing with such data by way of systematic and exhaustive comparison of words that are variants of each other. To test and develop the comparative methods presented here we use the *Anselm* Corpus (Dipper and Schultz-Balluff, 2013).

The paper is organized as follows. Section 2 addresses prior work done in this area. In Section 3, we introduce the *Anselm* Corpus that we used in our comparison. Sections 4 and 5 present the comparison and its results, followed by a conclusion in Section 6.

2 Related Work

In recent years, spelling variation in non-standard data, such as historical texts or texts from social media, has come into focus in Natural Language Processing. Most often, variation is dealt with by normalization, i.e. mapping variants to some standard form (for historical data, see Piotrowski (2012, chap. 6)). The main focus of this research has been on how to automatize the normalization process, which is often a preparatory step to facilitate further processing of historical language data, e.g. by search tools or taggers (e.g. Jurish (2010), Bollmann (2012)). Some work addresses the extent of variance found in the data (e.g. Baron et al. (2009)). However, the derived mappings themselves that map historical to modern word forms are usually not in the focus of interest (but see Barteld et al. (2016)).

In contrast, theoretical linguists researching language evolution and language varieties are interested in these mappings, which highlight the

Proceedings of the Fourth Workshop on NLP for Similar Languages, Varieties and Dialects, pages 36–45,
Valencia, Spain, April 3, 2017. ©2017 Association for Computational Linguistics

differences between the languages. Traditionally, historical linguistic research is mainly based on morphological and phonological properties. For instance, the relationships between the Indo-European languages have been established on the base of shared inflectional properties and phonetic relations, such as the first and second Germanic consonant shift. Similarly, dialect classification mainly depends on phonological and morphological features, with syntactic properties playing a minor role.

Language comparison in this spirit is based on specific language data: for sound-based comparison, lists of parallel words in different languages or language stages are usually used, such as the classical Swadesh list (Swadesh, 1955) or lists that have been compiled more recently for various languages (see, e.g., the data used in Jäger et al. (2017)). The challenge is then to identify related words, such as cognates and loan words, and unrelated words. The number of cognates between two languages serves as a measure of relatedness. In some approaches, no distinction is made between "real cognates", which are etymologically related, and words that are related due to some process other than strict inheritance.

In contrast to these approaches, we do not restrict our comparisons to single words from carefully-compiled word lists but aim at using as much data as possible from available corpora.

3 The Data

The data we use to test and refine our method has been extracted from the *Anselm* Corpus, which consists of about 50 versions of the medieval text *Interrogatio Sancti Anselmi de Passione Domini* ('Questions by Saint Anselm about the Lord's Passion'). The text is a dialogue between St. Anselm and the Virgin Mary, who recounts the events of the passion. The versions are from different language areas and time periods from Early New High German (1350–1600). Since they deal with the same topic, the overlap in content and vocabulary is large. Hence, the data provides a perfect basis for diatopic research. The map in Figure 1 gives an impression of the wide distribution of the different versions across the German language area.

Each word form in the *Anselm* Corpus has been manually annotated by its modern German translation (Bollmann et al., 2012). We define

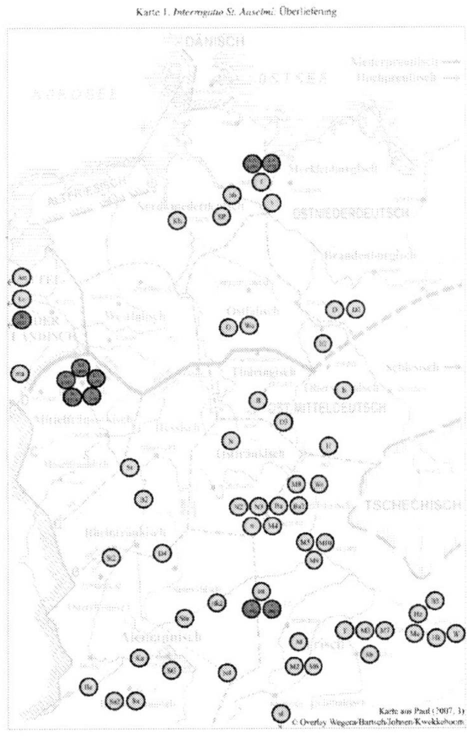

Figure 1: Distribution of the Anselm texts across the German-speaking area. Each marker represents one text (map taken from `https://www.linguistics.rub.de/anselm/corpus/map.html`).

as *shared* or *equivalent* all historical word forms whose modern translations are identical. For instance, *vffston* in an Alemannic text and *vpstain* in a Ripuarian text are considered equivalent because they both correspond to modern German *aufstehen* 'stand up'. The investigations we present in this paper are based on such shared, equivalent word forms occurring in different texts.

Table 1 gives an overview of the temporal and regional distribution of shared words in the *Anselm* data.[1] The table shows that the *Anselm* Corpus has a good coverage of the 15th century, and that *mbair* is the best-documented language area.

We selected seven texts from different language areas for diatopic comparison. The comparison starts with texts written in the same language area

---

[1] *14* means '14th century', *14.1* means 'first half of the 14th century' (i.e. 1300–1350), etc. The language areas are: *alem*: Alemannic, *hchalem*: High Alemannic, *mbair*: Central Bavarian, *nbair*: North Bavarian, *obs*: Upper Saxon, *rhfrk*: Rhine-Franconian, *rip*: 'Ripuarian', *schwaeb*: 'Swabian'; *thuer*: 'Thuringian'.

			14	14.1	14.2	15	15.1	15.2	16	16.1
Upper German	East	nbair					4143:2	12840:7		
		mbair			2119:1		7995:4	9915:6	2236:2	1535:1
	West	alem	2166:1			1991:1				
		hchalem		2497:1				6653:2		1976:1
		schwaeb					2102:1	4404:4		
Central German	West	rip						3507:2		5510:3
		rhfrk						4203:2		
	East	thuer				1250:1		1713:1		
		obs			777:1					2039:1

Table 1: Temporal and regional distributions of shared, equivalent words (number of types) in the *Anselm* Corpus. The numbers after the colon represent the number of texts that have been compared.

	nbair		mbair		schw	rhfrk	
	M4	*Ba2*	*M3*	*B3*	*D4*	*St*	*B2*
M4	–	1572	2407	1856	1732	2058	2141
Ba2		–	1744	1475	1552	1614	1585
M3			–	1954	1884	2220	2315
B3				–	1611	1734	1765
D4					–	1865	1779
St						–	2300

Table 2: Number of pairwise shared words (types) for diatopic comparison, all texts dating from 15.2.

Text 1	Text 2	Normalization
M4: bedürfen	*M3*: pedurffen	bedürfen 'require'
Ba2: pitten	*B3*: biten	bitten 'ask'
St: uch	*D4*: aüch	euch 'you (pl)'

Table 3: Examples of equivalent word forms.

(e.g. *mbair*) and proceeds with the comparison of adjacent language areas that belong to the same major dialect (*mbair* → *nbair*). Finally, texts from different dialects are compared, which are separated by the *Speyer line*, an isogloss separating the language areas called 'Central German' and 'Upper German' (*rhfrk* → *schwaeb/bair*).

Table 2 shows the overlap between the texts that we compared.[2]

4 Diatopic Comparison

As mentioned above, the diatopic comparisons are based on *equivalent* word forms. This section describes how these forms are found and how they form the base of comparison.

4.1 Finding Equivalent Word Forms

All original word forms in the *Anselm* Corpus have been manually normalized to the corresponding modern German word forms (Bollmann et al., 2012). All word forms with identical normalizations are considered equivalent.[3] For each pair of texts, equivalent word forms were collected and paired. Table 3 shows some sample pairs.

4.2 Deriving Rewrite Rules and Levenshtein-based Mappings

Similarities and differences between the equivalent word forms are modeled by means of 'Rewrite rules' and Levenshtein-based mappings (for detailed description and comparison of both methods, see Bollmann (2012)).

Rewrite rules Given a pair of equivalent word forms, both forms are first aligned at the character level, see (1a) which aligns the equivalent word forms *biten* and *pitten* (*bitten*, 'ask') (for details, see Bollmann et al. (2011)). (1b) is an alternative representation of the alignments. In the following,

---

[2]The identifiers used here (*M4* etc.) are the sigla of the individual texts, as defined in the *Anselm* corpus, see https://www.linguistics.ruhr-uni-bochum.de/anselm/corpus/german.html for a list. The sigla are derived from the respective repositories, e.g. *M4* is stored in Munich (Bayerische Staatsbibliothek).

[3]In order to diminish data sparseness, word forms with identical normalization but differing morphological properties were also considered equivalent, e.g. *chrawcze* (*M3*, mostly dative case) and *creucz* (*B3*, any case), both normalized as *kreuz* 'cross'.

the format of (1b) is used in the presentation of examples.

$$(1) \quad a. \quad \begin{array}{|c|c|c|c|c|c|}\hline \textit{B3} & b & i & & t & e & n \\\hline \textit{Ba2} & p & i & t & t & e & n \\\hline\end{array}$$

b. |b=p|i=i|t=t|=t|e=e|n=n|

From these character alignments, rewrite rules are derived that replace characters from the first word to arrive at the second word. The word pair in (1) gives rise to the context-aware replacement rules shown in (2). '#' indicates word boundaries, 'E' represents the empty string.

(2) a. b → p | # _ i
"Replace word-initial 'b' by 'p', if followed by 'i'"

b. E → t | i _ t
"Insert 't' between 'i' and 't'"

In addition to the replacement rules, "identity rules" are derived, recording the characters that are identical in both word forms, see (3) and (4) for the identity rules derived from (1).[4]

(3) a. i → i | p _ t

b. t → t | t _ e

c. e → e | t _ e

d. n → n | e _ #

(4) a. E → E | # _ p

b. E → E | p _ i

c. E → E | t _ e

d. E → E | e _ n

e. E → E | n _ #

The rules derived from a text pair are collected and counted. Table 4 shows the top five identity and non-identity rules with their frequencies, as derived from the equivalent word forms of *B3* and *Ba2*. The interpretation of these rules is addressed below.

---

[4]The left context is checked against the target word form, the right context against the source form. The rules can also map sequences of characters, thus considering larger context. For details see Bollmann et al. (2011).
The rules in (4) prevent the insertion of characters at specific positions.

Freq	Rule					
419	E	→	E	n	_	#
312	E	→	E	e	_	n
281	n	→	n	e	_	#
265	E	→	E	t	_	#
240	E	→	E	e	_	r
26	c	→	E	#	_	z
19	E	→	e	r	_	n
17	n	→	E	a	_	n
16	j	→	i	#	_	o
14	j	→	i	#	_	u

Table 4: Most frequent rewrite rules derived from *B3* → *Ba2* (top: identity rules; bottom: non-identity rules).

Weight	Seq 1 → Seq 2		
0.125245	nn	→	n
0.195926	j	→	i
0.202549	ei	→	ai
0.220936	te	→	tte
0.227544	enn	→	en

Table 5: Least weighted mappings derived from *B3* → *Ba2*.

Levenshtein-based mappings Another way of modeling the relation between both word forms is by means of weighted Levenshtein-based mappings, which map character sequences of varying length. The more often a certain mapping has been observed in the data, the smaller its weight or cost. According to Levenshtein, identity mappings are the cheapest mappings with zero costs.

Some sample mappings derived from the example pair in (1a) are provided in (5). Table 5 shows the top five cheapest mappings derived from *B3* and *Ba2*.

(5) a. b → p

b. bi → pi

c. te → tte

d. t → tt

4.3 Interpreting the Rules and Mappings

The notation of the rules and mappings makes use of '→', implying that there is a directed relation between the two word forms, which takes one of the forms as the input and produces the other form

Rule	Analysis
c → E | # _ z	Graphemic variation: <cz> or <z> representing /ts/ in initial position
E → e | r _ n	Syncope (loss) of <e> representing /ə/ before final <n>
n → E | a _ n	<n> or <nn> representing /n/
j → i | # _ o j → i | # _ u	Graphemic variation: <j> or <i> in initial position

Table 6: Top non-identity rewrite rules derived from *B3* → *Ba2*, along with a linguistic analysis.

as the output. This interpretation may seem adequate for diachronic changes where we can say that the later form evolves out of the former form. For diatopic relations, a bidirectional interpretation seems more sensible, simply stating that a certain character (or character sequence) in one language area corresponds to another one in the other language area.

The (non-identity) rules and mappings often encode interesting relations, such as b → p, which indicates (de)voicing of plosives. In the next section, we go through a set of selected rules and mappings, discussing the range of phenomena that can be observed.

Ultimately we aim at using the rules and mappings for automatic clustering of texts relating to the crucial factors in language variation, language area and time, as well as other parameters—if they are included in the metadata the corpus provides—such as text type/function. Speaking from the perspective of historical linguistics, we hope to further enhance methodology by facilitating exhaustive analyses of larger corpora. Of course, this approach must be able to bear comparison to previous non-exhaustive approaches. It should be able to reflect previous, well-substantiated findings, such as the results of the High German consonant shift, but it should also be able to allow for new insights and eventually to draw a more detailed picture. The examples discussed in the next section were selected in a way to show that our approach will be able to satisfy both criteria.

5 First Results

Before discussing some results in detail, we would like to begin this section by giving an impression of how to interpret the replacement rules extracted by the method described above.

Table 6 gives linguistic analyses for the top non-identity rules of the pairing *B3* → *Ba2* (listed in Table 4).

The interpretation of the rewrite rules has to take into account which texts have been paired, in particular their spatial and temporal relation. In the example, we have paired two texts from the same period and the same area (Bavarian), but from different regions: *Ba2* is a North Bavarian text, and *B3* a Central Bavarian text, so we do not expect to see any diachronic variation here, and diatopic variation only to some extent.

The rules derived from the corpus show variants which are related to different levels of linguistic variation on the word level: to morphological, phonological and graphemic variation. To classify the rules as morphological, phonological or graphemic, the underlying word forms have to be consulted. As an example, see the list of 26 alignments in Table 7 that the rule in (6) has been derived from. The list of alignments shows all word forms starting with an inital affricate /ts/, which is encoded by <cz> in *B3* on the one hand and by <z> in *Ba2* on the other hand. As can be seen, the graphematic variation <cz>/<z> concerns a variety of different lemmas but becomes visible as a pattern through the rewrite rule.

(6) *B3* → *Ba2*: c → E \| # _ z

In some cases (9 instances), *Ba2* also uses <cz>, like *B3*, triggering an identity rule, (7).

(7) *B3* → *Ba2*: c → c \| # _ z

Morphological variation When pairing a Central German text, *St* (from the Rhine-Franconian area (Mainz)) with any of the Bavarian Upper German texts (*Ba2*, *M4*, *M3*, *B3*) from the same time period—the latter in order to rule out diachronic variation—the rule shown in (8) sticks out in all comparisons, see Table 8. To give an impression of the type of rules and their frequencies that have been derived, the table provides the three top-ranked (non-identity) rules for each pairing.

(8) t → E \| n _ #

Alignments	Lemma
|c=|z=z|e=e|c=|h=h|e=e|r=r|=e|n=n|	*zeheren* '(to) weep'
|c=|z=z|e=e|c=c|h=h|e=e|r=r|=e|n=n|	
|c=|z=z|a=a|r=r|t=t|e=e|n=n|	*zart* 'sweet'
|c=|z=z|u=u|h=h|a=a|n=n|t=t|	*zuhand* ~ *zehant* 'at once'
|c=|z=z|u=u|h–h|a=a|n=n|=d|t=t|	
|c=|z=z|u=u|h=h|a=a|n=n|t=d|	
|c=|z=z|u=u|h=h|a=a|n=n|n=|t=t|	
|c=|z=z|u=u|h=h|a=a|n=n|n=d|t=t|	
|c=|z=z|u=u|h=h|a=a|n=n|n=|t=d|	
|c=|z=z|e=e|h=h|e=e|n=n|	*zehn* 'ten'
|c=|z=z|e=a|i=i|c=c|h=h|e=e|n=n|	*Zeichen* 'sign'
|c=|z=z|e=a|i=i|g=g|e=e|n=n|	*zeigen* '(to) show'
|c=|z=z|e=e|i=i|t=t|	*Zeit* 'time'
|c=|z=z|u=e|s=r|c=|h=s|l=l|a=a|h=g|e=e|n=n|	*zerschlagen* '(to) break'
|c=|z=z|u=e|s=s|p=p|i=i|=e|l=l|t=t|	*ze(r)spalten* '(to) split'
|c=|z=z|e=e|r=r|s=s|t=t|o=e|r=r|e=e|r=r|	*Zerstörer* 'destroyer'
|c=|z=z|u=u|g=c|k=h|t=t|	*ziehen* 'to pull'
|c=|z=z|u=o|g=c|k=h|t=|	
|c=|z=z|o=u|c=c|h=h|=t|	
|c=|z=z|o=o|c=c|h=h|	
|c=|z=z|u=u|g=g|e=e|n=n|	
|c=|z=z|o=o|r=r|=e|n=n|	*Zorn* 'anger'
|c=|z=z|u=u|	*zu* 'to'
|c=|z=z|w=w|u=e|=n|	*zwen* ~ *zwo* 'two'
|c=|z=z|w=w|u=o|	
|c=|z=z|e=e|r=r|t=t|l=l|i=i|c=c|h=h|e=e|n=n|	*zertlich* 'gentle'

Table 7: All 26 alignments underlying the replacement rule in (6).

Text pair	Rule					Freq
St → Ba2 (nbair)	t	→ E	|	n _ #		51
	e	→ E	|	t _ #		33
	d	→ t	|	# _ o		25
St → M4 (nbair)	t	→ E	|	n _ #		45
	e	→ E	|	t _ #		34
	e	→ E	|	d _ #		27
St → M3 (mbair)	t	→ E	|	n _ #		47
	E	→ h	|	c _ r		40
	E	→ e	|	l _ i		31
St → B3 (mbair)	t	→ E	|	n _ #		44
	e	→ E	|	t _ #		32
	i	→ E	|	o _ s		24

Table 8: Three top-ranked replacement rules, as derived from pairing a Central German text (*St*) with different Upper German texts.

Text pair	Se1 → Seq2	Weight
St → Ba2 (nbair)	y → i	0.136881
	yn → in	0.155339
	nt → n	0.167918
	d → t	0.171744
St → M4 (nbair)	y → i	0.13741
	yn → in	0.15568
	yn → ein	0.194489
	nt → n	0.213094
St → M3 (mbair)	cr → chr	0.117811
	b → p	0.146198
	nt → n	0.161911
	ent → en	0.168727

Table 9: Top four Levenshtein-based mappings of the Central text *St* with three texts from Upper German. The mappings corresponding to the replacement rule t → E | n _ # have been highlighted.

This rule is triggered mainly by varying inflectional verb forms, such as *gaben* vs. *gabent* '(they) gave', *haben* vs. *habent* '(they) have', *kommen* vs. *komment* '(they) come', *glauben* vs. *glaubent* '(they) believe', etc.

Rule (8) reflects a well-known case of diatopic morphological variation in the Early New High German period: Upper German strongly tends towards *-ent* as inflectional marker for plural verb forms, whereas Central German prefers *-en* (Dammers et al., 1988, §74ff.).

The Levenshtein-based mappings confirm the picture. Table 9 shows the top mappings for three of the pairings in Table 8. Only with the pairing *St → B3* (mbair), there is no respective mapping among the top-ranked ones.

B2 is another text from the Rhine-Franconian area but has been located further south than *St* (see Figure 2). If *B2* is paired with the same Upper German texts (*Ba2, M4, M3, B3*), the results do not contain rule (8) at all, or their frequency is much lower. This also reflects the findings presented in Dammers et al. (1988, §76ff.), who show that the distribution of the variants *-ent* vs. *-en* does not coincide completely with the isoglosse(s) separating Upper from Central German, and *-ent* is instead common farther to the north.

These examples show that the method proposed in this paper is able to confirm results of previous research, i.e. it is possible to derive constraints on the localization of these texts by means of their 'linguistic footprint' as mirrored in these rules.

Phonological variation We next look at a rule that is related to the High German consonant shift, see (9).

(9) *St → D4*: E → f | #p _ e
example: *penning* vs. *pfenni(n)g*

The rule in (9)[5] has been derived from pairing *St* with a Swabian text, *D4*. *D4* is a borderline case, i.e. located on the border between Upper and Central German, which is indicated by the isoglosse called *Germersheim Line*. This line marks the shift of Germanic /p/ to affricate /pf/ in initial position, see Figure 2. Rule (9) locates *D4* south of the *Germersheim Line*.

Another example of phonologically-based variation is the rule in (10)[6]. This rule clearly identifies *St* as a Rhine-Franconian text, showing /d/ instead of Upper German /t/ in initial or medial position, see Table 10.

(10) *St → D4*: t → d | # _ o
examples: *tochter* vs. *dochter, todes* vs. *dodes*

Graphemic variation The above examples confirmed results already known from the literature. The next examples illustrate that our new method also enables us to refine the picture of historical

---

[5] Rule rank: 30; rule frequency: 8.
[6] Rule rank: 8; rule frequency: 16.

Freq	Rule	Phonemes
26	E → c | # _ z	Initial affricate /ts/, <cz> vs. <z> e.g. *czehen* vs. *zehen*; *czu* vs. *zu*
15	u → ü | f _ r	Umlaut vowels with or without trema <¨> e.g. *für* vs. *fur*; *fürst* vs. *furst*; *füren* vs. *furen*
13	t → E | d _ #	Final alveolar stop <dt> vs. <t> e.g. *gesundt* vs. *gesund*; *kindt* vs. *kind*
11	z → E | s _ #	Final alveolar fricative <sz> or <s> e.g. *bisz* vs. *bis*; *dasz* vs. *das*; *schosz* vs. *schos*

Table 11: Selected rules and their frequencies, as derived from *Ba2 → M4*, both from North Bavaria, along with a description of the phonemes that are represented by the respective graphemes.

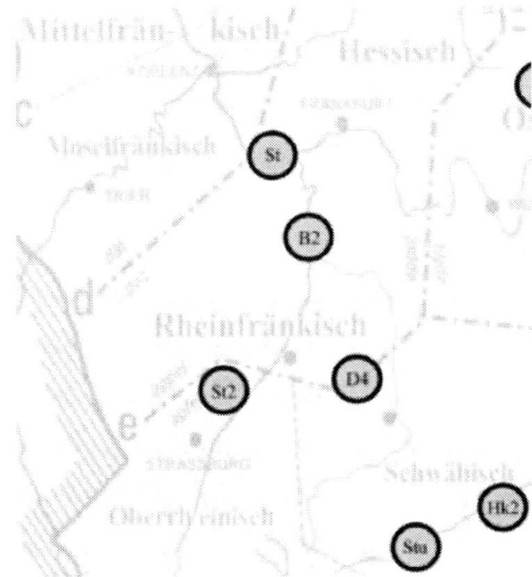

Figure 2: Localization of the texts. The *Speyer Line* is indicated by the letter 'e' on the left side. It coincides with the *Germersheim Line* in the Western part of the German language area. North of this line, Germanic */p/ is retained, south of the line, /pf/ is used instead.

Text pair	Freq	Rank
St → Ba2 (nbair)	25	3
St → M4 (nbair)	16	12
St → M3 (mbair)	21	8
St → B3 (mbair)	14	13

Table 10: Absolute frequencies and ranks of the replacement rule t → d \| # _ o, as derived from pairing a Central German text (*St*) with different Upper German texts.

variation, especially when it comes to graphemic variation.

Suitable examples come from pairing neighboring texts, e.g. *Ba2 → M4*, two texts from North Bavaria (*nbair*). This pairing generates rules which correspond mainly to graphemic variation, in contrast to pairings of different language areas, as in the previous section, see the examples in Table 11.

In applying the method proposed in this paper systematically and exhaustively, a highly nuanced picture of graphemic variation will become observable. In systematically assessing the replacement rules derived from a balanced corpus of historical texts we hope to be able to ascertain a complete picture of graphemic variation, i.e. which variants were available and were preferred by scribes in different areas.

6   Conclusion

We hope that our approach will help filling research gaps in historical linguistics. Thus far, research had to cope with a lack of corpora on the one hand, and the restrictedness of retrieval methods on the other hand. Therefore, previous studies in historical graphematics were inevitably restricted and of a merely exemplary nature.

Of course, the exemplary segments these studies have been focussing on—copies of one text in Glaser (1985), texts by one and the same author in Wiesinger (1996), German prints of the bible translated by Martin Luther in Rieke (1998), texts originating from one scribal office in Moser (1977) and texts from one specific place (Duisburg) in Mihm (2004) and Elmentaler (1998; 2001; 2003)—have been selected applying expedient criteria. The studies have been able to provide insight into a very small, if significant area, leaving the rest of the map to remain blank.

This is where our approach comes in. The characteristics of the bundle of methods described above is that we aim at capturing the whole range of variation documented in historical corpora, and that we do so by 'joining forces' and mustering expertise from NLP as well as from German historical linguistics. In this way we make sure that the results delivered by the computational methods fit the requirements of actual variation analysis and are therefore to be considered not only usable, but beneficial for future corpus-based historical linguistics. Our approach will be applicable to corpora with a normalization layer—which is the case for the reference corpora of historical German.

As Table 1 shows, the *Anselm* Corpus does not allow for comprehensive diachronic analyses. When applied to a corpus which covers a larger time period than the *Anselm* Corpus, we expect the proposed method to discover both diachronic and diatopic variation. Language change never occurs as a sudden change or replacement of one variant by the other but involves a period of co-existences of multiple variants. Hence, language change will become visible as changes in frequency of the variants involved (cf. Wegera and Waldenberger (2012, 25)), starting out with an increasing number of instances of the new variant and—if the process is successful—resulting in a decrease of the older variant. Such changes in frequency will translate into the rewrite rules generated by our method, specifically into the ratio between non-identity rules and their corresponding identity rules.

Acknowledgments

We would like to thank the anonymous reviewers for helpful comments. The research reported in this paper was supported by Deutsche Forschungsgemeinschaft (DFG), Grant DI 1558/4.

References

Alistair Baron, Paul Rayson, and Dawn Archer. 2009. Word frequency and key word statistics in historical corpus linguistics. *Anglistik: International Journal of English Studies*, 20(1):41–67.

Fabian Barteld, Ingrid Schröder, and Heike Zinsmeister. 2016. Dealing with word-internal modification and spelling variation in data-driven lemmatization. In *Proceedings of the 10th SIGHUM Workshop on Language Technology for Cultural Heritage, Social Sciences, and Humanities (LaTeCH)*, pages 52–62.

Marcel Bollmann, Florian Petran, and Stefanie Dipper. 2011. Rule-based normalization of historical texts. In *Proceedings of the RANLP-Workshop on Language Technologies for Digital Humanities and Cultural Heritage*, pages 34–42, Hissar, Bulgaria.

Marcel Bollmann, Stefanie Dipper, Julia Krasselt, and Florian Petran. 2012. Manual and semi-automatic normalization of historical spelling — case studies from Early New High German. In *Proceedings of the First International Workshop on Language Technology for Historical Text(s) (LThist2012), KONVENS*, Wien, Austria.

Marcel Bollmann. 2012. (Semi-)automatic normalization of historical texts using distance measures and the Norma tool. In *Proceedings of the Workshop on Annotating Corpora for Research in the Humanities (ACRH-2)*, Lisbon.

Ulf Dammers, Walter Hoffmann, and Hans-Joachim Solms. 1988. *Grammatik des Frühneuhochdeutschen 4: Flexion der starken und schwachen Verben*. Winter, Heidelberg.

Stefanie Dipper and Simone Schultz-Balluff. 2013. The *Anselm Corpus*: Methods and perspectives of a parallel aligned corpus. In *Proceedings of the NODALIDA Workshop on Computational Historical Linguistics*, pages 27–42, Oslo, Norway.

Karin Donhauser. 2015. Das Referenzkorpus Altdeutsch: Das Konzept, die Realisierung und die neuen Möglichkeiten. In Jost Gippert and Ralf Gehrke, editors, *Historical Corpora. Challenges and Perspectives*. Narr, Tübingen.

Michael Elmentaler. 1998. Die Schreibsprachgeschichte des Niederrheins. Ein Forschungsprojekt der Duisburger Universität. In Dieter Heimböckel, editor, *Sprache und Literatur am Niederrhein*, pages 15–34. Pomp, Bottrop.

Michael Elmentaler. 2001. Der Erkenntniswert der schreibsprachlichen Variation für die Sprachgeschichte. Überlegungen zu den Erkenntnissen eines Duisburger Graphematikprojektes. *Rheinische Vierteljahrsblätter*, 65:290–314.

Michael Elmentaler. 2003. *Struktur und Wandel vormoderner Schreibsprachen*. de Gruyter, Berlin, New York.

Elvira Glaser. 1985. *Graphische Studien zum Schreibsprachwandel vom 13. bis 16. Jahrhundert. Vergleich verschiedener Handschriften des Augsburger Stadtbuches*. Winter, Heidelberg.

Bryan Jurish. 2010. More than words: Using token context to improve canonicalization of historical German. *Journal for Language Technology and Computational Linguistics*, 25(1):23–39.

Gerhard Jäger, Johann-Mattis List, and Pavel Sofroniev. 2017. Using support vector machines and state-of-the-art algorithms for phonetic alignment to identify cognates in multi-lingual wordlists. In *Proceedings of the 15th Conference of the European Chapter of the Association for Computational Linguistics*.

Thomas Klein, Klaus-Peter Wegera, Stefanie Dipper, and Claudia Wich-Reif. 2016. Referenzkorpus Mittelhochdeutsch (1050–1350), Version 1.0. https://www.linguistics.ruhr-uni-bochum.de/rem/. ISLRN 332-536-136-099-5.

Arend Mihm. 2004. Zur Neubestimmung des Verhältnisses zwischen Schreibsprachen und historischer Mündlichkeit. In Franz Patocka and Peter Wiesinger, editors, *Morphologie und Syntax deutscher Dialekte und historische Dialektologie des Deutschen. Beiträge zum 1. Kongress der Internationalen Gesellschaft für Dialektologie des Deutschen, Marburg/Lahn, 5.-8. März 2003*, pages 340–382, Wien. Praesens.

Hans Moser. 1977. Die Kanzlei Kaiser Maximilians I. Graphematik eines Schreibusus. Univ. Innsbruck.

Robert Peters and Norbert Nagel. 2014. Das digitale 'Referenzkorpus Mittelniederdeutsch / Niederrheinisch (ReN)'. In Vilmos Ágel and Andreas Gardt, editors, *Paradigmen der Sprachgeschichtsschreibung*. de Gruyter, Berlin, Boston.

Michael Piotrowski. 2012. *Natural Language Processing for Historical Text*. Morgan & Claypool.

Ursula Rieke. 1998. *Studien zur Herausbildung der neuhochdeutschen Orthographie. Die Markierung der Vokalquantitäten in deutschsprachigen Bibeldrucken des 16.-18. Jahrhunderts*. Winder, Heidelberg.

Hans-Christian Schmitz, Bernhard Schröder, and Klaus-Peter Wegera. 2013. Das Bonner Frühneuhochdeutsch-Korpus und das Referenzkorpus 'Frühneuhochdeutsch'. In Ingelore Hafemann, editor, *Perspektiven einer corpusbasierten historischen Linguistik und Philologie. Internationale Tagung des Akademienvorhabens "Altägyptisches Wörterbuch" an der Berlin-Brandenburgischen Akademie der Wissenschaften, 12.–13. Dezember 2011*.

Morris Swadesh. 1955. Towards greater accuracy in lexicostatistic dating. *International Journal of American Linguistics*, 21:121–137.

Klaus-Peter Wegera and Sandra Waldenberger. 2012. *Deutsch Diachron. Eine Einführung in den Sprachwandel des Deutschen*. Erich Schmidt, Berlin.

Peter Wiesinger. 1996. *Schreibung und Aussprache im älteren Frühneuhochdeutschen. Zum Verhaltnis von Graphem – Phonem – Phon am bairisch-österreichischen Beispiel von Andreas Kurzmann um 1400*. de Gruyter, Berlin.

Author Profiling at PAN:
from Age and Gender Identification to Language Variety Identification
(invited talk)

Paolo Rosso
Natural Language Engineering Lab
PRHLT Research Center
Universitat Politècnica de València
Valencia, Spain
`prosso@dsic.upv.es`

1 Abstract

Author profiling is the study of how language is shared by people, a problem of growing importance in applications dealing with security, in order to understand who could be behind an anonymous threat message, and marketing, where companies may be interested in knowing the demographics of people that in online reviews liked or disliked their products. In this talk we will give an overview of the PAN[1] shared tasks that since 2013 have been organised at CLEF and FIRE evaluation forums, mainly on age and gender identification in social media, although also personality recognition in Twitter as well as in code sources was also addressed.

In 2017 the PAN author profiling shared task addresses jointly gender and language variety identification in Twitter where tweets have been annotated with authors' gender and their specific variation of their native language: English (Australia, Canada, Great Britain, Ireland, New Zealand, United States), Spanish (Argentina, Chile, Colombia, Mexico, Peru, Spain, Venezuela), Portuguese (Brazil, Portugal), and Arabic (Egypt, Gulf, Levantine, Maghrebi).

2 Biography

Paolo Rosso[2] is an associate professor of computer science at the Technical University of Valencia, Spain where he leads the NLE lab of the PRHLT research center. His research interests include author profiling and irony detection in social media, opinion spam detection, as well as text reuse and plagiarism detection. Since 2009 he has been involved in the organisation of PAN benchmark activities, since 2010 and 2011 in the framework of CLEF and FIRE evaluation forums, on plagiarism / text reuse detection and author profiling. He has been also co-organiser of the shared task on Sentiment analysis of figurative language in Twitter at SemEval-2015. Paolo Rosso has been PI in several national and international research projects. He is the co-author of 50+ articles in international journals and 400+ articles in conferences and workshops. He has been advisor of 17 PhD students. He has been chair of *SEM-2015, and organisation chair of CLEF-2013 and also of EACL-2017 both here in Valencia...

---

[1] `http://pan.webis.de/`

[2] `http://www.dsic.upv.es/~prosso/`

Proceedings of the Fourth Workshop on NLP for Similar Languages, Varieties and Dialects, page 46,
Valencia, Spain, April 3, 2017. ©2017 Association for Computational Linguistics

The Similarity and Mutual Intelligibility between Amharic and Tigrigna Varieties

Tekabe Legesse Feleke
Verona Univerisity
Verona, Italy
`hitakeleg@gmail.com`

Abstract

The present study has examined the similarity and the mutual intelligibility between Amharic and two Tigrigna varities using three tools; namely Levenshtein distance, intelligibility test and questionnaires. The study has shown that both Tigrigna varieties have almost equal phonetic and lexical distances from Amharic. The study also indicated that Amharic speakers understand less than 50% of the two varieties. Furthermore, the study showed that Amharic speakers are more positive about the Ethiopian Tigrigna variety than the Eritrean variety. However, their attitude towards the two varieties does not have an impact on their intelligibility. The Amharic speakers' familiarity to the Tigrigna varieties seems largely dependent on the genealogical relation between Amharic and the two Tigrigna varieties.

Keywords: Language Similarity, Language Distance, Mutual Intelligibility, Attitude, Language Contact

1 Introduction

1.1 Language in Ethiopia

More than 85 languages are spoken in Ethiopia (Demeke, 2001; Hetzron, 1972; Hetzron, 1977; Hudson, 2013). The languages are classified under four language families: Semitic, Cushitic, Omotic and Nilo-Saharan (Bender and Cooper, 1976; Demeke, 2001; Hornberger, 2002; Hudson, 2013). In each family, there are many related language varieties so that the speakers of one variety can sometimes communicate with the speakers of another variety in the same language family

without major difficulties (Demeke, 2001; Gutt, 1980). However, the similarity among the languages is often obscured by the attitude of the speakers since language is considered as a symbol of identity (Lanza and Woldemariam, 2008; Smith, 2008). Hence, there are cases where varieties of the same languages are considered as different languages (Hetzron, 1972; Hetzron, 1977; Hudson, 2013; Smith, 2008). Therefore, due to politics, sensitivity to ethnicity and the lack of commitment from the scholars, the exact number of languages in Ethiopia is not known (Bender and Cooper, 1976; Demeke, 2001; Leslau, 1969).Furthermore, except some studies for example, Gutt (1980) and Ahland (2003) cited in Hudson (2013) on the Gurage varieties, and Bender and Cooper (1971) on mutual intelligibility of Sidamo dialects, the degree of mutual intelligibility among various varieties and the attitude of the speakers towards each others' varieties has not been thoroughly investigated. Hence, the present study examined the distance and the mutual intelligibility between Amharic and two Tigrigna varieties together with the effect of the attitude on the mutual intelligibility.

Amharic and Tigrigna are members of the Ethiosemitic language family, a branch of proto-Semitic family (Bender and Cooper, 1976; Demeke, 2001; Hetzron, 1972; Hetzron, 1977). According to Demeke (2001), Hetzron (1972), Hetzron (1977) and Bender and Cooper (1971), Ethiosemitic languages are divided into North and South Ethiosemitc. While the Tigrigna varieties are North Ethiosemitic languages, Amharic is one of the South Ethiosemitic languages. Nowadays, Amharic is spoken only in Ethiopia, but Tigrigna is spoken both in Ethiopia and in Eritrea. Due to the genealogical and typological relationship between Amharic and Tigrigna (Demeke, 2001; Hetzron, 1972; Hetzron, 1977), Amharic speak-

Proceedings of the Fourth Workshop on NLP for Similar Languages, Varieties And Dialects, pages 47–54,
Valencia, Spain, April 3, 2017. ©2017 Association for Computational Linguistics

ers are supposed to understand the Tigrigna varieties to a certain degree. Since Amharic has been the national language of Ethiopia, it is a widely used language compared to Tigrigna (Getachew and Derib, 2008; Iyob, 2000; Lanza and Woldemariam, 2008; Smith, 2008). The use of Amharic as a national language helped many speakers of Ethiopian Tigrigna to learn Amharic as a second language (Smith, 2008). Moreover, Amharic has also been given as a subject for Ethiopian Tigrigna speakers, starting from elementary school. Some speakers of Eritrean Tigrigna variety used to speak Amharic before secession. However, after the independence, using Amharic in schools and in different offices was banned (Hailemariam and Walters, 1999; Rena, 2005). The relationship between the peoples of the two countries was also strained especially after Ethio-Eritrean war from 1988 to 2000. Hence, due to the border conflict, Eritrean Tigrigna speakers do not also have an access to Tigrigna speakers in Ethiopia and to the Amharic speakers.

Studies on the language attitude of the speakers of Amharic and the Tigrigna varieties are at scarce. However, language, ethnicity and politics are very interrelated in Ethiopia (Bulcha, 1997; May, 2011; Smith, 2008). The link has been accelerated by the ethnic-based federal system in Ethiopia (Lanza and Woldemariam, 2008; Young, 1996; Vaughan and Tronvoll, 2003).The atmosphere of politics in Eritrea and Ethiopia could also affect the attitude of the people in both countries. There has been an anti-Ethiopia sentiment in Eritrea since 1993 (Abbink, 2003; Assefa, 1996; Iyob, 2000). This hostile situation could have an effect on the attitude of the speakers of Amharic and the speakers of the Ethiopian Tigrigna.

The study of the similarity between Amharic and the Tigrigna varieties and the attitude of the speakers of one language towards another has a paramount significance in two ways. From practical point of view, there has been an attempt to standardize Tigrigna and use it widely in media and in schools. The study positively contributes to this effort. From theoretical perspective, there have been a number of attempts towards improving the enduring limitations of methods of dialectology. One of the positive contributions has been complementing the traditional lexicostatistics methods by the mutual intelligibility and perceptive distance measures. Very promising results have been reported by the studies conducted on the Scandinavian languages and the Chinese dialects in this regard (see (Gooskens and Heeringa, 2004; Gooskens, 2013; Gooskens, 2007; Tang and Heuven, 2007; Tang and Heuven, 2009; Tang and Heuven, 2015)). The present study is an addition to these contributions.

1.2 Measuring Language Distance and Mutual Intelligibility

The study of the distance among related languages has been a concern of many scholars for decades (Sokal, 1988). Several previous studies employed phonetic distance to measure the relative distance between various languages (Bakker, 2009; Cohn and Fienberg, 2003; Kessler, 1995). However, the emergence of the Levenshtein algorithm has enhanced the objective structural comparisons by introducing a computer-based distance computation (Heeringa, 2004; Gooskens and Heeringa, 2004). This has probably contributed a lot in terms of attracting many scholars towards the study of language variation (Gooskens, 2013). Recently, several studies have been conducted on European languages and on Chinese dialects, for example, (Gooskens and Heeringa, 2004; Heeringa, 2004; Tang and Heuven, 2007; Tang and Heuven, 2009; Tang and Heuven, 2015) by employing the Levenshtein algorithm together with the mutual intelligibility and perceptive distance measures. For instance, Gooskens (2007) compared data from Scandinavian languages (Danish, Swedish and Norwegian) with that of West Germanic languages (Dutch, Frisian and Afrikaans) and reported that mutual intelligibility can be predicted based on phonetic and lexical distances. Similarly, Bezooijen and Gooskens (2007) investigated the intelligibility of written Afrikaans and Frisian texts for Dutch speakers and reported the association between the Levenshtien distance and mutual intelligibility. Heeringa (2004) also employed the Levenshtein distance for the comparison of Dutch and Norwegian varieties.

The subjective measures often include perceptive distance and functional tests (Gooskens and Heeringa, 2004; Tang and Heuven, 2007; Tang and Heuven, 2009). According to Gooskens (2013), functional intelligibility between related languages can be measured by employing content questions, translation, recorded text testing, observations and performance tasks. Tang and Heuven (2009) employed word intelligibility test and word recognition in a sentence to examine the mutual intelligibility among the Chinese dialects. According to Gooskens (2013) and Tang and Heuven (2009) , opinion test can be designed without speech. For example, speakers of a certain variety can be requested to give their judgment on the speakers of other varieties who live in certain geographical areas (estimated linguistic distance). Bezooijen and Gooskens (2007) used cloze test to measure the functional ineligibility of written Afrikaans and Frisian for the native speakers of Dutch. Swarte and Gooskens (2014) employed a word translation to measure the importance of German for Dutch speaker to understand the Danish language. Hence, in the present study, the Levenshtein distance and the lexical distance were combined with intelligibility measure to determine the distance and the degree of intelligibility between Amharic and the Tigrigna varieties. Only the intelligibility of the Tigrigna varities for the native speakers of Amharic was examined; the intelligibility measure was one directional primarly since mesauring the degree of intelligibility of Amharic to the Tigrigna speakers was difficult as many Tigrigna speakrs have an access to Amharic.

To measure the phonetic and the lexical distances, a written short story 'The Baboon Chief' was transcribed using IPA. Amharic and both Tigrigna varieties use Ethiopic writing system which means that there is a correspondance between the phonemes and graphemes; the difference is only on a few supra-segmental features which may not be captured in the written form. After the transcription, cognates in the stories were identified and aligned. Then, the distance between the cognates of each language was computed using Levenshtein distance. Lexical distance was determined by dividing non-cognate words to the total number of words in each text. Word translation was employed to measure the mutual intelligibility between the languages. Word translation was used since it was suitable for on line administration. Due to the complex socio-political situation in Ethiopia, the attitude of Amharic speakers towards the two language varieties and the contact between Amharic speakers and the speakers of the two Tigrigna varieties were also examined. Questionnaire was employed since it is suitable for on line administration (Agheyisi and Fishman, 1970). Bezooijen

and Gooskens (2007) also used questionnaires to examine the language contact and language background of their participants.

2 Research objectives

The study was conducted to address, among others, the following four specific objectives. 1) To determine the distance between written Tigrigna varieties and Amharic. 2) To determine the attitude of the native Amharic speakers towards the Tigrigna varieties. 3) To identify which Tigrigna variety is more intelligible for the native speakers of Amharic. 4) To indicate the relationship between the attitude of the speakers and the degree of mutual intelligibility.

3 Method

3.1 Participants

The participants were 18 native Amharic speakers who were attending MA program at Groningen, Rotterdam and Wageningen universities. Four of them were females and the remaining 14 were males. The average age of the participants was 27 year. Students who lived outside Ethiopia for more than two years were not included in the study since the attrition of Amharic could affect their responses and their performances on the mutual intelligibility test. Those whose parents are from Tigray Regional State-where Tigrigna is spoken or from Eritrea were also not included in the study; all of them were working in different colleges in Ethiopia before joining the three universities. The attitude and contact questionnaires were sent to each participant via email.

3.2 Materials and Tests

To measure the phonetic distance, the lexical distance and the intelligibility of the two Tigrigna varieties for the native speakers of Amharic, a fable 'The Baboon Chief' was translated from Oromo to Amharic by the researcher who is a balanced bilingual. The translation was checked by two independent bilingual experts (one is Oromo language instructor at Haromaya University and the second one Amharic instructor at Mekelle University). The selection of the fable from Oromo was to minimize the priming effect that could happen if it were taken directly from Amharic, see Tang and Heuven (2009) for the priming effect. The Amharic version was translated to the two Tigrigna varieties. The translators were native speakers of the two varieties who were MA students at University of Groningen. The translated texts were checked by Tigrigna experts.

3.2.1 The Phonetic and Lexical Distance

The distances between Amharic and the two Tigrigna varieties were examined at two linguistic levels: phonetic and lexical. For the phonetic distance, the Levenshtein distance was employed. To apply the Levenshtein distance, the words in the translated written texts were transcribed using IPA symbols. To compute the phonetic distance, cognates both in Amharic and in the two Tigrigna texts were aligned. The distance between the corresponding cognates were determined based on a number of symbols which are inserted, deleted or substituted. The method of costs assignment was adopted from Gooskens (2007) with just a minor modification. The coast assignment is as follows: insertions and deletions 1 point, identical symbols 0 points, and substitutions of a vowel by a vowel or of a consonant by a consonant 0.5 point, substitutions of a vowel by a consonant or a consonant by a vowel 1 point. Below is an example of cost assignment which shows the distance between the cognates of Ethiopian Tigrigna and Amharic. In this example, the total cost (0.5 + 0.5) is one (1). The phonetic distance is the ratio of the total cost to the number of alignment (in this case 6). Thus, the phonetic distance is one divided by six (1/6) which is 0.167. In terms of percent, the distance between Tigrigna and Amharic cognates in this particular example is 16.7%.

k	u	l	l	o	m	Tigrigna
h	u	l	l	u	m	Amharic
.5	0	0	0	.5	0	Cost

The lexical distance between the two Tigrigna varieties and Amharic was determined based on the percentage of non-cognates in the total lexical items; the number of non-cognate words was divided to the total number of lexical items, based on Gooskens (2007). The cognates were identified based on two parameters which were suggested in Gooskens (2007): words in corresponding texts with common roots and cognate synonyms-words which are very similar in written form, but have slight meaning differences (e.g. hajal 'powerful' and hajl 'power'). Whether the pairs of words are cognates or not was determined by two Amharic and Ethiopian Tigrigna bilinguals and another two Amharic-Eritrean Tigrigna bilinguals.

3.2.2 Language Attitude and Contact

To examine the attitude of the Amharic speakers towards the two Tigrigna varieties, questionnaires were adopted from Bezooijen and Gooskens (2007). The questionnaires contained items which focus on the two Tigrigna varieties, on the speakers of the varieties and on areas where the two Tigrigna varieties are spoken. For each area of interest, three items and the total of eighteen items were constructed. The participants provided their responses on the items that contain five point scales. For example, they rate whether Tigrigna is an interesting language or not on the scale: 1 (interesting) to 5 (extremely boring).

Similarly, questionnaires were employed for the assessment of the participants' contact with the two Tigrigna varieties. The questionnaires included items related to the participants' frequency of contact with the speakers of the two varieties, media, movies, and newsletters of the two varieties. The participants rated the degree of contact by using five rating scales (very often, often, occasionally, very rarely and not at all). Ten questions were provided for each variety, and the items designed to measure each variety were evenly distributed.

3.2.3 The Mutual Intelligibility

Word translation was used for the mutual intelligibility measure due to its ease of administration. In the translation task, Tigrigna words in the translated fable were listed based on alphabetical order, and 100 words from each Tigrigna variety, a total of 200 words were selected. Since there were 136 Eritrean and 130 Ethiopian words in the translated texts, 36 words from Eritrean Tigrigna texts and 30 words from Ethiopian Tigrigna texts were randomly left out, and the remaining 100 words in each text were used for the test. Since translating 200 words could be a tiresome task for the participants, the 200 words in the two Tigrigna varieties were divided across the participants. Hence, among 18 participants who took part in the test, nine participants translated the first 50 words in the lists of each of the varieties, and the remaining nine participants translated the last 50 words in the lists of each variety. Using this procedure, each participant translated 100 words (50 from each variety) to Amharic. Since translating the list of words of one variety and shifting to the list of words of another variety could lead to priming (see Tang and Heuven (2009)), words from the two varieties were mixed, but were written in a slightly different font so that the researcher could identify to which variety each word belongs.

Then, the mixed words were evenly distributed in such a way that each translator received different word order. To achieve this, the mixed 100 words were initially randomly ordered and numbered. Then, different word orders were created using base ten as a point of classification. In this manner, the first order begins with No.1 and ends with No.100 (the default order). The second order begins with No.10 followed by from 11-100 and then from 1-9. The third order begins with No.20 followed by from 21-100 then from 1-19 and so on. In this manner nine different order for each group, and the total of 18 list of orders were created. The respondents were instructed to translate each word within 30 seconds. However, it is important to recognize that the participants could take less or more than the allotted time since the task was administered on line. The intelligibility measure is the number of words which was translated correctly. One (1) point was given for fully correct answer, and 0.5 point was given for correct answers but with tense, aspect, number and other morphological/grammatical errors. The appropriateness of the translation was checked by the researcher and by the native speakers of the two varieties.

4 Results

4.1 The Phonetic Distance

The two Tigrigna varieties have about 30% phonetic differences with Amharic. In other words, the two varieties have equal phonetic distance from Amharic; Ethiopian Tigrigna (M = 31%) and Eritrean Tigrigna (M = 28.5%); independent t-test, t = .023, p = .56. Among 136 total words, there were 51 Eritrean Tigrigna cognate words, and 85 non-cognates words. Hence, the lexical distance between Amharic and Eritrean Tigrigna variety is 62.5% (85/136). This means that the lexical similarity between Amharic and the Eritrean Tigrigna variety is 37.5%. The Ethiopian Tigrigna text contains 130 words. Among these, 59 (43.5 %) were cognates, and 71 (56.3) were non-cognates. This shows that the lexical distance between Amharic and the Ethiopian Tigrigna variety is 45.4% (71/130). The results indicate that

Amharic is more closer to Ethiopian Tigrigna variety than to the Eritrean Tigrigna Variety.

4.2 Language Attitude and Language Contact

The Amharic speakers are more positive about Ethiopian Tigrigna (M = 3.5) than the Eritrea Tigrigna (M = 3), paired sample t-test, t = -2.754, p = .01. The attitude of the Amharic speakers was also examined specifically in terms of the three areas of interest: attitude towards the language, attitude toward the people, and attitude towards the country. As Table 1 shows, Amharic speakers are more negative about Eritrea. The difference is significant in all cases except in their attitude towards the people (paired t-test t = .849, p = 0.42). With regard to the language contact, Amharic speakers have stronger contact to Ethiopian Tigrigna than to the Eritrean Tigrigna; paired sample t-test: t = -7.923, p = .00. Nothing is surprising about this finding since the speakers of Amharic do not have a direct contact with the Eritrean Tigrigna speakers due to the border conflict between the two countries. Though the contact between the speakers of Amharic and the speakers of Ethiopian Tigrigna is higher that the contact between the speakers of Amharic and that of the speakers of Eritrean Tigrigna, it does not seem that Amharic speakers have a frequent contact with Ethiopian Tigrigna speakers as the frequency of contact is very low (2.9 on 1-5 scale).

Focus	ERT	ETT	t	Sig
Lang	3.3	3.9	3.1	.01
Peop	3.6	3.7	.85	.40
Coun	1.9	2.8	2.8	.02
Mean	3.0	3.5	- 2.8	.01
Contact	1.8	2.9	-7.9	.00

The attitude of Amharic speakers towards the Tigrigna varieties measured on (1-5) Linker scale. 'ERT' refers to Eritrea Tigrigna, ETT refers to Ethiopian Tigrigna, 'Lang' is language, and 'Coun' refers to country.

4.3 Mutual Intelligibility

The mutual intelligibility test results indicate that Amharic speakers have equal performances on both languages; (M = 29.78%) on Ethiopian Tigrigna and (M = 26.11%) on Eritrean Tigrigna, paired sample t-test, p = 15. Besides, the attitude and contact results do not correlate with intelligibility results, r = -.267 and r = 0.181 respectively. Likewise, there is no correlation between Amharic speakers' contact with the Eritrean Tigrigna speakers and their performance on the Eritrean Tigrigna mutual intelligibility test.

5 Discussion

Results obtained from the phonetic and the lexical distance measures show that the two Tigrigna varieties have almost equal distance from Amharic. The lexical distance between Amharic and the Ethiopian Tigrigna is also similar with the one between Amharic and the Eritrean Tigrigna. The speakers of Amharic are more negative about Eritrean Tigrigna variety than the Ethiopian Tigrigna variety. The negative attitude towards Eritrea is not astonishing since there was political and ethnic hostility between the two countries which might have affected the Amharic speakers attitude towards Eritrea and Eritrean Tigrigna (Hailemariam and Walters, 1999; Rena, 2005).

Though the attitude of the Amharic speakers is more positive towards Ethiopian Tigrigna, the magnitude of the attitude is not high. This can be due to political reasons since there has been a fierce power struggle between the Amhara and the Tigray ethnic groups (Young, 1998). Amharic speaker have a stronger contact with the Ethiopian Tigrigna speakers than with the Eritrean Tigrigna speakers. However, in both cases, the frequency of contact is low. As presented earlier, contacting the Eritrean people is almost impossible for the Amharic speakers as the communication between the two countries has been blocked due to the border conflict. The contact between the Amharic speakers and the Ethiopian Tigrigna speakers is also small. This could be due to economic, language and social situation in the country. Tigray region is found in the northern tip of the country, very distant place from the capital. Usually, people move from Tigray region to the central part of the country where Amharic is used to seek job, education, recreation and other purposes. There is a less possibility for Amharic speakers to move to Tigray region.

The results obtained from the intelligibility test show that both Tigrigna varieties are almost equally difficult to the native Amharic speakers. This can have two possible interpretations. In one hand it shows that the two Tigrigna varieties have almost equal distance from Amharic. On the other hand, it indicates that native Amharic speakers cannot communicate with the speakers of both Tigrigna varieties using Tigrigna as a medium of communication since the Amharic speakers scored below the average on the mutual intelligibility tests. According to Gutt (1980), two languages are considered as intelligible if the speakers of one variety understand more than 80% of another variety. This means that the two Tigrigna varieties are not intelligible for the native Amharic speakers. Besides, Amharic speakers' intelligibility scores on both language varieties are not affected by both language contact and attitude. This finding is consistent with that of Bezooijen and Gooskens (2007) and Gooskens and Heeringa (2004) that there may not be a correlation between language attitude and language intelligibility. The absence of correlation between language contact and language mutual intelligibility shows that the distance and the magnitude of intelligibility which were reported in the present study are due to the genealogical relationship between Amharic and the two Tigrigna varieties.

In general, this study indicates that both the Ethiopian and the Eritrean Tigrigna varieties have almost a comparable phonetic and lexical distance from Amharic. Native Amharic speakers understand less than half of the two varieties which hints that the two Tigrigna varieties are not intelligible for the Amharic speakers. Furthermore, the speakers of Amharic are more positive about the Ethiopian Tigrigna variety than the Eritrean variety. Nevertheless, their attitude does not have an impact on their intelligibility of the two varieties. Moreover, the study has shown that Amharic speakers have more frequent contact with the Ethiopian Tigrigna speakers than with the Ethiopian Tigrigna speakers. However, their familiarity to the two Tigrigna varieties has nothing to do with the contact between the speakers of the two languages.

The present study is perhaps the first attempt towards establishing the mutual intelligibility and measuring the relative distance between Amharic and the two Tigrigna varieties. Future studies ought to consider a large scale research which includes all the Amharic and the Tigrigna dialects.

References

Abbink. 2003. Badme and the ethio-eritrean border: the challenge of demarcation in the post-war period. *Africa: Rivista trimestrale di studi e documentazione delllstituto italiano per lAfrica e lOriente*, 58(2):219–231.

Agheyisi and Fishman. 1970. Language attitude studies: A brief survey of methodological approaches. *Anthropological linguistics*.

Ahland. 2003. Interlectal intelligibility between gurage speech varieties. In *In North Conference on Afroasiataic Linguistics*, April.

Assefa. 1996. Ethnic conflict in the horn of africa: myth and reality. *Ethnicity and power in the contemporary world*.

Bakker. 2009. Adding typology to lexicostatistics: A combined approach to language classification. *Linguistic Typology,*, 13(1):169–181.

Bender and Cooper. 1971. Mutual intelligibility within sidamo. *Lingua*, 27(32-52).

Bender and Cooper. 1976. Language in ethiopia: Implications of a survey for sociolinguistic theory and method. *Pub date notes*, pages 75–191.

Bezooijen and Gooskens. 2007. Interlingual text comprehension: linguistic and extralinguistic determinants. *Hamburger Studies in Multilingualism*, (249-264).

Bulcha. 1997. The politics of linguistic homogenization in ethiopia and the conflict over the status of afaan oromo. *African affairs*, 96(384):325–352.

Ravikumar Cohn and Fienberg. 2003. A comparison of string distance metrics for name-matching task. . *In IIWeb*.

Demeke. 2001. The ethio-semitic languages (reexamining the classification. *Journal of Ethiopian Studies*, pages 57–93.

Getachew and Derib. 2008. Language policy in ethiopia: History and current trends. *Ethiopian journal of education and sciences*, 2(1).

Gooskens and Heeringa. 2004. Perceptive evaluation of levenshtein dialect distance measurements using norwegian dialect data. *Language variation and Change*, 16(03):189–207.

Gooskens. 2007. The contribution of linguistic factors to the intelligibility of closely related languages. *Journal of Multilingual and multicultural development*, 28(6):445–467.

Gooskens. 2013. *Experimental Methods for Measuring Intelligibility of Closely Related Language Varieties*. Oxford University Press.

Gutt. 1980. Intelligibility and interlingual comprehension among selected gurage speech varieties. *Journal of Ethiopian Studies*, 14:57–85.

Kroon Hailemariam and Walters. 1999. Multilingualism and nation building: Language and education in eritrea. *Journal of Multilingual and Multicultural Development*, 20(6):457–493.

Heeringa. 2004. *Measuring dialect pronunciation differences using Levenshtein distance*. Ph.D. thesis, University of Groningen.

Hetzron. 1972. *Ethiopian Semitic: studies in classification*. Manchester University Press.

Hetzron. 1977. *The Gunnn-Gurage Languages*, volume 2. Istituto orientale di Napoli.

Hornberger. 2002. Multilingual language policies and the continua of biliteracy: An ecological approach. . *Language policy*, 1(1):27–51.

Hudson. 2013. *Northeast African Semitic: Lexical Comparisons and Analysis*. Harrassowitz.

Iyob. 2000. The ethiopianeritrean conflict: diasporic vs. hegemonic states in the horn of africa, 19912000. *The Journal of Modern African Studies*, 38(04):659–682.

Kessler. 1995. Computational dialectology in irish gaelic. In *In Proceedings of the seventh conference on European chapter of the Association for Computational Linguistics*. Morgan Kaufmann Publishers Inc..

Lanza and Woldemariam. 2008. Language policy and globalization in a regional capital of ethiopia. In *Linguistic landscape*. Expanding the scenery.

Leslau. 1969. Toward a classification of the gurage dialects. *Journal of Semitic Studies*, 14(1):96–109.

May. 2011. *Language and minority rights: Ethnicity, nationalism and the politics of language*. Routledge.

Rena. 2005. Eritrean education-retrospect and prospect. *Journal of Humanities and Sciences*, 5(2):1–12.

Smith. 2008. The politics of contemporary language policy in ethiopia. *Journal of Developing Societies*, 24(2):207–243.

Sokal. 1988. Genetic, geographic, and linguistic distances in europe. In *Proceedings of the National Academy of Sciences*, volume 85 of 5, pages 1722–1726.

Schppert Swarte and Gooskens. 2014. Does german help speakers of dutch to understand written and spoken danish words? the role of second language knowledge in decoding an unknown but related language. in press.

Tang and Heuven. 2007. Mutual intelligibility and similarity of chinese dialects: Predicting judgments from objective measures. *Linguistics in the Netherlands*, 24(1):223–234.

Tang and Heuven. 2009. Mutual intelligibility of chinese dialects experimentally tested. *Lingua*, 119(5):709–732.

Tang and Heuven. 2015. Predicting mutual intelligibility in chinese dialects from subjective and objective linguistic similarity. *Interlinguistica*, 17:1019–1028.

Vaughan and Tronvoll. 2003. *The culture of power in contemporary Ethiopian political life*. Sida, Stockholm.

Young. 1996. Ethnicity and power in ethiopia. *Review of African Political Economy*, 23(70):531–542.

Young. 1998. Regionalism and democracy in ethiopia. *Third World Quarterly*, pages 191–204.

Why Catalan-Spanish Neural Machine Translation? Analysis, comparison and combination with standard Rule and Phrase-based technologies

Marta R. Costa-jussà
TALP Research Center
Universitat Politècnica de Catalunya, 08034 Barcelona
marta.ruiz@upc.edu

Abstract

Catalan and Spanish are two related languages given that both derive from Latin. They share similarities in several linguistic levels including morphology, syntax and semantics. This makes them particularly interesting for the MT task.

Given the recent appearance and popularity of neural MT, this paper analyzes the performance of this new approach compared to the well-established rule-based and phrase-based MT systems.

Experiments are reported on a large database of 180 million words. Results, in terms of standard automatic measures, show that neural MT clearly outperforms the rule-based and phrase-based MT system on in-domain test set, but it is worst in the out-of-domain test set. A naive system combination specially works for the latter.

In-domain manual analysis shows that neural MT tends to improve both adequacy and fluency, for example, by being able to generate more natural translations instead of literal ones, choosing to the adequate target word when the source word has several translations and improving gender agreement. However, out-of-domain manual analysis shows how neural MT is more affected by unknown words or contexts.

1 Introduction

Machine Translation (MT) is the application that allows to translate automatically from one source language to a target language. Approaches vary from rule-based to corpus-based. Rule-based MT systems have been the first largely commercialized MT systems (Douglas Arnold and Lorna Balkan and R. Lee Humphreys and Siety Meijer and Louisa Sadler, 1994). Years later, corpus-based approaches have reached both the interest in the scientific and industrial community (Hutchins, 1986). Recently, neural MT approach has been proposed. This corpus-based approach uses deep learning techniques (Kalchbrenner and Blunsom, 2013; Cho et al., 2014; Sutskever et al., 2014) and it may be taking over previous popular corpus-based approaches such as statistical phrase or hierarchical-based (Koehn et al., 2003; Chiang, 2007). As a result, large companies, such as Google, have been using rule-based MT, then statistical MT and just very recently, they are replacing some of their statistical MT engines by neural MT engines (Wu et al., 2016).

This paper analizes how standard neural MT techniques, which are briefly described in section 4.3, perform on the Catalan-Spanish task compared to popular rule-based and phrase-based MT. Additionally, we perform a naive system combination using the standard Minimum Bayes Risk (MBR) technique (Ehling et al., 2007) which reports slight improvements, in terms of standard automatic measures, in in-domain test set but large improvements in out-of-domain test set.

Catalan and Spanish are closely-related languages, which make them particularly interesting for MT and translation performance is quite high for rule-based and statistical-based systems.

Given these similarities, we want to test how neural MT behaves on such related language pairs. This leads us to the main question that this paper tries to solve:

Is neural MT competitive with current well-performing rule-based and phrase-based MT systems?

The answer to this question will be specially useful to industry, since they may decide over results shown if it is worth it to change their current

Proceedings of the Fourth Workshop on NLP for Similar Languages, Varieties and Dialects, pages 55–62,
Valencia, Spain, April 3, 2017. ©2017 Association for Computational Linguistics

paradigm which may be either rule or statistical or a combination of both. The aim of this study is to offer a comparison over these systems in terms of translation quality, terms of efficiency or computational cost are out-of-the-scope of this paper.

In this sense, the main contribution of this paper is the analysis and discussion on how the new neural MT approach addresses Catalan-Spanish MT compared to state-of-the-art systems and what are the remaining challenges for this particular language pair.

The rest of this paper is structured as follows. The next section briefly reports on the related work. Section 3 analyses details of this language pair. Section 4 briefly describes each MT approach: rule, phrase and neural-based, respectively. Section 5 details the experimental framework both in data description and in system parameters. Section 6 compares systems based on both automatic and manual analysis and discusses results. Finally, Section 7 reports the main conclusions of this paper.

2 Related work

Previous related publications on the Catalan-Spanish language pair are in rule-based MT (Canals-Marote et al., 2001; Alonso, 2005) and statitical MT (Poch et al., 2009; Costa-jussà et al., 2012). It is worth noting that given the similarity among Catalan and Spanish, Vilar et al (2007) proposed to build a statistical MT system that translated letters, whose underlying idea is similar to recent approaches in neural MT that are character-based (Costa-jussà and Fonollosa, 2016). As far as we are concerned, there are no previous works in neural MT covering Catalan-Spanish language pair.

3 Catalan and Spanish languages

This section reviews several aspects of the language pair we are addressing as a motivation of our study. We point out several social aspects covering language speakers and countries as well as commenting on situations of bilingualism. We also report linguistic aspects of both languages.

3.1 Social aspects

There are around 470 million native speakers for Spanish compared to 4 million for Catalan (as claimed in the Wikipedia). As a consequence, resources for Spanish are much larger than resources

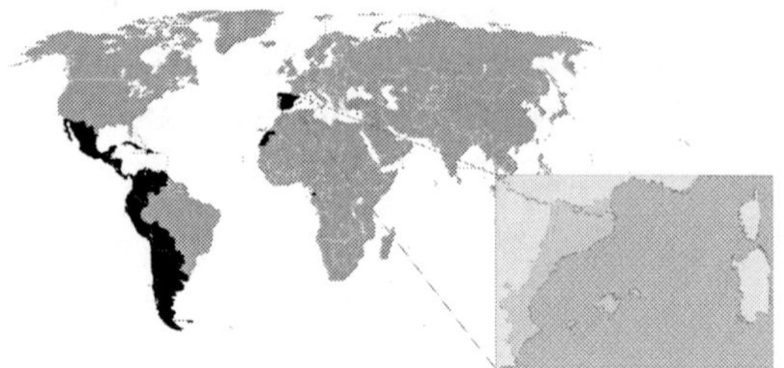

Figure 1: Map showing countries/regions where Spanish (blue) is official and Catalan is spoken (yellow).

for Catalan. Catalan is mainly spoken in Catalonia, Valencia and Balearic Islands, all regions of Spain. There are also some remaining speakers in the south of France and in the island of Sardinia. It is official language of the small country of Andorra. Spanish is official language in 20 countries including Mexico, Colombia and Spain. See Figure 1.

Catalan-Spanish bilingualism only occurs in the regions of Spain and in Andorra. The tendency is that all Catalan native speakers, in practice, also speak Spanish. However, it is not the same for Spanish native speakers. This leads us to a first example of use case for an MT system for this language pair: Spanish (native) speakers that do not understand Catalan. Other use cases include professional translations or web page translations.

3.2 Linguistic aspects

Catalan and Spanish belong to the romance languages which are the modern languages that evolved from Latin. Since both languages are from the same linguistic family, both share similar linguistic features such as morphological inflections or word reordering. Translation between both languages is quite straightforward since there are very few word reorderings and both vocabulary sizes and morphology inflection are quite similar.

4 MT Approaches

This section briefly reports standard baseline architectures for rule-based, phrase-based and neural-based MT. Description for all systems is done in a generic way, particular details from each one used in this work are described later in section 5.2. It is worth mentioning that the rule-based system significantly differs from the other two systems because it is not corpus-based. And

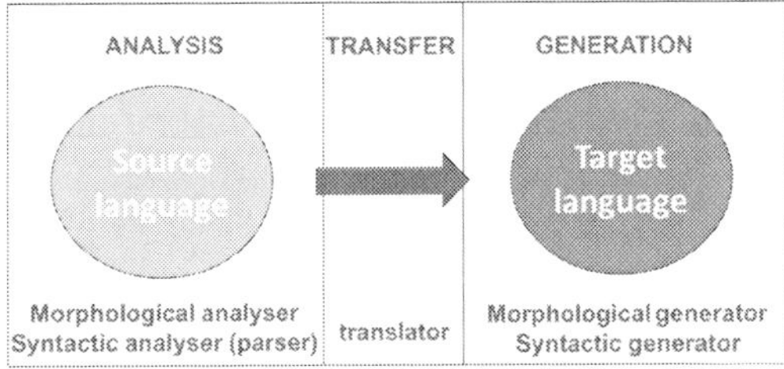

Figure 2: Standard architecture schema of a Rule-based MT system.

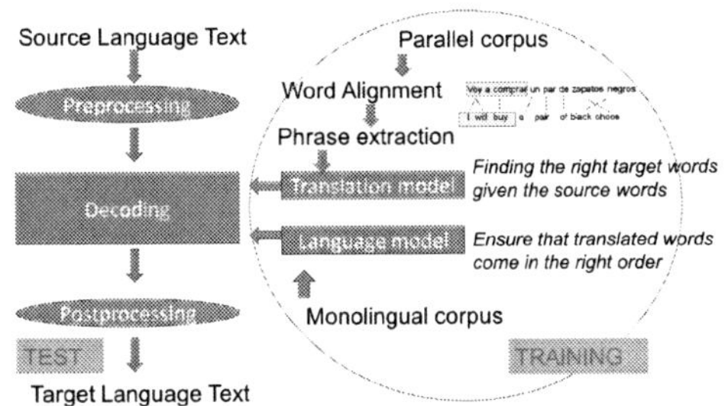

Figure 3: Standard architecture schema of a Phrase-based MT system.

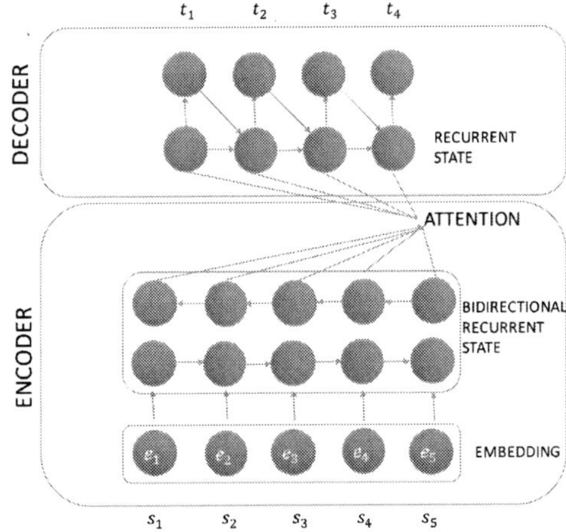

Figure 4: Standard architecture schema of a neural MT system.

phrase-based and neural-based, although both being corpus-based, they manage data very differently. The phrase-based system uses frequency counts and the neural-based system uses non-linear transformations. The main advantage from corpus-based approaches over the rule-based is that they learn from data. While the main advantage of neural-based over phrase-based is that the architecture allows for an end-to-end optimization.

4.1 Rule-based MT

Rule-based MT combines dictionaries and hand-made rules to generate the target output given the source input. Generally, a morphological and syntactic analysis of the source input is needed before doing the transfer into a simplified target. The final target is generated adding the appropriate morphology and/or syntax. See Figure 2 for an schematic representation of this approach.

4.2 Phrase-based Statistical MT

Standard phrase-based statitical MT (Koehn et al., 2003) focuses on finding the most probable target text given the source text by means of probabilistic techniques. Given a parallel corpus at the level of sentences, statistical co-ocurrences are studied to extract a bilingual dictionary of sequences of words (*phrases*) which are ranked using several features (i.e. conditional and posterior probabilities). Additionally to this bilingual dictionary, which is considered the translation model, other models such as reordering or language models are trained. Note that language modeling is trained on monolingual corpus and it gives information about the fluency of a sentence in the target language. All models are combined in the decoder which uses a beam search to extract the most probable target output given a source input. Note that the system is optimized in several steps since the word alignment is determined before building the translation model. See Figure 3 for an schematic representation of this approach.

4.3 Neural MT

Neural MT computes the conditional probability of the target sentence given the source sentence by means of an autoencoder architecture (Kalchbrenner and Blunsom, 2013; Sutskever et al., 2014; Cho et al., 2014). First, the encoder reads the source sentence $(s_1, s_2..., s_N)$ of N words, the encoder does a word embedding $(e_1, e_2, ...e_n)$ and encodes it into an intermediate representation (also refered to as context vector) by means of a recurrent neural network, which uses the gated recurrent unit (GRU) as activation function. The GRU function allows for a better performance with long sentences. Then, the decoder, which is also a recurrent neural network, generates a corresponding translation $(t_1, t_2...t_M)$ of M words based on this intermediate representation. Both encoder and decoder are jointly trained using the common statistical technique of Maximum (log-)likelihood Estimation (MLE).

This baseline autoencoder architecture is improved with an attention-based mechanism (Bahdanau et al., 2014), in which the encoder uses a bi-directional recurrent neural network. Now, the decoder predicts each target word with the intermediate representation plus the information of context given by the attention. See Figure 4.

5 Experimental Framework

This section reports details on the data used for training, optimizing and testing as well as a description of the parameters for each system in the comparison.

5.1 Data

We use a large corpus extracted from ten years of the paper edition of a bilingual Catalan newspaper, El Periódico (Costa-jussà et al., 2014). The Spanish-Catalan corpus is partially available via ELDA (Evaluations and Language Resources Dis-tribution Agency) in catalog number ELRA-W0053. Development and test sets are extracted from the same corpus, but additionally, to test system performance in out-of-domain, we use a test corpus within the medicine domain. This medical corpus was kindly provided by the Universal-Doctor project[1]. Preprocessing was limited to tokenization. Corpus statistics are shown in Table 1.

5.2 System details

Rule-based We use the Apertium rule-based system (Forcada et al., 2011). Apertium is open-source shallow-transfer MT system which was initially designed for the translation between related language pairs. In particular, this rule-based system does not do full syntactic parsing in contrast to the general rule-based architecture described in section 4.1. The system is available from Source-forge[2], and we use its last version 1.2.1.

Phrase-based We use Moses (Koehn et al., 2007) which is an open-source phrase-based MT system and it has a large community of developers behind. To build the system, we use stan-dard/default parameters which include: grow-diagonal-final-and word alignment symmetrization, lexicalized reordering, relative frequencies (conditional and posterior probabilities) with phrase discounting, lexical weights, phrase bonus, accepting phrases up to length 10, 5-gram language model with Kneser-Ney smoothing, word bonus and MERT (Minimum Error Rate Training) optimisation.

Neural-based The neural MT system was built using the open-source software available in github[3]. This code implements the auto-encoder with attention that we presented in section 4.3. We use the parameters defined in Table 2. Regarding vocabulary limitation, we use a vocabulary size of 90,000 both in Spanish and in Catalan. We replace out-of-vocabulary words (UNKs) using the standard methodology (Jean et al., 2015): we use the word-to-word translation model learned with 'fast-align' (Dyer et al., 2013) or, if not available, the aligned source word is used. We use an embedding of 512 and a dimension of 1024, a batch size of 32, and no dropout, learning-rate of 0.001 and adadelta optimization.

6 Results

This section evaluates the three systems in terms of standard automatic measures. Then, we show some examples of translation outputs and we do a manual comparison.

6.1 Automatic measures

Table 3 shows results in terms of METEOR (Lavie and Agarwal, 2007) and BLEU (Papineni et al., 2002). The best results for the in-domain test set are achieved when using the neural MT system for both translation directions. Best results for the out-of-domain corpus vary depending on the translation direction and measure: for Catalan-to-Spanish, best results are obtained with the phrase-based system; and for Spanish-to-Catalan, best results are obtained with the rule-based system in terms of BLEU, but with the phrase-based system in terms of METEOR. In all cases, results are statistically significant (99%) following the "pair bootstrap resampling" (Koehn, 2004).

To summarise, neural MT is significantly better in the in-domain translation, but it is left behind in out-of-domain. In this out-of-domain task, rule-

---

[1]http://www.universaldoctor.com

[2]https://sourceforge.net/projects/apertium/

[3]http://github.com/nyu-dl/dl4mt-tutorial/

	Set	Sentences	Words	Vocabulary	Singletons
	Training	6,5	179,9	713	336
Catalan	Development	2.2	60	11	8
	Test	2.2	60	12	7
	Test (Out-of-domain)	0.6	4	1	0.5
	Training	6,5	165,2	737	343
Spanish	Development	2.2	55	12	8
	Test	2.2	56	12	8
	Test (Out-of-domain)	0.6	4	1	0.5

Table 1: Corpus details (in thousands) for Catalan-Spanish.

Vocabulary	90,000
Embeddings	512
Dimension	1024
Batch	32
Dropout	none
Learning rate	0.001
Optimization	Adadelta

Table 2: Neural MT main parameters.

based becomes competitive with corpus-based approaches.

As expected, a simple naive system combination like MBR provides the best final translation results. This means that systems can complement each other, specially for the out-of-domain test set.

6.2 Manual analysis

Manual analysis in this section is intended to complement information provided by the automatic measures in previous section.

Table 4 shows several translation examples from the three systems for the in-domain test set. Examples show the advantages of the neural MT system compared to rule and/or phrase-based systems. Coherently with previous automatic results, neural MT shows best results. Each example in Table 4 specifically shows how neural MT is able to improve translation in the following terms:

1. *Better gender agreement* (compared to phrase-based MT), which clearly affects fluency of the final translation.

2. *No missing content words* (compared to phrase-based MT) and using the *right verb tense* (compared to the rule-based), which has an impact in adequacy of the translation.

3. *Avoiding redundant words* like "botar" produces a better translation since this would not sound fluent in this context in Catalan.

4. *Choosing the right translation from a polysemic word* improves adequacy and fluency at the same time, the verb "ser" in Catalan has mainly two different translations in Spanish which are "ser" o "estar", in this case, the correct one is the latter.

5. *Avoiding using literate translation*, if possible, improves translation, in particular, the obligation "s'ha de" in Catalan has to be translated to "hay que" or "han tenido que" in Spanish.

6. Right *preposition* translation.

7. *Adding words to make translation more fluent*. The use of "cuyas" which improves translation.

Finally, example 8 shows the main mistake that neural MT does systematically for this pair of languages: missing initial determiners.

Table 5 shows examples in the out-of-domain text. In this case, example 1 shows how the neural MT system correctly uses the pronoun but it does not coincide with the reference. Example 2, neural MT uses the wrong translation of "pedir" which would correspond to a correct translation in some contexts of the training material. Examples 3 shows how a new unnecessary (but also correct) word is added to the translation in the case of the neural MT. Finally, example 4 shows a missing translation of a word, which is an out-of-vocabulary.

Most of neural MT errors could be addressed by using already existing techniques. The example of missing determiners could be solved using

| System | CAES | | | | ESCA | | | |
| | In-domain | | Out-domain | | In-domain | | Out-domain | |
	METEOR	BLEU	METEOR	BLEU	METEOR	BLEU	METEOR	BLEU
Rule	87.11	75.20	67.22	50.53	83.92	70.15	63.77	**50.41**
Phrase	90.59	81.80	**72.31**	**57.20**	90.88	84.24	**64.31**	49.67
Neural	**90.65**	**83.01**	66.87	52.10	**92.15**	**86.31**	60.73	47.63
MBR	**91.51**	**83.35**	**73.15**	**58.07**	**92.25**	**86.33**	**66.73**	**53.20**

Table 3: METEOR and BLEU results. In bold, best results among individual systems and system combination.

1	SRC	una cosa lúdica y divertida
	Rule	una cosa **lúdica** i **divertida**
	Phrase	una cosa lúdic i divertit
	NN	una cosa **lúdica** i **divertida**
	REF	una cosa lúdica i divertida
2	SRC	los investigadores creen que el cuerpo pudo ser arrastrado desde otro lugar .
	Rule	els investigadors creuen que el cos va poder ser arrossegat des d'un altre lloc
	Phrase	els investigadors creuen que el cos va ser arrossegat des d un altre lloc .
	NN	els investigadors creuen que el cos **podria** haver estat arrossegat des d un altre lloc .
	REF	els investigadors creuen que el cos hauria pogut ser arrossegat des d un altre lloc .
3	SRC	cerca de 10.000 personas botaron al ritmo de Ruff down (...)
	Rule	prop de 10.000 persones van botar al ritme de Ruff down (...)
	Phrase	prop de 10.000 persones van botar al ritme de Ruff down (...)
	NN	prop de 10.000 persones **van al ritme** de Ruff down (...)
	REF	unes 10.000 persones van saltar al ritme de Ruff down (...)
4	SRC	quan el pilot ja era a l ' entrada del parc (...)
	Rule	cuando el piloto ya era a la entrada del parque (...)
	Phrase	cuando el piloto era ya a la entrada del parque (...)
	NN	cuando el piloto **estaba** ya a la entrada del parque (...)
	REF	cuando el pelotón ya se hallaba en la entrada del parque (...)
5	SRC	i s hi han d afegir dues querelles de particulars .
	Rule	y **han tenido que** añadir dos querellas de particulares .
	Phrase	y se han de añadir dos querellas de particulares .
	NN	(...) y **hay que** añadir dos querallas de particulares
	REF	a estos hay que añadir dos querellas de particulares .
6	SRC	(...) ja teníem als nostres magatzems un important estoc de peces
	Rule	(...) ya teníamos a nuestros almacenes un importante stock de piezas
	Phrase	(...) ya teníamos nuestros almacenes un importante estoc de piezas
	NN	(...) ya teníamos **en** nuestros almacenes un importante estoc de piezas
	REF	(...) ya teníamos en nuestros almacenes un importante estoc de piezas
7	SRC	va anunciar ahir el començament d un cicle de conferèncis que analitzaran l obra d Elliot . les conclusions es recolliran en un llibre .
	Rule	anunció ayer el comienzo de un ciclo de conferencias que analizarán la obra de Elliot . las conclusiones se recogerán en un libro .
	Phrase	(...) anunció ayer el inicio de un ciclo de conferencias que analizarán la obra de Elliot . las conclusiones se recogerán en un libro .
	NN	(...) anunció ayer el comienzo de un ciclo de conferencias que analizarán la obra de Elliot , **cuyas** conclusiones se recogerán en un libro .
	REF	anunció ayer el inicio de un ciclo de conferencias que analizarán la obra de Elliot y cuyas conclusiones se recogerán en un libro .
9	SRC	el cas dels profesionals és diferente .
	Rule	el caso de los profesionales es diferente .
	Phrase	en el caso de los profesionales es diferente
	NN	caso de los profesionales es diferente
	REF	el caso de los profesionales es diferente .

Table 4: Translation examples.

coverage neural MT (Tu et al., 2016); wrong translations may be reduced using a language model (Gulcehre et al., 2017); and out-of-vocabulary words may be reduced using existing approaches such as Byte Pair Encoding (BPE) (Sennrich et al., 2016) or character-based (Costa-jussà and Fonollosa, 2016). The integration of these new advances for Catalan-Spanish language pair is left for future work.

7 Discussion and Further Work

This paper shows a comparison between rule, phrase and neural MT systems in the Catalan-Spanish language pair. Performance is better in the case of the neural MT system when using the in-domain test set, but best performance in the out-of-domain test set is better for the rule-based system (Spanish-to-Catalan, in BLEU) and for the phrase-based sytem (Catalan-to-Spanish).

Regarding our research question: *Is neural MT competitive with current well-performing rule-based and phrase-based MT systems?* Based on the automatic and manual analysis from this paper, the answer is yes, specially, for in-domain sets. Therefore, it is worth it to use neural MT for Catalan-Spanish when building domain spe-

1	SRC	Debe ponerse el collarín .
	Rule	**Ha de posar-se** el collet .
	Phrase	ha de posar el collaret .
	NN	**S ' ha** de posar el collaret .
	REF	Ha de posar-se el collar .
2	SRC	Pedir un informe .
	Rule	**Demanar** un informe .
	Phrase	**Demanar** un informe .
	NN	*resumeixi* un informe .
	REF	Demanar un informe .
3	SRC	No hauria de consumir alcohol
	Rule	No tendría que consumir alcohol
	Phrase	No debería consumir alcohol
	NN	*yo* no tendría que consumir alcohol
	REF	No debería consumir alcohol
4	SRC	Ha sagnat per algun lloc del cos
	Rule	Ha **sangrado** por algún lugar de su cuerpo .
	Phrase	Ha **sangrado** por algún lugar del cuerpo .
	NN	Ha por algún lugar del cuerpo .
	REF	Ha sangrado por algún lugar de su cuerpo .

Table 5: Out-of-domain translation examples.

cific translation systems. And it is worth it to use system combination for the out-of-domain case. Again, mention that we do not consider efficiency and computational cost comparison in this study.

In this paper, we only implemented a baseline neural MT. Further work would be to show how recent improvements in neural MT like the ones mentioned in previous: Byte Pair Encoding (BPE) (Sennrich et al., 2016), character-based (Costa-jussà and Fonollosa, 2016), coverage (Tu et al., 2016), language model (Gulcehre et al., 2017), multilingual (Firat et al., 2017) and other strategies (Wu et al., 2016) affect this language pair.

Acknowledgments

The author wants to thank the anonymous reviewers for their valuable feedback which helped improving this paper. This work is supported by the Spanish Ministerio de Economía y Competitividad and European Regional Development Fund, through the postdoctoral senior grant *Ramón y Cajal* and the contract TEC2015-69266-P (MINECO/FEDER, UE).

References

Juan Alonso Alonso. 2005. Machine Translation for Catalan-Spanish The real case for productive MT. . In *Proceedings of EAMT*.

Dzmitry Bahdanau, Kyunghyun Cho, and Yoshua Bengio. 2014. Neural machine translation by jointly learning to align and translate. volume abs/1409.0473.

Raul Canals-Marote, Anna Esteve-Guillén, Alicia Garrido-Alenda, M Guardiola-Savall, Amaia Iturraspe-Bellver, Sandra Montserrat-Buendia, Sergio Ortiz-Rojas, Herminia Pastor-Pina, Pedro Pérez-Antón, and Míkel Forcada. 2001. The SpanishCatalan machine translation system interNOSTRUM. In *Proceedings of MT Summit VIII, Santiago de Compostela*, pages 73–76.

David Chiang. 2007. Hierarchical phrase-based translation. *Comput. Linguist.*, 33(2):201–228, June.

Kyunghyun Cho, Bart van Merrienboer, Çaglar Gülçehre, Dzmitry Bahdanau, Fethi Bougares, Holger Schwenk, and Yoshua Bengio. 2014. Learning phrase representations using RNN encoder-decoder for statistical machine translation. In *Proceedings of the 2014 Conference on Empirical Methods in Natural Language Processing, EMNLP 2014, October 25-29, 2014, Doha, Qatar, A meeting of SIGDAT, a Special Interest Group of the ACL*, pages 1724–1734.

Marta R. Costa-jussà and José A. R. Fonollosa. 2016. Character-based neural machine translation. In *Proceedings of the 54th Annual Meeting of the Association for Co mputational Linguistics (Volume 2: Short Papers)*, pages 357–361, Berlin, Germany, August. Association for Computational Linguistics.

Marta R. Costa-jussà, Mireia Farrús, José B. Mariño, and José A.R. Fonollosa. 2012. Study and comparison of rule-based and statistical Catalan-Spanish machine translation systems. *Computing and Informatics Journal*, 31:1001–1026, April.

Marta R. Costa-jussà, March Poch, José A.R. Fonollosa, Mireia Farrús, and José B. Mariño. 2014. A large Spanish-Catalna parallel corpus release for Machine Translation. *Computing and Informatics Journal*, 33.

Douglas Arnold and Lorna Balkan and R. Lee Humphreys and Siety Meijer and Louisa Sadler. 1994. *Machine Translation: An Introductory Guide (Clear Business Studies)*.

Chris Dyer, Victor Chahuneau, and Noah A. Smith. 2013. A Simple, Fast, and Effective Reparameterization of IBM Model 2. In *Proceedings of the 2013 Conference of the North American Chapter of the Association for Computational Linguistics: Human Language Technologies*, pages 644–648, Atlanta, Georgia, June. Association for Computational Linguistics.

Nicola Ehling, Richard Zens, and Hermann Ney. 2007. Minimum bayes risk decoding for bleu. In *Proceedings of the 45th Annual Meeting of the Association for Co mputational Linguistics Companion Volume Proceedings of the Demo and Poster Sessions*, pages 101–104, Prague, Czech Republic, June. Association for Computational Linguistics.

Orhan Firat, Kyunghyun Cho, Baskaran Sankaran, Fatos T.Ỹarman Vural, and Yoshua Bengio. 2017. Multi-Way, Multilingual Neural Machine Translation. *Accepted for publication in Computer Speech and Language, Specia l Issue in Deep learning for Machine Translation.*

Mikel L. Forcada, Mireia Ginestí-Rosell, Jacob Nordfalk, Jim OŘegan, Sergio Ortiz-Rojas, Juan Antonio Pérez-Ortiz, Felipe Sánchez-Martínez, Gema Ramírez-Sánchez, and Francis M. Tyers. 2011. Apertium: a free/open-source platform for rulebased machine translation". *Machine Translation*, 25.

Caglar Gulcehre, Orhan Firat, Kelvin Xu, Kyunghyun Cho, Loic Barrault, Huei-Chi Lin, Fethi Bougares, Holger Schwenk, and Yoshua Bengio. 2017. On Integrating a Language Model Into Neural Machine Translation. *Accepted for publication in Computer Speech and Language, Specia l Issue in Deep learning for Machine Translation.*

W. John Hutchins. 1986. *Machine Translation: Past, Present, Future.* John Wiley & Sons, Inc., New York, NY, USA.

Sébastien Jean, Kyunghyun Cho, Roland Memisevic, and Yoshua Bengio. 2015. On using very large target vocabulary for neural machine translation. In *Proceedings of the 53rd Annual Meeting of the Association for Computational Linguistics and the 7th International Joint Conference on Natural Language Processing (Volume 1: Long Papers)*, pages 1–10, Beijing, China, July. Association for Computational Linguistics.

Nal Kalchbrenner and Phil Blunsom. 2013. Recurrent continuous translation models. In *Proceedings of the 2013 Conference on Empirical Methods in Natur al Language Processing*, pages 1700–1709, Seattle, Washington, USA, October. Association for Computational Linguistics.

Philipp Koehn, Franz Josef Och, and Daniel Marcu. 2003. Statistical phrase-based translation. In *Proceedings of the 2003 Conference of the North American Chapter of the Association for Computational Linguistics on Human Language Technology - Volume 1*, NAACL '03, pages 48–54.

Philipp Koehn, Hieu Hoang, Alexandra Birch, Chris Callison-Burch, Marcello Federico, Nicola Bertoldi, Brooke Cowan, Wade Shen, Christine Moran, Richard Zens, Chris Dyer, Ondřej Bojar, Alexandra Constantin, and Evan Herbst. 2007. Moses: Open source toolkit for statistical machine translation. In *Proceedings of the 45th Annual Meeting of the ACL on Interactive Poster and Demonstration Sessions*, ACL '07, pages 177–180.

Philipp Koehn. 2004. Statistical Significance Tests For Machine Translation Evaluation. In *Proceedings of EMNLP*, volume 4, pages 388–395.

Alon Lavie and Abhaya Agarwal. 2007. Meteor: An Automatic Metric for MT Evaluation with High Levels of Correlation with Human Judgments. In *Proceedings of the Second Workshop on Statistical Machine Translation*, StatMT '07, pages 228–231.

Kishore Papineni, Salim Roukos, Todd Ward, and Wei-Jing Zhu. 2002. Bleu: A method for automatic evaluation of machine translation. In *Proceedings of the 40th Annual Meeting on Association for Computational Linguistics*, ACL '02, pages 311–318, Stroudsburg, PA, USA. Association for Computational Linguistics.

Marc Poch, Mireia Farrs, Marta R. Costa-jussà, José B. Mari no, Adolfo Hernández, Carlos A. Henríquez Q., and José A. R. Fonollosa. 2009. The TALP online Spanish-Catalan machine translation system. In *Speech and Language Technologies for Iberian Languages*, pages 105–105, September.

Rico Sennrich, Barry Haddow, and Alexandra Birch. 2016. Neural machine translation of rare words with subword units. In *Proceedings of the 54th Annual Meeting of the Association for Co mputational Linguistics (Volume 1: Long Papers)*, pages 1715–1725, Berlin, Germany, August. Association for Computational Linguistics.

Ilya Sutskever, Oriol Vinyals, and Quoc V. Le. 2014. Sequence to sequence learning with neural networks. In *Advances in Neural Information Processing Systems 27: Annual Conference on Neural Information Processing Systems 2014, December 8-13 2014, Montreal, Quebec, Canada*, pages 3104–3112.

Zhaopeng Tu, Zhengdong Lu, Yang Liu, Xiaohua Liu, and Hang Li. 2016. Coverage-based neural machine translation. *CoRR*, abs/1601.04811.

David Vilar, Jan-T. Peter, and Hermann Ney. 2007. Can we translate letters? In *Proceedings of the Second Workshop on Statistical Machine Translation*, StatMT '07, pages 33–39.

Yonghui Wu, Mike Schuster, Zhifeng Chen, Quoc V. Le, Mohammad Norouzi, Wolfgang Macherey, Maxim Krikun, Yuan Cao, Qin Gao, Klaus Macherey, Jeff Klingner, Apurva Shah, Melvin Johnson, Xiaobing Liu, Lukasz Kaiser, Stephan Gouws, Yoshikiyo Kato, Taku Kudo, Hideto Kazawa, Keith Stevens, George Kurian, Nishant Patil, Wei Wang, Cliff Young, Jason Smith, Jason Riesa, Alex Rudnick, Oriol Vinyals, Greg Corrado, Macduff Hughes, and Jeffrey Dean. 2016. Google's neural machine translation system: Bridging the gap between human and machine translation. *CoRR*, abs/1609.08144.

Kurdish Interdialect Machine Translation

Hossein Hassani
University of Kurdistan Hewlêr
Sarajevo School of Science and Technology
`hosseinh@ukh.edu.krd`
`hossein.hassani@stu.ssst.edu.ba`

Abstract

This research suggests a method for machine translation among two Kurdish dialects. We chose the two widely spoken dialects, Kurmanji and Sorani, which are considered to be mutually unintelligible. Also, despite being spoken by about 30 million people in different countries, Kurdish is among less-resourced languages. The research used *bi-dialectal* dictionaries and showed that the lack of parallel corpora is not a major obstacle in machine translation between the two dialects. The experiments showed that the machine translated texts are comprehensible to those who do not speak the dialect. The research is the first attempt for inter-dialect machine translation in Kurdish and particularly could help in making online texts in one dialect comprehensible to those who only speak the target dialect. The results showed that the translated texts are in 71% and 79% cases rated as *understandable* for Kurmanji and Sorani respectively. They are rated as *slightly understandable* in 29% cases for Kurmanji and 21% for Sorani.

1 Introduction

This paper discusses Intralanguage Machine Translation (IMT) among Kurdish dialects. The two most widely spoken Kurdish dialects are Kurmanji and Sorani which are considered to be mutually unintelligible (Hassanpour, 1992). Furthermore, the language is among less-resourced languages (Sheykh Esmaili, 2012; Sheykh Esmaili et al., 2014). However, this research shows that, in the absence of large parallel corpora, a word-for-word translation approach based on a bidialectal dictionary provides a reasonable translation output between the dialects. This improves mutual intelligibility among Kurmanji and Sorani users in the online textual environment.

Our aim is to show that lack of corpus is not a major obstacle for providing an inter-dialect (intralingual) machine translation between Sorani and Kurmanji. Our method intends to transfer the general meaning of texts in online media in one dialect to those audience who speak the other. To that extent, the output is not considered to be a literary translation nor it is able to transfer all grammatic features of the source to the target dialect.

Machine Translation (MT) is primarily understood as using computers for translating a language into another, or in other words, as automated *inter-language* translation. The main motive of MT is to make a language L_1 intelligible to whom who do not speak it by presenting it in a language L_2, which might be the audiences' own language or a language which they are able to understand. However, there are several languages such as Chinese, Arabic, and Kurdish that encompass several dialects which are mutually unintelligible (Tang et al., 2008; Farghaly and Shaalan, 2009; Sadat et al., 2014). In this respect, the translation between the dialects are of the *intralanguage* nature rather than *interlanguage*.

Kurdish is the name given to a number of distinct dialects of a language spoken in the geographical area touching on Iran, Iraq, Turkey, and Syria. However, Kurds have lived in other countries such as Armenia, Lebanon, Egypt, and some other countries since several hundred years ago. The population who speak the language is estimated about 30 million (Kurdish Academy of Languages, 2016; Hassani and Medjedovic, 2016).

Dialect diversity is an important characteristic of Kurdish. This diversity, the name of dialects, and their geographic distribution have been

Proceedings of the Fourth Workshop on NLP for Similar Languages, Varieties and Dialects, pages 63–72,
Valencia, Spain, April 3, 2017. ©2017 Association for Computational Linguistics

of interest for linguists who have been studying Kurdish. Kurdish is multi-dialect from the Indo-European root (Hassanpour, 1992). Although different scholars have categorized its dialects differently, a considerable majority refer to it as Northern Kurdish (Kurmanji), Central Kurdish (Sorani), Southern Kurdish, Gorani, and Zazaki that include several sub-dialects (Haig and Öpengin, 2014; Hassani and Medjedovic, 2016; Malmasi, 2016). The populations that speak different dialects of the language differ significantly. The majority of Kurmanji speakers are located in different countries, such as Turkey, Syria, Iraq, Iran, Armenia, Lebanon, just to name the mainlands. The second popular dialect is Sorani, which is mainly spoken among Kurds in Iran and Iraq. Zazaki is spoken in Turkey. Gorani is primarily spoken in Iran and Iraq (Izady, 1992; Hassanpour, 1992). Kurdish is written using four different scripts, which are modified Persian/Arabic, Latin, Yekgirtû(unified), and Cyrillic. The popularity of the scripts differ according to the geographical and geopolitical situations. Latin script uses a single character while Persian/Arabic and Yekgirtû in a few cases use two characters for one letter. The Persian/Arabic script is even more complex with its RTL and concatenated writing style auto(of Language, 2016).

We are facing the "knowledge acquisition bottleneck", which basically occurs in the early stages of Natural Language Processing (NLP) and Computational Linguistics (CL) studies (Schubert, 2015), hence we are interested in investigating of interdialect Kurdish translation in the absence of parallel corpora. Our hypothesis is that despite the mutual unintelligibility between the two dialects, a word-for-word translation would be able to transfer the core meaning of texts in one dialect into the other. To illustrate, Ballesteros and Croft (1996) have reported on the applicability using dictionaries in certain situations such as Information Retrieval (IR). This solution can be used while the necessary background knowledge is prepared for statistical MT.

The remainder of the article is organized in the following sections. Section 2 reviews the literature. Section 3 provide the method that is used in developing an IMT for Sorani-Kurmanji. Section 4 presents the performed experiments on the developed IMT and evaluates the results. Section 5 discusses the findings and the outcome of the experiments and analyzes the results. Finally, section 6 summarizes the findings, provides the conclusion, and addresses the future work.

2 Related Work

Zhang (1998) discusses inter-dialect MT between Cantonese and Mandarin as the two most important Chinese varieties, which are considered to be mutually unintelligible. Zhang (1998) discusses the differences between the two dialects at the level of sound systems, grammar rules, and vocabulary, based on which a method for inter-dialect MT between the two dialects has been provided. Zhang (1998) suggests that as the dialects of a language usually share a common standard written form, the target of inter-dialect MT is better to be the spoken dialects. The method has been implemented by using a Word collocation list, a Mandarin-Cantonese dictionary and a handful number of rules to handle syntactic differences. Zhang (1998) addresses the immediate purposes of the developed systems as to facilitate language communication and to help Hong Kong students to write standard Mandarin Chinese. However, he has not reported on the evaluation of the system and the level of intelligibility of the system's output by the targeted audience. Furthermore, the research reports that a Mandarin-Cantonese corpus has been built, but it does not mention how it has been created nor how it has been used in inter-dialect MT. Moreover, although it has been mentioned that the rules for the syntactic difference between the dialects are applied based on a knowledge base, it is not clear whether this knowledge base uses a Part-of-Speech (POS) tagger or an annotated corpus or it has applied another approach.

Peradin et al. (2014) suggest a shallow-transfer rule-based machine translation for Western group of South Slavic language using Apertium platform which is a modular machine translation system. Peradin et al. (2014) have used morphological lexicons available on Apertium repository.

Nakov and Tiedemann (2012) worked on Macedonian-Bulgarian machine translation as *close languages*. They have put their assumption based on the morphological and lexical similarities and have used statistical approach combined with word-for-word translation to show that MT is possible without having large corpora. Although the work technically could be of help for inter-dialect MT, it is not an IMT study in principle.

Our search for finding more work on automatic translation among dialects, which we called IMT, did not yield any other significant work beyond what has been done by Zhang (1998). To illustrate, we refer to a recent publication, a comprehensive handbook by Chan (2014), which covers different aspects of MT and MT technologies. However, although the book addresses the MT status with regard to different languages, for the work related to inter-dialect MT it only refers to the studies by Zhang (1998).

As another evidence for lack of noticeable study on IMT we refer to "The first workshop on Applying NLP Tools to Similar Languages, Varieties and Dialects" was conducted in 2014 (Zampieri et al., 2014) and consequently a "Joint Workshop on Language Technology for Closely Related Languages, Varieties and Dialects" (Ass, 2015) took place in 2015. Although these events fairly covered several areas of close languages, none of the papers discussed IMT.

However, the literature on mutual intelligibility has a longer background of scholarly work and is also closely related to our research area in a broad sense (Voegelin and Harris, 1951; Pierce, 1952; Yamagiwa, 1967).

Cheng (1997) has measured the relationship among dialects of Chinese . Also Szeto (2000) tested the intelligibility of Chinese using a tape-recorded text (RTT), asking the participant group members to write down the recognized vocabularies (Szeto, 2000). In a slightly recent attempt, Kluge (2006) suggested some improvements with regard to the question-answering approach of standard RTT. However, in none of theses studies the computational aspects of the process have been of concern to the researchers.

Tang and van Heuven (2009) have performed an experiment on Chinese and assessed intelligibility among a number of its dialects. They discuss the adequacy of mutual intelligibility testing "to determine how different two languages or language varieties are". Their method is based on speech recognition at both word and sentence intelligibility level.

Munday (2009) refers to intralingual translation as "rewording" and describes it as the process of summarizing or rewriting a text in the same language. However, the majority of this work has focused on interlingual, particularly bilingual translation.

From a different perspective, Beijering et al. (2008) have studied the dialectal and inter-language intelligibility and perceived linguistic distance among Scandinavian dialects using Levenshtein algorithm. According to Beijering et al. (2008) the Levenshtein algorithm is able to successfully predict intelligibility among different languages/dialects.

3 Methodology

We were not able to apply the probabilistic approach in inter-dialect machine translation because of the lack of required infrastructure in terms of parallel, annotated, and tagged corpora at the time of conducting this project. Therefore, we aimed to use a method for *intralingual* (inter-dialect) MT between Sorani and Kurmanji that is applicable in the absence of large data. As a result, we used a modified version of the method suggested by Zhang (1998) in which a word collocation list, a bidialectal dictionary and a series of rules to handle syntactic differences between the dialects are used to perform inter-dialect MT between Mandarin and Cantonese. In our adaptation, we have not considered the grammatic differences of Kurmanji. There are two reasons for this, first, lack of the required resources such as tagged corpora which does not allow us to implement an efficient syntactic analysis, and second, the regional variations in Kurmanji (Öpengin and Haig, 2014) makes the rules more complicated.

Therefore, we have based our method on the development of the two *bidialectal* dictionaries, one for Sorani to Kurmanji equivalents, and the other for Kuramnji to Sorani. We have implemented a word-for-word translation, which is also known as word-by-word (in a number of texts it is also called literal) or direct translation. This is an incremental transformation of the source-language text into a target-language text without having any knowledge about phrasing or grammatical structure in the source or target language (Jurafsky and Martin, 2008).

3.1 Dictionary Development

We used web data, mainly websites of Kurdish media and universities in Iraqi Kurdistan region, for our data collection. In terms of the genre, we selected the texts that were about art, literature, sport, and education. The reason was that we were interested in assessing the efficiency/adequacy of our method in helping Kurmanji users to be able to comprehend the online texts of ordinary day-to-day social genres written in Sorani and vice versa. We transliterated the texts in Persian/Arabic to Latin. We processed these texts and extracted their lexicon. We then used several Kurdish dictionaries to set the first sets of word equivalents, the lexicon, in the target dialect. For this purpose, we used (Demîrhan, 2007; Wîkîferheng and Ferhenga azad (*Azad Dictionary*), 2015; Ronahî, 2015; Mohammed Ali, 2008). The first three items are available online and the last one is in printed format. We also used our knowledge about the dialects and consulted language informants in the cases that the dictionaries could not resolve. This round of dictionary development process produced 6792 words out of which 2632 words are in Kurmanji and 4160 in Sorani.

3.2 Evaluation Method

We evaluated the efficiency of the implemented IMT by adapting the human raters method, which uses human experts to rate the translated texts. In this method several parameters are used such as fidelity or accuracy, intelligibility or clarity, and style (Fiederer and O´Brien, 2009; Ahsan et al., 2010). Although automated methods such as BLEU (bilingual evaluation understudy) (Papineni et al., 2002) have been implemented for MT evaluation, they perform more efficiently in the presence of proper corpora and language models, which were not available in our case.

We followed a combination of qualitative/quantitative approach for the evaluation process. In our adaptation of human raters, the translated texts are given to several speakers whose main dialects are not the same as the original text. Also some speakers will be chosen who have learned one of theses dialects as a second language and they do not have any familiarity, or at least any considerable familiarity, with the other dialect. The method then quantitatively evaluates the comprehensibility/understandability degree of the translated texts using this parameter. We also conduct a short interview with the human raters after they rated the text to qualitatively assess the result. We have not considered "style" parameter of human rating in our experiment because we have not evaluated the syntactic/parsing aspect of the translated texts.

For comprehensibility evaluation, Fiederer and O´Brien (2009) suggest 4 levels while Ahsan et al. (2010) suggest 5 levels. In our approach the translated texts is ranked in 5 categories: *not understandable*, *slightly understandable*, *understandable*, and *completely understandable*. Nevertheless, as it was mentioned, the translation evaluation is a subjective process no matter how one tries to quantify it. We briefly explain to the participants that they should rate a text as *not understandable* if they find that they cannot comprehend what the text is about; as *slightly understandable* if they know the meaning of a number of words and even a sentence but they do not have an overall comprehension of the text; as *understandable* if they comprehend the text but they do not know a few words; as *completely understandable* if they comprehend the text and they know the meaning of all words.

After rating process by each participant, we hold an interview to verify their understanding level. In this interview, we ask participants to tell us what the passages were about in their own words. Furthermore, if the given rate is *slightly understandable* or *understandable*, we ask the participant to explain what is the reason that they have not rated the text as *completely understandable*.

We also ask the participants to rank themselves with regard to their fluency in reading Kurdish texts in Latin, because many Kurdish speaking people in Iraqi Kurdistan either cannot read Kurdish texts in Latin or they are not fluent in reading this script [1]. We will ask more precise questions in the interview to verify the comprehensibility of the text, if a participant rates their Latin reading fluency below *good*.

Importantly, this study has not intended to consider the aesthetic aspects of the translation as an art, rather its intention is to evaluate the adequacy of this approach in the absence of large data that could support a high quality translation.

4 Experiments

We developed a transliterator to transliterate texts in Persian/Arabic script into Latin script. The dictionaries created in Latin script and where it was necessary the vocabulary was transliterated from Persian/Arabic into Latin. We manually removed

---

[1] In fact, most of the Kurdish speaking people, even if they are well-educated, might not be fluent in reading Kurdish texts either in Latin or Persian/Arabic or Cyrillic depending on the region who they live or have grown up.

Yekgirtû double-sign letters, such as "sh" in Yek-girtû and replaced with "ş" in Latin, when the source was created using Yekgirtû alphabet. We also uniformed the diacritics, for example by re-placing "ʼ" with "^".

For the evaluation of the implemented IMT, we arbitrarily chose 3 passages from Kurdish media. For the Sorani texts we transliterated the texts from Persian/Arabic script into Latin script. We then machine translated the texts and printed the output with the intelligibility rating printed along-side each translated text in the way that we men-tioned in Section 3. We gave the texts to our partic-ipants in the human rating process. Out of 11 par-ticipants who were all native Kurdish speakers, 3 could only speak in Kurmanji, 5 could only speak in Sorani, 2 could speak in both dialects. There was one participant who was not native Kurdish speaker and has learned basic Sorani dialect. Ex-cept the latter case, the other participant ranked their fluency in reading Latin texts at least *very good*. Although one participant rated their Latin reading fluency as *beginner*, we verified the eval-uation in the interview and found it appropriate. During the evaluation process, we did not explain to the participants that the texts were a machine translated results and only asked them to rate the text based on their understanding. We did not in-tervene or help in any case until the rating was fin-ished.

The interviews showed that in all cases the rat-ing was almost conforming with what had been assigned. However, when we asked participants who had rated a text *understandable* about why they did not find it *completely understandable*, we realized this was coming from the grammatical is-sues of the translated text. The participants replied that they had found the text not fluent from gram-matical perspective.

Figures 1 and 2 show two snapshots of parts the documents used in the IMT evaluation.

The results of this experiment is show in Table 1.

The evaluation shows that none of the human raters rated the output to be *not understandable*. Importantly, the result shows that a significant per-centage of the human raters have rated the output as *understandable*. However, 8% of the partici-pants in the test, ranked the results as *completely

Understandability	Sorani to Kurmanji	Kurmanji to Sorani
Not Understandable	0%	0%
Slightly Understandable	29%	21%
Understandable	63%	71%
Completely Understandable	8%	8%

Table 1: Understandability of the IMT output - The table shows that 82% of the human raters, rated the output of IMT to be quite understand-able.

understandable.

To the best of our knowledge, there is no base-line or golden-standard available for inter-dialect translations at the time of writing this paper. To illustrate, in the work by Zhang (1998) on inter-dialect MT, neither a quantitative evaluation of the developed system, nor any measures and baselines with which the system's performance could have been evaluated, have been provided. This is, per-haps, because this work seems to be the first study of the kind. As an another example, Nakov and Tiedemann (2012) who have studied MT among closely-related languages have used BLEU (Pap-ineni et al., 2002) as an evaluation method and compared their suggested approaches using the mentioned method. However, we were not able to apply BLEU for the reasons we mentioned in Section 3.2. Also in a recent work Shah and Boitet (2015) have used raw machine translation for translating Hindi tweets into English and have used the measure of *understandability* without re-ferring to a certain baseline. Therefore we based our evaluation on the definitions that we suggested in Section 3.2.

5 Discussion

The experiment showed that the system performs at an acceptable level as about 82% of human raters rated the results as understandable. The evaluation also shows that none of the human raters rated the output to be *not understandable*. However, this rate for Sorani to Kurmanji is less than the rate for Kurmanji to Sorani outputs. The reason for this, as participants in the evaluation also confirm it, is because in the translation pro-cess, as the consequence of lack of underlying language resources, we could not apply the tech-niques of reordering the words and word align-ment to make the output to completely conform with the Kurmanji structure. This causes the out-

I am fluent □ very good □ good □ beginner □ in reading Sorani Kurdish texts in Latin script.

Text 1

emro termî nûsar û romannûsêkî kurd yaşar kemal le şari estenbolê dête şardnewe Dête çawerêkirdin - jimareyêk mezin - kesayetî ast berz û kesayetî edebî yan cîhanê beşdari merasîmi şardnewey yaşar kemal bibin yaşar kemal 28ê mangi derbaz bû le nexwoşxaneyek le şari estenbolê le 92 saliy xoyan da koçî diwayî kirdibû

The above text was:
not-understandable □ slightly-understandable □ understandable □ completely_understandable □

Fig. 1: IMT Evaluation - Kurmanji to Sorani

I am fluent □ very good □ good □ beginner □ in reading Kurmanji Kurdish texts in Latin script.

Text 1

êwarê 30 12 2014 yek-ji-perlemantarên mêvanê bernameya rûdawê îro bû le kenalê rûdaw. ezîş giwê bû şilikrbû bizanim ev perlemantare çawa welamê pirsên pêşkeşkarê dide u bernameya çawaye bû çareser-kirinê brînên gringên ev welatê. lê-belê pir cihê sosretê bû ji-bu-min rasttir wihaye bêjim tûşî şok hatîm demê-kû binîm yek-ji-perlemantaran mûçeyên xwê berhev dekir di-gel mûçeyên pêşkeşkarê u digot ez kû serokê 24 perlemantarime be pileî wezîr mûçey-xwe kemtire le î hûn kû karmendekî televzîonêkî.

The above text was:
not-understandable □ slightly-understandable □ understandable □ completely_understandable □

Fig. 2: IMT Evaluation - Sorani to Kurmanji

put to be seemed as an artificial and influent text which makes the evaluation rate different for Sorani to Kurmanji translation. But, because Sorani does not recognize genders and also its structure is more flexible as a result of borrowing more structures from other dialects, particularly, in the Iraqi Kurdistan region, where the evaluation has been conducted, the translated texts into Sorani have received better ratings.

The results showed that the method performs at an applicable level. However, we are also interested in finding the justifications for this fact from computational perspective. As Table 2 shows, the two bidialectal dictionaries do not share a high percentage common vocabulary. That is, perhaps the common vocabulary is not the only reason that justifies the acceptable performance of the system. Therefore, we will look into the Levenshtein distance between our bidialectal dictionaries to assess whether there is any correlation between this parameter and the our hypothesis about the efficiency of IMT.

Count	**Total**	**Kurmanji**	**Sorani**
Words	6792	2632	4160
Common Words	208	208	208
Percentage	3%	7%	5%

Table 2: The table shows the number of words attributed to each dialect alongside the common words among the dialects. It also shows the percentage of the common words to all words and total words in each dialect dictionary.

5.1 Levenshtein Distance and Intelligibility

We studied the results of our experiments from the perspective of Levenshtein distance in both bidalectal dictionaries in order to find any correlations between the efficiency of the suggested method and the similarities among the dialects vocabulary. Researchers in the NLP and CL have addressed the issue of intelligibility and similarity among languages and dialects from different points of view. For instance, Casad (1992) states that "the set of variables that underlie linguistic similarity are largely distinct from those that underlie intelligibility". Unlike "linguistic similarity", word similarity and word synonymy is one of the most computationally developed ideas. It has applications in several areas of NLP and CL such as Information Retrieval (IR), summarization, and MT. Two words are considered as similar if they share common meaning elements (Jurafsky and Martin, 2008). Word similarity has been investigated in different contexts. As a related example to this research subject, Bondi Johannessen et al. (2005) have investigated word similarity in the Scandinavian languages which are assumed as mutually intelligible dialects. Also Ljubšić and Kranjčić (2015) have studied Language Identification (LI) on Twitter using word similarity (Ljubšić and Kranjčić, 2015).

Word distance is another perspective of word similarity. From this perspective, one can measure the differences between two words (the "distance") instead of their similarities. That is, the less the distance between the words, the more similar the words are and the more the distance between te words, the less similar the words are. The Levenshtein distance measures the distance between the two words by counting the number of deletions, substitutions, and insertions that transfers one sequence into the other (Jurafsky and Martin, 2008). In the context of our experiment, Beijering et al. (2008) have applied this method in their study about the dialectal and inter-language intelligibility.

We calculated the Levenshtein distance among our bi-dialectal dictionaries entries. Figures 3 and 4 show the results of this calculation for Kurmanji-Sorani and Sorani-Kurmanji dictionaries respectively.

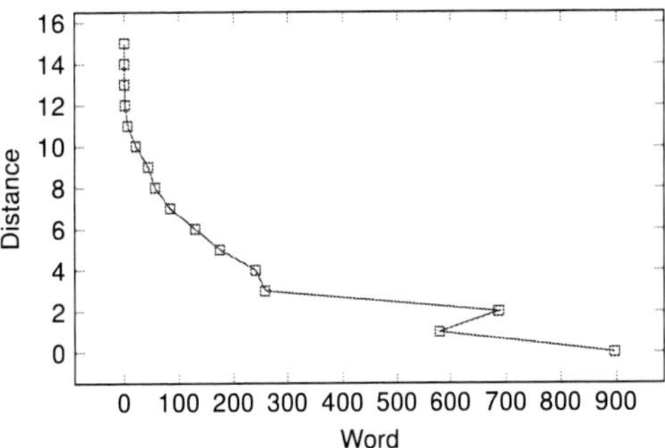

Fig. 3: Levenshtein Distance, Kurmanji-Sorani Bidialectal Dictionary - The plot shows the numbers of words with a certain distance in the dictionary.

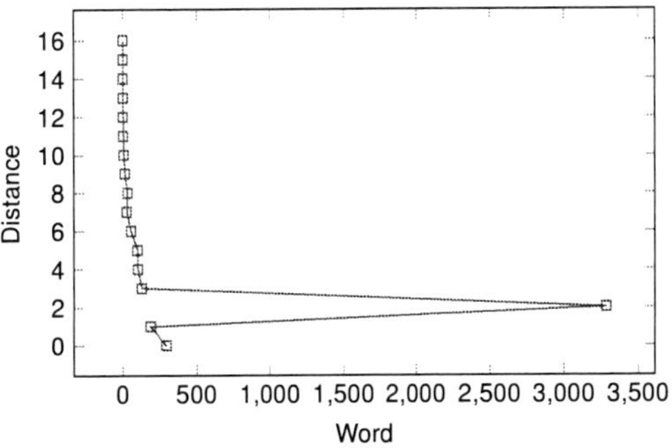

Fig. 4: Levenshtein Distance, Sorani-Kurmanji Bidialectal Dictionary - The plot shows the numbers of words with a certain distance in the dictionary.

As the Figures 3 and 4 show, except in a few cases, the plots indicate that majority of vocabulary of the two dialects have no more than 2 to 3 distances with each other. Based on this figures and the data of in Table 2 we suggest two reasons for the competency of our method. First, the Kurmanji and Sorani dialects are sharing a common vocabulary that although does not form a large portion of their lexicon, plays an important role as the basis for their lexicon structure. Second, the differences in a majority of the vocabulary that is used in social conversations differ by one or two letters, or sometimes just phonemes, for example, "ştêk" and "şêwezmanî" in Sorani versus "tştêk" and "şêwezimanî" in Kurmanji. Further investigation is required perhaps with the help of Kurdish linguists to come up with solid conclusion in the future studies.

6 Conclusion

We implemented an Intralingual Machine Translation for translating texts in Kurmani to Sorani. We used word-for-word translation (literal or direct translation) among the dialects. The results were tested using human raters method. The experiments, according to different human raters, showed that this naive approach could provide a significantly intelligible results according to different human raters. The experiment also showed that this approach might be able to be considered as an immediate remedy for the current lack of corpus issue. In fact, the approach, if incorporated to the online resources, allow the speakers of one dialect to have access to the resources of the others with a reasonable degree of understandability. It also allows Kurdish computational linguists to focus on other aspects of the computational dialectology through studying the intelligibility issues.

Nevertheless, this study has not intended to consider the aesthetic aspects of the translation as an art, rather its intention is to evaluate the adequacy of this approach in the absence of large data that could support a high quality translation. Moreover, the outcome of this study might help other linguistics studies about the relation of the diverse dialects of a language such as Kurdish. The experiments showed that translated texts are understandable according to readers in 71% cases for Kurmanji and 79% for Sorani. They are slightly understandable in 29% cases for Kurmanji and 21% for Sorani.

However, there are several areas that we believe might be of interest as future work. For example, to investigate the extent to which the word-for-word translation of Kurdish dialect could be beneficial. For instance, to develop a system based on a shallow-transfer and rule-based approach using Apertium platform (Peradin et al., 2014) and to compare this method with the previous one in terms of the quality of the output, the speed of the system and the simplicity of reapplying the method to other Kurdish dialects. In addition, the evaluation approach can be changed from human rating to automated methods for example, BLEU (Papineni et al., 2002). Also to assess whether these approaches eliminates the role of parallel corpus in **intralingual** translation by adding grammatic rules, can be conducted as another research. Moreover, to analyze the case of word ambiguity in the implemented IMT, more investigation on the role of the Levenshtein distance, the implication of phonological/morphological differences, and similarities between the dialects are other areas that need to be studied further. Finally, the implementation of the method for translation between other Kurdish dialects could reveal more enlightening facts about the mutual intelligibility among these dialects. This also helps in better understanding the role of IMT with respect to making these dialects comprehensible among different audience, particularly web users.

Acknowledgments

We would like to express our warm appreciations to Dr. Dzejla Medjedovic an Assistant Professor and Vice Dean of Graduate Program at the University Sarajevo School of Science and Technology (SSST) for reviewing this paper and providing influential recommendations. We would also like to thank the anonymous reviewers who have provided constructive suggestions that have improved the final version of this paper.

References

Arafat Ahsan, Prasanth Kolachina, Sudheer Kolachina, Dipti Misra Sharma, and Rajeev Sangal. 2010. Coupling Statistical Machine Translation with Rule-based Transfer and Generation. In *Proceedings of the 9th Conference of the Association for Machine Translation in the Americas*.

Association for Computional Linguistics. 2015. *Joint Workshop on Language Technology for Closely Related Languages, Varieties and Dialects*. Association for Computational Linguistics (ACL), September.

Lisa Ballesteros and Bruce Croft. 1996. Dictionary Methods for Cross-lingual Information Retrieval. In *Database and Expert Systems Applications*, pages 791–801. Springer.

Karin Beijering, Charlotte Gooskens, and Wilbert Heeringa. 2008. Predicting intelligibility and perceived linguistic distances by means of the Levenshtein algorithm. *Linguistics in the Netherlands*, 15:13–24.

Janne Bondi Johannessen, Kristin Hagen, Åsne Haaland, Andra Björk Jónsdottir, Anders Nøklestad, Dimitris Kokkinakis, Paul Meurer, Eckhard Bick, and Dorte Haltrup. 2005. Named entity recognition for the mainland Scandinavian languages. *Literary and Linguistic Computing*, 20(1):91–102.

Eugene H. Casad. 1992. *Windows on bilingualism*. Summer Institute of Linguistics.

Sin-wai Chan. 2014. *Routledge Encyclopedia of Translation Technology*. Routledge.

Chin-Chuan Cheng. 1997. Measuring relationship among dialects: DOC and related resources. *Computational Linguistics & Chinese Language Processing*, 2(1):41–72.

Umîd Demîrhan. 2007. *Ferhenga Destî -kurdî bi kurdî - çapa duyem a berfireh (Kurdish to Kurdish Dictionary, expanded 2nd ed)*. weşanên SEWADê (*SEWAD Publication*). In Kurdish.

Ali Farghaly and Khaled Shaalan. 2009. Arabic natural language processing: Challenges and solutions. *ACM Transactions on Asian Language Information Processing (TALIP)*, 8(4):14.

Rebecca Fiederer and Sharon O´Brien. 2009. Quality and Machine Translation: A Realistic Objective. *Journal of Specialised Translation*, 11:52–74.

Geoffrey Haig and Ergin Öpengin. 2014. Introduction to Special Issue-Kurdish: A critical research overview. *Kurdish Studies*, 2(2):99–122.

Hossein Hassani and Dzejla Medjedovic. 2016. Automatic Kurdish Dialects Identification. *Computer Science & Information Technology*, 6(2):61–78.

Amir Hassanpour. 1992. *Nationalism and language in Kurdistan, 1918-1985*. Edwin Mellen Pr.

Mehrdad R. Izady. 1992. *The Kurds: A concise handbook*. Taylor & Francis.

Daniel Jurafsky and James H. Martin. 2008. *Speech and Language Processing*. Prentice Hall, 2 edition.

Angela Kluge. 2006. RTT retelling method: An Alternative Approach to Intelligibility Testing. *Occasional paper. Dallas: SIL International*.

Kurdish Academy of Languages. 2016. The Kurdish Population.

Nikola Ljubšić and Denis Kranjčić. 2015. Discriminating between closely related languages on twitter. *Informatica*, 39(1):1.

Shervin Malmasi. 2016. Subdialectal differences in sorani kurdish. In *Proceedings of the VarDial Workshop*, Osaka, Japan, December.

Ayishe Mohammed Ali. 2008. *Kurdish-Kurdish Dictionary*. Ministry of Culture-KRG. In Kurdish.

Jeremy Munday. 2009. *Introducing translation studies: Theories and applications*. Routledge.

Preslav Nakov and Jörg Tiedemann. 2012. Combining Word-level and Character-level Models for Machine Translation Between Closely-related Languages. In *Proceedings of the 50th Annual Meeting of the Association for Computational Linguistics: Short Papers - Volume 2*, ACL '12, pages 301–305, Stroudsburg, PA, USA. Association for Computational Linguistics.

Kurdish Academy of Language. 2016. KAL Featured Articles.

Ergin Öpengin and Geoffrey Haig. 2014. Regional variation in Kurmanji: A preliminary classification of dialects. *Kurdish Studies*, 2(2):143–176.

Kishore Papineni, Salim Roukos, Todd Ward, and Wei-Jing Zhu. 2002. BLEU: a method for automatic evaluation of machine translation. In *Proceedings of the 40th annual meeting on association for computational linguistics*, pages 311–318. Association for Computational Linguistics.

Hrvoje Peradin, Filip Petkovsky, and Francis M. Tyers. 2014. Shallow-transfer rule-based machine translation for the Western group of South Slavic languages. In *Proceedings of the 9th SaLTMiL Workshop on Free/open-Source Language Resources for the Machine Translation of Less-Resourced Languages*, pages 25–30.

Joe E. Pierce. 1952. Dialect distance testing in algonquian. *International Journal of American Linguistics*, 18(4):203–210.

Erdal Ronahî. 2015. Lîsteya soranî-kurmancî (Sorani-Kurmanji Dictionary). In Kurdish.

Fatiha Sadat, Farnazeh Kazemi, and Atefeh Farzindar. 2014. Automatic Identification of Arabic Dialects in Social Media. In *Proceedings of the First International Workshop on Social Media Retrieval and Analysis*, pages 35–40. ACM.

Lenhart Schubert. 2015. Computational linguistics. *The Stanford Encyclopedia of Philosophy*. Spring 2015 Edition.

Ritesh Shah and Christian Boitet. 2015. Understandability of machine-translated Hindi tweets before and after post-editing: perspectives for a recommender system. In *Tweet Translation Workshop 2015*, pages 44–50. CEUR-WS.org.

Kyumars Sheykh Esmaili, Shahin Salavati, and Anwitaman Datta. 2014. Towards kurdish information retrieval. *ACM Transactions on Asian Language Information Processing (TALIP)*, 13(2):7.

Kyumars Sheykh Esmaili. 2012. Challenges in Kurdish Text Processing. *arXiv preprint arXiv:1212.0074*.

Cecilia Szeto. 2000. Testing intelligibility among Sinitic dialects. In *Proceedings of ALS2K, the 2000 Conference of the Australian Linguistic Society*. Citeseer.

Chaoju Tang and Vincent J. van Heuven. 2009. Mutual intelligibility of Chinese dialects experimentally tested. *Lingua*, 119:24.

Chaoju Tang, Vincent J. van Heuven, et al. 2008. Mutual intelligibility of Chinese dialects tested functionally. *Linguistics in the Netherlands*, 25(1):145–156.

Carl F. Voegelin and Zellig S. Harris. 1951. Methods for determining intelligibility among dialects of natural languages. *Proceedings of the American Philosophical Society*, 95(3):322–329.

Wîkîferheng and Ferhenga azad (*Azad Dictionary*). 2015. Pêvek:soranî-kurmancî (*Amendment: Sorani-Kurmanji*). In Kurdish.

Joseph K. Yamagiwa. 1967. On dialect intelligibility in Japan. *Anthropological Linguistics*, pages 1–17.

Marcos Zampieri, Liling Tan, Nikola Ljubešić, and Jörg Tiedemann, editors. 2014. *The 1 st Workshop on Applying NLP Tools to Similar Languages, Varieties and Dialects*, Dublin, Ireland, August. Association for Computational Linguistics (ACL).

Xiaoheng Zhang. 1998. Dialect mt: a case study between cantonese and mandarin. In *Proceedings of the 17th international conference on Computational linguistics-Volume 2*, pages 1460–1464. Association for Computational Linguistics.

Twitter Language Identification Of Similar Languages And Dialects Without Ground Truth

Jennifer Williams and Charlie K. Dagli[*]
Human Language Technology Group
Massachusetts Institute of Technology, Lincoln Laboratory
244 Wood Street, Lexington, MA 02420, USA
`{jennifer.williams,dagli}@ll.mit.edu`

Abstract

We present a new method to *bootstrap filter* Twitter language ID labels in our dataset for automatic language identification (LID). Our method combines geo-location, original Twitter LID labels, and Amazon Mechanical Turk to resolve missing and unreliable labels. We are the first to compare LID classification performance using the MIRA algorithm and *langid.py*. We show classifier performance on different versions of our dataset with high accuracy using only Twitter data, without ground truth, and very few training examples. We also show how Platt Scaling can be use to calibrate MIRA classifier output values into a probability distribution over candidate classes, making the output more intuitive. Our method allows for fine-grained distinctions between similar languages and dialects and allows us to rediscover the language composition of our Twitter dataset.

1 Introduction

Every second, the Twitter microblogging webservice relays as many as 6,000[1] short written messages (less than 140 characters), called tweets, from people around the world. The tweets are created and viewed publicly by anyone with internet access. Tweets obtained from the Twitter API are tagged with metadata such as language ID and geo-location (Graham et al, 2014).

Currently there is a mismatch between the built-in language identification support provided by the Twitter API and the needs of the natural language processing (NLP) community. While there are around 7,000[2] human languages spoken today, only 34 of the most common languages are currently recognized and tagged by Twitter[3] using automatic methods for language identification (LID). In addition to Twitter's low-coverage of languages, Twitter's default language tags are not always accurate (Zubiaga et al, 2015; Lui and Baldwin, 2014; Bergsma et al, 2012) making it very challenging to obtain the necessary ground-truth for training a language classifier.

Twitter data is linguistically diverse and has tremendous global reach and influence. Discriminating languages and dialects automatically is a critical pre-processing step for more advanced NLP applications (Dagli et al, 2016). Heavy, worldwide use of Twitter has created a very rich landscape for developing NLP applications such as support for disaster relief (Sakaki et al., 2010; Kumar et al., 2011), sentiment analysis (Volkova et al., 2013), as well as recognizing named entities (Ritter et al., 2011) and temporal reasoning for events and habits (Williams and Katz, 2012).

In this work we show how geo-location can be used to identify the language of a tweet when appropriate language tags are seemingly incorrect, or absent. Specifically, we are interested in discriminating similar languages English, Malay and Indonesian (en, ms, id) as well as dialects of Spanish from Europe and Mexico $(es\text{-}ES, es\text{-}MX)$ and dialects of Portuguese from Europe and Brazil $(pt\text{-}PT, pt\text{-}BR)$. Language names are represented using the ISO-639-2 language codes and 2-letter country abbreviation added for dialects. The methods we present in this paper provide a fast, low-cost approach to filtering Twitter LID la-

[*] This material is based upon work supported by the Defense Advanced Research Projects Agency under Air Force Contract No. (FA8721-05-C-0002 and/or FA8702-15-D-0001). Any opinions, findings and conclusions or recommendations expressed in this material are those of the author(s) and do not necessarily reflect the views of the Defense Advanced Research Projects Agency.

[1] http://www.internetlivestats.com/twitter-statistics/

[2] https://www.ethnologue.com/

[3] https://dev.twitter.com/web/overview/languages

Proceedings of the Fourth Workshop on NLP for Similar Languages, Varieties and Dialects, pages 73–83,
Valencia, Spain, April 3, 2017. ©2017 Association for Computational Linguistics

bels. It is very important to have data with reliable language labels because it allows us to make fine-grained distinctions between dialects and similar languages, in order to expand the linguistic scope of NLP applications.

This paper is organized as follows: Section 2 describes related work, Section 3 describes the data collection and preparation, Section 4 describes classification algorithms, Section 5 shows our re-annotation experiments and results, Section 6 presents results using Platt Scaling, and finally Section 7 is discussion and future work.

2 Related Work

Language identification has a rich history in natural language processing (Cavnar and Trenkle, 1994; Dunning, 1994). Recently, many different language combinations have appeared in benchmark shared tasks, most notably in the DSL (Discriminating Similar Languages) Shared Task 2014, 2015, and 2016 (Lui et al, 2014; Zampieri et al, 2014; Zampieri et al, 2015, Malmasi et al, 2016). In these shared-tasks the train/test data is not composed entirely of social media while simultaneously providing support for the languages and dialects that we are interested in. Additionally, English is sometimes used by Twitter users within the country geo-boundaries of Indonesia and Malaysia. Therefore we cannot rely on user profile settings as in previous work (Saloot et al., 2016), including Kevin Scannell's ongoing Indigenous Tweets Project[4] which relies on self-reported minority language usage but does not guarantee homogeneity of labeled language collections.

Ranaivo-Malançon (2006) was the first to work on Malay-Indonesian LID using n-gram profiling and other linguistic features. While their work capitalizes on nuanced linguistic differences between Malay and Indonesian, it does not address whether or not this technique can be expanded to include English, or dialect pairs, and the results for classifier accuracy are not reported. We are also interested in discriminating dialects of Spanish and Portuguese, as these are widely spoken languages with important dialect distinctions (Zampieri et al, 2016; Çöltekin and Rama, 2016).

The 2014 DSL Shared-Task was the first large-scale task for distinguishing between similar languages and dialects in a language group, including: Malay/Indonesian, Brazilian Por-

tuguese/Portuguese, and Spanish/Mexican Spanish. The data for this shared-task, compiled by Tan et al (2014), was collected from the web, cleaned, and consists of 18,000 training sentences per language group. Performance results per language group are reported for the top 8 systems, with the best performing system, NRC-CNRC (Goutte et al, 2014), achieving overall accuracy between 91%-99% on the language groups that we are interested in. Our work is distinct from the DSL Shared-Tasks for language and dialect identification because we are interested in learning a classifier using only Twitter data, without ground truth, using very few training examples.

3 Data Collection

We collected tweets from Twitter using the 10% firehose that we obtained from GNIP[5] between January 2014 and October 2014. The 10% firehose is a real-time random sampling of all tweets as they are relayed through the Twitter webservice. As part of their service, GNIP provided a filtering with geo-tagging enabled, so that all of the tweets in our collection were geographically tagged with longitude and latitude, allowing us to pin-point the exact location of the tweet. Initially, we collected over 25.6 million tweets during that time period. In our collection, 24 languages were automatically identified by the Twitter API using the ISO-639-2 and ISO-639-3 language codes[6].

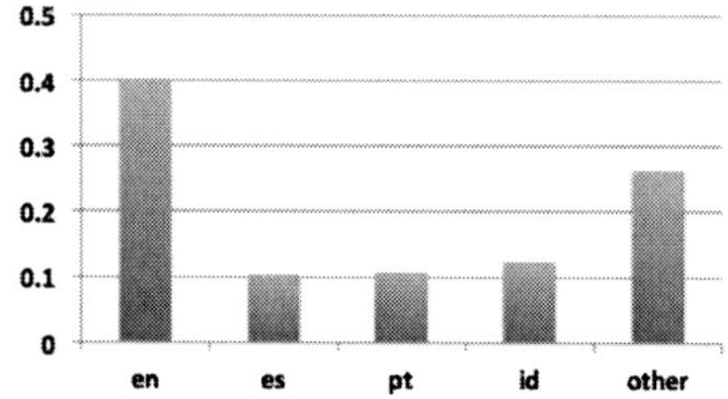

Figure 1: Twitter LID label composition (relative frequency) for our collected Twitter dataset

The most commonly occurring languages in our dataset were English, Spanish, Indonesian, and Portuguese. We note that our dataset did not contain any tweets initially identified as being in the Malay language. Figure 1 shows the distribution of languages relative to the overall collection. The

---

[4]http://indigenoustweets.com/

[5]https://gnip.com/
[6]https://dev.twitter.com/rest/reference/get/help/languages

language distribution in our data does not accurately represent the languages used on Twitter for two reasons: 1) Twitter's own language ID codes are not always accurate in identifying the language of a tweet, and 2) this distribution in Figure 1 represents 10% geo-enabled firehose from GNIP collected during a specific time period. Furthermore without adequate language ID technology and reliable language labels, the true distribution of languages on Twitter is not known with certainty.

4 Classification Algorithms

In this section we describe two classification algorithms that we used in our experiments. We compared performance of the MIRA algorithm with the popular pre-trained software called *langid.py*.

4.1 MIRA

Advances in statistical learning theory have made it possible to expand beyond binary classification with perceptrons (Rosenblatt, 1958) to multiclass online learners such as the Margin Infused Relaxed Algorithm (MIRA) from Crammer and Singer (2003). The MIRA algorithm is formulated as a multiclass classifier which maintains one prototype weight vector for each class. MIRA performs similar to Support Vector Machines (SVM) without batch training (Crammer et al, 2006).

For multiclass classification, MIRA is formulated as shown in equation (1):

$$c^* = \arg\max_{c \in \mathbf{C}} f_c(\mathbf{d}) \qquad (1)$$

where

$$f_c(\mathbf{d}) = \mathbf{w} \cdot \mathbf{d} \qquad (2)$$

and $\mathbf{w}$ is the weight vector which defines the model for class c. The output of the classifier, for each class, is the dot product between a document vector $\mathbf{d}$ and the weight vector for each class c, shown in equation (2). Therefore the predicted class is chosen by selecting the $argmax$. The values for each class, from equation (2) are neither normalized or scaled, and so they do not represent a probability distribution over candidate classes. We discuss this in greater depth in Section 6 with regard to calibrating the classifier output.

To train MIRA, we swept values for the margin slack (0.0005 to 0.00675) and number of training epochs (5 to 30). The value for training epochs denoted a hard-stop for training iterations and served as the stopping criterion. The feature vectors contained log-normalized frequency counts for word and character n-grams, with values for n swept separately for words (1 to 5) and characters (1 to 5), to allow various word and character-level n-gram combinations. After sweeping all possible feature combinations, we report experiment results based on the highest achieved overall accuracy. Words were defined by splitting on whitespace and we did not do any pre-processing or text normalization of the original tweets, similar to Lui and Baldwin (2014). For MIRA we used the open-source software suite called LLClass[7], which proved useful for other types of text categorization tasks (Shen et al, 2013).

4.2 langid.py

For comparison, we used the off-the-shelf tool *langid.py* from Lui and Baldwin (2012). This tool employs a multinomial näive Bayes classifier, and n-gram feature set. The n-gram features are selected using information gain to maximize information with respect to language while minimizing information with respect to data source. A pre-trained model also comes off-the-shelf and covers 97 languages, including the specific languages that we use for this work. At the time of this writing the pre-trained model does not include support for dialect distinction. While we did not sweep parameters for the *langid.py* software, as we wanted to evaluate off-the-shelf performance, we did use their built-in feature "label constraint" which restricts the multinomial distribution to a specified set of target labels, rather than all 97 supported languages. For example, with experiments involving English/Malay/Indonesian, we restricted the language label set to these three languages.

5 Re-Annotation Experiments

In this section we present our method to *bootstrap filter* our Twitter dataset to re-annotated data and arrive at ground truth labels. Our data processing technique is fast, easy, cheap, and independent of the classification algorithm. We also present classification results for each dataset using MIRA and *langid.py* classifiers. All classification results are reported as the overall average accuracy with an 80/20 train/test split. Each experiment is based on N total tweets per target language and classes were stratified irrespective of tweet length.

---

[7]https://github.com/mitll/LLClass

5.1 Exp 1: Twitter Labels

First for Experiment 1, we used Twitter API labels as ground truth for language classification. Unfortunately, our dataset did not contain Twitter LID labels for Malay, or the Portuguese and Spanish dialects.

Languages	N/class	MIRA	langid.py
en, id	500	98.0	90.1
pt, es, en, id	500	93.5	85.95

Table 1: Exp 1 results using Twitter API language labels as ground truth

The performance shown for the English/Indonesian pair in Table 1 is competitive with the DSL Shared Task performance for this language pair (Zampieri et al, 2016). We also used Twitter labels to evaluate multiclass classification for pt, es, en, id and note that the MIRA classifier outperforms langid.py for this set.

5.2 Exp 2: Geo-Boundary Filtering

In Experiment 2, we filtered our Twitter dataset by establishing geo-bounding boxes to geographically define countries where the language of interest is suspected to be most prominent. For example, we used the country Malaysia as a representative geo-source for Malaysian tweets. We used a free website to set up the latitudinal and longitudinal geo-bounding boxes around the countries [8] and there are additional alternative websites to obtain similar geo-boundaries[9][10]. Each bounding box corner was defined by a latitude/longitude coordinate pair corresponding to SW, NW, SE, NE. Multiple bounding boxes were used for approximating the shape of each country and we made every effort to include major metropolitan cities within the bounds. In some cases, our bounding boxes were slightly overspecified and slightly underspecified depending on the geometric shape of the country as shown for Portugal in Figure 2.

We recognize that Twitter users in each of the geo-bounded countries are able to tweet in any language. Our data filtering method was based on the assumption that the majority of tweets from a country would be composed in that country's most common language. We calculated how frequently different Twitter API language labels occurred within the bounds of the target country de-

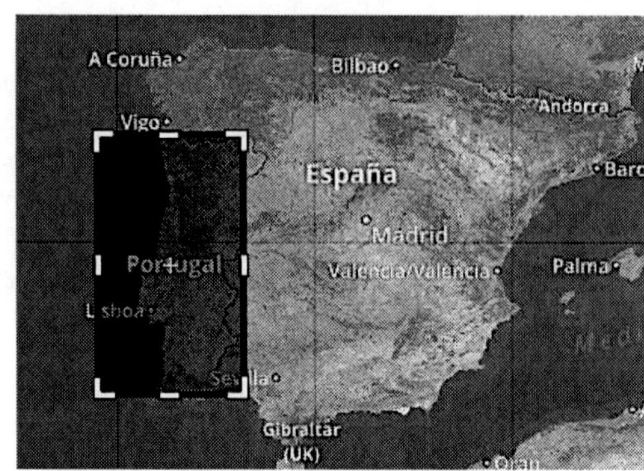

Figure 2: Example of geo-bounding box to identify tweets that originated from Portugal

fine a target label *purity*, with respect to the expected majority language. This is the conditional probability of the target Twitter LID label occurring in the target country, shown in equation (3)

$$\mathbf{p(label|country)} = \frac{count_{label}}{count_{country}} \quad (3)$$

Geo-Bound Country	Language	Label	Purity
Malaysia	Malaysian	ms	0%
Indonesia	Indonesian	id	63%
United States	English	en	85%
Portugal	Portuguese	pt	68%
Brazil	Portuguese	pt	71%
Spain	Spanish	es	72%
Mexico	Spanish	es	69%

Table 2: Twitter LID label purity within geographic country boundaries

The majority of tweets originating from Malaysia were tagged as id and en. We observed similar scarcity of Malay tweets in Twitter's publicly released language identification datasets [11]. In fact, Malay tweets make up less than 0.001% of Twitter's uniformly sampled dataset despite API support for Malay language identification. Our estimates of label purity, in addition to Twitter's dataset coverage of Malay, emphasize the persisting need for automatic language disambiguation. We compared classifier performance using geo-boundary as a stand-in for ground truth labels, and our results are shown in Table 3.

5.3 Exp 3: Geo Filtering + Twitter Labels

To generate ground truth in Experiment 3, we took the intersection of labels from geo-bounds and

---

[8] http://boundingbox.klokantech.com/

[9] http://www.naturalearthdata.com/

[10] https://help.openstreetmap.org/

[11] https://blog.twitter.com/2015/evaluating-language-identification-performance

Languages	N/class	MIRA	langid.py
en, id, ms	1000	80.8	54.2
en, id	1000	93.5	79.5
id, ms	1000	86.3	51.7
en, ms	1000	86.0	76.6
pt-PT, pt-BR	1000	75.0	–
es-ES, es-MX	1000	66.8	–
en, id, ms, pt-PT, pt-BR, es-ES, es-MX	1000	68.5	–

Table 3: Exp 2 results using geo-boundaries to represent ground truth LID labels (i.e. country labels = language labels)

original Twitter LID labels. For example, we extracted all tweets from Brazil that the Twitter API had labeled as *pt* for Portuguese, and re-labeled them as Brazilian Portuguese, *pt-BR*. We repeated the classification experiment using a separate subset of tweets and these new labels. As shown in Table 4, the classification results for MIRA in Experiment 3 are competitive with results from related benchmarking tasks, such as DSL 2016 (Malmasi et al, 2016).

Languages	N/class	MIRA	langid.py
en, id, ms	1000	85.5	60.7
en, id	1000	99.5	92.8
id, ms	1000	90.5	49.0
en, ms	1000	88.7	78.9
pt-PT, pt-BR	1000	80.5	–
es-ES, es-MX	1000	67.2	–
en, id, ms, pt-PT, pt-BR, es-ES, es-MX	1000	77.2	–

Table 4: Exp 3 results using combined geo-boundary definitions and Twitter LID labels

5.4 Exp 4: Mechanical Turk-Verified Labels

Finally, in Experiment 4 we further refined the ground truth labels obtained from earlier experiments. We verified the target language of tweets using Amazon Mechanical Turk Human Intelligence Tasks (HITs), using the same train/test data from Experiment 3 (before classification). Each HIT contained one tweet. We assigned 3 workers per HIT at the rate of $0.02 USD per HIT and the total cost for MTurk annotation in this work was $360.00 USD. In an effort to ensure that workers were qualified for the task, we allowed only workers who had an MTurk approval rating >95%, however we did not administer a language performance test in this work. To complete a HIT, workers selected one answer to a multiple-choice question, described below, and we did not inform workers that the text was from Twitter.

Instructions: *Please indicate which language the text is in. Some text snippets are full sentences while others are partial sentences or phrases. If the text contains more than one language, indicate that in your response. Note that you can ignore URLs, punctuation, and emoticons to decide the language. In order to be paid you must answer each question correctly.*

The authors would like to note that this final statement of the instructions to workers was to motivate them to complete the task meaningfully. All workers who completed tasks in the allotted time frame were paid automatically.

Workers were asked to select one of the following three statements, where language X the language label used for train/test in Experiment 3.

A1. The text is entirely composed in language X

A2. The text is composed in language X and at least one other language

A3. None of the text is composed in language X

Target	# HITs	A1	A2	A3
ms	900	**614**	205	81
id	912	**736**	158	18
pt-PT	904	**816**	66	22
pt-BR	874	**778**	66	30
es-ES	889	**845**	36	8
es-MX	838	**762**	72	4

Table 5: MTurk annotations per language

The annotation results of our MTurk experiment are shown in Table 5. Columns $A1$, $A2$, and $A3$ show the frequency that at least 2 of 3 human annotators agreed on the language condition. We began with 1000 tweets per language for annotation. If fewer than 2 annotators agreed on a condition, the HIT for that tweet was not counted in this analysis. This method of filtering both reduced the amount of data and simultaneously increased our confidence in the labels as ground truth. Our analysis with MTurk shows that the majority of train/test tweets in Experiment 3 were composed entirely in the target language X, with some instances of code-mixing of two or more languages. We used the tweets verified by Mechanical Turk to learn another set of classifiers for Experiment 4, shown in Table 6. The number of tweets per language class is reduced in this dataset, because we used only tweets verified as being 100% in the target language (column A1 from Table 5). While the classifier accuracy between Experiment 3 and Experiment 4 is similar, we believe that the performance is lower in Experiment 4 because of fewer training examples.

Languages	N/class	MIRA	langid.py
en, id, ms	600	92.5	63.8
id, ms	600	87.9	53.4
pt-PT, pt-BR	750	79.6	–
es-ES, es-MX	750	70.3	–
en, id, ms, pt-PT, pt-BR, es-ES, es-MX	1000	79.3	–

Table 6: Exp 4 results using MTurk verified labels

6   MIRA Classifier Calibration

Classifier output scores for MIRA and similar algorithms, like SVM, do not correspond to probabilities. For example, the raw score cannot guide the researcher or end user to knowing if a tweet is 80% likely to be English or 50% likely to be English. The ability to transform raw classifier scores into probabilities is very important if the technology is to be used as a consumable for text analytics or as part of an advanced NLP pipeline. In this section, we show how we calibrated scores using output from the MIRA classifier for 3 different experiments from Section 5. As with many classifiers, the raw score output can be difficult to interpret intuitively since the scalar values for each class do not represent a probability distribution over the classes. We used a technique called Platt Scaling, which learns logistic regression from the raw score output of the MIRA classifier. The Platt Scaling technique provides us with a probability distribution on classes and is easy to train and test. For our reliability plots and calibration, we used classifier output scores of test sets from experiments described in Section 5. For the purpose of brevity, we describe classifier scaling using results for one language pair: Indonesian and Malay.

6.1   Score Reliability Plots

Reliability plots show how well a classifier's output is calibrated when the true probability distribution for classes is not known (Niculescu-Mizil and Caruana, 2005; Zadronzy and Elkan, 2002; DeGroot and Feinberg, 1983). For this visualization, the classifier output scores, also called *predicted values*, are normalized between 0 and 1 and then values are binned into 10 bins. The values plotted are the binned scores s versus the conditional probability of correct class prediction given the score, $P(c|s(x) = s)$. A classifier that is well-calibrated will have values that fall close to the diagonal line $x = y$.

We normalized the raw classifier output values so that the scores fell between 0 and 1, using exponent-normalization as in equation (4), for a given tweet:

$$\mathbf{exp_c} = \frac{e^{s_c}}{\sum_{c \in C} e^s} \qquad (4)$$

where $\mathbf{exp_c}$ is the normalized score for class c, and s_c is the raw classifier output score for class c. We further divide by the sum, so that the normalized class scores for a given tweet sum to 1.

We created reliability plots for the id, ms prediction task from Experiments 2, 3, and 4. Figures 3 - 11 show the histogram distribution of normalized classifier scores with the corresponding reliability plot. Recall that each experiment was based on different kinds of ground truth. All of the reliability plots before Platt-scaling exhibit a sigmoidal distribution. The prevalence of our observed sigmoidal distribution is similar to findings from Niculescu-Mizil and Caruana (2005), who noted this shape for learning algorithms based on maximum margin methods, such as SVM. MIRA and SVM both use maximum margin principles and are known to perform similarly, with the additional benefit that MIRA does not require batch training because it is online (Crammer et al., 2006)

6.2   Platt Scaling

Platt scaling uses logistic regression to learn a mapping between classifier output scores and probability estimates (Platt, 1999). The output of Platt scaling is a probability distribution over candidate classes, rather than raw scores from the classifier which are often non-intuitive and difficult to interpret (Zadronzy and Elkan, 2002). Platt scaling is traditionally used in binary problems, and adapted to multiclass problems by developing the original classifier as an ensemble of one-vs-all classifiers, then fitting logistic regression for each binary model (Niculescu-Mizil and Caruana, 2005; Zadronzy and Elkan, 2002). We trained and tested logistic regression on a binary class problem with MIRA output using the Logistic Regression library in Python Scikit-Learn, which is designed to handle binary, one-vs-rest, and multinomial logistic regression (Pedregosa et al, 2011).

To build and evaluate logistic regression, we used the test data from our previous experiments, as in Section 6.1, and divided that data into train and test sets with an 80/20 split. For example, the test data from Experiment 2 for id, ms consisted

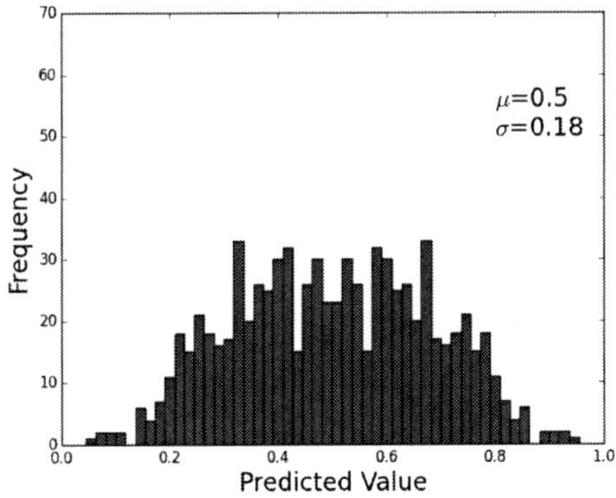

Figure 3: Geo-only, normalized scores

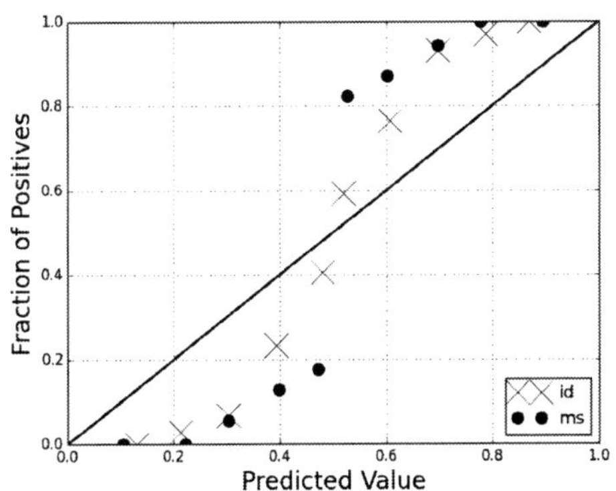

Figure 4: Geo-only, reliability plot

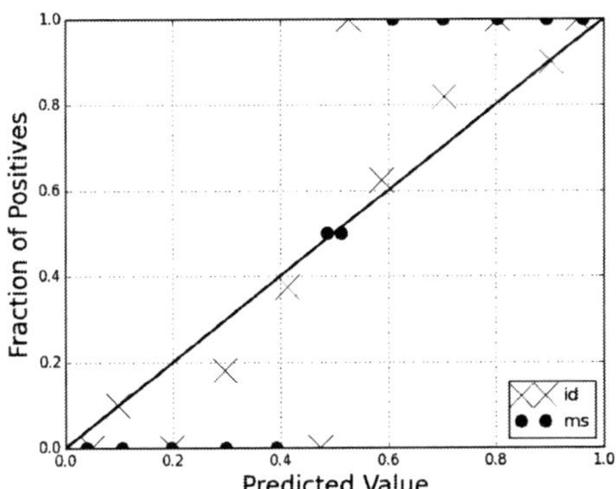

Figure 5: Geo-only, with Platt-scaling

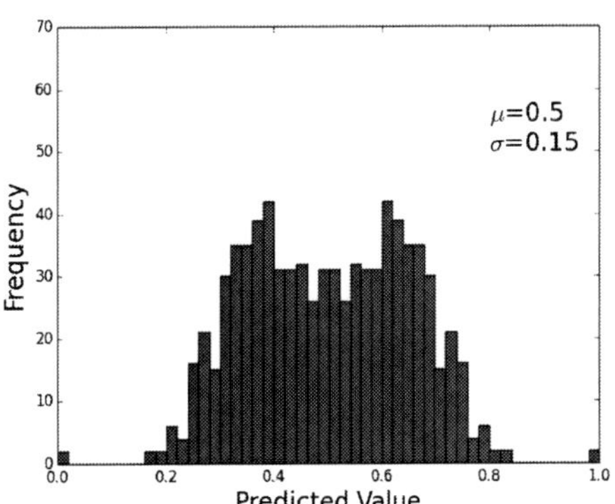

Figure 6: Geo+Twitter, normalized scores

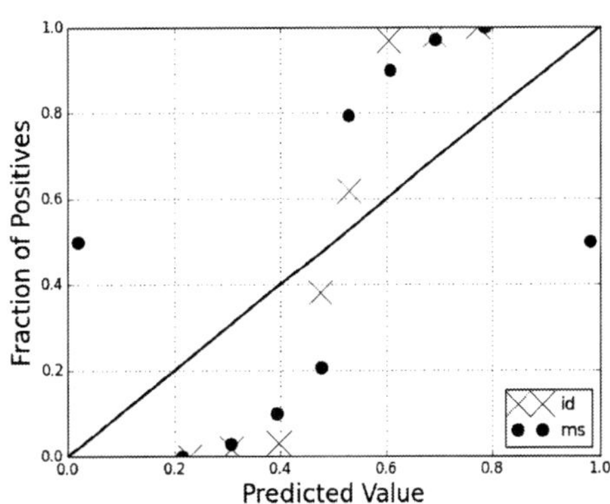

Figure 7: Geo+Twitter, reliability plot

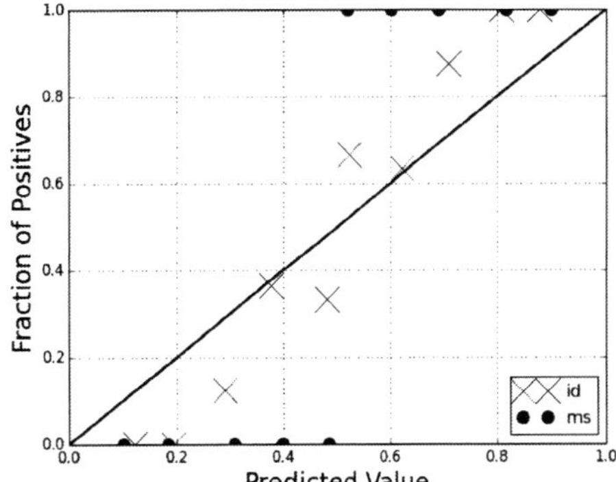

Figure 8: Geo+Twitter, with Platt-scaling

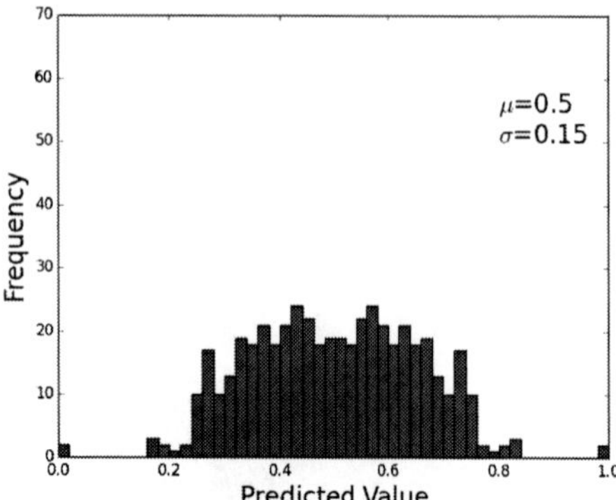

Figure 9: MTurk, normalized scores

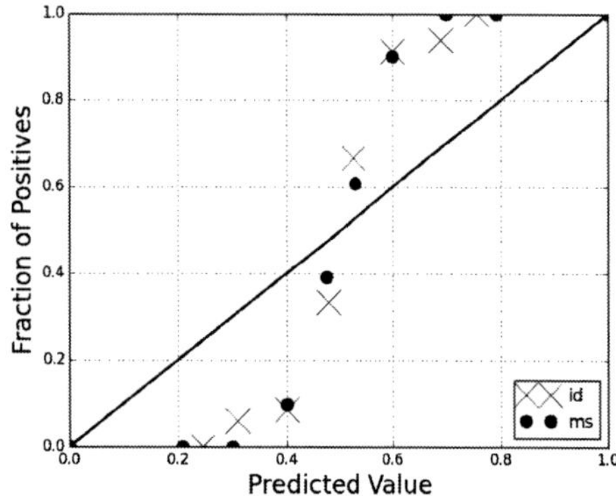

Figure 10: MTurk, reliability plot

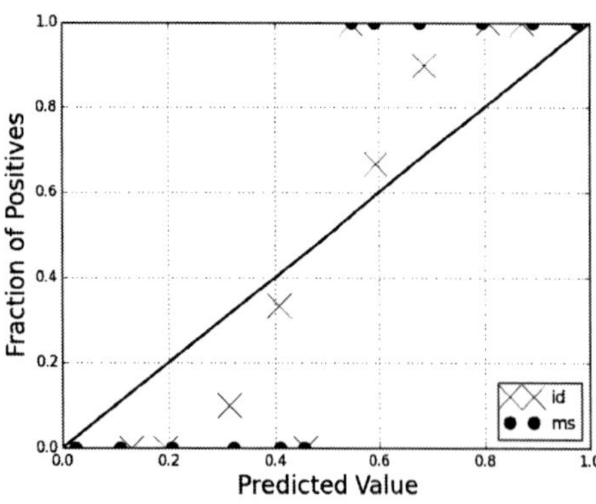

Figure 11: MTurk, with Platt-scaling

of 200 tweets per class. To do Platt scaling on this dataset, we used 160 tweets per class for training and 40 per class for testing.

With each of the datasets, Platt-scaling tends to affect calibration probabilities for Indonesian tweets more than for Malay tweets. This is observed as Indonesian data points are closer to the diagonal line. At the same time, the Platt-scaling plots also reveal that predicted values, especially for Malay, are pushed closer to 0 and 1. For example, logistic regression will always correctly predict ms for Malay, when the probability of Malay is > 0.5, but not for Indonesian. This could indicate a need for further data purification.

We examined the accuracy of logistic regression, where the predicted class is taken to be the $argmax$ class probability. In Figure 12, the overall classification accuracy on each dataset is similar for MIRA with and without Platt-scaling. We think this is an important finding because it shows that LID classifier output can be converted into probability distributions without loss of accuracy.

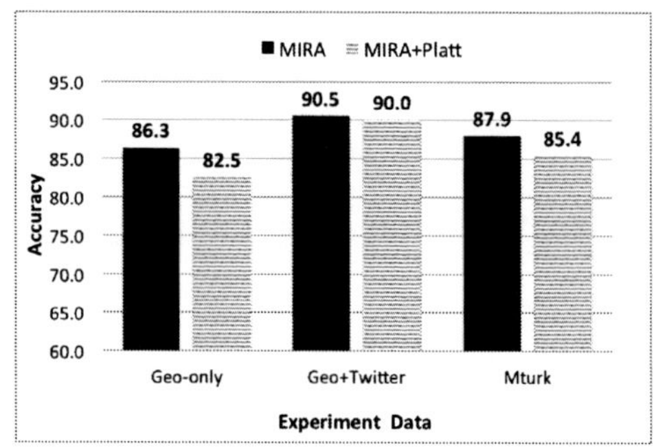

Figure 12: MIRA and Platt-scaling Test Accuracy

What do scores look like for a given tweet? In Table 7 we show raw classifier output scores, normalized scores, and probabilities from Platt-scaling for the following Malay tweet:

Malay: *Nak tengok wayang. Rindu tempat kerja. Hehehe*

English[12]**:** *Want to see a movie. Miss work. hehehe*

	ma	id
Raw scores	0.514	-0.514
Exponent Normalized	0.737	0.263
Platt + Exponent Normalized	0.535	0.465

Table 7: Score distribution for Malay tweet

---

[12]Translation obtained from https://translate.google.com/

The raw output scores from MIRA, while clearly separating binary classes, are not easily interpreted as a measure of certainty or probability. While the exponent normalized scores do sum to 1, and appear to situate probability mass towards the predicted class, it is not a true probability. The probabilities that are output during Platt-scaling are true probabilities and this method preserves the original MIRA classifier accuracy, thus it is a valid and meaningful technique, especially when language ID is a consumable pre-processing technology for NLP pipelines.

7   Discussion and Future Work

In this work, we showed that geo-bounding combined with "best-guess" language labels can be used to annotate language labels on easily confused language pairs and dialects, when ground truth is unreliable. In each experiment, we showed how our data purification method resulted in increasing accuracy and classifier performance for both classifiers, MIRA and *langid.py*. Further, our method to purify language labels is easy to implement for tweets that are geo-tagged with latitude and longitude. Once a model has been learned from geo-tagged tweets, the model can also be used for tweets that are not geo-tagged.

We uncovered hidden Malay tweets in our dataset with high accuracy. We also showed that MIRA is useful for LID, with performance accuracy near state-of-the-art on very few training examples without pre-processing or text cleaning. While previous work has shown that Malay/Indonesian can be learned using 18,000 training sentences with accuracy as high as 99.6% (Goutte et al., 2014), our result of 90.5% trained on 1600 tweets is competitive with previous work. We believe performance will further increase as more training examples are added with high confidence ground truth labels. Using geo-bounding, we were also able to separate dialects of Spanish and Portuguese to achieve finer-grained distinctions at the dialect level, which the Twitter API does not currently provide.

The highest weighted MIRA n-gram features correspond to high-frequency characters in each target language, suggesting that MIRA is learning features of languages and not Twitter artifacts (URLs, hashtags, @mentions, emoticons, etc).

In future work, we want to explore other easily confused language pairs, such as Ukrainian and Russian. Also, since MIRA is well-formulated for multiclass classification, we are interested in seeing how well it performs on a large multi-language dataset that includes several easily confused language pairs. Sometimes a single tweet will be written in more than one language, for example with code-switching or code-mixing (Barman et al, 2014). We are especially interested in adapting the MIRA classifier for code-switching and language segmentation problems. In the case of code-switching, it may be possible to utilize raw scores from classifier output or the results of Platt-scaling to construct a model that predict language mixture in a single utterance.

References

Ustab Barman, Amitava Das, Joachim Wagner, and Jennifer Foster. "Code Mixing: A Challenge for Language Identification in the Language of Social Media". In Proceedings of *First Workshop on Computational Approaches to Code Switching, Empirical Mdethods in Natural Language Processing (EMNLP)*, Doha, Qatar, (2014): 13-23.

Shane Bergsma, Paul McNamee, Mossaab Bagdouri, Clayton Fink, and Theresa Wilson. "Language Identification for Creating Language-Specific Twitter Collections." In Proceedings of *North American Chapter of the Association for Computational Linguistics (NAACL-HLT)* 2012.

William B. Cavnar and John M. Trenkle. "N-gram Based Text Categorization". *Ann Arbor, MI, 48113(2)*, 1994, 161-175.

Çagri Çöltekin, and Taraka Rama. "Discriminating similar languages: experiments with linear SVMs and neural networks". In Proceedings of *3rd Workshop on Language Technology for Closely Related Languages, Varieties and Dialects (VarDial)*, Osaka, Japan. 2016.

Koby Crammer and Yoram Singer. "Ultraconservative Online Algorithms for Multiclass Problems". In *Journal of Machine Learning Research*, 2003, Jan(3): 951-991.

Koby Crammer, Ofer Dekel, Joseph Keshet, Shai Shalev-Schwartz, and Yoram Singer. "Online Passive-Aggressive Algorithms". In *Journal of Machine Learning Research*, 2006, Mar(7): 551-585.

Charlie K. Dagli, William M. Campbell, Lin Li, Jennifer Williams, Kelly Geyer, Gordon Vidaver, Joel Acevedo-Aviles, Esther Wolf, Jonathan Taylor, Joseph P. Campbell "LLTools: Machine Learning for Human Language Processing. In Proceedings of *Neural Information Processing Systems (NIPS) Workshop on Machine Learning Systems*, Barcelona, Spain, December 2016.

Morris H. DeGroot and Stephen E. Feinberg. "The comparison and evaluation of forecasters.". The Statistician (1983): 12-22.

Ted Dunning. "Statistical Identification of Language". Computing Research Laboratory, New Mexico State University, 1994, 10-03.

Cyril Goutte, Serge Léger, Marine Carpuat. "The NRC System for Discriminating Similar Languages". In Proceedings of *First Workshop on Applying NLP Tools to Similar Languages, Varieties, and Dialects*, 139-145, Dublin, Ireland, August 2014.

Cyril Goutte, Serge Lger, Shervin Malmasi and Marcos Zampieri. "Discriminating Similar Languages: Evaluations and Explorations". In Proceedings of *10th International Conference on Language Resources and Evaluation (LREC)*, 2016.

Mark Graham, Scott A. Hale, and Devin Gaffney "Where in the world are you? Geolocation and language identification in Twitter". *The Professional Geographer*, 66, no. 4 (2014): 568-578.

Shamanth Kumar, Geoffrey Barbier, Mohammad Ali Abbasi, and Huan Liu. "TweetTracker: An Analysis Tool for Humanitarian and Disaster Relief." In Proceedings of *International Conference on Weblogs and Social Media (ICWSM)*, AAAI, 2011.

Marco Lui and Tim Baldwin. "langid. py: An off-the-shelf language identification tool.". In Proceedings of *ACL 2012 system demonstrations*, pp. 25-30. Association for Computational Linguistics, 2012.

Marco Lui and Tim Baldwin. "Accurate Language Identification of Twitter Messages". In Proceedings of *Joint Workshop on Language Technology for Closely Related Languages, Varieties and Dialects (LT4VarDial)*, 2015, 35-43.

Marco Lui, Ned Letcher, Oliver Adams, Long Duong, Paul Cook, Timothy Baldwin. "Exploring methods and resources for discriminating similar languages". In Proceedings of *First Workshop on Applying NLP Tools to Similar Languages, Varieties and Dialects*, pp. 129-138. 2014.

Shervin Malmasi and Mark Dras "Language Identification Using Classifier Ensembles". In Proceedings of *Fifth Workshop on Language Analysis for Social Media (LASM), European Association for Computational Linguistics (EACL)*, Gothenburg, Sweden, 2014: 17-25.

Shervin Malmasi, Marcos Zampieri, Nikola Ljubešic, Preslav Nakov, Ahmed Ali, and Jörg Tiedemann. "Discriminating between similar languages and arabic dialect identification: A report on the third dsl shared task". In Proceedings of *3rd Workshop on Language Technology for Closely Related Languages, Varieties and Dialects (VarDial)*, Osaka, Japan. 2016.

Alexandru Niculescu-Mizil, and Rich Caruana. "Predicting good probabilities with supervised learning". In Proceedings of *22nd International Conference on Machine learning (ICML)*, Opp. 625-632. ACM, 2005.

Fabian Pedregosa, Gaël Varoquaux, Alexandre Gramfort, Vincent Michel, Bertrand Thirion, Olivier Grisel, Mathieu Blondel et al. "Scikit-learn: Machine learning in Python". In *Journal of Machine Learning Research*, 12, no. Oct (2011): 2825-2830.

John Platt. "Probabilistic outputs for support vector machines and comparisons to regularized likelihood methods". In *Advances in large margin classifiers*, 10.3 (1999): 61-74.

Bali Ranaivo-Malançon. "Automatic Identification of Close Languages - Case Study: Malay and Indonesian." In *ECTI Transaction on Computer and Information Technology*, 2006, 2(2): 126-133.

Alan Ritter, Sam Clark, and Oren Etzioni. "Named Entity Recognition in Tweets: An Experimental Study." In Proceedings of *Conference on Empirical Methods in Natural Language Processing (EMNLP)*, 2011, 1524-1534.

Frank Rosenblatt. "The Perceptron: A Probabilistic Model For Information Storage and Organization in the Brain". In *Psychological Review*, 1958, 65(6): 386.

Takeshi Sakaki, Makoto Okazaki, and Yutaka Matsuo. "Earthquake Shakes Twitter Users: Real-Time Event Detection by Social Sensors." In Proceedings of the *19th International Conference on World Wide Web*, Association for Computing Machinery, 2010, 851-860.

Mohammad Arshi Saloot, Norisma Idris, AiTi Aw, and Dirk Thorleuchter. "Twitter Corpus Creation: The Case Of A Malay Chat-Style Text Corpus (MCC)". *Digital Scholarship in the Humanities* 2016, 31(2), 227-243.

Wade Shen, Jennifer Williams, Tamas Marius, and Elizabeth Salesky. "A language-independent approach to automatic text difficulty assessment for second-language learners". In Proceedings of *Second Workshop on Predicting and Improving Text Readability for Target Reader Populations (PITR), Association for Computational Linguistics (ACL)* 2013, 30-38.

Thamar Solorio, Elizabeth Blair, Suraj Maharjan, Steven Bethard, Mona Diab, Mahmoud Gohneim, Abdelati Hawwari, Fhad AlGhamdi, Julia Hirschberg, Alison Chang, and Pascale Fung. "Overview for the First Shared Task on Language Identification in Code-Switched Data". In Proceedings of *First Workshop on Computational Approaches to Code Switching, Empirical Methods in Natural Language Processing (EMNLP)* 2014, 62-72.

Liling Tan, Marcos Zampieri, Nikola Ljubešic, and Jörg Tiedemann. "Merging comparable data sources for the discrimination of similar languages: The DSL corpus collection". In Proceedings of *7th Workshop on Building and Using Comparable Corpora (BUCC)*, pp. 11-15. 2014.

Svitlana Volkova, Theresa Wilson, and David Yarowsky. "Exploring Demographic Language Variations to Improve Multilingual Sentiment Analysis in Social Media". In Proceedings of *Empirical Methods in Natural Language Processing (EMNLP)*, 2013, 1815-1827.

Jennifer Williams and Graham Katz. "Extracting and modeling durations for habits and events from Twitter." In Proceedings of *Proceedings of the 50th Annual Meeting of the Association for Computational Linguistics: Short Papers-Volume 2*, Association for Computational Linguistics, 2012.

Yin-Lai Yeong and Tien-Ping Tan. "Language Identification of Code Switching Sentences and Multilingual Sentences of Under-Resourced Languages by Using Multi-Structural Word Information". In Proceedings of *INTERSPEECH* 2014, 3052-3055.

Bianca Zadronzy and Charles Elkan. "Transforming classifier scores into accurate multiclass probability estimates.". In Proceedings of *Eighth ACM SIGKDD International Conference on Knowledge Discovery and Data Mining* pp. 694-699. ACM, 2002.

Marcos Zampieri and Binyam Gebrekidan Gebre. "Automatic identification of language varieties: The case of Portuguese". In Proceedings of *KONVENS2012 - The 11th Conference on Natural Language Processing*. Österreichischen Gesellschaft für Artificial Intelligende (ÖGAI), 2012, 233-237.

Marcos Zampieri, Liling Tan, Nikola Ljubešic, and Jörg Tiedemann. "A report on the DSL shared task 2014." In Proceedings of *First Workshop on Applying NLP Tools to Similar Languages, Varieties and Dialects* 2014, 58-67.

Marcos Zampieri, Liling Tan, Nikola Ljubešic, and Jörg Tiedemann. "Overview of DSL Shared Task 2015". In Proceedings of *Joint Wokrshop on Closely Related Languages, Varieties, and Dialects* 2015.

Marcos Zampieri, Shervin Malmasi, Octavia-Maria Sulea and Liviu P. Dinu. "A Computational Approach to the Study of Portuguese Newspapers Published in Macau". In Proceedings of *Workshop on Natural Language Processing Meets Journalism (NLPMJ)* 2016, 47-51.

Arkaitz Zubiaga, Iñaki San Vincente, Pablo Gamallo, José Ramon Pichel, Iñaki Alegria, Nora Aranberri, Aitzol Ezeiza, and Víctor Fresno. "TweetLID: A Benchmark For Tweet Language Identification." In Proceedings of *Language Resources and Evaluation Conference (LREC)* 2015: 1-38.

Multi-source morphosyntactic tagging for Spoken Rusyn

Yves Scherrer
Department of Linguistics
University of Geneva
Switzerland
`yves.scherrer@unige.ch`

Achim Rabus
Department of Slavonic Studies
University of Freiburg
Germany
`achim.rabus@`
`slavistik.uni-freiburg.de`

Abstract

This paper deals with the development of morphosyntactic taggers for spoken varieties of the Slavic minority language Rusyn. As neither annotated corpora nor parallel corpora are electronically available for Rusyn, we propose to combine existing resources from the etymologically close Slavic languages Russian, Ukrainian, Slovak, and Polish and adapt them to Rusyn. Using MarMoT as tagging toolkit, we show that a tagger trained on a balanced set of the four source languages outperforms single language taggers by about 9%, and that additional automatically induced morphosyntactic lexicons lead to further improvements. The best observed accuracies for Rusyn are 82.4% for part-of-speech tagging and 75.5% for full morphological tagging.

1 Introduction

This paper addresses the development of morphosyntactic taggers for spoken varieties of the Slavic minority language Rusyn by leveraging the resources available for the neighboring, etymologically related languages. Due to the lack of annotated and parallel Rusyn data, we propose to create Rusyn taggers by combining training data from related resource-richer languages such as Ukrainian, Polish, Slovak and Russian.

We start by giving a brief introduction to the characteristics of Rusyn and present related work in the domain of low-resource language tagging. After describing the training and test data, we present a set of experiments on different multi-source tagging approaches. In particular, we investigate the impact of majority voting, Brown clustering, training corpus adaptation, and the ad-

dition of automatically induced morphosyntactic lexicons. Finally, we give an outlook on future work.

2 Status of Rusyn and corpus data

Rusyn is a Slavic linguistic variety spoken predominantly in Transcarpathian Ukraine, Eastern Slovakia, and Southeastern Poland, and is linguistically close to the Ukrainian language. Its sociolinguistic status is disputed insofar as some scholars see Rusyn as a dialect of Ukrainian, others claim it to be an independent – the fourth East Slavic – language. Despite its closeness to Ukrainian, Rusyn exhibits numerous distinct features on all linguistic levels, which make Rusyn look more "West Slavic" as compared to Ukrainian.[1]

Nowadays, most speakers of Rusyn are bilingual and have native-like command of, e.g., Polish or Slovak. This has an impact on their Rusyn speech and leads to new divergences within the old Rusyn dialect continuum, which can be investigated using the Corpus of Spoken Rusyn (`www.russinisch.uni-freiburg.de/corpus`) that is currently in the process of being built up. The corpus comprises several hours of transcribed Rusyn speech from the different countries where Rusyn is spoken. This means that both diatopic and individual speaker variation is reflected in the transcription, which is one reason for the fact that the corpus data is orthographically (and morphologically) heterogeneous. Another reason is that variation in transcription practices due to several individual transcribers could not completely be avoided.

The goal of the research presented here is to automatically provide morphosyntactic annotations

---

[1]For further details on the status and the features of Rusyn see, e.g., Magocsi (2004), Plishkova (2009), Pugh (2009), Skrypnyk (2013), Teutsch (2001).

Proceedings of the Fourth Workshop on NLP for Similar Languages, Varieties and Dialects, pages 84–92,
Valencia, Spain, April 3, 2017. ©2017 Association for Computational Linguistics

PL	Na początku było Słowo a Słowo było u Boga, i Bogiem było Słowo.
Cyrillicized	На почутку было Слово а Слово было у Бога, и Богем было Слово.
RU	В начале было Слово, и Слово было у Бога, и Слово было Богом.
SK	Na počiatku bolo Slovo a Slovo bolo u Boha a Boh bol to Slovo.
Cyrillicized	На почиатку боло Слово а Слово боло у Бога а Бог бол то Слово.
UK	На початку було Слово, а Слово в Бога було, і Бог було Слово.
RUE	На початку было Слово, а Слово было у Бога, і Бог было Слово.

Figure 1: John 1:1 in the Slavic languages used for the experiments.

for the Corpus of Spoken Rusyn. However, there are virtually no NLP resources (annotated corpora or tools) available for Rusyn at the moment. The different types of variation present in the data complicate the task of developing NLP tools even more. Crucially, there is no parallel corpus available for Rusyn, which means that the popular projection-based approaches cannot be applied (see below).

Considering the lack of annotated Rusyn data and the etymological situation of Rusyn, our approach consists in training taggers for several related languages – namely, the East Slavic languages Ukrainian and Russian and the West Slavic languages Polish and Slovak – and combining and adapting them to Rusyn. This multi-source setting makes sense, because the Rusyn dialect continuum features both West Slavic and East Slavic linguistic traits to a different extent, depending on both the dialect region and the impact of the respective umbrella language. In order to get an idea of the similarities and differences of the Slavic languages involved, compare the different versions of John 1:1 in Figure 1.

3 Related work

The task of creating taggers for languages lacking manually annotated training corpora has inspired a lot of recent research. The most popular line of work, initiated by Yarowsky and Ngai (2001), draws on parallel corpora. They annotate the source side of a parallel corpus with an existing tagger, and then project the tags along the word alignment links onto the target side of the parallel corpus. A new tagger is then trained on the target side, with some smoothing to reduce the noise caused by alignment errors. Follow-up work has focused on the inclusion of several source languages (Fossum and Abney, 2005), more accu-

rate projection algorithms (Das and Petrov, 2011; Duong et al., 2013), the integration of external lexicon sources (Li et al., 2012; Täckström et al., 2013), the extension from part-of-speech tagging to full morphological tagging (Buys and Botha, 2016), and the investigation of truly low-resource settings by resorting to Bible translations (Agić et al., 2015). A related approach (Aepli et al., 2014) uses majority voting to disambiguate tags proposed by several source languages. However, these projection approaches are not adapted to our setting as no parallel corpora – not even the Bible[2] – are electronically available for Rusyn.

Another approach consists in training a model for one language and applying it to another, closely related language. In this process, the model is trained not to focus on the exact shape of the words, but on more generic, language-independent cues, such as part-of-speech tags for parsing (Zeman and Resnik, 2008), or word clusters for part-of-speech tagging (Kozhevnikov and Titov, 2014). A related idea consists in translating the words of the model to the target language, either using a hand-written morphological analyzer and a list of cognate word pairs (Feldman et al., 2006), or using bilingual dictionaries extracted from parallel corpora (Zeman and Resnik, 2008) or induced from monolingual corpora (Scherrer, 2014).

Our work mostly follows the second approach: we train taggers on four resource-rich Slavic languages and adapt them to Rusyn using a variety of techniques.

4 Training data

While morphosyntactically annotated corpora exist for all four source languages, e.g. in the form

---

[2] We did not find any Rusyn material in the sources given by Christodouloupoulos and Steedman (2015) and Mayer and Cysouw (2014). The sentence cited in Figure 1 has been taken from the printed edition Krajnjak and Kudzej (transl.) (2009).

ID	Origin		Training data			Test data		
			Sentences	Tokens	Tags	Sentences	Tokens	Tags
PL	UD 1.4 Polish	train / dev	6 800	69 499	920	700	6 887	448
RU1	UD 1.4 Russian	train / dev	4 029	79 772	704	502	10 044	410
RU2	UD 1.4 SynTagRus	train / dev	48 171	850 689	580	6 250	109 694	501
SK	UD 1.4 Slovak	train / dev	8 483	80 575	657	1 060	12 440	426
UK	UD 1.4 Ukrainian train / dev+test		200	1 281	1 040	55	395	92
	Additional data		3 962	70 299				
RUE1	Manually annotated gold standard					104	1 050	96
RUE2	Corpus of Spoken Rusyn					5 922	75 201	—

Table 1: Sizes of the training and test corpora used in our experiments.

of national corpora,[3] they use disparate tagsets and are often difficult to obtain in full-text format. The MULTEXT-East project (Erjavec et al., 2010; Erjavec, 2012)[4] provides annotated versions of the novel *1984* for several Eastern European languages, but Ukrainian and Russian versions are not available.

Fortunately, since version 1.4, the Universal Dependencies project[5] contains treebanks for the four relevant languages with unified part-of-speech tags and morphosyntactic descriptions (Nivre et al., 2016; Zeman, 2015). Two corpora are available for Russian, but the Ukrainian corpus is still rather small (see Table 1). Additionally, we were able to obtain more Ukrainian data developed by the non-governmental Institute of Ukrainian[6] and planned to be included in one of the upcoming Universal Dependencies releases; we converted these additional data from the MultextEast-style tags to universal tags and morphological features.

As Rusyn is written in Cyrillic script, we converted the Slovak and Polish corpora into Cyrillic script. During this process, we applied certain transformation rules in order to "rusynify" our training data (e.g., transform Polish *ć* to Cyrillic *ть* or Polish *ą* to Cyrillic *у*, which is in line with well-known historical phonological processes).

Initial experiments have shown that additional morphological dictionaries, such as those made available for the four languages within the MULTEXT-East project, do not have a positive impact on Rusyn tagging. We therefore do not include these additional resources (except for the derived lexicons discussed in Section 5.5).

We evaluate our methods on a small hand-annotated sample of Rusyn containing 104 sentences and 1 050 tokens and 96 distinct tags (henceforth RUE1). At the time of conducting the experiments, the Corpus of Spoken Rusyn (RUE2), which we aim to annotate with the presented methods, contains 5 922 sentences with 75 201 tokens. We also report OOV rates on the latter and use it as additional unlabeled data for some of the adaptation processes described below.

5 Experiments

5.1 The MarMoT tagger

We use the MarMoT tagger for all of our experiments. MarMoT (Mueller et al., 2013) is a state-of-the-art toolkit for morphological tagging based on Conditional Random Fields (CRFs). It has been shown to work well on full morphological tagging with hundreds of tags (as opposed to part-of-speech tagging, which typically only uses a few dozen tags), thanks to pruning and coarse-to-fine decoding. Unless stated otherwise, we use the default parameters for morphological tagging.

We evaluate the different models on the development sets of the five source corpora as well as on RUE1. A token is considered correctly tagged if its part-of-speech tag is correct and if all morphological features present in the gold annotation are found with the same value.[7]

---

[3]Ukrainian National Corpus: www.mova.info; Russian National Corpus: www.ruscorpora.ru; Polish National Corpus: www.nkjp.pl/; Slovak National Corpus: http://korpus.juls.savba.sk/index_en.html.

[4]http://hdl.handle.net/11356/1043

[5]www.universaldependencies.org

[6]https://mova.institute

[7]The gold annotation of RUE1 does not distinguish proper from common nouns, auxiliary from main verbs, and coordinating from subordinating conjunctions; these mismatches were not penalized.

	Accuracy (%)						OOV rate (%)						
	PL	SK	UK	RU1	RU2	RUE1	PL	SK	UK	RU1	RU2	RUE1	RUE2
PL	**85.87**	49.08	39.2	40.47	43.15	49.5 ±1.0	**20.02**	60.61	59.0	65.56	60.87	50.5	46.00
SK	46.77	**79.87**	37.2	41.94	45.54	43.3 ±0.4	58.05	**33.87**	57.7	63.72	58.56	53.1	43.73
UK	38.25	35.71	**79.8**	41.24	44.81	**63.4** ±0.4	63.13	67.98	**15.4**	69.11	66.07	**37.1**	**39.67**
RU1	39.19	42.60	36.5	**85.73**	79.39	46.0 ±0.6	64.93	65.14	62.0	24.53	27.51	54.1	46.58
RU2	40.79	46.33	40.8	80.68	**93.79**	50.9 ±0.0	59.36	60.35	55.7	**19.73**	**7.98**	49.1	42.72

Table 2: Tagging accuracies and OOV rates for single-language taggers. Rows represent models, columns represent test sets.

5.2 Single-language taggers

We start by training five distinct taggers on the five training corpora and apply these taggers to the five source-language test corpora as well as to the Rusyn corpora. The results are shown in Table 2.

Unsurprisingly, each test set is best tagged with the tagger based on its own training set. Polish and Russian fared somewhat better than Slovak and Ukrainian. The differences between RU1 and RU2 give an indication of the loss resulting from annotation/conversion differences as well as domain differences within the same language. For Rusyn, the best accuracy is obtained using the Ukrainian tagger, which is in line with the claims on linguistic proximity made above, followed by RU2, which is due to its large size rather than to small etymological distance. Also note that for none of the models, Rusyn is the worst-performing test language, hinting at its role as a bridge language between East and West Slavic.

In order to quantify the reliability of the Rusyn tagging results given the somewhat small test corpus, we split it into two equally-sized parts and computed the accuracies on both parts. The deviation of the accuracy values of these parts from the mean accuracy is indicated after the ± sign in Table 2.

While no single-language tagger achieves satisfactory accuracy on Rusyn, the results suggest that a combination of the five taggers (or of their training data) could yield improved accuracy on Rusyn. There are essentially two ways of combining taggers: using the five source language taggers and choosing the majority vote, or using a single tagger trained on merged data from the five source corpora.

5.3 Majority-vote tagging

Aepli et al. (2014) develop a tagger for Macedonian by transferring morphosyntactic annotations from multiple source languages by word alignment, choosing one annotation by majority vote, and training a new tagger on the annotated corpus. We follow a similar method. We start by annotating the Rusyn data with the five source language taggers. A majority annotation is determined in two steps: first, the majority part-of-speech tag is determined, and second, the majority morphological features are determined on the basis of the taggers that have predicted the majority part-of-speech tag. We propose two ways of dealing with ties: we either randomly resolve ties (*Random*) or weight the tags on the basis of *a priori* knowledge about the etymological distances of the languages (*Weighted*).[8]

We report results on this direct annotation (see Table 3, rows MAJ-D), but also use the annotated RUE2 corpus to retrain a new tagger (see Table 3, rows MAJ-R). Only the weighted method yields similar tagging accuracies as the best single-language tagger. The impact of retraining is negative, probably due to the fact that the OOV rate on RUE1 hardly decreases. While we could have tuned the weights of the majority-vote models to further improve their accuracy, this option did not look worthwhile in the light of the better results obtained with the approaches discussed below.

5.4 Creating multi-source taggers

For the multi-source tagger, we concatenate the five training sets, using only the first 10% of RU2 in order to keep the distribution better balanced. As shown in Table 3 (row MS), this simple combination of training resources yields better accuracy than all majority-vote systems and outperforms the best single-language model (UK) by nearly 9%, although with a high variance between the two parts of the corpus. If only parts-of-speech are eval-

---

[8]The following weights are used: PL: 1.5, SK: 3, UK: 4, RU1: 1, RU2: 1.

	Accuracy (%)						OOV rate (%)						
	PL	SK	UK	RU1	RU2	RUE1	PL	SK	UK	RU1	RU2	RUE1	RUE2
Majority-vote – direct annotation (R=random, W=weighted):													
MAJ-D-R	55.35	59.13	46.3	70.31	75.34	54.9 ±0.7	18.08	28.17	11.9	13.37	7.33	24.9	23.83
MAJ-D-W	51.91	57.55	64.1	49.93	55.12	63.4 ±1.3							
Majority-vote – after retraining (R=random, W=weighted):													
MAJ-R-R	47.38	45.82	42.0	48.30	52.37	54.7 ±0.3	55.34	61.45	31.7	63.54	58.34	23.5	0.00
MAJ-R-W	44.62	43.36	57.2	41.29	46.07	63.0 ±1.2							
Multi-source tagger (B=with Brown clusters):													
MS	84.23	**79.61**	81.5	85.91	88.00	72.0 ±1.3	18.66	29.08	13.2	20.17	16.40	26.4	24.99
MS-B	84.07	79.32	**83.3**	86.44	**88.31**	72.3 ±2.0							
Taggers with additional lexicons (R=rules, L=Levenshtein):													
LEX-R	83.72	79.34	81.8	86.03	88.06	73.9 ±0.1	18.51	28.82	11.7	20.03	16.31	9.6	7.94
LEX-L	83.65	79.54	82.0	86.25	88.04	**75.5** ±0.0						1.1	1.01
Taggers trained on adapted corpora (R=rules, L=Levenshtein, B=with Brown clusters):													
COR-R	83.04	78.30	80.3	85.16	86.68	71.3 ±0.6	20.75	31.54	14.2	22.88	19.81	23.2	22.04
COR-L	80.83	77.59	79.2	84.01	85.71	70.6 ±0.8	26.32	34.22	19.2	26.15	22.69	12.8	12.83
COR-L-B	**84.27**	78.79	82.3	**86.53**	88.30	73.0 ±0.9							

Table 3: Tagging accuracies and OOV rates for the multi-source tagging experiments.

uated, the multi-source tagger achieves 79.2% of accuracy, compared to 69.7% for the best single-language model (UK).

Following e.g. Owoputi et al. (2013), we include word clusters as an additional feature for tagging. We obtain hierarchical word clusters (c=1 000) with the Brown clustering algorithm (Brown et al., 1992) on the concatenation of all source language and Rusyn texts (1.5M running tokens), and add the clusters as an additional feature to the tagger. This addition yields small improvements for some source languages and for Rusyn (see Table 3, row MS-B), although the latter impact is inconclusive due to the high variance between the two corpus parts. We observe that all word clusters spread over words from more than one language, suggesting that the clustering algorithm generalizes well over data from different languages. While larger amounts of unlabeled data will undoubtedly further increase source language tagging, it is less clear whether this will also have a positive impact on Rusyn tagging. In any case, larger Rusyn corpora will be hard to come by.

The idea behind tagger combination was that a lot of Rusyn words can be found in one of the source languages. This has been confirmed, as the OOV rates of the combined taggers (around 24% for Rusyn, see Table 3, rows MAJ-D and MS) are much lower than those of the single language taggers (between 37% and 54% for Rusyn, see Table 2). However, we assume that even more Rusyn words could be found in a source language if some transformations were applied. In the following two subsections, we investigate two different approaches.

5.5 Adding automatically induced lexicons

In Rabus and Scherrer (2017), we describe the automatic induction of morphosyntactic lexicons for Rusyn. In a nutshell, we match Rusyn words extracted from RUE1 and RUE2 with source language words extracted from the Polish, Slovak, Ukrainian and Russian MULTEXT-East lexicons as well as the morphological dictionary of UGtag[9] (Kotsyba et al., 2011), using vowel-sensitive Levenshtein distance, hand-written rules, and a combination of both. The Rusyn words are then associated with the morphosyntactic descriptions of the matched source-language words. The resulting lexicon contains 51 600 token-tag tuples when induced with Levenshtein distance, and 28 900 tuples when induced with rules.

Table 3 (rows LEX-R and LEX-L) reports tagging results, where one of the induced lexicons is added to the multi-source tagger. As expected, the OOV rates drop considerably.[10] Both the

---

[9]UGtag is a tagger specifically developed for Ukrainian, but essentially consists of a large morphological dictionary and a simple disambiguation component.

[10]OOV rates do not completely drop to 0 because the induction methods failed to find correspondences for a few Rusyn

rule-induced and the Levenshtein-induced lexicon improve accuracy, the latter by 3.5% to 75.5%, the best observed result. Moreover, these results are stable between the two parts of the RUE1 corpus, with only 0.2% difference for the rule-induced lexicon and less than 0.1% difference for the Levenshtein-induced lexicon. If evaluated on the parts-of-speech only, the accuracies increase from 79.2% to 81.3% for the rule-induced lexicon and to 82.4% for the Levenshtein-induced lexicon. Combinations of rule-induction and Levenshtein-induction do not lead to further tagging improvements with respect to the Levenshtein model.

5.6 Adapting the corpora to Rusyn

An alternative to adding Rusyn data in the form of lexicons is to modify the source language training corpora directly by making them look more Rusyn-like. The idea behind this method is to provide the tagger with additional Rusyn tokens in sentential context. We proceed as follows: for each source language word, we search for the most similar Rusyn word in the RUE1 and RUE2 corpora, again using Levenshtein distance or the hand-written rules. If the most similar Rusyn word is different from the source word, we replace the source word with the former.[11]

As the number of known Rusyn words is small in comparison with the number of source words, there is a risk of replacing a source word by a non-related Rusyn word because the related one simply is not known. In this case, we prevent the replacement whenever another source word is closer to the Rusyn candidate. For example, the word *презыдент* in the Polish corpus (converted from *prezydent* 'president') would be replaced by the most similar Rusyn word, which happens to be the word *презенти* but which is unrelated. This replacement is blocked because another Polish word, *презенты* (< *prezenty* 'gifts'), is even closer to *презенти*. When more than one Rusyn word exists with the same distance, no replacement takes place. This phenomenon mostly occurs with Levenshtein distance, where 3-5% of tokens are concerned, but more rarely with the rules, where 1-3% of tokens are concerned. In the end, between 8% and 12% of source tokens are replaced with Lev-

enshtein, and between 1% and 5% of source tokens with the rules.

The results presented in Table 3 (rows COR-R and COR-L) show that these conversions slightly decrease tagging accuracy for the source languages (which is expected, as training corpora now look less like the source languages), but do not improve the accuracy for Rusyn either compared to the simple multi-source model. We also reran the word clustering tool on the Levenshtein-converted data, under the assumption that the increased frequency of the Rusyn words would improve the reliability of the induced clustering. This assumption was indeed borne out with an accuracy increase of 2.4% absolute (row COR-L-B). However, this result did not surpass the one obtained with induced lexicons.

6 Conclusion and future work

We have investigated several approaches to morphosyntactic tagging of spoken Rusyn without relying on annotated Rusyn training data nor on annotation projection from aligned parallel data. Instead, we argued that fair tagging accuracy could be achieved by training taggers on the etymologically related languages Ukrainian, Slovak, Polish and Russian. The experiments also showed that although Ukrainian is most closely related to Rusyn, all four related languages are useful for tagging. We have shown that a multi-source tagger trained on a balanced set of source language corpora performs rather well and even outperforms majority vote approaches. In contrast, Brown clustering has only been modestly useful in our setting, which may be due to the low amount of unlabeled data used.

We have presented two additional techniques to adapt the taggers to the specificities of Rusyn: adding automatically induced morphosyntactic lexicons, or adapting the training corpora. We oriented the first technique towards maximising recall (e.g., keeping all possible readings of a Rusyn word in the induced lexicons) and the second towards high precision (e.g., only replacing unambiguous words in the corpus). The first approach turned out to be more successful.

However, we believe that further improvements can be achieved. First, the RUE1 corpus – currently our only gold standard – is not completely representative of the material found in RUE2. In fact, the RUE1 test set may actually underesti-

---

words.

[11] For relative Levenshtein distance, we introduce a threshold at 0.25 – as already in the lexicon induction experiments – above which word matches are considered noise and are discarded.

mate the impact of the tagger adaptation methods, as it contains only Rusyn varieties spoken in Ukraine, with a low amount of orthographic variation, whereas RUE2 also contains Rusyn from Poland and Slovakia. As an illustration, compare the OOV rates of the UK tagger (Table 2), which is 2.5% higher in RUE2 than in RUE1. A cursory evaluation of the results confirms this hypothesis, but we cannot quantify it at the moment. Only the manual annotation of a balanced subset of the different RUE2 parts would provide us with a broader data basis for evaluation.

Second, it is crucial to keep in mind that both RUE1 and RUE2 – as opposed to the training corpora – are oral corpora with distinct features such as corrections, repetitions, incomplete sentences, unintelligible words or phrases, markers for pauses, etc. Any tagger trained on written data and applied to oral data will inevitably perform worse than when applied to written data (Nivre and Grönqvist, 2001; Westpfahl, 2014).

The final annotation of the Rusyn corpus is not only expected to consist of morphosyntactic descriptions, but also of lemmas. Therefore, we intend to train a separate lemmatization model on the tagged Rusyn corpora. The multi-source approach will be more problematic here, as we do not want the predicted lemmas to be a mix of the four source languages. The prediction of Rusyn lemmas is prevented by two factors: none of our Rusyn data are annotated with Rusyn lemmas, and the orthographic variation would also carry over to the lemmas, which we would like to avoid. Therefore, one goal could be to annotate the Rusyn tokens with Ukrainian lemmas such as those available in the UGtag lexicon.

Finally, all source language corpora used in our experiments are annotated with syntactic dependencies. We assume that a Rusyn dependency parser could be created using similar methods as those presented here for morphosyntactic tagging.

Acknowledgments

We would like to thank Christine Grillborzer, Natalia Kotsyba, Bohdan Moskalevskyi, Andrianna Schimon, Peter Schwarz, and Ruprecht von Waldenfels. The usual disclaimers apply.

Sources of external funding for our research include the German Research Foundation (DFG).

References

Noëmi Aepli, Ruprecht von Waldenfels, and Tanja Samardžić. 2014. Part-of-speech tag disambiguation by cross-linguistic majority vote. In *Proceedings of the First Workshop on Applying NLP Tools to Similar Languages, Varieties and Dialects*, pages 76–84, Dublin, Ireland, August. Association for Computational Linguistics and Dublin City University.

Željko Agić, Dirk Hovy, and Anders Søgaard. 2015. If all you have is a bit of the Bible: Learning POS taggers for truly low-resource languages. In *Proceedings of the 53rd Annual Meeting of the Association for Computational Linguistics and the 7th International Joint Conference on Natural Language Processing (Volume 2: Short Papers)*, pages 268–272, Beijing, China, July. Association for Computational Linguistics.

Peter F. Brown, Peter V. de Souza, Robert L. Mercer, Vincent J. Della Pietra, and Jenifer C. Lai. 1992. Class-based n-gram models of natural language. *Computational Linguistics*, 18(4):467–479.

Jan Buys and Jan A. Botha. 2016. Cross-lingual morphological tagging for low-resource languages. In *Proceedings of the 54th Annual Meeting of the Association for Computational Linguistics (Volume 1: Long Papers)*, pages 1954–1964, Berlin, Germany, August. Association for Computational Linguistics.

Christos Christodouloupoulos and Mark Steedman. 2015. A massively parallel corpus: the Bible in 100 languages. *Language Resources and Evaluation*, 49(2):375–395.

Dipanjan Das and Slav Petrov. 2011. Unsupervised part-of-speech tagging with bilingual graph-based projections. In *Proceedings of the 49th Annual Meeting of the Association for Computational Linguistics: Human Language Technologies*, pages 600–609, Portland, Oregon, USA, June. Association for Computational Linguistics.

Long Duong, Paul Cook, Steven Bird, and Pavel Pecina. 2013. Simpler unsupervised pos tagging with bilingual projections. In *Proceedings of the 51st Annual Meeting of the Association for Computational Linguistics (Volume 2: Short Papers)*, pages 634–639, Sofia, Bulgaria, August. Association for Computational Linguistics.

Tomaž Erjavec, Ana-Maria Barbu, Ivan Derzhanski, Ludmila Dimitrova, Radovan Garabík, Nancy Ide, Heiki-Jaan Kaalep, Natalia Kotsyba, Cvetana Krstev, Csaba Oravecz, Vladimír Petkevič, Greg Priest-Dorman, Behrang QasemiZadeh, Adam Radziszewski, Kiril Simov, Dan Tufiş, and Katerina Zdravkova. 2010. MULTEXT-east "1984" annotated corpus 4.0. Slovenian language resource repository CLARIN.SI.

Tomaž Erjavec. 2012. MULTEXT-East: Morphosyntactic resources for Central and Eastern European languages. *Language Resources and Evaluation*, 1(46):131–142.

Anna Feldman, Jirka Hana, and Chris Brew. 2006. A cross-language approach to rapid creation of new morpho-syntactically annotated resources. In *Proceedings of the Fifth International Conference on Language Resources and Evaluation (LREC 2006)*, pages 549–554, Genoa, Italy.

Victoria Fossum and Steven Abney. 2005. Automatically inducing a part-of-speech tagger by projecting from multiple source languages across aligned corpora. In *Proceedings of the Second International Joint Conference on Natural Language Processing*, page 862–873, Jeju Island, Korea.

Natalia Kotsyba, Andriy Mykulyak, and Ihor V. Shevchenko. 2011. UGTag: morphological analyzer and tagger for the Ukrainian language. In Stanisław Goźdź-Roszkowski, editor, *Explorations across Languages and Corpora*, pages 69–82, Frankfurt a. M.

Mikhail Kozhevnikov and Ivan Titov. 2014. Cross-lingual model transfer using feature representation projection. In *Proceedings of the 52nd Annual Meeting of the Association for Computational Linguistics (Volume 2: Short Papers)*, pages 579–585, Baltimore, Maryland, June. Association for Computational Linguistics.

František Krajnjak and Josif Kudzej (transl.). 2009. *Tetrajevanhelije*. Svitovŷj kongres Rusyniv, Prešov.

Shen Li, João Graça, and Ben Taskar. 2012. Wiki-ly supervised part-of-speech tagging. In *Proceedings of the 2012 Joint Conference on Empirical Methods in Natural Language Processing and Computational Natural Language Learning*, pages 1389–1398, Jeju Island, Korea, July. Association for Computational Linguistics.

Paul R. Magocsi, editor. 2004. *Rusyn'skŷj jazŷk*. Najnowsze dzieje języków słowiańskich. Uniw. Opolski Inst. Filologii Polskiej, Opole.

Thomas Mayer and Michael Cysouw. 2014. Creating a Massively Parallel Bible Corpus. In *Proceedings of the Ninth International Conference on Language Resources and Evaluation (LREC'14)*, pages 3158–3163, Reykjavik, Iceland.

Thomas Mueller, Helmut Schmid, and Hinrich Schütze. 2013. Efficient higher-order CRFs for morphological tagging. In *Proceedings of the 2013 Conference on Empirical Methods in Natural Language Processing*, pages 322–332, Seattle, Washington, USA, October. Association for Computational Linguistics.

Joakim Nivre and Leif Grönqvist. 2001. Tagging a corpus of spoken Swedish. *International Journal of Corpus Linguistics*, 6(1):47–78.

Joakim Nivre, Marie-Catherine de Marneffe, Filip Ginter, Yoav Goldberg, Jan Hajič, Christopher D. Manning, Ryan McDonald, Slav Petrov, Sampo Pyysalo, Natalia Silveira, Reut Tsarfaty, and Daniel Zeman. 2016. Universal dependencies v1: A multilingual treebank collection. In *Proceedings of the Tenth International Conference on Language Resources and Evaluation (LREC 2016)*, pages 1659–1666, Portorož, Slovenia.

Olutobi Owoputi, Brendan O'Connor, Chris Dyer, Kevin Gimpel, Nathan Schneider, and Noah A. Smith. 2013. Improved part-of-speech tagging for online conversational text with word clusters. In *Proceedings of the 2013 Conference of the North American Chapter of the Association for Computational Linguistics: Human Language Technologies*, pages 380–390, Atlanta, Georgia, June. Association for Computational Linguistics.

Anna Plishkova. 2009. *Language and national identity: Rusyns south of Carpathians*, volume 14 of *Classics of Carpatho-Rusyn scholarship*. Columbia University Press and East European Monographs, New York.

Stefan M. Pugh. 2009. *The Rusyn language: A grammar of the literary standard of Slovakia with reference to Lemko and Subcarpathian Rusyn*, volume 476 of *Languages of the World/Materials*. Lincom Europa, München.

Achim Rabus and Yves Scherrer. 2017. Lexicon induction for spoken Rusyn – challenges and results. In *Proceedings of the 6th Workshop on Balto-Slavic Natural Language Processing*, Valencia, Spain.

Yves Scherrer. 2014. Unsupervised adaptation of supervised part-of-speech taggers for closely related languages. In *Proceedings of the First Workshop on Applying NLP Tools to Similar Languages, Varieties and Dialects*, pages 30–38, Dublin, Ireland, August. Association for Computational Linguistics and Dublin City University.

H. A. Skrypnyk, editor. 2013. *Ukrajinci-Rusyny: Etnolinhvistyčni ta etnokul'turni procesy v istoryčnomu rozvytku*. Instytut mystectvoznavstva, fol'klorystyky ta etnolohiji im. M.T. Ryl's'koho, Kyjiv.

Oscar Täckström, Dipanjan Das, Slav Petrov, Ryan McDonald, and Joakim Nivre. 2013. Token and type constraints for cross-lingual part-of-speech tagging. *Transactions of the Association for Computational Linguistics*, 1:1–12.

Alexander Teutsch. 2001. *Das Rusinische der Ostslowakei im Kontext seiner Nachbarsprachen*, volume 12 of *Heidelberger Publikationen zur Slavistik. A, Linguistische Reihe*. Lang, Frankfurt am Main, Berlin, Bern.

Swantje Westpfahl. 2014. STTS 2.0? Improving the tagset for the part-of-speech-tagging of German spoken data. In *Proceedings of LAW VIII - The 8th Linguistic Annotation Workshop*, pages 1–10, Dublin, Ireland.

David Yarowsky and Grace Ngai. 2001. Inducing multilingual POS taggers and NP bracketers via robust projection across aligned corpora. In *Proceedings of NAACL '01*, pages 200–207.

Daniel Zeman and Philip Resnik. 2008. Cross-language parser adaptation between related languages. In *Proceedings of the IJCNLP '08 Workshop on NLP for Less Privileged Languages*, pages 35–42.

Daniel Zeman. 2015. Slavic languages in Universal Dependencies. In *Slovko 2015: Natural Language Processing, Corpus Linguistics, E-learning*, pages 151–163, Bratislava, Slovakia.

Identifying dialects with textual and acoustic cues

Abualsoud Hanani, Aziz Qaroush
Electrical & Computer Engineering Dept
Birzeit University
West Bank, Palestine
{ahanani,qaroush}@birzeit.edu

Stephen Taylor
Computer Science Dept
Fitchburg State University
Fitchburg, MA, USA
staylor@fitchburgstate.edu

Abstract

We describe several systems for identifying short samples of Arabic or Swiss-German dialects, which were prepared for the shared task of the 2017 DSL Workshop (Zampieri et al., 2017). The Arabic data comprises both text and acoustic files, and our best run combined both. The Swiss-German data is text-only. Coincidently, our best runs achieved a accuracy of nearly 63% on both the Swiss-German and Arabic dialects tasks.

1 Introduction

The 2017 Distinguishing Similar Languages Workshop sponsored four shared tasks, and our team participated in two of them: Arabic dialect identification, and Swiss-German dialect identification. The Arabic dialect data includes Automatic Speech Recognition transcripts of broadcasts, as well as the most helpful audio features, which were provided as 400-dimensional I-vector files. The raw audio data was also available for download. The Swiss-German data consists of transcripts only, transcribed to indicate pronunciation by human linguists.

The training set for Arabic comprises 14000 lines, totaling 1.7MB, each line labeled for one of five dialect groups. In addition, 1524 lines totaling 318KB of development data were also provided. The test set is 1492 lines.

We did not use the IS2016 data or the varDial3 shared task data, which have similar characteristics, and might have improved the efficacy of training.

For the three Arabic runs, we prepared six different text-based classifiers, and five wave-file-based classifiers, in addition to the two baseline word and I-vector systems, and combined them in two groups of four and one group of five classifiers.

Our best run on the Arabic test data has a weighted F1 score of 0.628; this run combined some of our classifiers with the provided `svm_multiclass` baseline classifiers.

The Swiss-German data consists of 14478 lines of data, totalling 700KB, labeled with one of four dialects. We divided this into a 13032 line training set, and two 723-line files for development. The test set is 3638 lines.

Only two of the classifiers prepared for Arabic were deployed on the Swiss-German test data. Our best run on this data has an accuracy of 0.63 and a weighted F1 score of 0.61.

2 Related Work

In Ferguson (1959), which introduced the term *diglossia* into English, two of his four principal examples are Arabic and Swiss-German. In these languages, every educated native speaker has two distinct languages, the mother tongue, and the language of education.

In both instances, the languages have a prestigous written form with a unified literary tradition, in which native speakers of all dialects are educated. In some registers, the spoken language of various regions is mutually unintelligible. At more formal registers, the distinctions between dialects include vocabulary shifts and phonemic variations, but vocabulary is more similar to the written language and communication is less difficult. For example, speakers using the more formal registers of Arabic dialects often claim to be speaking classical Arabic, albeit with an 'accent' – an accent which drops classical case markings, changes the vowels, and reassigns many phonemes.

Among other applications for dialect recogni-

Proceedings of the Fourth Workshop on NLP for Similar Languages, Varieties and Dialects, pages 93–101,
Valencia, Spain, April 3, 2017. ©2017 Association for Computational Linguistics

tion, it might serve as a selector for acoustic and language models for ASR, as shown in Najafian et al. (2014), which achieved a 44% improvement in word error rate after 43 seconds of accent identification for British dialects.

Biadsy et al. (2009) distinguish four Arabic dialects and MSA[1] based on (audio) phone sequences; the phones were obtained by phone recognizers for English, German, Japanese, Hindi, Mandarin, Spanish, and three different MSA phone-recognizer implementations. The dialects were distinguished by phoneme sequences, and the results of classifications based on each phone-recognizer were combined using a logistic regression classifier. They train on 150 hours per dialect of telephone recordings. They report 61% accuracy on 5-second segments, and 84% accuracy on 120 second segments.

Zaidan and Callison-Burch (2011) describe building a text corpus, based on reader commentary on newspaper websites, with significant dialect content; the goal is to provide a corpus to improve machine translation for Arabic dialects. They used Amazon Mechanical Turk to provide annotation for a portion of the corpus. Zaidan and Callison-Burch (2014) describe the same work in greater detail, including dialect classifiers they built using the Mechanical Turk data for classes and origin metadata as additional features. They say these classifiers are 'approaching human quality.'

ElFardy and Diab (2013) classify EGY[2] and MSA sentences from the Zaidan and Callison-Burch (2011) corpus, that is, from text. Not only is this a binary task, but orthographic hints, including repeated long vowels, emojis and multiple punctuation, give strong clues of the register, and hence whether MSA is being employed. They do a number of experiments comparing various preprocessing schemes and different training sizes, ranging from 2-28 million tokens. They achieve 80% – 86% accuracy for all of their attempts.

Malmasi et al. (2015) do Arabic dialect identification from text corpora, including the Multi-Dialect Parallel Corpus of Arabic (Bouamor et al., 2014) and the Arabic Online Commentary database (Zaidan and Callison-Burch, 2011).

Hanani et al. (2015) perform recognition of several Palestinian regional accents, evaluating four different acoustic models, achieving 81.5% accuracy for their best system, an I-vector framework with 64 Gaussian components.

Ali et al. (2016) developed the corpus on which the DSL Arabic shared task is based. Their own dialect detection efforts depended largely on acoustical cues.

Arabic dialect recognition appeared in the 2016 edition of the workshop's shared task (Malmasi et al., 2016). The shared task data was text-only. Our classifiers (Hanani et al., 2016) for that task gave middling performance relative to other entrants, but the best classifiers (Malmasi and Zampieri, 2016; Ionescu and Popescu, 2016) for the shared task performed far below the best results reported by some of the preceding researchers. Part of the reason must be that the amount of training data for the workshop is much smaller than that used by some of the other researchers; the workshop data also did not include the audio recordings on which the transcripts are based.

3 Methodology and Data

The Arabic training and test data are excerpted from the corpus described in Ali et al. (2016). The provided `.ivec` files contain selected audio features; a list of `.wav` files was also provided with the training data, but not included in the distribution, presumably for reasons of space. We also downloaded the `.wav` files, and build several classifiers using them, which were combined into our run3 on the test data.

The Swiss-German data is excerpted from Samardzic et al. (2016).

The two data sources differ in their presentation. The Arabic data seems to attempt to present words in dictionary spelling, independent of how they were pronounced. If a word is not present in the dictionary, the transcript shows <UNK>, not a phonetic transcription. For example, the particle

هذا h*A *that*, which is frequently pronounced هدا hdA *that* in Levantine, is always presented in its MSA written form, which is of course how Levantine speakers would write it – since they are educated to write standard Arabic, not to indicate their regional dialect.

---

[1] Modern Standard Arabic – the language of television news programs.

[2] Egyptian dialect

In contrast, the Swiss-German transcripts are intended for scholarly study of the contrasts between dialects. They use the transcription guidelines of Dieth (1986) for this purpose. The spellings of words attempt to present those dialect contrasts, so that the same standard German word may be spelled in numerous different ways, depending on the pronunciation. There is an attempt in the transcription toward standardization, but it is within the dialect, not aimed toward unifying dialects. The result is that there is a large apparent vocabulary difference between Swiss-German dialects, whereas the corresponding vocabulary differences between Arabic dialects correspond to usage shifts, rather than pronunciation shifts.

In the subsections which follow, we present the methodology of each of our classifiers. We combined several classifiers for each run, and we present the fusion classifiers as well.

3.1 Word-focused baseline

This baseline classifier was provided with the training data. It treats each training or test segment as a bag of words and n-grams. The script which runs it preprocesses each segment into a line of integers and occurrence counts, with each integer representing a single word or bigram. (The setup program can be configured to use n-grams as features up to n=6. However, if n is greater than 3, the accuracy of the classifier declines; the difference between n=2 and n=3 doesn't look significant, so we followed the default, using n=2.) The resulting files are processed by Thorsten Joachim's `svm_multiclass_learn` (Tsochantaridis et al., 2004; Joachims, 2008) program which produces a model file. This can be used with the `svm_multiclass_classify` program to provide an output for each test segment with a best guess for the segment class and the scores for all classes.

This word-focused baseline classifier was combined with the I-vector baseline classifier, the word-entropy classifier, and the character string entropy classifier for ADI run1.

Applying the word-focussed baseline classifier to the ADI development data gives an accuracy of 48%.

3.2 I-vector baseline

This baseline classifier was also provided with the training data. It also uses `svm_multiclass`. The input files consist of one line per training or test segment, with the class as the first integer on the line, and the integers from 1 to 400, in order, each with a real-valued feature value. The output file, like that of the word-focused baseline classifier, contains one line for each test segment, with the first integer on the line the class with the highest score, followed by scores for this segment for each class.

This classifier, applied standalone to the ADI development data, gets an accuracy of 57%.

3.3 Word entropy

This classifier reads through the training file, and builds a table of word, bigram, and trigram frequencies for each dialect.[3]

Using the frequencies as estimates of the true probability of the n-gram occurring in a test sample if the sample is in the corresponding dialect, it estimates the probability that the sample is in each of the dialects which appeared in training. In other words, it creates n-gram language models for each dialect, and for each test sentence chooses the dialect with the best cross-entropy. The classifier can be configured to ignore words which occur less than m times. It can write files either in vardial3 submission format, or in the input format used by the Focal Multiclass toolkit, for combining its results with other classifiers.

This classifier is used alone for our GDI run1, and in combination for our ADI run1.

On the ADI development data, this classifier gives an accuracy of 52%, and on 723 lines of reserved GDI data, it gives an accuracy of 84%.

On the test data, it is used standalone only on GDI run1, where it shows an accuracy of 56%.

3.4 Character-string entropy

This classifier ignores word boundaries.[4] It accumulates statistics for all of the strings up to twenty-five bytes long in the training file, except for those strings which end in a UTF-8 sequence which is broken by the 25-byte boundary. For each dialect, it greedily attempts to pave the test strings with strings from training, trying the longest strings first. Once the test segment is completely covered by strings seen in training, a log-probability is

---

[3] The classifier is implemented by the file `https://github.com/StephenETaylor/vardial4/blob/master/wordfreq.py`.

[4] The character-string entropy classifier is implemented by `https://github.com/StephenETaylor/vardial4/blob/master/chars.c`.

computed by adding log-frequencies for the covering strings. The dialect with the largest log-probability for the segment is selected as the dialect. When the classifier is configured for saving scores, the log-probabilities for each dialect are the scores for the test segment.

On the ADI development data, this classifier has an accuracy of 44%. On the 723 lines of reserved GDI training data, this classifier has an accuracy of 79%.

For the test runs, it is used standalone on GDI run2, where it achieves an accuracy of 63%.

3.5 Fusing estimates

To combine the estimates of the four classifiers used for ADI run1, we used the Focal Multiclass Toolkit (Brümmer, 2007), which is written in MATLAB. We ported it to Octave (Eaton and others, 2012), a trivial effort.[5]

The toolkit script calibrates the scores of the four classifiers (the winning class is always the largest, but the scores aren't necessarily in the same range, let alone a probability distribution) then applies logistic regression to fit the various scores to the known correct answers for the development data. The same fitting is then used to combine the scores of the classifiers on the test data.

It accepts files in precisely the format produced by the baseline classifiers, so we modified the word-entropy classifier and the character n-gram entropy classifier to produce files in the same format. We wrote python scripts to convert the output to the expected format for the workshop test runs.

3.6 ADI run2 combination

We used a combination of 4 classifiers on the system level. All four of these classifiers used the same features: character unigrams, bigrams, and trigrams derived from the training data, presented to the software as a feature vector.

Systems are:

- Naive Bayes with multinomial distribution

- SVM with RBF kernel

- Linear logistic regression

- Random forests with 300 trees

All these classifiers were trained on the training dataset part and tested on the development dataset part. The feature vector used was built based on character trigram model combined with word unigram model and word bigram model. The final output was generated by applying voting (max was chosen) on output of the four classifiers for each class label. To build the language models (character trigram, word unigram, and word bigram) to prepare the feature vector and to do the classification process we used the Weka toolkit (Hall et al., 2009), which is written in java.

On the ADI development data, this system gave an accuracy of 52.03%. It is used in ADI run2, where it achieves an accuracy of 32%.

3.7 Acoustic processing: ADI run3

3.7.1 Front-end Processing

Each utterance is divided into short frames by a 20-ms window progressing at a 10-ms frame rate; then 19 Mel-scale Cepstral Coefficients (MFCC) are extracted from each speech frame. Next, Shifted-Delta Cepstra (SDC) with 7-3-1-7 configuration, are computed and appended to the MFCC feature vectors resulting in feature vectors with dimension equal to 68. RASTA filtration is applied to the power spectra. A simple energy-based voice activity detection (VAD) was performed to discard the non-speech frames.

Finally, Cepstral mean and variance normalization (CMVN) was applied on the resulting 68-dimensional feature vectors.

3.7.2 GMM-UBM AID

A Universal Background Model (UBM) GMM (Gaussian Mixture Model) is trained on the acoustic features (68 feature vectors) extracted from all training dataset of all Arabic dialects. The K-means clustering algorithm is used for finding initial parameters of UBM GMM (means, diagonal covariance matrices and weights).

A dialect-dependent GMM is obtained by MAP adaptation (means only) of the UBM using the dialect specific enrollment features. This results in one UBM model and one dialect-dependent model for each of the target dialects. We have tried different numbers of Gaussians: 64, 256 and 2048. Applying these three systems to the ADI development data gives an accuracy of 35.6%, 36% and 40.16%, respectively.

---

[5]See the goal `test.f4` in the file `https://github.com/StephenETaylor/vardial4/blob/master/v17/dialectID/Makefile`

3.7.3 GMM Tokenization

This system is similar to the Phonotactic systems in which a sequence of phones is extracted from the speech waveform using a phone recognizer. In GMM tokenization, the phone recognizer is replaced by a Multi-Dialect Model (MDM), which is a GMM trained on training data of all dialects (same UBM used in the GMM-UBM system described above). For each utterance, a sequence of GMM components (tokens) is extracted by representing each acoustic vector with the GMM component which gives the highest log likelihood.

The n-gram components of the sequence of tokens generated from an utterance U can be represented as a D-dimensional vector p where, D is the number of all n-grams (in our case GMM components), C_j is the jth n-gram and the probability p_j of C_j is estimated using counts of n-grams,

$$p_j = \frac{Count(C_j)}{\sum_i Count(C_i)} \quad (1)$$

where the sum in (1) is performed over all n-grams and $Count(C_j)$ is the number of times the n-gram C_j occurs in the produced sequence of tokens.

Before we apply the SVM, the probabilities of the n-grams are estimated for each utterance. Then, these probabilities are weighted to emphasize the most discriminative components (i.e. those which occur frequently in one dialect and infrequently in others). The n-gram components which are common in most dialects, such as silence or common phones, contain little discriminative information and are de-emphasized. Numerous weighting techniques are available for this purpose, such as the Inverse Document Frequency (IDF) from Information Retrieval (IR) and the Log-Likelihood Ratio (LLR) weighting. The LLR weighting w_j for component C_j is given by:

$$w_j = g_j \left(\frac{1}{P(C_j|all)} \right) \quad (2)$$

where g_j is a function used to smooth and compress the dynamic range (for example, $g_j(x) = \sqrt{x}$, or $g_j(x) = log(x) + 1$). $p(C_j/all)$ is the probability of n-gram component C_j across all dialects. The components which have zero occupancy in all dialects are removed since they do not carry any useful information. A benefit of discarding these non-visited components is that it reduces the feature dimension dramatically, particularly for the high order n-gram system as the dimension of the n-gram increases exponentially $O(M^n)$ with GMM model order (M).

In addition, a feature selection technique is needed to minimize the number of n-gram components by keeping only those which are most discriminative. This is particularly necessary in high order n-gram systems because the dimension is increased exponentially. Consequently, reducing the number of n-gram components decreases the computational cost and the required amount of memory. A powerful iterative feature selection algorithm based on the SVM is proposed by Guyon et al. (2002). This is applied to phone-based language recognition with discriminative keyword selection in Richardson and Campbell (2008), where more details can be found. A similar algorithm is applied on the bigram data of the GMM tokens.

For GMM tokenization, we have used UBM with 256 and 2048 order. Due to resources limitation, bigram and unigram of UBM with 256 components, but only unigram of UBM with 2048 components have been implemented. When applied to the ADI development data, the unigram, bigram of 256 UBM and unigram of 2048 are 42%, 45.15% and 46.85%, respectively.

3.7.4 I-vector based system

I-vectors is a technique introduced in Dehak et al. (2011) for speaker identification. This technique has also been proven to work well in language and dialect identification (Martínez et al., 2011; Hanani et al., 2015). An I-vector classifier is based on a configuration determined by the size of the UBM, the number of factor dimensions for the total variability subspace, as well as the various compensation methods to attenuate within-dialect variability.

Feature vectors of each utterance in the training data are used for adapting means of UBM (which is trained on all available training data) in order to estimate an utterance dependent GMM using eigenvoice adaptation technique.

The eigenvoice adaptation technique assumes that all the pertinent variability is captured by a low rank rectangular, total variability matrix T. Then the GMM supervector (vector created by concatenating all mean vectors from the utterance dependent GMM) for a given utterance can be modeled as follows:

$$M = m + Tx + \epsilon \quad (3)$$

where m is the UBM supervector, the I-vector x is a random vector having a normal distribution $N(0, I)$, and the residual noise term $\epsilon \sim N(0, \Sigma)$ models the variability not captured by the matrix T. In training total variability matrix for dialect recognition, we assume that every utterance for a given dialect is considered a different class. Additional details on the I-vector extraction procedure are described in Dehak et al. (2011).

Linear Discriminant Analysis (LDA) is used for reducing I-vectors dimension. The LDA procedure consists of finding the basis that maximizes the between classes variability while minimizing the intra-dialect variability.

Recently, Gaussian-PLDA has been used to make the I-vector distribution more normal, which improves performance of I-vector system based on standard LDA Bousquet et al. (2012). A Gaussian-PLDA model has been trained on dimensionally-reduced I-vectors of training data, and then used for scoring in our I-vector system. In addition to the text transcription and wav files of each utterance, 400-dimensional I-vectors are provided with the dataset released for VarDial 2017. These I-vectors are extracted using a UBM with 2048 components and Bottleneck features instead of the traditional MFCC and SDC (Shifted Delta Cepstral) acoustic features. More details about the provided I-vectors can be found in Ali et al. (2016). When applied to the ADI development data and with setting LDA dimension to four, the accuracy is 58%.

3.7.5 Acoustic Overall system

The best four acoustic sub-systems: GMM-UBM with 2048 components; bigram of GMM tokenization with 256 components; unigram with 2048 components; and I-vector system, are fused together to get the overall acoustic system, using Focal multi-class linear logistic regression (Brümmer, 2007). The fusion parameters were trained on the ADI Development data. The resulting system was used to classify the ADI testing data (run 3 in the results of ADI task). In order to have an idea how well the overall acoustic system compared with the sub-systems, we divided the development data of each dialect into two parts (nearly equally). The fusion parameters were estimated using one part and applied to the second part and vice versa. In this way, we got the system performance on the development data without overlapping between training and evaluation data. The accuracy of the fused (overall acoustic) sys-

tem on the development data was 61%.

Table 1: Classifier Accuracy on ADI Development Data, Test Sest

Section Described	Dev. Set	Test Set
3.1	0.48	
3.2	0.57	
3.4	0.44	
3.3	0.52	
3.5		0.63
3.6	0.52	0.32
3.7.2	0.40	
3.7.3 (256 bigrams)	0.45	
3.7.3 (2048 unigrams)	0.47	
3.7.4	0.58	
3.7.5	0.61	0.59

4 Results

There were six teams participating in the Arabic Dialect Identification task for 2017; in contrast, there were eighteen for 2016.

Given the reduced field, the rise of our team, AHAQST, from 14th to 4th place, can be ascribed in part to decreased competition! However, all the teams who entered both shared tasks posted scores for 2017 much better than their scores for 2016.

Table 2 shows the best results for each team for the two years.

Table 2: 2017 versus 2016 ADI results

Team	F1 2017	F1 2016
unibuckernel	0.763	0.5131[6]
MAZA	0.717	0.5132[7]
tubasfs	0.697	0.472[8]
ahaqst	0.628	0.426[9]
qcri_mit	0.616	-new-
deepCybErNet	0.574	-new-

In our own case, some of the improvement is due to combining the acoustic and the text data. Table 3 shows our three ADI runs. run1 and run3 both use acoustic data, whereas run2 does not; run3 uses only acoustic data, while run1 uses both kinds.

The Swiss-German task was new this year, and attracted attention from teams who also entered other tasks, as shown in Table 4.

---

[6]Ionescu and Popescu (2016)
[7]Malmasi and Zampieri (2016)
[8]Çöltekin and Rama (2016)
[9]Hanani et al. (2016)

Table 3: Performance of our merged classifiers

Run (Data)	Accuracy	F1 (mic)	F1 (wt'd)
2 (Text)	0.3231	0.3231	0.3137
3 (Acoust.)	0.5932	0.5932	0.5861
1 (both)	0.6287	0.6287	0.628

Table 4: Participation of Swiss-German teams in other tasks

Team	GDI	DSL	ADI
MAZA	1		2
CECL	2	1	
CLUZH	3		
qcri_mit	4		5
unibuckernel	5		1
tubasfs	6	4	3
ahaqst	7		4
Citius_Ixa_Imaxin	8	9	
XAC_Bayesline	9	3	
deepCybErNet	10	11	6

It's interesting to note the imperfect correlations between the tasks, but they are less interesting than the table makes them look, because on the GDI task the accuracy for the best run of all the teams except for the first and the last is within a range of four percentage points.

Table 5 shows our two runs were more widely separated than that, but only the best run for each team contributes to the rank above.

Table 5: AHAQST results on GDI task

Run	Accuracy	F1 (micro)	F1 (weighted)
run1	0.5621	0.5621	0.5484
run2	0.6289	0.6289	0.6143

The top run for the GDI task had an accuracy of 68%, and the bottom an accuraccy of 26%. Omitting the bottom outlier, the weighted F1 scores of the other nine teams are all within 1.35 standard deviations of the mean. The range of values is not nearly so interesting as we see for the ADI task.

We would expect the GDI task to be easier, since only four classes need be distinguished, versus five for the ADI task, but it looks like there are other factors at work. Since only the CLUZH team entered only the GDI task, it may be that other teams devoted less effort to the task, focussing their primary attention on one of the other tasks. Or it may be that there is something else at work.

Since our own classifiers performed much better on our reserved training data, it may be that the Swiss-German corpus is inhomogenous, and that the test data is drawn from a part of the corpus which is different in some way from the training data.

However, a simpler theory for differing performance is a topic bias. If the training sentences are drawn from coherent conversation, one would expect neighboring sentences to have theme words in common. Since both turns of a conversation will normally be entirely in one dialect, rare theme words are trained as dialect-unique, when in fact they may have no relevance to dialect. Of course, even when not dialect-specific, theme words may still be helpful for distinguishing dialect. In the training data, "Zürich" occurs only in instances of the ZH dialect. While someone from Berne may talk about Zürich, Berne is far more likely to come up in their conversation. Similarly a particular restaurant or street is probably indicative of their neighborhood.

5 Discussion

We were pleased to be able to so quickly put into practice some of the ideas we considered for the 2016 workshop. But we ran out of time to implement others. For example, deep learning has fared poorly in the shared tasks in the past, including in our 2016 submission, but considering its success in other machine learning tasks, it seems possible that there is an approach which will fare better, even if the (relatively small by neural-network standards) 1-2 megabyte training sets typical of the two ADI tasks and one GDI task we've seen continue to prevail.

Some of our negative results seem surprising. Why does including larger word n-grams actually hurt recall? At worst it is noise, and there are plenty of other sources of noise.

We'd like to revisit tools which can provide explanations of their behavior. For example, for 2016, one of our classifiers reported that the word

يعني yEny *that is* which is very common in all varieties of Arabic was actually a useful predictor for dialect, because although it is not uncommon in MSA, it is *very* common in all the dialects. The explanation doesn't greatly improve the class discrimination, but it is a nice converational tidbit.

References

Ahmed Ali, Najim Dehak, Patrick Cardinal, Sameer Khurana, Sree Harsha Yella, James Glass, Peter Bell, and Steve Renals. 2016. Automatic dialect detection in Arabic broadcast speech. In *Proceedings of Interspeech 2016*, pages 2934–2938.

Fadi Biadsy, Julia Hirschberg, and Nizar Habash. 2009. Spoken arabic dialect identification using phonotactic modeling. In *Proceedings of the EACL Workshop on Computational Approaches to Semitic Languages*, pages 53–61.

Houda Bouamor, Nizar Habash, and Kemal Oflazer. 2014. A multidialectal parallel corpus of Arabic. In *Proceedings of the Ninth International Conference on Language Resources and Evaluation (LREC14)*. European Language Resources Association (ELRA), May.

Pierre-Michel Bousquet, Anthony Larcher, Driss Matrouf, Jean-François Bonastre, and Oldrich Plchot. 2012. Variance-spectra based normalization for i-vector standard and probabilistic linear discriminant analysis. In *Odyssey: The Speaker and Language Recognition Workshop*, pages 157–164.

Niko Brümmer. 2007. Focal multi-class: Toolkit for evaluation, fusion and calibration of multi-class recognition scores   tutorial and user manual.   downloaded in January 2017 from https://sites.google.com/site/nikobrummer/focalmulticlass.

Çağri Çöltekin and Taraka Rama. 2016. Discriminating Similar Languages with Linear SVMs and Neural Networks. In *Proceedings of the Third Workshop on NLP for Similar Languages, Varieties and Dialects (VarDial3)*, pages 15–24, Osaka, Japan.

Najim Dehak, Patrick J. Kenny, Réda Dehak, Pierre Dumouchel, and Pierre Ouellet. 2011. Front end factor analysis for speaker verification. *IEEE Transactions on Audio, Speech and Language Processing*, 19:788–798.

Eugen Dieth. 1986. *Schwyzertütschi Dialäktschrift: Dieth-Schreibung*. Sauerländer Verlage, Aarau, Switzerland.

John W. Eaton et al. 2012. Gnu octave program for scientific calculation. current version available from http://www.octave.org.

Heba ElFardy and Mona Diab. 2013. Sentence level dialect identification in Arabic. In *Proceedings of the 51st Annual Meeting of the Association for Computational Linguistics (ACL)*, pages 456–461.

Charles A. Ferguson. 1959. Diglossia. *WORD*, 15(2):325–340.

Isabelle Guyon, Jason Weston, Stephen Barnhill, and Vladimir Vapnik. 2002. Gene selection for cancer classification using support vector machines. *Machine Learning*, 46(1-3):389–422.

Mark Hall, Eibe Frank, Geoffrey Holmes, Bernhard Pfahringer, Peter Reutemann, and Ian H. Witten. 2009. The WEKA data mining software: An update. *SIGKDD Explorations*, 11(1).

Abualsoud Hanani, Hanna Basha, Yasmeen Sharaf, and Stephen Taylor. 2015. Palestinian Arabic regional accent recognition. In *The 8th International Conference on Speech Technology and Human-Computer Dialogue*.

Abualsoud Hanani, Aziz Qaroush, and Stephen Taylor. 2016. Classifying ASR Transcriptions According to Arabic Dialect. In *Proceedings of the Third Workshop on NLP for Similar Languages, Varieties and Dialects (VarDial3)*, pages 126–134, Osaka, Japan.

Radu Tudor Ionescu and Marius Popescu. 2016. UnibucKernel: An Approach for Arabic Dialect Identification Based on Multiple String Kernels. In *Proceedings of the Third Workshop on NLP for Similar Languages, Varieties and Dialects (VarDial3)*, pages 135–144, Osaka, Japan.

Thorsten Joachims. 2008. Multi-class support vector machine. downloaded in January 2017 from http://www.cs.cornell.edu/people/tj/svm_light/svm_multiclass.html.

Shervin Malmasi and Marcos Zampieri. 2016. Arabic Dialect Identification in Speech Transcripts. In *Proceedings of the Third Workshop on NLP for Similar Languages, Varieties and Dialects (VarDial3)*, pages 106–113, Osaka, Japan.

Shervin Malmasi, Eshrag Refaee, and Mark Dras. 2015. Arabic dialect identification using a parallel multidialectal corpus. In *Proceedings of the 14th Conference of the Pacific Association for Computational Linguistics (PACLING 2015)*, pages 209–217, Bali, Indonesia, May.

Shervin Malmasi, Marcos Zampieri, Nikola Ljubešić, Preslav Nakov, Ahmed Ali, and Jörg Tiedemann. 2016. Discriminating between similar languages and Arabic dialect identification: A report on the third DSL shared task. In *Proceedings of the 3rd Workshop on Language Technology for Closely Related Languages, Varieties and Dialects (VarDial)*, Osaka, Japan.

David Martínez, Oldrich Plchot, Lukás Burget, Ondrej Glembek, and Pavel Matejka. 2011. Language recognition in i-vectors space. In *Interspeech*, pages 861–864.

Maryam Najafian, Andrea DeMarco, Stephen Cox, and Martin Russell. 2014. Unsupervised model selection for recognition of regional accented speech. In *Proceedings of Interspeech 2014*.

Fred S. Richardson and William M. Campbell. 2008. Language recognition with discriminative keyword selection. In *ICASSP'08*, pages 4145–4148.

Tanja Samardzic, Yves Scherrer, and Elvira Glaser. 2016. ArchiMob–A corpus of spoken Swiss German. In *Proceedings of the Language Resources and Evaluation (LREC)*, pages 4061–4066, Portoroz, Slovenia).

Ioannis Tsochantaridis, Thomas Hofmann, Thorsten Joachims, and Yasemin Altun. 2004. Support vector machine learning for interdependent and structured output spaces. In *Proceedings of the Twenty-first International Conference on Machine Learning*, ICML '04, pages 104–, New York, NY, USA. ACM.

Omar F. Zaidan and Chris Callison-Burch. 2011. The Arabic Online Commentary dataset: An annotated dataset of informal Arabic with high dialectal content. In *Proceedings of ACL*, pages 37–41.

Omar F. Zaidan and Chris Callison-Burch. 2014. Arabic dialect identification. *Computational Linguistics*, 40(1):171–202.

Marcos Zampieri, Shervin Malmasi, Nikola Ljubešić, Preslav Nakov, Ahmed Ali, Jörg Tiedemann, Yves Scherrer, and Noëmi Aepli. 2017. Findings of the VarDial Evaluation Campaign 2017. In *Proceedings of the Fourth Workshop on NLP for Similar Languages, Varieties and Dialects (VarDial)*, Valencia, Spain.

Evaluating HeLI with Non-linear Mappings

Tommi Jauhiainen
University of Helsinki
`@helsinki.fi`

Krister Lindén
University of Helsinki
`@helsinki.fi`

Heidi Jauhiainen
University of Helsinki
`@helsinki.fi`

Abstract

In this paper we describe the non-linear mappings we used with the Helsinki language identification method, HeLI, in the 4th edition of the Discriminating between Similar Languages (DSL) shared task, which was organized as part of the VarDial 2017 workshop. Our SUKI team participated in the closed track together with 10 other teams. Our system reached the 7th position in the track. We describe the HeLI method and the non-linear mappings in mathematical notation. The HeLI method uses a probabilistic model with character n-grams and word-based back-off. We also describe our trials using the non-linear mappings instead of relative frequencies and we present statistics about the back-off function of the HeLI method.

1 Introduction

The 4th edition of the Discriminating between Similar Languages (DSL) shared task (Zampieri et al., 2017) was divided into an open and a closed track. In the closed track the participants were allowed to use only the training data provided by the organizers, whereas in the open track the participants could use any data source they had at their disposal. This year we did not participate in the open track, so we did not use any additional sources for training and development. The creation of the earlier DSL corpora has been described by Tan et al. (2014). This year's training data consisted of 18,000 lines of text, excerpts of journalistic texts, for each of the 14 languages. The corresponding development set had 2,000 lines of text for each language. The task had a language selection comparable to the 1st (Zampieri et al., 2014), 2nd (Zampieri et al.,

2015), and 3rd (Malmasi et al., 2016) editions of the shared task. The languages and varieties are listed in Table 1. The differences from the previous year's shared task were the inclusion of Persian and Dari languages, as well as replacing the Mexican Spanish variety with Peruvian Spanish.

Country	Language
Bosnia and Herzegovina	Bosnian
Croatia	Croatian
Serbia	Serbian
Malaysia	Malay
Indonesia	Indonesian
Iran	Persian
Afghanistan	Dari
Canada	French
France	French
Brazil	Portuguese
Portugal	Portuguese
Argentina	Spanish
Spain	Spanish
Peru	Spanish

Table 1: The languages and varieties of the 4th edition of the Discriminating between Similar Languages (DSL) shared task.

For the 4th edition, we were interested in modifying the HeLI method and use the TF-IDF scores and some non-linear mappings instead of relative frequencies. We were inspired by the successful use of TF-IDF scores by Barbaresi (2016). He was able to significantly boost the accuracy of his identifier after the 3rd edition of the shared task by using the TF-IDF scores. Earlier, Brown (2014) managed to boost several language identification methods using non-linear mappings.

2 Related Work

Automatic language identification of digital text has been researched for more than 50 years. The first article on the subject was written by Mustonen (1965), who used multiple discriminant anal-

Proceedings of the Fourth Workshop on NLP for Similar Languages, Varieties and Dialects, pages 102–108,
Valencia, Spain, April 3, 2017. ©2017 Association for Computational Linguistics

ysis to distinguish between Finnish, English and Swedish. For more of the history of automatic language identification the reader is suggested to take a look at the literature review chapter of Marco Lui's doctoral thesis (Lui, 2014).

There has also been research directly involving the language groups present in this year's shared task. Automatic identification of South-Slavic languages has been researched by Ljubešic et al. (2007), Tiedemann and Ljubešic (2012), Ljubešic and Kranjcic (2014), and Ljubešic and Kranjcic (2015). Brown (2012) presented confusion matrices for the languages of the former Yugoslavia (including Bosnian and Croatian) as well as for Indo-Iranian languages (including Western and Eastern Farsi). Chew et al. (2009) experimented distinguishing between Dari and Farsi, as well as Malay and Indonesian, among others. Distinguishing between Malay and Indonesian was studied by Ranaivo-Malançon (2006). Automatic identification of French dialects was studied by Zampieri et al. (2012) and Zampieri (2013). Discriminating between Portuguese varieties was studied by Zampieri and Gebre (2012), whereas Zampieri et al. (2012), Zampieri (2013), Zampieri et al. (2013), and Maier and Gómez-Rodríguez (2014) researched language variety identification between Spanish dialects.

The system description articles provided for the previous shared tasks are all relevant and references to them are provided by Zampieri et al. (2014), Zampieri et al. (2015), and Malmasi et al. (2016). Detailed analysis of the first two shared tasks was done by Goutte et al. (2016).

The language identification method used by the system presented in this article, HeLI, was first introduced by Jauhiainen (2010) and it was also described in the proceedings of the 2nd edition of the DSL shared task (Jauhiainen et al., 2015). The complete description of the method was first presented in the proceedings of the 3rd VarDial workshop (Jauhiainen et al., 2016). The language identifier tool using the HeLI method is available as open source from GitHub[1]. The non-linear mappings evaluated in this article were previously tested with several language identifiers by Brown (2014).

[1]https://github.com/tosaja/HeLI

3 Methodology

In this paper, we re-present most of the description of the HeLI method from the last year's system description paper (Jauhiainen et al., 2016). We leave out the mathematical description of the words as features, as they were not used in the submitted runs. We tried several combinations of words, lowercased words, n-grams, and lowercased n-grams with the development set. The best results of these trials can be seen in Table 2. In the table, "l. n_{max}" refers to the maximum number of lowercased n-grams, "c. n_{max}" to the n-grams with also capital letters, "l. w." to lowercased words, and "c. w." to words with original capitalization. We did similar tests with different combinations of the language models when choosing the models to be used with the loglike-function described later.

rec.	l. n_{max}	c. n_{max}	l. w.	c. w.
0.9107	0	8	no	no
0.9107	8	8	no	no
0.9099	0	8	yes	no
0.9098	8	0	yes	yes
0.9098	8	8	yes	yes
0.9092	0	8	no	yes
0.9060	8	8	yes	no
0.9059	8	0	yes	no
0.9052	8	0	no	no

Table 2: Testing the different combinations of language models on the development set.

3.1 On Notation

A corpus C is a finite sequence, $u_1, ..., u_l$, of individual tokens u_i, which may be words or characters. The total count of all individual tokens u in the corpus C is denoted by l_C. A feature f is some countable characteristic of the corpus C. When referring to all features F in a corpus C, we use C^F and the count of all features is denoted by l_{C^F}. The count of a feature f in the corpus C is referred to as $c(C, f)$. An n-gram is a feature which consists of a sequence of n individual tokens. An n-gram of the length n starting at position i in a corpus is denoted u_i^n. If $n = 1$, u is an individual token. When referring to all n-grams of length n in a corpus C, we use C^n and the count of all such n-grams is denoted by l_{C^n}. The count of an n-gram u in a corpus C is referred to as $c(C, u)$ and is defined by Equation 1.

$$c(C, u) = \sum_{i=1}^{l_C+1-n} \begin{cases} 1 & \text{, if } u = u_i^n \\ 0 & \text{, otherwise} \end{cases} \qquad (1)$$

The set of languages is G, and l_G denotes the number of languages. A corpus C in language g is denoted by C_g. A language model O based on C_g is denoted by $O(C_g)$. The features given values by the model $O(C_g)$ are the domain $dom(O(C_g))$ of the model. In a language model, a value v for the feature f is denoted by $v_{C_g}(f)$. For each potential language g of a corpus C in an unknown language, a resulting score $R_g(C)$ is calculated. A corpus in an unknown language is also referred to as a mystery text.

3.2 HeLI Method

The goal is to correctly guess the language $g \in G$ in which the monolingual mystery text M has been written, when all languages in the set G are known to the language identifier. In the method, each language $g \in G$ is represented by several different language models based on character n-grams from one to n_{max}. Only one of the language models is used for every word t found in the mystery text M. The model used is selected by its applicability to the word t under scrutiny. If we are unable to apply the n-grams of the size n_{max}, we back off to lower order n-grams. We continue backing off until character unigrams, if needed.

A development set is used for finding the best values for the parameters of the method. The three parameters are the maximum length of the used character n-grams (n_{max}), the maximum number of features to be included in the language models (cut-off c), and the penalty value for those languages where the features being used are absent (penalty p). The penalty value has a smoothing effect in that it transfers some of the probability mass to unseen features in the language models.

3.2.1 Creating the Language Models

The training data is tokenized into words using non-alphabetic and non-ideographic characters as delimiters. The relative frequencies of character n-grams from 1 to n_{max} are calculated inside the words, so that the preceding and the following space-characters are included. The n-grams are overlapping, so that for example a word with three characters includes three character trigrams.

The c most common n-grams of each length in the corpus of a language are included in the language models for that language. We estimate the probabilities using relative frequencies of the character n-grams in the language models, using only the relative frequencies of the retained to-

kens. Then we transform those frequencies into scores using 10-based logarithms.

The derived corpus containing only the n-grams retained in the language models is called C'^n. The domain $dom(O(C'^n))$ is the set of all character n-grams of length n found in the models of all languages $g \in G$. The values $v'_{C'^n_g}(u)$ are calculated similarly for all n-grams $u \in dom(O(C'^n))$ for each language g, as shown in Equation 2

$$v'_{C'^n_g}(u) = \begin{cases} -\log_{10}\left(v_{C_g}(u)\right) & \text{, if } c(C'^n_g, u) > 0 \\ p & \text{, if } c(C'^n_g, u) = 0 \end{cases} \quad (2)$$

In the first run of the shared task we used relative frequencies of n-grams as values $v_{C_g}(u)$. They are calculated for each language g, as in Equation 3

$$v_{C_g}(u) = \frac{c(C'^n_g, u)}{l_{C'^n_g}} \quad (3)$$

where $c(C'^n_g, u)$ is the number of n-grams u found in the derived corpus of the language g and $l_{C'^n_g}$ is the total number of the n-grams of length n in the derived corpus of language g.

Brown (2014) experimented with five language identifiers using two non-linear mappings, the gamma and the loglike functions. We tested applying the two non-linear mappings to the relative frequencies. Both functions have a variable (*gamma* or *tau*), the value of which has to be empirically found using the development set.

The value $v_{C_g}(u)$ using the gamma function is calculated as in Equation 4

$$v_{C_g}(u) = \left(\frac{c(C'^n_g, u)}{l_{C'^n_g}}\right)^\gamma \quad (4)$$

The value $v_{C_g}(u)$ using the loglike function is calculated as in Equation 5

$$v_{C_g}(u) = \frac{\log(1 + 10^\tau \frac{c(C'^n_g, u)}{l_{C'^n_g}})}{\log(1 + 10^\tau)} \quad (5)$$

3.2.2 Scoring N-grams in the Mystery Text

When using n-grams, the word t is split into overlapping n-grams of characters u_i^n, where $i = 1, ..., l_t + 1 - n$, of the length n. Each of the n-grams u_i^n is then scored separately for each language g.

If the n-gram u_i^n is found in $dom(O(C'^n_g))$, the values in the models are used. If the n-gram u_i^n

is not found in any of the models, it is simply discarded. We define the function $d_g(t, n)$ for counting n-grams in t found in a model in Equation 6.

$$d_g(t, n) = \sum_{i=1}^{l_t+1-n} \begin{cases} 1 & , \text{if } u_i^n \in dom(O(C'^n)) \\ 0 & , \text{otherwise} \end{cases} \quad (6)$$

When all the n-grams of the size n in the word t have been processed, the word gets the value of the average of the scored n-grams u_i^n for each language, as in Equation 7

$$v_g(t, n) = \begin{cases} \frac{1}{d_g(t,n)} \sum_{i=1}^{l_t+1-n} v'_{C'^n_g}(u_i^n) & , \text{if } d_g(t, n) > 0 \\ v_g(t, n-1) & , \text{otherwise} \end{cases} \quad (7)$$

where $d_g(t, n)$ is the number of n-grams u_i^n found in the domain $dom(O(C'^n_g))$. If all of the n-grams of the size n were discarded, $d_g(t, n) = 0$, the language identifier backs off to using n-grams of the size $n - 1$. If no values are found even for unigrams, a word gets the penalty value p for every language, as in Equation 8.

$$v_g(t, 0) = p \quad (8)$$

3.2.3 Language Identification

The mystery text is tokenized into words using the non-alphabetic and non-ideographic characters as delimiters. After this, a score $v_g(t)$ is calculated for each word t in the mystery text for each language g. If the length of the word l_t is at least $n_{max} - 2$, the language identifier uses character n-grams of the length n_{max}. In case the word t is shorter than $n_{max} - 2$ characters, $n = l_t + 2$.

The whole mystery text M gets the score $R_g(M)$ equal to the average of the scores of the words $v_g(t)$ for each language g, as in Equation 9

$$R_g(M) = \frac{\sum_{i=1}^{l_{T(M)}} v_g(t_i)}{l_{T(M)}} \quad (9)$$

where $T(M)$ is the sequence of words and $l_{T(M)}$ is the number of words in the mystery text M. Since we are using negative logarithms of probabilities, the language having the lowest score is returned as the language with the maximum probability for the mystery text.

4 Experiments

In order to find the best possible parameters (n_{max}, c, and p), we applied a simple form of the greedy algorithm using the development set. The best recall for the original HeLI method, 0.9105, was reached using $n_{max} = 8$, $c = 170,000$, and p of 6.6.

4.1 TF-IDF

We made a small experiment trying to adapt the HeLI method to use TF-IDF scores (product of term frequency and inverse document frequency). TF-IDF scores were successfully used to boost the performance of a Naive Bayes identifier by Barbaresi (2016). Also Malmasi et al. (2015) used character n-grams from one to four, which were weighted with TF-IDF. There are several variations of TF-IDF weighting scheme and Malmasi et al. (2015) do not specify whether they used the basic formula or not. We calculated the TF-IDF as in Equation 10

$$v_{C_g}(u) = c(C_g, u) log \frac{l_G}{df(C_G, u)} \quad (10)$$

where $df()$ is defined as in Equation 11. Let l_G be the number of languages in a language segmented corpus C_G. We define the number of languages in which an n-gram u appears as the document frequency df of u as

$$df(C_G, u) = \sum_{g=1}^{l_G} \begin{cases} 1 & , \text{if } c(C_g, u) > 0 \\ 0 & , \text{otherwise} \end{cases} \quad (11)$$

We used the $v_{C_g}(u)$ values from Equation 10 instead of relative frequencies in Equation 2, but we were unable to come even close to the accuracy of our original method. We did not submit a run using the TF-IDF weighting.

4.2 Gamma Function

Using the gamma function in his experiments, Brown (2014) was able to reduce the error rate of his own language identifier by 83.9% with 1366 languages and 76.7% with 781 languages. We tested using the gamma function with the development set, which did not manage to improve our results. It seems that the penalty value p of the HeLI method and the γ variable have at least partly the same effect. If we fix one of the values we are able to reach almost or exactly the same results by varying the other. Table 3 shows some of the results on the development set. When using γ of 1.0 the method is identical to the original HeLI method. As there were no improvements on the results at all, we decided not to submit a run using the gamma function.

4.3 Loglike Function

Table 4 shows some of the results on the development set when using the loglike function, $n_{max} =$

Recall	Penalty p	Gamma γ
0.9105	*3.3*	*0.5*
0.9102	4.6	0.7
0.9103	5.3	0.8
0.9105	**6.6**	**1.0**
0.9104	7.9	1.2
0.9104	8.6	1.3
0.9105	*9.9*	*1.5*
0.9104	11.2	1.7

Table 3: Testing the gamma on the development set.

8, and c = 170,000. There seemed to be a local optimum at around τ = 2.9, so we experimented with a bit different n_{max} and c around it as well. The best recall of 0.9109 was provided by n_{max} = 7, c = 180,000, and τ = 3.0. The loglike funtion seemed to make a tiny (about half a percent) improvement on the error rate when using the development set. Using the loglike function, Brown (2014) was able to reduce the errors made by his own identifier by 83.8% with 1366 languages and 76.7% with 781 languages. Even though our error reduction was far from Brown's numbers, we still decided to submit a second run using the loglike function.

Recall	Penalty p	Tau τ
0.9104	6.5	0
0.9103	5.2	2.0
0.9104	4.7	2.7
0.9107	4.6	2.8
0.9106	4.5	2.9
0.9107	4.4	3.0
0.9104	4.3	3.2
0.9101	4.1	3.5
0.9075	3.0	4.5
0.9058	1.2	6.5

Table 4: Testing the loglike function on the development set.

5 Results

Our SUKI team submitted two runs for the closed track. For both of the runs we used all of the training and the development data to create the language models. The first run was submitted using the relative frequencies as in Equation 3. In the second run, we used the loglike function as in Equation 5. The results and the parameters for each run can be seen in Tables 5 and 6. We have also included the results and the name of the winning team CECL (Bestgen, 2017).

For the 3rd edition of the task, we used the HeLI-method without any modifications and the

Run	Accuracy	F1 (macro)
CECL run1	0.9274	0.9271
SUKI run 2	0.9099	0.9097
SUKI run 1	0.9054	0.9051

Table 5: Results for the closed training.

Run	n_{max}	c	p
SUKI run 1	8	170,000	6.6
SUKI run 2	7	180,000	4.7

Table 6: Parameters for the closed training.

first run of the 4th edition was run with an identical system. This year the Peruvian Spanish replaced the Mexican Spanish. It seems that it is more easily distinguished, at least with the HeLI method, from the Argentinian or Peninsular varieties, as the average F1-score for the Spanish varieties rose from last year's 0.80 to 0.86. Also the inclusion of the languages using the Arabic script helped to raise the overall average F1-score from 0.888 to 0.905.

6 Discussion

After this year's shared task we also looked into the backoff function of the HeLI method and calculated how often each of the n-gram lengths were used with the test set. These calculations can be seen in Table 7.

Number of words	n
176,635	8
57,252	7
56,361	6
56,243	5
88,054	4
27,975	3
3	2
0	1

Table 7: Number of words identified with each length of n-gram.

Table 8 shows the number of words of each length after removing non-alphabetic characters and adding extra space before and after the word. When comparing the two tables it seems that the backoff function was used only with a small fraction of words.

7 Conclusions

Using the loglike function with the actual test set improved the result much more than with the development set. The reduction on the error rate of the accuracy was 4.8%, which was around ten

Number of words	length
60,108	¿10
33,243	10
41,731	9
46,448	8
56,229	7
54,611	6
54,912	5
87,385	4
27,856	3

Table 8: Number of words of each length.

times higher than with the development set. In the future, we will be making further experiments trying to introduce discriminating features into the HeLI method. As it is now, it is still a generative method, not relying on finding discriminating features between languages.

Acknowledgments

We would like to thank Kimmo Koskenniemi for many valuable discussions and comments. This research was made possible by funding from the Kone Foundation Language Programme.

References

Adrien Barbaresi. 2016. An Unsupervised Morphological Criterion for Discriminating Similar Languages. In *Proceedings of the Third Workshop on NLP for Similar Languages, Varieties and Dialects (VarDial3)*, pages 212–220, Osaka, Japan.

Yves Bestgen. 2017. Improving the character ngram model for the dsl task with bm25 weighting and less frequently used feature sets. In *Proceedings of the 4th VarDial Workshop*, Valencia, Spain.

Ralf D. Brown. 2012. Finding and identifying text in 900+ languages. *Digital Investigation*, 9:S34–S43.

Ralf D. Brown. 2014. Non-linear mapping for improved identification of 1300+ languages. In *Proceedings of the 2014 Conference on Empirical Methods in Natural Language Processing (EMNLP 2014)*, pages 627–632, Doha, Qatar.

Yew Choong Chew, Yoshiki Mikami, Chandrajith Ashuboda Marasinghe, and S. Turrance Nandasara. 2009. Optimizing n-gram order of an n-gram based language identification algorithm for 68 written languages. *International Journal on Advances in ICT for Emerging Regions (ICTer)*, 2(2):21–28.

Cyril Goutte, Serge Léger, Shervin Malmasi, and Marcos Zampieri. 2016. Discriminating Similar Languages: Evaluations and Explorations. In *Proceedings of the 10th International Conference on Language Resources and Evaluation (LREC 2016)*.

Tommi Jauhiainen, Heidi Jauhiainen, and Krister Lindén. 2015. Discriminating similar languages with token-based backoff. In *Proceedings of the Joint Workshop on Language Technology for Closely Related Languages, Varieties and Dialects (LT4VarDial)*, pages 44–51, Hissar, Bulgaria.

Tommi Jauhiainen, Krister Lindén, and Heidi Jauhiainen. 2016. HeLI, a Word-Based Backoff Method for Language Identification. In *Proceedings of the Third Workshop on NLP for Similar Languages, Varieties and Dialects (VarDial3)*, pages 153–162, Osaka, Japan.

Tommi Jauhiainen. 2010. Tekstin kielen automaattinen tunnistaminen. Master's thesis, University of Helsinki, Helsinki, Finland.

Nikola Ljubešic and Denis Kranjcic. 2014. Discriminating between very similar languages among twitter users. In *Proceedings of the Ninth Language Technologies Conference*, pages 90–94, Ljubljana, Slovenia.

Nikola Ljubešic and Denis Kranjcic. 2015. Discriminating between closely related languages on twitter. *Informatica*, 39.

Nikola Ljubešic, Nives Mikelic, and Damir Boras. 2007. Language indentification: How to distinguish similar languages? In *Information Technology Interfaces, 2007. ITI 2007. 29th International Conference on*, pages 541–546, Cavtat/Dubrovnik, Croatia.

Marco Lui. 2014. *Generalized language identification*. Ph.D. thesis, The University of Melbourne.

Wolfgang Maier and Carlos Gómez-Rodríguez. 2014. Language variety identification in spanish tweets. In *Proceedings of the EMNLP'2014 Workshop: Language Technology for Closely Related Languages and Language Variants (LT4CloseLang 2014)*, pages 25–35, Doha, Qatar.

Shervin Malmasi, Eshrag Refaee, and Mark Dras. 2015. Arabic dialect identification using a parallel multidialectal corpus. In *Proceedings of the 14th Conference of the Pacific Association for Computational Linguistics, PACLING'15*, pages 209–217, Bali, Indonesia.

Shervin Malmasi, Marcos Zampieri, Nikola Ljubešić, Preslav Nakov, Ahmed Ali, and Jörg Tiedemann. 2016. Discriminating between similar languages and arabic dialect identification: A report on the third dsl shared task. In *Proceedings of the 3rd Workshop on Language Technology for Closely Related Languages, Varieties and Dialects (VarDial)*, Osaka, Japan.

Seppo Mustonen. 1965. Multiple discriminant analysis in linguistic problems. *Statistical Methods in Linguistics*, 4:37–44.

Bali Ranaivo-Malançon. 2006. Automatic identification of close languages–case study: Malay and indonesian. *ECTI Transaction on Computer and Information Technology*, 2(2):126–133.

Liling Tan, Marcos Zampieri, Nikola Ljubešic, and Jörg Tiedemann. 2014. Merging comparable data sources for the discrimination of similar languages: The dsl corpus collection. In *Proceedings of the 7th Workshop on Building and Using Comparable Corpora*, Reykjavik.

Jörg Tiedemann and Nikola Ljubešic. 2012. Efficient discrimination between closely related languages. In *Proceedings of COLING 2012*, pages 2619–2634, Mumbai.

Marcos Zampieri and Binyam Gebrekidan Gebre. 2012. Automatic identification of language varieties: The case of portuguese. In *11th Conference on Natural Language Processing (KONVENS) - Empirical Methods in Natural Language Processing - Proceedings of the Conference on Natural Language Processing 2012*, pages 233–237, Vienna.

Marcos Zampieri, Binyam Gebrekidan Gebre, and Sascha Diwersy. 2012. Classifying pluricentric languages: Extending the monolingual model. In *Proceedings of the Fourth Swedish Language Technlogy Conference (SLTC2012)*, pages 79–80, Lund.

Marcos Zampieri, Binyam Gebrekidan Gebre, and Sascha Diwersy. 2013. N-gram language models and pos distribution for the identification of spanish varieties. In *Actes de TALN'2013 : 20e conférence sur le Traitement Automatique des Langues Naturelles*, pages 580–587, Sables d'Olonne.

Marcos Zampieri, Liling Tan, Nikola Ljubešić, and Jörg Tiedemann. 2014. A report on the dsl shared task 2014. In *Proceedings of the First Workshop on Applying NLP Tools to Similar Languages, Varieties and Dialects (VarDial)*, pages 58–67, Dublin, Ireland.

Marcos Zampieri, Liling Tan, Nikola Ljubešić, Jörg Tiedemann, and Preslav Nakov. 2015. Overview of the dsl shared task 2015. In *Proceedings of the Joint Workshop on Language Technology for Closely Related Languages, Varieties and Dialects (LT4VarDial)*, pages 1–9, Hissar, Bulgaria.

Marcos Zampieri, Shervin Malmasi, Nikola Ljubešić, Preslav Nakov, Ahmed Ali, Jörg Tiedemann, Yves Scherrer, and Noëmi Aepli. 2017. Findings of the VarDial Evaluation Campaign 2017. In *Proceedings of the Fourth Workshop on NLP for Similar Languages, Varieties and Dialects (VarDial)*, Valencia, Spain.

Marcos Zampieri. 2013. Using bag-of-words to distinguish similar languages: How efficient are they? In *Computational Intelligence and Informatics (CINTI), 2013 IEEE 14th International Symposium on*, pages 37–41, Budapest.

A Perplexity-Based Method for Similar Languages Discrimination

Pablo Gamallo
CiTIUS
Univ. of Santiago de Compostela
Galiza
pablo.gamallo@usc.es

Jose Ramom Pichel
imaxin|software,
Santiago de Compostela,
Galiza
jramompichel@imaxin.com

Iñaki Alegria
IXA group
Univ. of the Basque Country
UPV/EHU
i.alegria@ehu.eus

Abstract

This article describes the system submitted by the Citius_Ixa_Imaxin team to the VarDial 2017 (DSL and GDI tasks). The strategy underlying our system is based on a language distance computed by means of model perplexity. The best model configuration we have tested is a voting system making use of several n-grams models of both words and characters, even if word unigrams turned out to be a very competitive model with reasonable results in the tasks we have participated. An error analysis has been performed in which we identified many test examples with no linguistic evidences to distinguish among the variants.

1 Introduction

Language detection is not a solved problem if the task is applied to the identification of similar languages and varieties. Closely related languages or language varieties are much more difficult to identify and separate than languages belonging to different linguistic families. In this article, we describe the system submitted by the Citius_Ixa_Imaxin team to the VarDial 2017. We have participated in two task: Discriminating between Similar Languages (DSL) and German Dialect Identification (GDI). The strategy underlying our system is based on comparing language models using perplexity. Perplexity is defined as the inverse probability of the test text given the model. Most of the best systems for language identification use probability-based metrics with n-grams models. This report paper (Zampieri et al., 2017) describes the shared task and compares all the presented systems.

DSL is focused on discriminating between similar languages and national language varieties, including six different groups of related languages or language varieties:

- Bosnian, Croatian, and Serbian

- Malay and Indonesian

- Persian and Dari

- Canadian and Hexagonal French

- Argentine, Peninsular, and Peruvian Spanish

- Brazilian and European Portuguese

The objective of GDI is the identification of German varieties (four Swiss German dialect areas: Basel, Bern, Lucerne, Zurich) based on speech transcripts.

Analysis about previous results on the two scenarios can be found in Goutte et al. (2016) and Malmasi et al. (2015). The latter is focused on Arabic varieties but the scenario is similar to the GDI task.

2 Related Work

2.1 Language Identification and Similar Languages

Two specific tasks for language identification have attracted a lot of research attention in recent years, namely discriminating among closely related languages (Malmasi et al., 2016) and language detection on noisy short texts such as tweets (Zubiaga et al., 2015).

The Discriminating between Similar Languages (DSL) workshop (Zampieri et al., 2014; Zampieri et al., 2015; Goutte et al., 2016) is a shared task where participants are asked to train systems to discriminate between similar languages, language

Proceedings of the Fourth Workshop on NLP for Similar Languages, Varieties and Dialects, pages 109–114,
Valencia, Spain, April 3, 2017. ©2017 Association for Computational Linguistics

varieties, and dialects. In the three editions organized so far, most of the best systems were based on models built with high-order character n-grams ($>= 5$) using traditional supervised learning methods such as SVMS, logistic regression, or Bayesian classifiers. By contrast, deep learning approaches based on neural algorithms did not perform very well (Bjerva, 2016).

In our previous participation (Gamallo et al., 2016) in the DSL 2016 shared task we presented two very basic systems: classification with ranked dictionaries and Naive Bayes classifiers. The results showed that ranking dictionaries are more sound and stable across different domains while basic Bayesian models perform reasonably well on in-domain datasets, but their performance drops when they are applied on out-of-domain texts. We also observed that basic n-gram models of characters and words work pretty well even if they are used with simple learning systems. In the current participation we decided to use basic n-grams with a very intuitive strategy: to measure the distance between languages on the basis of the perplexity of their models.

2.2 Perplexity

The most widely-used evaluation metric for language models is the perplexity of test data. In language modeling, perplexity is frequently used as a quality measure for language models built with n-grams extracted from text corpora (Chen and Goodman, 1996; Sennrich, 2012). It has also been used in very specific tasks, such as to classify between formal and colloquial tweets (González, 2015).

3 Methodology

Our method is based on perplexity. Perplexity is a measure of how well a model fits the test data. More formally, the perplexity (called PP for short) of a language model on a test set is the inverse probability of the test set. For a test set of sequences of characters $CH = ch_1, ch_2, ..., ch_n$ and a language model LM with n-gram probabilities $P(\cdot)$ estimated on a training set, the perplexity PP of CH given a character-based n-gram model LM is computed as follows:

$$PP(CH, LM) = \sqrt[n]{\prod_{i}^{n} \frac{1}{P(ch_i|ch_1^{i-1})}} \quad (1)$$

where n-gram probabilities $P(\cdot)$ are defined in this way:

$$P(ch_n|ch_1^{n-1}) = \frac{C(ch_1^{n-1}ch_n)}{C(ch_1^{n-1})} \quad (2)$$

Equation 2 estimates the n-gram probability by dividing the observed frequency (C) of a particular sequence of characters by the observed frequency of the prefix, where the prefix stands for the same sequence without the last character. To take into account unseen n-grams, we use a smoothing technique based on linear interpolation.

A perplexity-based distance between two languages is defined by comparing the n-grams of a text in one language with the n-gram model trained for the other language. Then, the perplexity of the test text CH in language $L2$, given the language model LM of language $L1$, can be used to define the distance, $Dist_{perp}$, between $L1$ and $L2$:

$$Dist_{perp}(L1, L2) = PP(CH_{L2}, LM_{L1}) \quad (3)$$

The lower the perplexity of CH_{L2} given LM_{L1}, the lower the distance between languages $L1$ and $L2$. The distance $Dist_{perp}$ is an asymmetric measure.

In order to apply this measure to language identification given a test text, we compute the perplexity-based distance for all the language models and the test text, and the closest model is selected.

4 Experiments

4.1 Runs and Data

In the DSL task we have taken part in both tracks: closed and open. The open model was trained with the datasets released in previous DSL tasks (Malmasi et al., 2016; Zampieri et al., 2015; Zampieri et al., 2014).

We prepared three runs for each task. All of them are based on perplexity but using different model configuration:

- Run1 uses perplexity with a voting system over 6 n-gram models: 1-grams, 2-grams and 3-grams of words, and 5-grams, 6-grams and 7-grams of characters. We observed that short n-grams of words clearly outperform longer word n-grams, while long n-grams of

Run	Accuracy	F1 (micro)	F1 (macro)	F1 (weighted)
run1	0.903	0.903	0.9025	0.9025
run2	0.9016	0.9016	0.9013	0.9013
run3	0.8791	0.8791	0.8787	0.8787

Table 1: Results for the DSL task (closed).

Run	Accuracy	F1 (micro)	F1 (macro)	F1 (weighted)
run1	0.9028	0.9028	0.9016	0.9016
run2	0.9069	0.9069	0.9065	0.9065
run3	0.8788	0.8788	0.8773	0.8773

Table 2: Results for the DSL task (open).

characters perform better than shorter ones. In previous experiments, this system configuration reached a similar score to the best system in the DSL Task 2016, namely 0.8926 accuracy, very close to 0.8938 reached by the best system in task A (Çöltekin and Rama, 2016).

- Run2 uses perplexity with just 1-grams of words. In the development tests, we observed that this simple model is very stable over different situations and tasks.

- Run3 also uses perplexity but with 7-grams of characters, since long n-grams of characters tend to perform better than short ones.

4.2 Results

In the first task (Discriminating between Similar Languages) we submitted systems generated with both closed and open training.

4.2.1 DSL Closed

The results obtained by our runs in the DSL task are shown in Table 1. The random baseline (14 classes) is 0.071 and the references from the best system in 2016 is 0.8938 accuracy. However, it is worth noticing that 2016 and 2017 DSL tasks are not comparable because the varieties proposed for the two shared tasks are not exactly the same.

The table shows that best results are obtained using the two first configurations: Run1 and Run2. Let us notice that the second one reaches good results even if it is based on a very simple models (just words unigrams). This is also true for the GDI task (see below in the Discussion section).

Our best run in task DSL achieved 0.903 accuracy (9th position out of 11 systems) while the best system in this task reached 0.927.

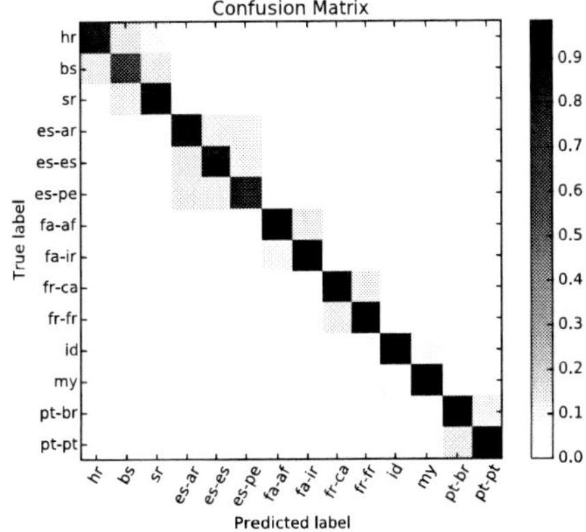

Figure 1: Confusion matrix: DSL run2

The confusion matrix for Run2 is shown in Figure 1. Bosnian and Peruvian Spanish seem to be the most difficult languages/varieties to be distinguished.

Comparing confusion matrices for Spanish variants between Run1 and Run2, we can observe that although the results are similar in both cases, they guess and fail in a different way (Table 3). So, they seem to be quite complementary strategies.

4.3 DSL Open Training

We tried to improve the results by adding more training data from previous shared tasks. Table 2 shows that the simplest configuration (Run2) gets better results than in the closed training task, but only a slight improvement (0.5 %) was obtained. No comparison can be made with other systems because the other participants did not take part in this track.

	run1			**run2**		
	es-ar	es-es	es-pe	es-ar	es-es	es-pe
es-ar	892	67	36	861	81	56
es-es	88	871	35	78	870	48
es-pe	111	126	763	87	104	809

Table 3: Confusion matrices in run1 and run2 for variants of Spanish

Run	Accuracy	F1 (micro)	F1 (macro)	F1 (weighted)
run1	0.6262	0.6262	0.6118	0.6108
run2	0.6308	0.6308	0.613	0.612
run3	0.5921	0.5921	0.5785	0.5774

Table 4: Results for the GDI task.

4.4 GDI

The results for the GDI task are shown in Table 4. The majority class baseline is 0.258 and there were no previous results to compare with. However, the best results for Arabic dialects in VarDial 2016 (in similar conditions to GDI) were 0.513 (F-score).

The results are much lower than in DSL task. Several factors which can influence these results are the following:

- the GDI task has unbalanced test sets,

- the data are from speech transcription,

- the task itself is more difficult given the strong similarity of the varieties.

In this task, our best configuration is Run2, which, in spite of its simple model, improves the voting-based system. The confusion matrix for Run2 (see Figure 2) shows that the scores obtained for Lucerne dialect are very poor.

Run2 achieved 0.630 accuracy (8th position out of 10 systems) while the best system in this task reached 0.680. It is worth noticing that only two systems also involved in DSL 2016 task improve our results in GDI.

5 Discussion

The results show that our system, despite its simplicity, performs reasonably well. For the DSL task 2016 we obtained the second best performance even if the results are more discrete in 2017; and for the GDI task the results are better than the best score in 2016 for the Arabic Dialectal Identification task.

It can be underlined that the configuration of our run2 is very simple (just unigrams of words) and

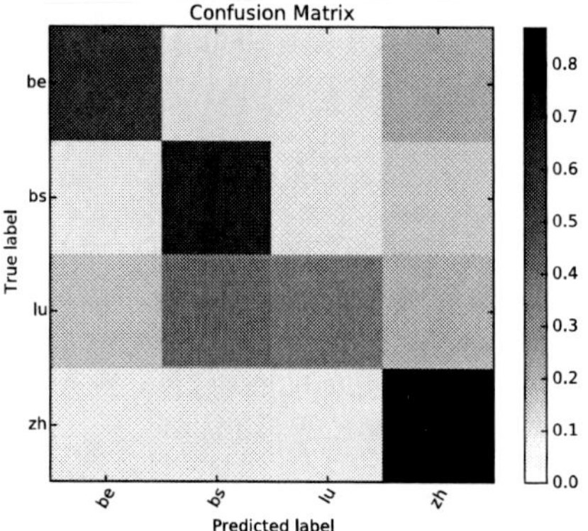

Figure 2: confusion matrix: GDI run2

results using perplexity are very competitive. It could be considered as a baseline for the future.

In order to find key elements for further improvement, we decided to carry out an analysis of errors on variants that we know quite well (variants of Spanish).

5.1 Analysis of errors in Spanish

From the list of errors among Spanish texts extracted from the evaluation carried on the development corpus we selected randomly 50 cases.

We decided to classify these texts on the following categories:

- Not distinguishable: the dialect is impossible or very difficult to classify. There are no specific language features allowing to make a distinction. For instance: *La propuesta de reunir en un mismo lugar a las etiquetas premium de las principales bodegas del país ha*

Cases	number	freq.
not distinguishable	18	0.36
distinguishable by named entities	17	0.34
distinguishable by dialectal uses	7	0.14
others	8	0.16

Table 5: Figures from error analysis on Spanish texts.

logrado cautivar al público amante del buen vino, siendo hoy el evento del sector más esperado del año. is classified by our system as Spanish from Argentina (es-AR) but it was annotated as Spanish from Spain (es-ES). However, the text has no relevant dialectal characteristic.

- Distinguishable by named entities: including geographical names (*Argentina, Galicia, ...*), organizations (*PP, PSOE*), localization information (*euro, peso, peruano, Buenos Aires*, etc.). For instance: *Los ingresos tributarios totales de la provincia ascendieron en marzo a 1.305.180.533,54 pesos, un 10,37 por ciento por encima del monto presupuestado para ese mes* is classified by our system as es-ES, but it contains the term *pesos* which refers to the Argentinian currency.

- Distinguishable by dialectal uses. These are cases in which it is possible to find words such as *mamá* or *tercerizar* that are more frequent in some of the variants.

- Others: more complex cases in which it is difficult to make a decision since there are no clear language features from one particular variety. In some of the examples, several hypotheses were possible.

The figures for each case are shown in Table 5. We can observe that the first two cases (i.e not distinguishable and distinguishable by named entities) are the more frequent in the test test.

5.2 Future Work

Based on the error analysis we are planning to test a variant of our system with two new features:

- The system will be provided with the *none* category for those cases where there is no enough evidence to make a decision. This can increase the precision of the system.

- The system will be enriched with lists (gazetteers) of named entities linked to the dialects or geographical locations. These gazetteers could be used to assign weights to n-grams or as new features in the voting system. However, it will be necessary to consider the interferences that this new information might add to the system. For instance, in the following example (*Es indudable que los que utilice en los partidos amistosos que jugaremos contra España, en Huelva el 28 de mayo, y ante México...*), the use of localized named entities could generate a false positive for Spanish from Spain (es-ES).

Additionally we intend to test the perplexity strategy to measure the distance among the language or dialects in a diachronic mode. This would allow us to observe the quantitative transformations of the languages/dialects and the relations among them.

Finally, we will perform further experiments with different voting systems in order to find the most appropriate for our models.

Our perplexity-based system to measure the distance between languages is freely available at `https://github.com/gamallo/Perplexity`.

Acknowledgments

This work has been supported by a 2016 BBVA Foundation Grant for Researchers and Cultural Creators, by TelePares (MINECO, ref:FFI2014-51978-C2-1-R) and TADeep (MINECO, ref: TIN2015-70214-P) projects. It also has received financial support from the Consellería de Cultura, Educación e Ordenación Universitaria (accreditation 2016-2019, ED431G/08) and the European Regional Development Fund (ERDF).

The authors thanks the referees for thoughtful comments and helpful suggestions.

References

Johannes Bjerva. 2016. Byte-based language identification with deep convolutional networks. In *Proceedings of the 3rd Workshop on Language Technology for Closely Related Languages, Varieties and Dialects (VarDial)*, Osaka, Japan.

Çağri Çöltekin and Taraka Rama. 2016. Discriminating Similar Languages with Linear SVMs and Neural Networks. In *Proceedings of the Third Workshop on NLP for Similar Languages, Varieties and Dialects (VarDial3)*, pages 15–24, Osaka, Japan.

Stanley F. Chen and Joshua Goodman. 1996. An empirical study of smoothing techniques for language modeling. In *Proceedings of the 34th Annual Meeting on Association for Computational Linguistics*, ACL '96, pages 310–318, Stroudsburg, PA, USA. Association for Computational Linguistics.

Pablo Gamallo, Iñaki Alegria, José Ramom Pichel, and Manex Agirrezabal. 2016. Comparing Two Basic Methods for Discriminating Between Similar Languages and Varieties. In *Proceedings of the Third Workshop on NLP for Similar Languages, Varieties and Dialects (VarDial3)*, pages 170–177, Osaka, Japan.

Meritxell González. 2015. An analysis of twitter corpora and the differences between formal and colloquial tweets. In *Proceedings of the Tweet Translation Workshop 2015*, pages 1–7.

Cyril Goutte, Serge Léger, Shervin Malmasi, and Marcos Zampieri. 2016. Discriminating Similar Languages: Evaluations and Explorations.

Shervin Malmasi, Eshrag Refaee, and Mark Dras. 2015. Arabic Dialect Identification using a Parallel Multidialectal Corpus. In *Proceedings of the 14th Conference of the Pacific Association for Computational Linguistics (PACLING 2015)*, pages 209–217, Bali, Indonesia, May.

Shervin Malmasi, Marcos Zampieri, Nikola Ljubešić, Preslav Nakov, Ahmed Ali, and Jörg Tiedemann. 2016. Discriminating between similar languages and arabic dialect identification: A report on the third dsl shared task. In *Proceedings of the 3rd Workshop on Language Technology for Closely Related Languages, Varieties and Dialects (VarDial)*, Osaka, Japan.

Rico Sennrich. 2012. Perplexity minimization for translation model domain adaptation in statistical machine translation. In *Proceedings of the 13th Conference of the European Chapter of the Association for Computational Linguistics*, EACL '12, pages 539–549, Stroudsburg, PA, USA. Association for Computational Linguistics.

Marcos Zampieri, Liling Tan, Nikola Ljubešić, and Jörg Tiedemann. 2014. A report on the dsl shared task 2014. In *Proceedings of the First Workshop on Applying NLP Tools to Similar Languages, Varieties*

and Dialects (VarDial), pages 58–67, Dublin, Ireland.

Marcos Zampieri, Liling Tan, Nikola Ljubešić, Jörg Tiedemann, and Preslav Nakov. 2015. Overview of the dsl shared task 2015. In *Proceedings of the Joint Workshop on Language Technology for Closely Related Languages, Varieties and Dialects (LT4VarDial)*, pages 1–9, Hissar, Bulgaria.

Marcos Zampieri, Shervin Malmasi, Nikola Ljubešić, Preslav Nakov, Ahmed Ali, Jörg Tiedemann, Yves Scherrer, and Noëmi Aepli. 2017. Findings of the VarDial Evaluation Campaign 2017. In *Proceedings of the Fourth Workshop on NLP for Similar Languages, Varieties and Dialects (VarDial)*, Valencia, Spain.

Arkaitz Zubiaga, Iñaki San Vicente, Pablo Gamallo, José Ramom Pichel, Iñaki Alegria, Nora Aranberri, Aitzol Ezeiza, and Víctor Fresno. 2015. Tweetlid: a benchmark for tweet language identification. *Language Resources and Evaluation*, pages 1–38.

Improving the Character Ngram Model for the DSL Task with BM25 Weighting and Less Frequently Used Feature Sets

Yves Bestgen

Centre for English Corpus Linguistics
Université catholique de Louvain
Place du cardinal Mercier, 10 B-1348 Louvain-la-Neuve Belgium
`yves.bestgen@uclouvain.be`

Abstract

This paper describes the system developed by the Centre for English Corpus Linguistics (CECL) to discriminating similar languages, language varieties and dialects. Based on a SVM with character and POStag n-grams as features and the BM25 weighting scheme, it achieved 92.7% accuracy in the Discriminating between Similar Languages (DSL) task, ranking first among eleven systems but with a lead over the next three teams of only 0.2%. A simpler version of the system ranked second in the German Dialect Identification (GDI) task thanks to several ad hoc postprocessing steps. Complementary analyses carried out by a cross-validation procedure suggest that the BM25 weighting scheme could be competitive in this type of tasks, at least in comparison with the sublinear TF-IDF. POStag n-grams also improved the system performance.

1 Introduction

This paper presents the participation of the Centre for English Corpus Linguistics (CECL) in the fourth edition of the VarDial Evaluation Campaign, which deals with the automatic identification of similar languages (such as excerpts of journalistic texts in Malay and Indonesian), language varieties (such as excerpts of Canadian and Hexagonal French) and dialects (such as Swiss German dialects) (Zampieri et al., 2017). The VarDial tasks share many similarities with the Native Language Identification (NLI) Task (Tetreault et al., 2013) so that several teams (Gebre et al., 2013; Goutte et al., 2013) relied on their participation in the NLI task to develop a system for VarDial. As we achieved an excellent level of performance

in the NLI task (Jarvis et al., 2013), we decided to reuse the approach developed on that occasion, which was based on n-grams of characters, words and part of speech (POS) tags, and on global statistical indices such as the number of tokens per documents or the word mean length.

In the NLI task, n-grams of characters had proved to be as effective as the combination of n-grams of words and POStags. The character n-grams also obtained the best results in the 2016 Discriminating between Similar Languages (DSL) shared task (Malmasi et al., 2016) as well as in previous editions (Goutte et al., 2014; Malmasi and Dras, 2015). These performances led us to privilege this approach especially since we did not have an off-the-shelf POS-tagger for some of the languages to be discriminated. We nevertheless used POStag n-grams in addition to character n-grams for the three languages for which a version of TreeTagger is available (Schmid, 1994).

The CECL system was specifically developed for the DSL task in which it obtained the best performance (0.927) according to the weighted F1 measure, but it should be noted that its lead on the system ranked second is only 0.002. A simplified version, due to the different nature of the material to be processed, was applied to a second task, the German Dialect Identification (GDI) task which was organized for the first time. The task aim was to distinguish manually annotated speech transcripts from four Swiss German dialect areas: Basel (BS), Bern (BE), Lucerne (LU) and Zurich (ZH). This task is particularly difficult because many transcripts are very short and because it is not unusual to find in the learning material identical transcripts (e.g., *aber*) belonging to the four categories. In this task, the CECL system came second, obtaining a weighted F1 of 0.661, 0.001 less than the system ranked first.

The next section presents the main characteris-

Proceedings of the Fourth Workshop on NLP for Similar Languages, Varieties and Dialects, pages 115–123,
Valencia, Spain, April 3, 2017. ©2017 Association for Computational Linguistics

tics of the system within the context of previous research. The third section describes the material of each task in which we participated and the technical characteristics of the system. The fourth section reports the results obtained on the test set, but also an evaluation of the benefits/losses brought by the various components of the system by means of a cross-validation procedure. In the conclusion, we discuss the main limits of this work and consider a few avenues for improvement.

2 System Characteristics in Relation to Previous Work

Character n-grams are the main features of the system. In the previous VarDial campaigns, a large number of systems obtained excellent performances using them (Çöltekin and Rama, 2016; Goutte et al., 2014; Zampieri et al., 2015a). Regarding the n-gram length, we choose a span of one to seven characters as in Çöltekin and Rama (2016), but the possibility to use more characters for some languages was left open.

In previous editions, named entities received much attention to such an extent that, in the 2015 edition, the documents of one of the test sets was preprocessed so as to mask them (Zampieri et al., 2015b). Their impact on performance is undoubtedly complex. On the one hand, as the material is composed of excerpts of journalistic texts, the named entities should reflect at least partially the origin of the texts. On the other hand, they could also introduce some noise since some of them can be used in any language. We decided to try to identify them (at a lower cost) so they could be processed in different ways. The solution we ended in is very similar to that used by King et al. (2014) which is based on the fact that the first letter of a named entities is usually capitalised. The goal was to determine whether performance could be improved by eliminating them. As the initial analyses refuted this hypothesis, we evaluated the opposite option, that is adding them as a supplementary feature set. The idea was that when these words are encoded in standard character n-grams, they are merged with n-grams from common words. For example, *bec* (*beak*) is included in *Québec* and in *Québecquois*.

Many previous systems developed for the DSL task also used word n-grams (Purver, 2014; Zampieri et al., 2014). We have not explored this option because there is a partial overlap between them and character n-grams. Such a situation does not occur for POStag n-grams whose usefulness has been advocated by Lui et al. (2014). There were added thus to the feature sets for each language for which we had a POS-tagger at our disposal.

The last set of features used is composed of global statistical indices similar to those employed in previous work (Bestgen, 2012; Jarvis et al., 2013). They are computed on the basis of the number of characters, spaces, uppercase letters and punctuation marks in each document.

An important characteristic of the developed system lies in the weighting function used for scaling every n-gram feature. The best performing systems in the previous VarDial editions often employed TF-IDF (see Zampieri et al. (2015a) for a detailed presentation) whose most classical formula is:

$$\text{TF-IDF} = tf \times \log \frac{N}{df} \qquad (1)$$

where tf refers to the frequency of the term in the document, N is the number of documents in the set and df the number of documents that include the term. Zampieri et al. (2015a) and Çöltekin and Rama (2016) took advantage of a variant called Sublinear TF-IDF:

$$(\text{sl})\text{TF-IDF} = (1 + \log(tf)) \times \log \frac{N}{df} \qquad (2)$$

Other weighting schemes have been proposed in the literature, some of them are simpler and some more complex (Ács et al., 2015). In the NLI task, we choose the log-entropy weighting scheme often used in latent semantic analysis (Piérard and Bestgen, 2006). In Information Retrieval, the BM25 (for Best Match 25, also called *Okapi BM25*) weighting scheme is considered one of the most efficient (Manning et al., 2008) to the point that it is strongly advocated by Claveau (2012). Our first analyses having shown that BM25 surpassed log-entropy, we opted for this weighting scheme for all the n-gram based features.

BM25 is a kind of TF-IDF with specific choices for each of the two components, but above all it takes into account the length of the document. Its classic formula is (Robertson and Zaragoza,

2009):

$$\text{BM25} = \frac{tf}{tf + k_1 * (1 - b + b * \frac{dl}{dl - avg_{dl}})}$$
$$\times \log \frac{N - df + 0.5}{df + 0.5} \quad (3)$$

in which

- $\frac{tf}{tf + k_1}$ is the TF component which, contrarily to the usual TF-IDF, has an asymptotic maximum tuned by the k_1 parameter.

- $(1 - b + b * \frac{dl}{dl - avg_{dl}})$, where dl is the length of the document and avg_{dl} the average length of the documents in the set, is the document length normalization factor whose impact is tuned by parameter b (and by k_1).

- The second part of the formula is a variant of the usual IDF, proposed by Robertson and Spärck Jones (Robertson and Zaragoza, 2009).

In our analyses, k_1 was set to 2 and b to 0.75 (Claveau, 2012).

3 Data and System Detailed Description

This section first describes the data provided by the organizers for each of the two tasks in which we participated and then the implementation of the various components of the system. Since the system set up for the GDI task was a simplified version of the one developed for the DSL task, the emphasis is placed on the latter.

3.1 Data

DSL Task: The organizers have made available to participants of the task a multilingual dataset (Tan et al., 2014) containing excerpts of journalistic texts in six groups of languages, each composed of two or three varieties:

- Bosnian (bs), Croatian (hr), and Serbian (sr)

- Malay (my) and Indonesian (id)

- Persian (fa-IR) and Dari (fa-AF)

- Canadian (fr-CA) and Hexagonal French (fr-FR)

- Brazilian (pt-BR) and European Portuguese (pt-PT)

- Argentine (es-AR), Peninsular (es-ES), and Peruvian Spanish (es-PE)

For each of the 14 varieties, the learning set consists of 18000 documents and development set of 2000 documents, for a total of 280000 documents.

GDI Task: The dataset for the German Dialect Identification task, described in Samardzic et al. (2016), consists of manually annotated speech transcripts from four Swiss German dialect areas: 3411 from Basel (BS), 3889 from Bern (BE), 3214 from Lucerne (LU), and 3964 from Zurich (ZH), for a total of 14478 documents. For each area, speeches were collected from several speakers and retranscribed by several annotators using a writing system designed to express the phonetic properties of different Swiss German dialects.

3.2 Detailed System Description

The extraction of all the features described below was performed by means of a series of custom SAS programs running in SAS University (freely available for research at http://www.sas.com/en_us/software/university-edition.html). To construct the predictive models during the development and test phases, we used LibSVM (with a linear kernel) (Chang and Lin, 2011), which is significantly slower than LibLIN-EAR developed by the same authors. This unfortunate choice prevented further optimization trials.

DSL Task: As Goutte et al. (2014), we used a hierarchical approach with a first model for discriminating language groups and then a specific model for each language group. From our point of view, this approach has two advantages. First, since distinguishing different languages (such as Persian and French) is much simpler than distinguishing language varieties (such as Canadian and Hexagonal French), the first model can be based on a reduced number of features and is thus easier to handle even though it is applied to a much larger dataset. Then, different models can be constructed for each language group in order to try to optimize their effectiveness both in selecting the sets of features and in setting the regularization parameter (C) of the SVM.

1. *Features for the identifying the language groups*: This model is based on the character n-grams of length one to four, which occurs at least 100 times in the whole dataset, weighted by means of BM25. These character n-grams were substrings of the documents

Features	bs-hr-sr	es	fa	fr	id-my	pt
CharNgram	1-7	1-7	1-8	1-7	1-7	1-7
CapCharNgram	1-7	1-7	no	1-7	1-7	1-7
POStagNgram	no	1-5	no	1-5	no	1-5
GlobStat	yes	yes	yes	yes	yes	yes
C	0.30	0.0001	0.00005	0.001	0.00005	0.00005

Table 1: Set of features and C value for the six language groups.

and include whitespace, punctuation, digits and symbols. A special character was used to signal the beginning and the end of the document.

2. *Features for the language specific models*:

   (a) *Character n-grams*: They were extracted exactly as explained above, but they contained from 1 to 7 or 8 characters.

   (b) *Capitalized word character n-grams*: Every word that starts with a capital letter was extracted from each document and the character n-grams it contains were used as supplementary features. Consideration was given to not taking into account the first word of each sentence, but since the material consisted of excerpts from newspaper articles, this criterion would have eliminated many named entities as in *Ottawa demande tout de même à la Cour suprême comment....* This approach does not work for Persian since it does not use capital letters.

   (c) *POStag n-grams*: We used the Tree-Tagger (Schmid, 1994) to collect the parts of speech associated with each token in a document for each language for which a parameter file for TreeTagger (http://www.cis.uni-muenchen.de/ schmid/tools/TreeTagger/) was available, that is French, Spanish and Portuguese. It might be useful to note that each of these parameter files has been built for a language group (i.e., French) and not for a language variety (i.e., Canadian French), and that they are not used to identify the language groups.

   (d) *Global statistics*: We also extracted five global statistics from each document: the proportions of capitalized letters, punctuation marks, spaces, and numerals, and the proportion of characters that are not a space, a numeral or a punctuation mark.

The feature sets and the value of the parameter C used during the test phase are given in Table 1. They were determined by means of (non-systematic) cross-validation analyses using one fifth of the data for learning and the remaining for testing.

GDI Task: Since this task was not our priority, we simply adapted the model designed for the DSL task by removing all the sets of features that were not relevant, that is the capitalized word character n-grams, the POStag n-grams, and the global statistics. Thus, only the character n-grams and the BM25 weighting scheme remain.

4 Analyses and Results

4.1 DSL Task

Performance on the Test Set: A single run was submitted because no attempt to optimize the predictions was possible due to the use of LibSVM. We got an accuracy of 92.74% and a weighted F1 of 0.9271. The system ranked first of the eleven systems that participated in the task but with a lead over the next three teams of only 0.002 (weighted F1).

Table 2 gives the confusion matrix on the test set. As can be seen, the language group of 29 documents was incorrectly identified during the first step, which corresponds to a 99.79% accuracy. It is noteworthy that a document in Persian was incorrectly categorized as in Portuguese whereas these are two totally different writing systems. It is also noted that the varieties within the different language groups did not exhibit the same level of difficulty, the triplet *bs-hr-sr* being much more difficult for the system than the others.

The Good (and the Bad) of the System: After

	bs-hr-sr			es			fa		fr		ma		pt	
	bs	hr	sr	ar	es	pe	af	ir	ca	fr	id	my	br	pt
bs	784	112	102	0	0	0	0	0	0	1	0	0	0	1
hr	119	865	15	0	0	0	0	0	0	1	0	0	0	0
sr	71	7	921	0	0	0	0	0	0	0	0	0	1	0
es-ar	0	2	0	855	70	68	0	0	0	0	0	0	3	2
es-es	0	2	0	69	892	34	0	0	0	1	0	0	0	2
es-pe	0	0	0	11	24	965	0	0	0	0	0	0	0	0
fa-af	0	0	0	0	0	0	968	32	0	0	0	0	0	0
fa-ir	0	0	0	0	0	0	32	967	0	0	0	0	1	0
fr-ca	0	0	0	0	0	0	0	0	956	44	0	0	0	0
fr-fr	1	0	0	0	0	0	0	0	53	946	0	0	0	0
id	0	0	0	1	1	0	0	0	0	1	980	17	0	0
my	0	0	0	0	0	1	0	0	0	0	10	989	0	0
pt-br	0	0	0	1	0	1	0	0	0	2	0	0	939	57
pt-pt	0	0	0	0	0	1	0	0	0	2	0	0	41	956

Table 2: Confusion matrix for the DSL task.

the test period (and because we remembered having used LibLINEAR in Jarvis et al. (2013)), we conducted a series of experiments on the learning and development sets to determine the gains/losses made by each component of the system. These experiments were carried out independently for each language group. Since the optimum values for the C parameter had not been determined using a cross-validation procedure, 17 values distributed between 0.000001 and 4 were tested. The results given below corresponds to the average accuracy calculated over all these C values[1]

The first experiment aimed at comparing the effectiveness of the BM25 weighting scheme with that of the sublinear TF-IDF scheme used in the best performing systems of previous years (Çöltekin and Rama, 2016; Zampieri et al., 2015a). In order to be the closest to Çöltekin and Rama (2016) system, only characters n-grams were used. Table 3 show that BM25 produced a superior accuracy in five language groups out of six, the only exception being Malay with an advantage for TF-IDF of 0.08, but it is also the language group for which performance is nearly perfect. The average benefit is 0.47%.

The second experiment used the ablation approach to assess the independent contribution of each set of features to the overall performance of the system. It consists in removing one feature of

Language	BM25	TF-IDF	Diff.
bs-hr-sr	85.06	84.45	0.61
es	90.30	89.70	0.60
fa	96.32	95.98	0.34
fr	94.72	93.96	0.76
id-my	98.27	98.35	-0.08
pt	93.55	92.99	0.56

Table 3: Accuracy for the two weighting schemes (DSL).

the system at a time and re-evaluating the model. The results indicated that, in each language group, the most comprehensive model (see Table 1) was always the best. Concerning the different sets of features (see Table 4):

- Deleting the global statistics reduced the accuracy in a minimal way since the difference is at most 0.02% and it is even null in three language groups out of 6.

- Deleting capitalized word character n-grams reduced accuracy by 0.09% to 0.27% depending on the language group, with an average decrease of 0.16%.

- Deleting POStag n-grams had a somewhat greater effect since the decrease is at least 0.23% and can be as high as 0.70%.

4.2 GDI Task

Specificity and Performance of the Three Runs:
The system for the GDI task was developed using

---

[1]The analyses were also performed on the maximum accuracy obtained by each model, assuming that an oracle allowed to know the ideal value of the C parameter, and produced very similar results.

Features	bs-hr-sr	es	fa	fr	id-my	pt
GlobStat	0.02	0.002	0.001	0	0	0
CapCharNgram	0.23	0.27		0.09	0.12	0.10
POStagNgram		0.70		0.23		0.30

Table 4: Benefits in accuracy for the three complementary sets of features (DSL).

Source	BE	BS	LU	ZH
Learning set	26.86	23.56	22.20	27.38
Run 1	26.25	26.36	8.74	38.65
Run 2	24.41	29.49	11.00	35.10
Run 3	23.86	25.12	23.69	27.32

Table 5: Percentage breakdown of the documents into the four categories (GDI).

BE	BS	LU	ZH	#	%
0	0	0	0	297	8.16
0	0	0	1	877	24.11
0	0	1	0	615	16.90
0	0	1	1	33	0.91
0	1	0	0	794	21.83
0	1	1	0	112	3.08
1	0	0	0	756	20.78
1	0	1	0	150	4.12
1	1	0	0	4	0.11

Table 6: Categorisation of the documents according to the probability estimate ranking (GDI).

a 5-fold cross-validation procedure. It led to select a model based on n-grams of 1 to 5 characters and a value of 0.0003 for the C parameter. This model was used to produce the first submitted run. It got the seventh place[2] with a weighted F1 of 0.625, close enough to the system ranked sixth but at 0.012 of the fifth place.

When taking a look at the predictions of this model during the submission period, it appeared that it attributed an unequal breakdown of the documents into the four categories, as shown in the second row of Table 5, and quite different from the breakdown in the learning set (see first row in Table 5). Even if such a distribution were possible, it does not look optimal. A few additional analyses were quickly carried out to try obtaining a more balanced breakdown.

First, we obtained from LibSVM the probability estimates of each document for each class, an option not available in LibLINEAR for SVMs. Since the solution proposed with or without probability estimation is not exactly the same for a given value of C, this solution was submitted as the second run. As shown in the third row of Table 5, the breakdown into the categories is somewhat more homogeneous. This run ranked fifth, with a weighted F1 of 0.638, almost tied with the team ranked fourth since the difference is only 0.0006 but at 0.015 from third place.

These probabilities were then used to try to equalize the headcounts in the four categories. To do this, the 910 documents[3] with the highest probability estimate of belonging to a category were tentatively assigned to this category. Obviously, this procedure allows the classification of a document into several categories as shown in Table 6. A set of ad hoc rules was then applied to take the final decision. The most obvious one was that documents categorized into only one category were assigned to that one. Other rules apply to documents that were not assigned to any category or to documents that were assigned to two categories by giving priority to the least populated one. The last row of Table 5 confirms that this procedure made it possible to obtain a more homogeneous breakdown into the categories compared to the two other runs.

The resulting submission ranked second in the GDI task with a weighted F1 of 0.661, close to the performance of the team ranked first since the difference is only 0.0013. Thus, these simple changes in the category breakdown, only justified by the fact that one of the objectives of a shared task is to obtain the best performance, made it possible to gain 0.035 in weighted F1 and to climb from the seventh place to the second.

Benefits Brought by BM25: In order to determine whether the use of BM25 instead of sublinear TF-IDF provided a benefit, a 5-fold cross-

---

[2]To determine this place, we used the ranking provided by the organizers, which only contains the highest score of each team, and inserted our different runs. The rank given therefore includes only the best run of each of the other teams.

[3]That is a quarter of the test set. We could also have relied on the percentages in the learning set given in Table 4.

C	BM25	TF-IDF	Diff.
0.0001	82.62	80.58	2.04
0.0002	84.26	82.52	1.73
0.0003	84.68	83.22	1.46
0.0004	84.57	83.46	1.11
0.0005	84.50	83.46	1.05
0.0006	84.43	83.44	0.99
0.0007	84.26	83.42	0.85
0.0008	83.99	83.29	0.70
0.0009	83.87	83.17	0.70
0.0010	83.69	83.11	0.58

Table 7: Accuracy for the two weighting schemes (GDI).

validation procedure was used to first find the best C value for each weighting scheme and then to compare the levels of accuracy achieved. For both BM25 and sublinear TF-IDF, the optimum value of C was between 0.001 and 0.0001. Table 7 gives, for different C, the average accuracy on the 5 folds for the two weightings. As can be seen, BM25 always performed better than sublinear TF-IDF and the gain in the area where the two weightings got the best results was in the range of 1 to 1.5% accuracy. This gain may seem rather low, but it is obtained at the cost of a minimal modification of the system.

Specific Difficulties with this Task: The preceding analyses and the 2017 VarDial report (Zampieri et al., 2017) show that the performances obtained by a cross-validation procedure on the learning set (accuracy = 84%) were clearly superior to those obtained on the test set by any of the teams (maximum accuracy = 68%). This means that, although no information had been provided on this subject in the task description, the transcripts in the test set were quite different from those in the learning set.

5 Conclusion

This paper describes the system developed by the Centre for English Corpus Linguistics for participating in the fourth edition of the VarDial Evaluation Campaign (Zampieri et al., 2017). It was mainly based on characters n-grams, known for their effectiveness in this kind of task, to which less frequently used sets of features were added. These features were weighted by means of the BM25 scheme. In the two tasks we participated in, the CECL system ranked at least second. The

good performance in the GDI task was due to several ad hoc adjustments of the breakdown of the test documents in the categories and cannot therefore be seen as a proof of the intrinsic superiority of the system.

The results obtained and the complementary analyses carried out by means of a cross-validation procedure suggest that the BM25 weighting scheme could be competitive in this type of tasks, at least when compared to the sublinear TF-IDF. However, it should be noted that gains were relatively small. Due to the lack of time, a detailed analysis of BM25 was not carried out to optimize the two parameters, to evaluate alternative formulas (Trotman et al., 2014) or to determine which difference between BM25 and the sub-linear TF-IDF is responsible for the performance gain.

Other options for improving the system include removing the words in English (King et al., 2014) and pre-processing the sentences entirely in capital letters. It would also be interesting to determine whether POStag n-grams could be as effective in the other languages as they were in French, Spanish and Portuguese.

Acknowledgments

This work was supported by the Fonds de la Recherche Scientifique (FRS-FNRS) under Grant J.0025.16. The author is a Research Associate of this institution. Computational ressources have been provided by the supercomputing facilities of the Université catholique de Louvain (CISM/UCL) and the Consortium des Equipements de Calcul Intensif en Fédération Wallonie Bruxelles (CECI) funded by the FRS-FNRS.

References

Judit Ács, László Grad-Gyenge, and Thiago Bruno Rodrigues de Rezende Oliveira. 2015. A two-level classifier for discriminating similar languages. In *Proceedings of the Joint Workshop on Language Technology for Closely Related Languages, Varieties and Dialects (LT4VarDial)*, pages 73–77, Hissar, Bulgaria.

Yves Bestgen. 2012. DEFT2009 : essais d'optimisation d'une procédure de base pour la tâche 1. In C. Grouin and D. Forest, editors, *Expérimentations et évaluations en fouille de textes: un panorama des campagnes DEFT*, pages 135–151. Hermes Lavoisier, Paris, France.

Çağri Çöltekin and Taraka Rama. 2016. Discriminating Similar Languages with Linear SVMs and Neural Networks. In *Proceedings of the Third Workshop on NLP for Similar Languages, Varieties and Dialects (VarDial3)*, pages 15–24, Osaka, Japan.

Chih-Chung Chang and Chih-Jen Lin. 2011. LIBSVM: A library for support vector machines. *ACM Transactions on Intelligent Systems and Technology*, 2:27:1–27:27. Software available at http://www.csie.ntu.edu.tw/~cjlin/libsvm.

Vincent Claveau. 2012. Vectorisation, Okapi et calcul de similarité pour le TAL : pour oublier enfin le TF-IDF. In *Actes de la conférence conjointe JEP-TALN-RECITAL 2012*, pages 85–98, Grenoble, France.

Binyam Gebrekidan Gebre, Marcos Zampieri, Peter Wittenburg, and Tom Heskes. 2013. Improving native language identification with TF-IDF weighting. In *Proceedings of the 8th NAACL Workshop on Innovative Use of NLP for Building Educational Applications (BEA8)*, pages 216–223.

Cyril Goutte, Serge Léger, and Marine Carpuat. 2013. Feature space selection and combination for native language identification. In *Proceedings of the 8th NAACL Workshop on Innovative Use of NLP for Building Educational Applications (BEA8)*, pages 96–100.

Cyril Goutte, Serge Léger, and Marine Carpuat. 2014. The NRC system for discriminating similar languages. In *Proceedings of the First Workshop on Applying NLP Tools to Similar Languages, Varieties and Dialects (VarDial)*, pages 139–145, Dublin, Ireland.

Scott Jarvis, Yves Bestgen, and Steve Pepper. 2013. Maximizing classification accuracy in native language identification. In *Proceedings of The 8th Workshop on Innovative Use of NLP for Building Educational Applications (NAACL-HLT)*, pages 111–118.

Ben King, Dragomir Radev, and Steven Abney. 2014. Experiments in sentence language identification with groups of similar languages. In *Proceedings of the First Workshop on Applying NLP Tools to Similar Languages, Varieties and Dialects (VarDial)*, pages 146–154, Dublin, Ireland.

Marco Lui, Ned Letcher, Oliver Adams, Long Duong, Paul Cook, and Timothy Baldwin. 2014. Exploring methods and resources for discriminating similar languages. In *Proceedings of the First Workshop on Applying NLP Tools to Similar Languages, Varieties and Dialects (VarDial)*, pages 129–138, Dublin, Ireland.

Shervin Malmasi and Mark Dras. 2015. Language identification using classifier ensembles. In *Proceedings of the Joint Workshop on Language Technology for Closely Related Languages, Varieties and Dialects (LT4VarDial)*, pages 35–43, Hissar, Bulgaria.

Shervin Malmasi, Marcos Zampieri, Nikola Ljubešić, Preslav Nakov, Ahmed Ali, and Jörg Tiedemann. 2016. Discriminating between similar languages and arabic dialect identification: A report on the third dsl shared task. In *Proceedings of the 3rd Workshop on Language Technology for Closely Related Languages, Varieties and Dialects (VarDial)*, Osaka, Japan.

Christopher D. Manning, Prabhakar Raghavan, and Hinrich Schtze. 2008. *An Introduction to Information Retrieval*. Cambridge University Press.

Sophie Piérard and Yves Bestgen. 2006. Validation d'une méthodologie pour l'étude des marqueurs de la segmentation dans un grand corpus de textes. *TAL: Traitement Automatique du Langage*, 47(2):89–110.

Matthew Purver. 2014. A simple baseline for discriminating similar languages. In *Proceedings of the First Workshop on Applying NLP Tools to Similar Languages, Varieties and Dialects (VarDial)*, pages 155–160, Dublin, Ireland.

Stephen Robertson and Hugo Zaragoza. 2009. The probabilistic relevance framework: BM25 and beyond. *Foundations and Trends in Information Retrieval*, 3(4):333–389, April.

Tanja Samardzic, Yves Scherrer, and Elvira Glaser. 2016. ArchiMob–A corpus of spoken Swiss German. In *Proceedings of the Language Resources and Evaluation (LREC)*, pages 4061–4066, Portoroz, Slovenia).

Helmut Schmid. 1994. Probabilistic part-of-speech tagging using decision trees. In *Proceedings of the International Conference on New Methods in Language Processing*, Manchester, UK.

Liling Tan, Marcos Zampieri, Nikola Ljubešic, and Jörg Tiedemann. 2014. Merging comparable data sources for the discrimination of similar languages: The DSL corpus collection. In *Proceedings of the 7th Workshop on Building and Using Comparable Corpora (BUCC)*, pages 11–15, Reykjavik, Iceland.

Joel R. Tetreault, Daniel Blanchard, and Aoife Cahill. 2013. A report on the first native language identification shared task. In Joel R. Tetreault, Jill Burstein, and Claudia Leacock, editors, *Proceedings of the Eighth Workshop on Innovative Use of NLP for Building Educational Applications*, pages 48–57. The Association for Computer Linguistics.

Andrew Trotman, Antti Puurula, and Blake Burgess. 2014. Improvements to BM25 and language models examined. In *Proceedings of the 2014 Australasian Document Computing Symposium*, ADCS '14, pages 58–65, New York, NY, USA. ACM.

Marcos Zampieri, Liling Tan, Nikola Ljubešić, and
Jörg Tiedemann. 2014. A report on the DSL shared
task 2014. In *Proceedings of the First Workshop on
Applying NLP Tools to Similar Languages, Varieties
and Dialects (VarDial)*, pages 58–67, Dublin, Ireland.

Marcos Zampieri, Binyam Gebrekidan Gebre, Hernani
Costa, and Josef van Genabith. 2015a. Comparing approaches to the identification of similar
languages. In *Proceedings of the Joint Workshop
on Language Technology for Closely Related Languages, Varieties and Dialects (LT4VarDial)*, pages
66–72, Hissar, Bulgaria.

Marcos Zampieri, Liling Tan, Nikola Ljubešić, Jörg
Tiedemann, and Preslav Nakov. 2015b. Overview
of the DSL shared task 2015. In *Proceedings of
the Joint Workshop on Language Technology for
Closely Related Languages, Varieties and Dialects
(LT4VarDial)*, pages 1–9, Hissar, Bulgaria.

Marcos Zampieri, Shervin Malmasi, Nikola Ljubešić,
Preslav Nakov, Ahmed Ali, Jörg Tiedemann, Yves
Scherrer, and Noëmi Aepli. 2017. Findings of the
VarDial Evaluation Campaign 2017. In *Proceedings
of the Fourth Workshop on NLP for Similar Lan-
guages, Varieties and Dialects (VarDial)*, Valencia,
Spain.

Discriminating between Similar Languages with Word-level Convolutional Neural Networks

Marcelo Criscuolo and **Sandra Maria Aluísio**
Institute of Mathematical and Computer Sciences
University of São Paulo
{mcrisc,sandra}@icmc.usp.br

Abstract

Discriminating between Similar Languages (DSL) is a challenging task addressed at the VarDial Workshop series. We report on our participation in the DSL shared task with a two-stage system. In the first stage, character n-grams are used to separate language groups, then specialized classifiers distinguish similar language varieties. We have conducted experiments with three system configurations and submitted one run for each. Our main approach is a word-level convolutional neural network (CNN) that learns task-specific vectors with minimal text preprocessing. We also experiment with multi-layer perceptron (MLP) networks and another hybrid configuration. Our best run achieved an accuracy of 90.76%, ranking 8th among 11 participants and getting very close to the system that ranked first (less than 2 points). Even though the CNN model could not achieve the best results, it still makes a viable approach to discriminating between similar languages.

1 Introduction

Language identification is the task of detecting the language of a given text segment. Although methods that are able to achieve an accuracy of over 99% for clearly distinct languages like English and Spanish do exist (Dunning, 1994), it is still a major problem to distinguish between closely related languages, like Bosnian and Croatian, and language varieties, like Brazilian and European Portuguese (Goutte et al., 2016). The problem of discriminating between similar languages was addressed in the DSL shared task at VarDial 2017. In

DSL 2017, participants were asked to develop systems that could distinguish between 14 language varieties, distributed over 6 language groups. Two participation tracks were available: closed and open training. In closed track, systems should be trained exclusively in the DSL Corpus Collection (Tan et al., 2014), provided by the organizers (see Section 3), while in open training the use of external resources was allowed. For a detailed description of the VarDial workshop and of DSL 2017, refer to the shared task report (Zampieri et al., 2017).

This paper describes our system and the results of our submissions for closed track at DSL 2017. Our goal was to experiment with deep neural networks in language variety distinction, in particular word-level Convolutional Neural Networks (CNN). This kind of network has been successfully applied to several natural language processing tasks, such as text classification (Kim, 2014) and question answering (Severyn and Moschitti, 2015; Wang et al., 2016).

Like other participants did in previous editions of the DSL shared task (Zampieri et al., 2015), we chose to use two-stage classification. First, each sentence gets a group label, that guides the selection of a model especially trained for that group. Then, it goes through a classifier that predicts the final language variety. We experimented with different machine learning techniques for variety prediction while the language group classifier was kept the same. This allowed us to compare, not only the overall accuracy of each classifier, but also its accuracy within each language group.

To distinguish between language groups, the efficiency of character n-grams was leveraged (Vatanen et al., 2010), while three configurations had their performances comparared for language variety prediction. One run was submitted for each of the following configurations: (a) run1: a word-

Proceedings of the Fourth Workshop on NLP for Similar Languages, Varieties and Dialects, pages 124–130,
Valencia, Spain, April 3, 2017. ©2017 Association for Computational Linguistics

level CNN that learns word vectors from scratch; (b) `run2`: a multi-layer perceptron (MLP) fed by tf-idf vectors of word n-grams, and (c) `run3`: a hybrid configuration composed by word-level MLP models and character-level Naive Bayes models. Our best run (`run3`) was positioned 8th among 11 participants, with 90.76% of accuracy in the test set and with a difference of 1.98 percentage points from the first system in the rank.

Although our word-level CNN did not outperform the other two configurations, it scored very close to our best run. We also found that combinations of unigrams and bigrams produce higher scores than unigrams alone. This was observed in both convolutional networks and multi-layer perceptron networks.

2 Related Work

Many approaches to discriminating between similar languages have been attempted in previous DSL shared tasks, and best results were achieved by simpler machine learning methods like SVMs and Logistic Regression (Malmasi et al., 2016). However, since deep neural networks have been successfully applied to many NLP tasks such as question answering (Severyn and Moschitti, 2015; Santos et al., 2015; Rao et al., 2016), we wanted to experiment with similar network architectures, particularly CNNs, in the task of discriminating between similar languages.

In the last shared task (DSL 2016), four teams used some form of convolutional neural network. The team *mitsls* (Belinkov and Glass, 2016) developed a character-level CNN, meaning that each sentence character was embedded in vector space. Their system ranked 6th out of seven rank positions, with 0.830 of overall accuracy, while the 1st system scored 0.894 using SVMs and character n-grams.

Cianflone and Kosseim (2016) used a character-level convolutional network with a bidirectional long short term memory (BiLSTM) layer. This approach achieved accuracy of 0.785.

A similar approach was used by the team *Resident* (Bjerva, 2016). They developed a residual network (a CNN combined with recurrent units) and represented sentences at byte-level, arguing that UTF-8 encodes non-ascii symbols with more than one byte, which potentially allows for more disambiguating power. This system achieved accuracy of 0.849. The fourth team used a word-

level CNN (Malmasi et al., 2016), but details are not available since a paper was not submitted.

In DSL 2015, Franco-Salvador et al. (2015) used logistic regression and SVM models fed by pre-trained distributed vectors. Two strategies were explored for sentence representation: sentences represented as an average of its word vectors trained by word2vec (Mikolov et al., 2013), and sentences represented directly as vectors trained by Paragraph Vector (Le and Mikolov, 2014). This system ranked 7th out of 9 participants.

Collobert et al. (2011) propose avoiding task-specific engineering by learning features during model training. In that work, several NLP tasks were used as benchmarks to measure the relevance of the internal representations discovered by the learning procedure. One of these benchmarks used a convolutional layer to produce local features around each word in a sentence.

We intended to experiment with learning word vectors in the target task, in an approach similar to that of Collobert et al. (2011). We are particulary interested in local features captured by convolutional networks. We believe these networks can learn words and language constructions commonly used in particular language varieties.

3 Data

Since we participated in the closed track, all models were trained and tested in the DSL Corpus Collection (Tan et al., 2014), provided by the organizers. This corpus was composed by merging different corpora subsets, for the purpose of the DSL shared task, and comprises news data of various language varieties.

New versions of the DSL Corpus Collection (DSLCC) are build upon lessons learned by the organizers. Thus, an overview of the version used in DSL 2017 is provided in Table 1. It encompasses 14 language varieties distributed over 6 language groups. Since its first release, the DSLCC contains 18,000 training sentences, 2,000 development sentences and 1,000 test sentences for each language variety; each sentence contains at least 20 tokens (Tan et al., 2014).

4 Methodology

Three system configurations were experimented, and one run was submitted for each. We use two-stage classification, and apply different machine

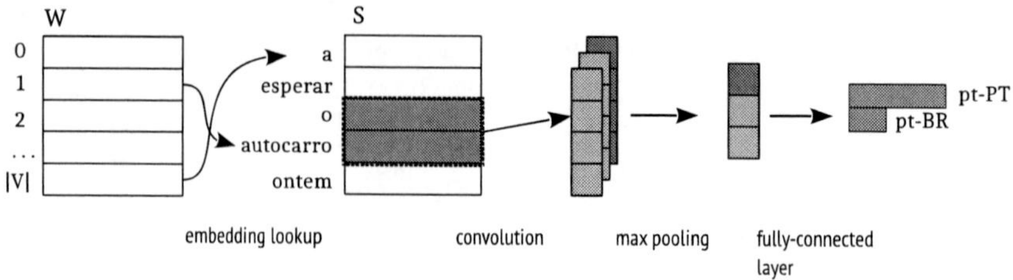

Figure 1: Architecture of the convolutional neural network.

Group	Language/Variety	Code
A	Bosnian	bs
	Croatian	hr
	Serbian	sr
B	Indonesian	id
	Malay	my
C	Persian	fa-IR
	Dari	fa-AF
D	Canadian French	fr-CA
	Hexagonal French	fr-FR
E	Brazilian Portuguese	pt-BR
	European Portuguese	pt-PT
F	Argentine Spanish	es-AR
	Peninsular Spanish	es-ES
	Peruvian Spanish	es-PE

Table 1: Language groups and language varieties contained in DSL Corpus Collection provided for DSL 2017.

learning techniques to train one classifier per language group in each configuration.

Our pipeline starts with language group prediction. After getting a group label, each sentence is forwarded to the corresponding variety classifier. In all configurations, the group classifier was kept fixed.

Character n-grams are used to train a Naive Bayes classifier[1] that distinguishes between language groups. Before training, language codes are replaced with the respective group code (*bs*, *hr*, or *sr* becomes *A*, for example), sentences are tokenized, and each token gets an end mark ($). Tokens are defined as character segments delimited by whitespaces. Better results were achieved in the development set when letter case was kept original, so it was not changed. Named entities were not changed either. We found 5 to be the best size for n-grams, with accuracy of 0.9981 in the

development set. Values greater than 5 also give good results, but training is much slower.

In the first system configuration, language varieties are classified using convolutional neural networks. This is our main approach.

4.1 Convolutional Neural Network

The model, shown in Figure 1, is similar to one of the architectures experimented by Kim (2014). It takes raw sentences as input and generates class probabilities as output. The highest probability is selected as the predicted class.

Let $s = \{w_1, w_2, w_3, \ldots, w_L\}$ be a sentence of fixed length L. Each word w_j must be mapped to a row vector $x_j \in \mathbb{R}^d$ embedded in matrix $W_{|V|+1 \times d}$, where $|V|$ is the number of distinct words in the language group. Rows in W follow the same order as words in the vocabulary, so that the i-th row in W represents the vector of the i-th word in the vocabulary V. Words are mapped to vectors by looking up their corresponding indexes in W (*embedding lookup*). Words that are not found in the vocabulary V are skipped.

Matrix $S_{L \times d}$ represents the sentence s and is obtained by concatenation of word vectors x_j. Notice that W has $|V| + 1$ rows. The first row corresponds to a special token PAD, used to fill up sentences shorter than L.

Convolution filters are slid over S to generate intermediate feature vectors known as *feature maps*. Filters are always of width d, but there may be different filter lengths and multiple filters of each length.

Formally, each feature c_i in a feature map c is computed as

$$c_i = f(w \cdot S_{i:i+h-1} + b) \qquad (1)$$

where $w \in \mathbb{R}^{h \times d}$ is a convolution filter, $b \in \mathbb{R}$ is a bias term, $f(\cdot)$ is a non-linear function such as the hyperbolic tangent, and h is the filter length.

---

[1] We use scikit-learn multinomial Naive Bayes.

The convolution of 3 filters of length 2 is represented in Figure 1. Each filter generates one feature map.

Max-over-time pooling is applied to each feature map c to take the maximum value $\hat{c} = \max(c)$. Those pooled values are concatenated to form a final feature vector that is fed to a fully-connected layer followed by softmax. For regularization, dropout is applied to the fully-connected layer. The final output is a probability distribution over the class labels.

4.1.1 Model Training

To train the model, sentences are tokenized and all digits (0-9) are replaced with zeros. Letter case is not changed. Tokens are delimited by whitespaces, but no end marker is appended to them. Maximum sentence length L is set to 80, since the longest sentence found in the training set had 77 tokens.

One model is trained for each language group. The vocabulary V is the set of unique tokens found in the training set for the current group. Vocabulary sizes are shown in in Table 2.

Group	Languages	# of tokens
A	bs, hr, sr	175,665
B	id, my	74,654
C	fa-AF, fa-IR	38,145
D	fr-CA, fr-FR	66,891
E	pt-BR, pt-PT	72,694
F	es-AR, es-ES, es-PE	92,062

Table 2: Vocabulary size for each language group.

Word vectors (matrix W) are initialized randomly and updated by backpropagation along with other network weights. Since we intend to minimize the dependence of our model on external resources, that may not be readily available for specific languages, the use of pre-trained word embeddings is entirely avoided.

The model hyperparameters are: vector dimension $d = 200$, filters of lengths (h) 1 and 2 with 100 feature maps each, hyperbolic tangent for non-linearity, drop-rate of 0.20 (or keeping probability of 0.80) for dropout, and shuffled mini-batches of size 50. Parameter values were found by grid search on the development set. All models are trained for 3 epochs, using Adam optimizer (Kingma and Ba, 2014) to minimize the cross-entropy, without early stopping. We use

TensorFlow (Abadi et al., 2016) for implementation.

Group	Code	Precision	Recall	F1
A	bs	0.74	0.72	0.73
	hr	0.83	0.84	0.84
	sr	0.85	0.88	0.86
B	id	0.98	0.97	0.97
	my	0.97	0.98	0.98
C	fa-ir	0.95	0.94	0.95
	fa-af	0.94	0.95	0.95
D	fr-ca	0.89	0.91	0.90
	fr-fr	0.90	0.89	0.89
E	pt-br	0.93	0.91	0.92
	pt-pt	0.91	0.93	0.92
F	es-ar	0.85	0.80	0.82
	es-es	0.85	0.84	0.85
	es-pe	0.82	0.88	0.85

Table 3: Performance of run1 (CNN) in each language variety.

4.2 Multi-Layer Perceptron

A vanilla Multi-Layer Perceptron[2] (MLP) was used to compare the CNN performance with that of another neural model.

In this approach, one classifier is trained for each language group, just as before. Sentences are represented as bag of word n-grams structured as high-dimensional tf-idf vectors. To make n-grams comparable to filters in the CNN models, they are extracted from sentences in sizes of 1 and 2 words (unigrams and bigrams). Letter case is not changed and no transformation is done on digits.

The model has a hidden layer of size 30 and each language variety corresponds to one unit in the output layer. The activation function is hyperbolic tangent. Models are trained for 10 epochs without early stopping by stochastic gradient descent with mini-batches of 200 examples. Optimization is carried out by having Adam optimizer to minimize the cross entropy.

4.3 Hybrid System Configuration

Considering the lower performance of both previous configurations in group A, relatively to other groups, we came up with a hybrid system configuration in which all language varieties are predicted by MLP classifiers, except for group A. For that

---

[2]We use the MLP classifier implemented in scikit-learn.

group, a standard character *n*-gram model is applied. It is exactly the model described in Section 4 as the first component of our pipeline.

This change caused little impact on performance, as discussed later in Section 6.

5 Results

Table 3 shows the performance of our convolutional neural network (`run1`) in each language variety, while Table 4 shows the corresponding confusion matrix. In Table 4, the horizontal axis indicates predicted labels, while true labels are indicated on the vertical axis. For example, it can be understood that 28 *hr* sentences were wrongly predicted as *sr*. For fine grained results, we opted to report on our main approach (CNN) instead of reporting on our best performing system.

The overall results of our three submitted runs, along with a random baseline, are summarized on Table 5. The result of the best performing system is also reported, and an extra column was appended to the table to report on development set accuracy. Our best run (`run3`) ranked 8th out of 11 participants according to the official evaluation. It achieved an accuracy of 0.9076, with a small difference of 0.0198 percentage points to the best system. Our deep neural network (`run1`) achieved an accuracy of 0.8878, indicating that the CNN scored close to our best run, but could not outperform it. Accuracy values computed on the development set behave similarly to that of the official evaluation.

The result of a traditional single-stage character *n*-gram model is also reported in Table 5 as a baseline for the development set. This is the Naive Bayes model described in Section 4, used to distinguish between language groups, but trained over all 14 language varieties.

6 Discussion

Although we focus on results of our main approach, all three runs behaved similarly. We can see in Table 4 that the confusion between language groups is minimal. This is due to the two-stage architecture that separates sentences in groups before discriminating between varieties.

The group classifier performs its task almost perfectly. In the development set, the group classifier achieved accuracy of 99.81%. We have conducted an error analysis by sampling misclassified sentences, and found that most of them really

seems to belong to the predicted language group. In the following example, the classifier predicted group D (French) instead of the true label F (Spanish):

> *Jean-Paul Bondoux, chef propietario de*
> *La Bourgogne & Jérôme Mathe, chef de*
> *Le Café des Arts (Figueroa*

In most examples, the classifier is misguided by proper nouns in foreign languages, like names of soccer players commonly found in news texts.

Prior classification of language groups narrows down the set of output classes for variety classifiers, allowing for their optimization in a single language. We believe this raises the accuracy within language groups.

However, some language groups are more challenging than others, as is shown in Table 3. Groups A and F are responsible for the lowest scores. Group A, particulary, contains the most difficult language to discriminate (*bs*) for our three system configurations. Even the change from a neural to a statistical approach in our hybrid configuration had little impact in that group performance (Table 5). This was observed both in the development set and the official runs.

The vocabulary of group A may lead to more sparse language models that hinders performance of classifiers. Group A contains almost 2 times the number of tokens in group F, the second largest group which also comprises 3 language varieties (Table 2).

Overall, our hybrid configuration showed the best performance, which is very close to the MLP. In fact, we would still rank the same position if the MLP configuration (`run2`) were considered instead.

Although the MLP scored higher than the CNN, difference was small. Also, the convolutional model is trained relatively fast in appropriate hardware, considering that pre-trained word vectors are not used and all model values are initialized randomly. With its minimum preprocessing requirements, these characteristics make our word-level CNN a viable model for discriminating between similar languages.

7 Conclusion

In this work we explored word-level convolutional neural networks to discriminate between similar languages and language varieties. Our intuition

	hr	bs	sr	es-ar	es-es	es-pe	fa-af	fa-ir	fr-ca	fr-fr	id	my	pt-br	pt-pt
hr	837	131	28	0	1	0	0	0	0	1	2	0	0	0
bs	156	718	125	0	0	0	0	0	0	1	0	0	0	0
sr	10	114	876	0	0	0	0	0	0	0	0	0	0	0
es-ar	0	0	0	798	77	123	0	0	0	0	0	0	2	0
es-es	0	0	0	90	842	63	0	1	1	0	0	0	0	3
es-pe	0	0	0	55	67	878	0	0	0	0	0	0	0	0
fa-af	0	0	0	0	0	0	953	47	0	0	0	0	0	0
fa-ir	0	0	0	0	0	0	59	940	0	1	0	0	0	0
fr-ca	0	0	0	0	0	0	0	0	909	91	0	0	0	0
fr-fr	0	1	2	0	1	0	0	0	110	885	0	0	0	1
id	0	0	0	0	1	0	0	0	0	1	971	27	0	0
my	0	0	0	0	0	0	0	0	0	1	19	980	0	0
pt-br	0	0	0	0	0	2	0	0	0	2	0	0	913	83
pt-pt	0	0	0	0	1	1	0	0	0	1	0	0	68	929

Table 4: Confusion matrix for the DSL task, run1 (CNN). The horizontal axis indicates predicted labels, while true labels are on the vertical axis.

Run	Config.	Accuracy	F1 (micro)	F1 (macro)	F1 (weighted)	Dev Accuracy
Random baseline		0.0710				
Best system		0.9274				
run1	CNN	0.8878	0.8878	0.8876	0.8876	0.8954
run2	MLP	0.9033	0.9033	0.9029	0.9029	0.9107
run3	Hybrid	0.9076	0.9076	0.9075	0.9075	0.9120
NB baseline						0.8976

Table 5: Results for the DSL task. Last column shows results computed on the development set.

is that language varieties can be distinguished by particular words and common language constructions. Even though we argue for avoiding task-specific feature engineering, we believe this kind of linguistic bias is fundamental to the success of methods that address the task of discriminating between similar languages. We believe both the CNN and the MLP models were able to capture particular words and common language constructions as features.

Acknowledgements

The work of Marcelo Criscuolo was fully funded by Federal Institute of Education, Science and Technology of São Paulo (IFSP).

References

Martín Abadi, Ashish Agarwal, Paul Barham, Eugene Brevdo, Zhifeng Chen, Craig Citro, Greg S Corrado, Andy Davis, Jeffrey Dean, Matthieu Devin, et al. 2016. Tensorflow: Large-scale machine learning on heterogeneous distributed systems. *arXiv preprint arXiv:1603.04467*.

Yonatan Belinkov and James Glass. 2016. A Character-level Convolutional Neural Network for Distinguishing Similar Languages and Dialects. In *Proceedings of the Third Workshop on NLP for Similar Languages, Varieties and Dialects (VarDial3)*, pages 145–152, Osaka, Japan.

Johannes Bjerva. 2016. Byte-based Language Identification with Deep Convolutional Networks. In *Proceedings of the Third Workshop on NLP for Similar Languages, Varieties and Dialects (VarDial3)*, pages 119–125, Osaka, Japan.

Andre Cianflone and Leila Kosseim. 2016. N-gram and Neural Language Models for Discriminating Similar Languages. In *Proceedings of the Third Workshop on NLP for Similar Languages, Varieties and Dialects (VarDial3)*, pages 243–250, Osaka, Japan.

Ronan Collobert, Jason Weston, Léon Bottou, Michael Karlen, Koray Kavukcuoglu, and Pavel Kuksa. 2011. Natural language processing (almost) from scratch. *Journal of Machine Learning Research*, 12(Aug):2493–2537.

Ted Dunning. 1994. *Statistical Identification of Language*. Computing Research Laboratory, New Mexico State University.

Marc Franco-Salvador, Paolo Rosso, and Francisco Rangel. 2015. Distributed representations of words and documents for discriminating similar languages. In *Proceedings of the Joint Workshop on Language Technology for Closely Related Languages, Varieties and Dialects (LT4VarDial)*, pages 11–16, Hissar, Bulgaria.

Cyril Goutte, Serge Léger, Shervin Malmasi, and Marcos Zampieri. 2016. Discriminating Similar Languages: Evaluations and Explorations.

Yoon Kim. 2014. Convolutional neural networks for sentence classification. In *Proceedings of the 2014 Conference on Empirical Methods in Natural Language Processing, EMNLP 2014, October 25-29, 2014, Doha, Qatar, A meeting of SIGDAT, a Special Interest Group of the ACL*, pages 1746–1751.

Diederik Kingma and Jimmy Ba. 2014. Adam: A method for stochastic optimization. *arXiv preprint arXiv:1412.6980*.

Quoc V Le and Tomas Mikolov. 2014. Distributed representations of sentences and documents. In *ICML*, volume 14, pages 1188–1196.

Shervin Malmasi and Marcos Zampieri. 2016. Arabic Dialect Identification in Speech Transcripts. In *Proceedings of the Third Workshop on NLP for Similar Languages, Varieties and Dialects (VarDial3)*, pages 106–113, Osaka, Japan.

Shervin Malmasi, Marcos Zampieri, Nikola Ljubešić, Preslav Nakov, Ahmed Ali, and Jörg Tiedemann. 2016. Discriminating between similar languages and arabic dialect identification: A report on the third dsl shared task. In *Proceedings of the 3rd Workshop on Language Technology for Closely Related Languages, Varieties and Dialects (VarDial)*, Osaka, Japan.

Tomas Mikolov, Kai Chen, Greg Corrado, and Jeffrey Dean. 2013. Efficient estimation of word representations in vector space. *arXiv preprint arXiv:1301.3781*.

Jinfeng Rao, Hua He, and Jimmy Lin. 2016. Noise-contrastive estimation for answer selection with deep neural networks. In *Proceedings of the 25th ACM International on Conference on Information and Knowledge Management*, pages 1913–1916. ACM.

Cícero dos Santos, Luciano Barbosa, Dasha Bogdanova, and Bianca Zadrozny. 2015. Learning hybrid representations to retrieve semantically equivalent questions. In *Proceedings of the 53rd Annual Meeting of the Association for Computational Linguistics and the 7th International Joint Conference on Natural Language Processing*, volume 2, pages 694–699.

Aliaksei Severyn and Alessandro Moschitti. 2015. Learning to rank short text pairs with convolutional deep neural networks. In *Proceedings of the 38th International ACM SIGIR Conference on Research and Development in Information Retrieval*, pages 373–382. ACM.

Liling Tan, Marcos Zampieri, Nikola Ljubešic, and Jörg Tiedemann. 2014. Merging comparable data sources for the discrimination of similar languages: The dsl corpus collection. In *Proceedings of the 7th Workshop on Building and Using Comparable Corpora (BUCC)*, pages 11–15, Reykjavik, Iceland.

Tommi Vatanen, Jaakko J. Väyrynen, and Sami Virpioja. 2010. Language identification of short text segments with n-gram models. In Nicoletta Calzolari (Conference Chair), Khalid Choukri, Bente Maegaard, Joseph Mariani, Jan Odijk, Stelios Piperidis, Mike Rosner, and Daniel Tapias, editors, *Proceedings of the Seventh International Conference on Language Resources and Evaluation (LREC'10)*, Valletta, Malta, may. European Language Resources Association (ELRA).

Zhiguo Wang, Haitao Mi, and Abraham Ittycheriah. 2016. Sentence similarity learning by lexical decomposition and composition. *CoRR*, abs/1602.07019.

Marcos Zampieri, Liling Tan, Nikola Ljubešić, Jörg Tiedemann, and Preslav Nakov. 2015. Overview of the dsl shared task 2015. In *Proceedings of the Joint Workshop on Language Technology for Closely Related Languages, Varieties and Dialects (LT4VarDial)*, pages 1–9, Hissar, Bulgaria.

Marcos Zampieri, Shervin Malmasi, Nikola Ljubešić, Preslav Nakov, Ahmed Ali, Jörg Tiedemann, Yves Scherrer, and Noëmi Aepli. 2017. Findings of the VarDial Evaluation Campaign 2017. In *Proceedings of the Fourth Workshop on NLP for Similar Languages, Varieties and Dialects (VarDial)*, Valencia, Spain.

Cross-Lingual Dependency Parsing for Closely Related Languages – Helsinki's Submission to VarDial 2017

Jörg Tiedemann
Department of Modern Languages
University of Helsinki
first.lastname@helsinki.fi

Abstract

This paper describes the submission from the University of Helsinki to the shared task on cross-lingual dependency parsing at VarDial 2017. We present work on annotation projection and treebank translation that gave good results for all three target languages in the test set. In particular, Slovak seems to work well with information coming from the Czech treebank, which is in line with related work. The attachment scores for cross-lingual models even surpass the fully supervised models trained on the target language treebank. Croatian is the most difficult language in the test set and the improvements over the baseline are rather modest. Norwegian works best with information coming from Swedish whereas Danish contributes surprisingly little.

1 Introduction

Cross-lingual parsing is interesting as a cheap method for bootstrapping tools in a new language from resources in another language. Various approaches have been proposed in the literature, which can mainly be divided into data transfer (i.e. annotation projection, e.g. (Hwa et al., 2005)) and model transfer approaches (e.g. delexicalized models such as (McDonald et al., 2013)). We will focus on data transfer in this paper using annotation projection and machine translation to transform source language treebanks to be used as training data for dependency parsers in the target language. Our previous work has shown that these techniques are quite robust and show better performance than simple transfer models based on delexicalized parsers (Tiedemann and Agić, 2016). This is especially true for real-world test

cases in which part-of-speech (PoS) labels are predicted instead of given as gold standard annotation while testing the parsing models (Tiedemann, 2015a).

Cross-lingual parsing assumes strong syntactic similarities between source and target language which can be seen at the degradation of model performance when using distant languages such as English and Finnish (Tiedemann, 2015b). The task at VarDial, therefore, focuses on closely related languages, which makes more sense also from a practical point of view. Many pools of closely related languages and language variants exist and, typically, the support in terms of resources and tools is very biased towards one of the languages in such a pool. Hence, one can say that the task at VarDial simulates real-world cases using existing resources from the universal dependencies project (Nivre et al., 2016) and promotes the ideas for practical application development. The results show that this test is, in fact, not only a simulation but actually improves the results for one of the languages in the test set: Slovak. Cross-lingual models outperform the supervised upper bound, which is a great result in favor of the transfer learning ideas.

More details about the shared task on cross-lingual parsing at VarDial 2017 can be found in (Zampieri et al., 2017). In the following, we will first describe our methodology and the data sets that we have used, before jumping to the results and some discussions in relation to our main findings.

2 Methodology and Data

Our submission is based on previous work and basically applies models and techniques that have been proposed by (Hwa et al., 2005; Tiedemann, 2014; Tiedemann et al., 2014). We made very lit-

Proceedings of the Fourth Workshop on NLP for Similar Languages, Varieties and Dialects, pages 131–136,
Valencia, Spain, April 3, 2017. ©2017 Association for Computational Linguistics

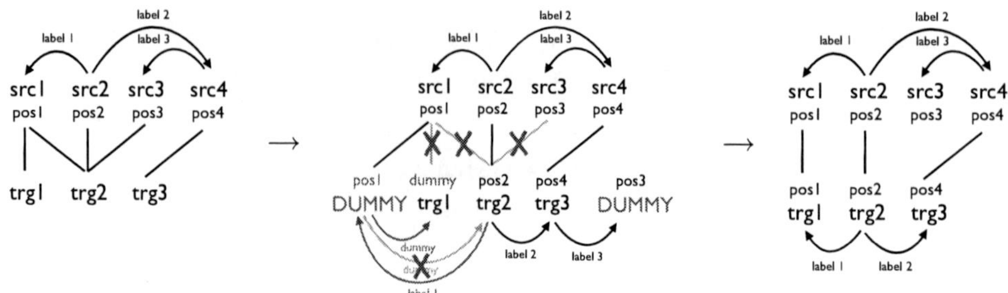

Figure 1: Annotation projection heuristics with *dummy* nodes: One-to-many alignments create dummy nodes that govern the linked target language tokens. Many-to-one alignments are resolved by removing links from lower nodes in the source language tree. Non-aligned source language tokens are covered by additional dummy nodes that take the same incoming and outgoing relations. The final picture to the right illustrates that dumme leaf nodes can safely be deleted and internal dummy nodes with single daughters can be removed by collapsing relations.

tle changes to the basic algorithms but emphasized a systematic evaluation of different methods and parameters which we tested on the development data provided by VarDial 2017. All our results are, hence, scored on data sets with predicted PoS labels. In particular, we used three different cross-lingual model types:

Projection: Annotation projection across word-aligned parallel corpora using the data sets provided by the workshop organizers (the subtitle corpora). Source language parts are tagged and parsed automatically with supervised taggers and parsers.

PBSMT: Treebank translation using a phrase-based model of statistical machine translation (SMT). Annotation are then projected from the original source language treebank to the translations to create a synthetic target language treebank. Alignment is taken directly from the translation model. The translation and language models are trained on the provided parallel corpora. No extra resources are used.

SyntaxSMT: Treebank translation using a tree-to-string hierarchical SMT model. Dependencies are transformed into constituency representations using the spans defined by the yield of each word in the sentence with respect to the dependency relations. Constituency labels are taken from the dependency relations and PoS labels are used as well for the labels of leaf nodes. After translation, we project the annotation of the source

language treebank using the same procedures as for the other two approaches. Translation models are trained on the provided parallel corpora with automatically parsed source language sentences.

There are various improvements and heuristics for the projection of dependency trees. We applied two of them: (1) *collapseDummy*, which deletes leaf nodes that are labeled as "dummy" and also removes dummy nodes with just one daughter node by collapsing the parent and daughter relations. (2) *noDummy*, which discards all sentences that still include dummy nodes after applying collapseDummy. Dummy nodes appear with the projection heuristics introduced by (Hwa et al., 2005), which we also use for handling non-one-ot-one word alignments. For example, unaligned source language tokens are projected on dummy target nodes to ensure the proper connection of the projected dependency tree. This can lead to dummy leaf nodes that can be ignored or dummy nodes with single daughters, which can be removed by collapsing the relations to head and dependent. Figure 1 illustrates the projection heuristics and the *collapseDummy* procedures. More details and examples are given in (Tiedemann and Agić, 2016). Overall, *noDummy* leads to a drop in performance and, therefore, we do not consider those results in this paper. The differences were small and most problems arose with smaller data sets where the reduction of training data has a negative impact on the performance.

For annotation projection, we used various sizes of parallel data to test the impact of data on parsing performance. The translation models are trained on the entire data provided by VarDial. Language models are simply trained on the target side of the parallel corpus.

We also tested cross-lingual models that exploit language similarities on the lexical level without translating or projecting annotation. The idea is similar to delexicalized models that are trained on generic features on the source language treebank, which are then applied to the target languages without further adaptation. With closely related languages, we can assume substantial lexical overlaps, which can be seen at the relative success of the second baseline in the shared task (also shown in Table 1). In particular, we used substrings such as prefixes (simulating simple stemming) and suffixes (capturing inflectional similarities) to add lexical information to delexicalized models. However, those models did not perform very well and we omit the results in this paper.

For training the parsers, we used mate-tools (Bohnet, 2010), which gave us significantly better results than UDPipe (Straka et al., 2016) without proper parameter optimization except for some delexicalized models. Table 1 compares the baseline models with the two different toolkits. We still apply UDPipe for PoS and morphological tagging using the provided tagger models for the target languages and similar ones trained on the UD treebanks for the source languages except for Czech, which did not work with standard settings due to the complexity of the tagset and limitations of the implementation of UDPipe. Instead, we apply Marmot (Müller and Schütze, 2015) for Czech, which also provides efficient model training for PoS and morphology.

The only "innovation" compared to our previous work is the inclusion of target language tagging on top of annotation projection. Earlier, we only used projected annotation even for PoS information. In this paper, we also test the use of target language taggers (which are part of the provided setup) to (i) over-rule projected universal PoS tags and (ii) add morphological information to the data. Especially the latter makes a lot of sense especially for highly-inflecting languages like Slovak and Croatian. However, the risk of this procedure is that noisy projection of dependency label may not fit well together with the tags created by independent tools that are probably less noisy and make different kinds of mistakes. This may mis-

lead the training algorithm to learn the wrong connections and we can see that effect in our experiments especially in connection with the tagging of universal PoS labels. This actually degrades the parsing performance in most cases. More details will be presented in the following section in connection with the results of our experiments.

3 Results

We considered all language pairs from the VarDial campaign and here we present the relevant results from our experiments. First of all, we need to mention that we created new baselines using the mate-tools to have fair comparisons of the cross-lingual models with respect to baseline approaches. The new figures (on development data) are given in Table 1. The same table also summarizes our basic results for all language pairs using the three approaches for data transfer as introduced in the previous section. All projections are made in collapseDummy mode as explained above.

Target	Croatian	Slovak	Norwegian	
Source	Slovenian	Czech	Danish	Swedish
UDPipe				
supervised	74.27	70.27	78.10	
delex	53.93	53.66	54.54	56.71
cross	56.85	54.61	54.11	55.85
mate-tools				
supervised	79.68	71.89	81.37	
delex	53.39	55.80	50.07	56.27
cross	60.29	62.21	56.85	59.63
Projected				
100,000	58.82	60.29	57.19	63.03
500,000	59.86	62.23	57.58	64.61
1,000,000	**62.92**	63.57	57.82	64.59
PBSMT	60.81	**65.97**	57.87	65.96
SyntaxSMT	58.57	63.13	58.36	**66.31**

Table 1: Basic results of cross-lingual parsing models in terms of labeled attachment scores (LAS) on development data: Annotation projection on automatically parsed bitexts of varying sizes (projected: number of sentence pairs); treebank translation models (PBSMT and SyntaxSMT); compared to three baselines: delexicalized models (delex), source language models without adaptation (cross) and fully-supervised target language models (supervised).

The first observation is that all cross-lingual models beat the delexicalized baseline by a large margin. This is, at least, self-assuring and motivates further developments in the direction of annotation projection and treebank translation. Another observation is that Croatian is surprisingly hard to improve in comparison to the cross-lingual model that applies a parser for Slovenian without any adaptation.

Another surprise is the quality of the Norwegian models coming from Danish. Both languages are very close to each other especially in writing (considering that we use bokmål in our data sets for Norwegian). Projection and translation should work well and should at least be on-par with using Swedish as the source language. However, the differences are quite significant between Danish and Swedish as the source language and this points to some substantial annotation differences between Danish and the other two languages that must be the reason behind this mystery. This conclusion is even more supported by the results of the cross-lingual baseline model without adaptation, which should perform better for Danish as the lexical overlap is large, greater than the overlap with Swedish. Yet another indication for the annotation differences is the result of the delexicalized parsers. There is also a big gap between Danish and Swedish as the source language. The result of these experiments demonstrate the remaining difficulties of cross-linguistically harmonized data sets, which is a useful outcome on its own.

We can also see, that treebank translation works rather well. For most language pairs, the performance is better than for annotation projection but the differences are rather small in many cases. An exception is Croatian for which annotation projection on parallel corpora works best, whereas translation is on par with Slovenian models applied to Croatian data.

In contrast to our previous findings, we can also see that the amount of data that is useful for annotation projection is bigger. Our prior work indicated that small corpora of around 40,000 sentence pairs are sufficient and that the learning curve levels out after that (Tiedemann and Agić, 2016). In this paper, we see increasing model performance until around one million sentence pairs before the scores converge (additional runs confirm this, even though they are not reported in the paper). A reason for this behaviour is that we now rely on movie subtitles instead of sentences from the European parliament proceedings. Subtitles are shorter in general and the domain may be even further away than parliament data, which explains the increased

amount of data to obtain reasonable lexical coverage.

Our next study looks at the impact of tagging the target language with supervised models. Our previous work on annotation projection and treebank translation relied entirely on annotation transfer from source to target when training target language parsing models. This means that we discarded any language-specific features and modeled parsing exclusively around universal PoS tags and lexical information. For highly-inflecting languages, this is not very satisfactory and the performance drops significantly compared to models that have access to morphological features. Therefore, we now test models that use projected data with additional annotation from automatic taggers. Table2 summarizes the results of those experiments.

| | projected | target-tagged | |
	PoS	morph	PoS+morph
Projected			
sl-hr	**62.92**	62.10	56.42
cs-sk	63.57	–	70.68
da-no	57.82	58.08	61.40
sv-no	64.59	64.78	62.35
PBSMT			
sl-hr	60.81	61.60	61.10
cs-sk	67.81	–	**73.90**
da-no	57.87	58.46	63.67
sv-no	65.96	66.44	64.15
SyntaxSMT			
sl-hr	58.57	60.15	56.85
cs-sk	63.13	64.05	65.02
da-no	58.36	58.59	64.74
sv-no	66.31	66.64	65.43
da+sv-no	–		**67.80**

Table 2: Added PoS and morphological tagging to projected data sets: LAS scores on development data. Only morphological tagging added (morph) or tagging both, PoS and morphology (PoS+morph).

There are two models that we evaluate: (i) A model that adds morphological features to the projected annotation, and (ii) a model that even overwrites the universal PoS tags created through projection. The first variant adds information that may contradict the PoS labels transferred from the source. For example, it may assign nominal inflection categories to a word labeled as verb through projection. The latter model should be more consistent between PoS and morphology but has the problem that those categories may not fit the dependency relations attached to the corresponding words when projecting from the source. This can also greatly confuse the learning procedures.

As it turns out, overwriting the projected PoS labels is more severe in most cases except Slovak and Norwegian (only when projected from Danish). There, it seems to be beneficial to run complete tagging after projection. In almost all other cases the performance drops, often quite dramatical. On the other hand, adding morphology always helps, except for Croatian annotation projection (which is a bit surprising again).

There is no clear winner between phrase-based and syntax-based SMT. For Slovak and Croatian, phrase-based systems seem to work best whereas Norwegian performs better with syntax-based models. A combination of Danish and Swedish data gives another significant boost (retagging projected Danish including PoS and adding morphology to projected Swedish).

We then used the best results on development data for each of the three target languages to run the cross-lingual models on the test set. No further adjustments were done after tuning the models on development data. The final results of the official test are shown in Table 3.

LAS	hr	no	sk
supervised	73.37	81.77	71.41
delex	50.05	58.13	53.87
cross	56.91	60.22	61.17
CUNI	60.70	70.21	78.12
our model	57.98	68.60	73.14

UAS	hr	no	sk
supervised	80.16	85.59	78.73
delex	63.29	67.86	64.55
cross	68.52	69.31	70.60
CUNI	69.73	77.13	84.92
our model	69.57	76.77	82.87

Table 3: Final results on the test set (*our model*) compared to baselines and fully supervised models. *CUNI* refers to a competing system – the winning team of VarDial. For the Norwegian baselines we report the results for Swedish as the source language, which is much better than using Danish.

The results on test data mainly confirm the findings from the development phase. Slovak performs clearly best in the cross-lingual scenario. This is the only language pair for which the cross-lingual model even outperforms the fully super-

vised "upper bound". This is quite fascinating and rather unexpected. Certainly, the Czech treebank is by far the largest one in the collection and much bigger than the corresponding Slovak treebank. The languages are also very close to each other and their morphological complexity requires sufficient resources. This may explain why the large Czech training data can compensate for the shortcomings of the small Slovak training data. Other factors for the positive result may also include the similarity in domains covered by both treebanks and the closeness of annotation principles. The performance for the other target languages is less impressive. Norwegian performs similar to the scores that we have seen in related work on annotation projection and cross-lingual parsing. Croatian is rather disappointing even though it also beats the cross-lingual baselines.

The main scores in our evaluations is LAS but it is also interesting to look at unlabelled attachment scores (UAS). Table 3 lists those scores as well and we can see that labelling seems to be a major problems for our models. The difference to LAS scores is dramatic, much more than the absolute difference we see between UAS and LAS in the fully supervised models. Compared to the winning submission at VarDial (*CUNI*, see (Rosa et al., 2017)), we can also see that the main difference is in LAS whereas UAS are rather similar. This seems to be a shortcoming of our approach that we should investigate more carefully.

4 Conclusions

Our experiments demonstrate the use of annotation projection and treebank translation techniques. The models perform well, especially for Slovak, which even outperforms the fully supervised "upper bound" model. In this paper, we have discussed the use of target language tagging on top of annotation projection with the conclusion that adding morphological information is almost always useful. We observe a large gap between LAS and UAS, which would require some deeper investigations. A possible reason is the use of language-specific dependency labels that are not available from the projection. However, we actually doubt that explanation looking at the success of the winning team. In their results, LAS did not suffer that much. Some surprising results could be seen as well, for example, the fact that Danish does not work as well as a source for Norwegian as

Swedish does. This cannot be explained in terms of linguistic grounds but need to refer to unexpected annotation differences or possibly a larger domain mismatch. Croatian as a target language was also surprisingly difficult and the performance is the worst in the final among all test cases. This improvement over the non-adapted Slovenian parser is only very modest whereas large gains can be observed for the other language pairs.

References

Bernd Bohnet. 2010. Top Accuracy and Fast Dependency Parsing is not a Contradiction. In *Proceedings of COLING*, pages 89–97.

Rebecca Hwa, Philip Resnik, Amy Weinberg, Clara Cabezas, and Okan Kolak. 2005. Bootstrapping Parsers via Syntactic Projection across Parallel Texts. *Natural Language Engineering*, 11(3):311–325.

Ryan McDonald, Joakim Nivre, Yvonne Quirmbach-Brundage, Yoav Goldberg, Dipanjan Das, Kuzman Ganchev, Keith Hall, Slav Petrov, Hao Zhang, Oscar Täckström, Claudia Bedini, Núria Bertomeu Castelló, and Jungmee Lee. 2013. Universal Dependency Annotation for Multilingual Parsing. In *Proceedings of ACL*, pages 92–97.

Thomas Müller and Hinrich Schütze. 2015. Robust morphological tagging with word representations. In *Proceedings of NAACL*.

Joakim Nivre, Marie-Catherine de Marneffe, Filip Ginter, Yoav Goldberg, Jan Hajic, Christopher D Manning, Ryan McDonald, Slav Petrov, Sampo Pyysalo, Natalia Silveira, et al. 2016. Universal dependencies v1: A multilingual treebank collection. In *Proceedings of Language Resources and Evaluation (LREC)*, pages 1659–1666, Portoroz, Slovenia.

Rudolf Rosa, Daniel Zeman, David Mareček, and Zdeněk Žabokrtský. 2017. Slavic Forest, Norwegian Wood. In *Proceedings of the VarDial Workshop*.

Milan Straka, Jan Hajič, and Straková. 2016. UDPipe: trainable pipeline for processing CoNLL-U files performing tokenization, morphological analysis, pos tagging and parsing. In *Proceedings of the Tenth International Conference on Language Resources and Evaluation (LREC'16)*, Paris, France, May. European Language Resources Association (ELRA).

Jörg Tiedemann and Željko Agić. 2016. Synthetic treebanking for cross-lingual dependency parsing. *Journal of Artificial Intelligence Research*, 55:209–248, January.

Jörg Tiedemann, Željko Agić, and Joakim Nivre. 2014. Treebank translation for cross-lingual parser induction. In *Proceedings of the 18th Conference Natural Language Processing and Computational Natural Language Learning (CoNLL)*, Baltimore, Maryland, USA.

Jörg Tiedemann. 2014. Rediscovering annotation projection for cross-lingual parser induction. In *Proceedings of COLING 2014*, Dublin, Ireland, August.

Jörg Tiedemann. 2015a. Cross-lingual dependency parsing with universal dependencies and predicted PoS labels. In *Proceedings of the Third International Conference on Dependency Linguistics (Depling 2015)*, pages 340–349, Uppsala, Sweden, August. Uppsala University, Uppsala, Sweden.

Jörg Tiedemann. 2015b. Improving the cross-lingual projection of syntactic dependencies. In *Proceedings of the 20th Nordic Conference of Computational Linguistics (NODALIDA 2015)*, pages 191–199, Vilnius, Lithuania, May. Linköping University Electronic Press, Sweden.

Marcos Zampieri, Shervin Malmasi, Nikola Ljubešić, Preslav Nakov, Ahmed Ali, Jörg Tiedemann, Yves Scherrer, and Noëmi Aepli. 2017. Findings of the VarDial Evaluation Campaign 2017. In *Proceedings of the Fourth Workshop on NLP for Similar Languages, Varieties and Dialects (VarDial)*, Valencia, Spain.

Discriminating between Similar Languages Using a Combination of Typed and Untyped Character N-grams and Words

Helena Gómez-Adorno[1], Ilia Markov[1], Jorge Baptista[2], Grigori Sidorov[1], David Pinto[3]

[1]Instituto Politécnico Nacional, Center for Computing Research,
Av. Juan de Dios Bátiz, C.P. 07738, Mexico City, Mexico
[2]Universidade do Algarve/FCHS and INESC-ID Lisboa/L2F,
Campus de Gambelas, P-8005-139, Faro, Portugal
[3]Benemérita Universidad Autónoma de Puebla, Faculty of Computer Science,
Av. San Claudio y 14 Sur, C.P. 72570, Puebla, Mexico
helena.adorno@gmail.com, markovilya@yahoo.com,
jbaptis@ualg.pt, sidorov@cic.ipn.mx, dpinto@cs.buap.mx

Abstract

This paper presents the CIC_UALG's system that took part in the Discriminating between Similar Languages (DSL) shared task, held at the VarDial 2017 Workshop. This year's task aims at identifying 14 languages across 6 language groups using a corpus of excerpts of journalistic texts. Two classification approaches were compared: a single-step (all languages) approach and a two-step (language group and then languages within the group) approach. Features exploited include lexical features (unigrams of words) and character n-grams. Besides traditional (untyped) character n-grams, we introduce typed character n-grams in the DSL task. Experiments were carried out with different feature representation methods (binary and raw term frequency), frequency threshold values, and machine-learning algorithms – Support Vector Machines (SVM) and Multinomial Naive Bayes (MNB). Our best run in the DSL task achieved 91.46% accuracy.

1 Introduction

Discriminating between Similar Languages (DSL) is a Natural Language Processing (NLP) task aiming at automatically identifying the language in which a text is written. From the machine-learning perspective, DSL can be viewed as a multi-class, single-label classification problem, in which automatic methods have to assign class labels (languages) to objects (texts). DSL can be used in a variety of applications, including security and

forensics, when, for example, identifying the language/dialect in which a given threat is written can help limit the search space of the author of this threat. Moreover, automated DSL is a useful aid for machine translation and information retrieval systems.

Discriminating between Similar Languages (DSL) shared task[1] provides a common platform for researchers interested in evaluating and comparing their systems' performance on discriminating between similar languages. The DSL 2017 edition (Zampieri et al., 2017) focuses on a set of 14 language varieties within 6 language groups using short text excerpts extracted from journalistic texts. Similar languages or language varieties are grouped by similarity or by their common origin.

According to (Malmasi and Dras, 2015; Çöltekin and Rama, 2016; Jauhiainen et al., 2016; Zirikly et al., 2016), high-order character n-grams and their combinations have proved to be highly discriminative for the DSL task, hence this study examines the variation of n from 1 to 6 on untyped (traditional) n-grams, but foremost this work introduces in this task the use of typed character n-grams (with n varying between 3 and 4), that is, character n-grams classified into the categories introduced by Sapkota *et al.* (2015). The authors defined 10 different character n-gram categories based on affixes, words, and punctuation. Typed character n-grams have shown to be predicative features for other classification tasks, such as Authorship Attribution (Sapkota et al., 2015) and Author Profiling (Maharjan and Solorio, 2015), including a cross-genre scenario (Markov et al., 2016). To the best of our knowledge, this is the

---

[1] http://ttg.uni-saarland.de/vardial2017/sharedtask2017.html

137

Proceedings of the Fourth Workshop on NLP for Similar Languages, Varieties and Dialects, pages 137–145,
Valencia, Spain, April 3, 2017. ©2017 Association for Computational Linguistics

first time typed character n-grams are used in the DSL task.

Furthermore, a single-step and a two-step classification approaches were built. In the single-step approach, all 14 languages are discriminated against each other. In the two-step approach, first, the language group is predicted, and then the language variety within the group. Besides, two different feature representation methods were tested, namely, binary feature representation and term frequency weighting scheme. Several threshold values were evaluated in order to fine-tune the feature set for the final submission. Finally, the performance of two popular machine-learning algorithms was examined: Support Vector Machines (SVM) and Multinomial Naive Bayes (MNB).

The remainder of the paper is organized as follows: Section 2 discusses the related work. Section 3 presents the proposed methodology. First, subsection 3.1 provides some characteristics of the DSL 2017 corpus, and subsection 3.2 describes the conducted experiments. Section 4 provides the obtained results and their evaluation. Next, Section 5 discusses these results in the light of the typed n-gram features, newly introduced in the DSL task, and based on the results from the experiments carried out on the development set. Section 6 draws the conclusions and points to possible directions of future work.

2   Related Work

The task of identifying the language of a text has been largely studied, and it is considered a solved problem. However, recent studies have shown that the task is more difficult when the texts are from different domains and have different lengths (Lui and Baldwin, 2011), when they contain code-switching (Solorio et al., 2014), or when the texts are very similar (Tan et al., 2014).

Motivated by the shared task on Discriminating between Similar Languages (DSL), there has been an increasing number of published papers in this research field. The organizers of the task compiled and released the DSL *Corpus Collection* (DSLCC) (Tan et al., 2014), which includes short excerpts from journalistic texts. It is divided, according to the version, in groups of languages. The different versions of the corpus can be found in the corresponding overview papers of the DSL task (Zampieri et al., 2014; Zampieri et al., 2015; Malmasi et al., 2016). The DSL shared task of-fers closed and open tracks; the open track allows the use of additional information or material apart from the provided training corpus, whereas the closed track only allows the use of the provided training corpus. The rest of the section will focus on the related work on the closed DSL tasks.

Most of the work on the DSL research topic addresses the task as a classification problem, using supervised machine-learning algorithms. The best performing methods for DSL use high-order character n-gram and word n-gram features (Goutte et al., 2016; Ionescu and Popescu, 2016). For a complete guide of the approaches developed for the DSL shared task, please refer to the overview papers of each edition (Zampieri et al., 2014; Zampieri et al., 2015; Malmasi et al., 2016).

In the fist edition of the DSL shared task (Zampieri et al., 2014), the best performance was achieved by the NRC-CNRC (Goutte et al., 2014) team. They proposed a two-step classification approach to predict first the language group and then the languages within the group. For both steps, they used Support Vector Machines (SVM) with word and character n-gram features. In the 2015 edition of the DSL shared task, the best performing system (Malmasi and Dras, 2015) proposed an ensemble of SVM classifiers, each trained on a single feature type. The used feature types include character n-grams ($n = 1$–6), word unigrams, and word bigrams. In the 2016 edition of the task, the winning approach (Çöltekin and Rama, 2016) used a single SVM classifier with linear kernel trained on character n-gram features of length from 1 to 7. The winning team also reported additional experiments with deep learning architectures, concluding that the linear models perform better in the DSL task.

In summary, DSL approaches can be divided into single- and two-step classification; the most popular machine-learning algorithms for this task are SVM, Logistic Regression, and ensemble classifiers. Other techniques have been also explored in the DSL task, including token-based back-off (Jauhiainen et al., 2016), prediction by partial matching (Bobicev, 2015), and word and sentence vectors (Franco-Salvador et al., 2015). It is worth mentioning that most of the deep learning-based approaches performed poorly in the DSL shared task when compared to traditional classifiers, with one exception, the character-level CNN used by the MITSLS team (Belinkov and Glass, 2016).

3   Methodology

This section presents the corpus and the experiments performed in the DSL 2017 task by the system.

3.1   Corpus

The corpus compiled for the DSL 2017 shared task is composed of excerpts of journalistic texts, and it is divided into training, development, and test subsets. For this work, the training and development subsets were joined to train the system. The corpus is balanced in terms of sentences per language. For each of the 14 languages (classes) considered in the task, the training set consists of 18,000 sentences and the development set of 2,000 sentences. The entire corpus contains 252,000 sentences for training, 28,000 for development, and 14,000 for testing (1,000 sentences per language/variety).

As mentioned above, languages are grouped by similarity or common origin. Six groups are considered (each language code is indicated in brackets): (A) Bosnian (`bs`), Croatian (`hr`), and Serbian (`sr`); (B) Malay (`my`) and Indonesian (`id`); (C) Persian (`fa-IR`) and Dari (`fa-AF`); (D) Canadian (`fr-CA`) and Hexagonal French (`fr-FR`); (E) Brazilian (`pt-BR`) and European Portuguese (`pt-PT`); and (F) Argentinian (`es-AR`), Peruvian (`es-PE`), and Peninsular Spanish (`es-ES`).

3.2   Experimental settings

Let us now move to describe the experimental settings for the three runs submitted to the competition. Table 1 summarizes the experimental settings presented below.

For runs 1 and 2, a two-step classification approach was examined, since it has previously been proved to be a useful strategy for this task (Goutte et al., 2014; Goutte et al., 2015). In this approach, the language group is predicted first, and then the closely-related languages are discriminated within the group. This approach was compared against a single-step classification (run 3), where all the 14 languages of the corpus are discriminated, irrespective of their grouping.

The performance of two machine-learning classifiers was compared using their WEKA's (Witten et al., 2016) implementation with default parameters: Support Vector Machines (SVM) and Multinomial Naive Bayes (MNB). These classification algorithms are considered among the best for text categorization tasks (Kibriya et al., 2005;

Zampieri et al., 2015). Moreover, SVM was the classifier of choice of the majority of the teams in the previous edition of the DSL shared task (Malmasi et al., 2016).

In the two-step approach (runs 1 and 2), the first step is the language group discrimination, which was performed using SVM classifier. Due to time constraints, in the second step (language/variety discrimination within a group) these two runs were set differently. In run 1, different algorithms were used for different language groups: SVM was used for groups B (Malay and Indonesian), C (Persian and Dari), and D (Canadian and Hexagonal French); while MNB was used for groups A (Bosnian, Croatian, and Serbian), E (Brazilian and European Portuguese), and F (Argentine, Peninsular, and Peruvian Spanish). In run 2, all language groups were discriminated using only MNB. For language group classification (runs 1 and 2), we increased the number of instances for training the classifier by duplicating and in some cases triplicating the training instances. In the single-step approach (run 3), only MNB was used to discriminate between the 14 languages (without group classification).

The performance of different feature sets was examined, using term frequency (*tf*) weighting scheme. Only features with $tf \geq 5$ were selected, that is, only those features that occur at least five times in the training corpus. The features used are the following: (i) unigrams of words, (ii) untyped (traditional) character n-grams, and (iii) typed character n-grams, that is, character n-grams classified into the categories introduced by Sapkota *et al.* (2015). The authors defined 10 different character n-gram categories based on affixes, words, and punctuation. In more detail, there are 3 main types, and each one has sub-categories as explained below:

- **Affix character n-grams**

  prefix An n-gram that covers the first n characters of a word that is at least $n + 1$ characters long.

  suffix An n-gram that covers the last n characters of a word that is at least $n + 1$ characters long.

  space-prefix An n-gram that begins with a space and that does not contain any punctuation mark.

Experimental settings		Run 1	Run 2	Run 3
Approach		two-step (6 groups; 14 languages)		single-step (14 languages)
ML algorithm (WEKA implementation, default parameters)	1st step	SVM	SVM	MNB
	2nd step	SVM: groups B, C, and D MNB: groups A, E, and F	MNB: all groups	
Features		untyped char. n-grams (n = 3–5), typed char. 3-grams (Sapkota et al., 2015), word unigrams.	same as run 1	same as run 1
Settings		*tf* weighting scheme; *frq*$\geq$5	same as run 1	same as run 1

Table 1: Experimental settings in the three runs of the system.

space-suffix An n-gram that ends with a space, that does not contain any punctuation mark, and whose first character is not a space.

- **Word character n-grams**

  whole-word An n-gram that encompasses all the characters of a word, and that is exactly n characters long.

  mid-word An n-gram that contains n characters of a word that is at least $n + 2$ characters long, and that does not include neither the first nor the last character of the word.

  multi-word An n-gram that spans multiple words, identified by the presence of a space in the middle of the n-gram.

- **Punctuation character n-grams**

  beg-punct An n-gram whose first character is a punctuation mark, but the middle characters are not.

  mid-punct An n-gram whose middle character is a punctuation mark (for n =3).

  end-punct An n-gram whose last character is a punctuation mark, but the first and the middle characters are not.

In this approach, instances of the same untyped n-gram may refer to different typed n-gram features. For example, in the phrase *the mother*, the first instance of the 3-gram *the* is assigned to a *whole-word* category and the second instance to a *mid-word* category. As an example, let us consider the following sample sentence:

(1) *Ana said, "Tom will fix it tomorrow."*

The character n-grams (n = 3) for the sample sentence (1) for each of the categories are shown in Table 2.

SC	Category	N-grams
affix	*prefix*	sai wil tom
	suffix	aid ill row
	space-prefix	_sa _wi _fi _it _to
	space-suffix	na_ om_ ll_ ix_ it_
word	*whole-word*	Ana Tom fix
	mid-word	omo mor orr rro
	multi-word	a_s m_w l_f x_i t_t
punct	*beg-punct*	,_" "To
	mid-punct *	_,_ _"_ _._ _"_
	end-punct	id, ow.

* In our approach, punctuation marks are separated from adjacent words and from each other by space for this category. This enables to capture their frequency.

Table 2: Character 3-grams per category for the sample sentence (1) after applying the algorithm by Sapkota *et al.* (2015).

Different lengths of character n-grams were tested. Besides, and following previous studies (Malmasi and Dras, 2015), we examine whether the performance of the proposed models could be enhanced when combining different feature sets, i.e., typed and untyped character n-grams and words. In all the runs, the combination of untyped character n-grams with n from 3 to 5, typed character 3-grams, and words was selected for the final submission.

Finally, several authors (Franco-Salvador et al., 2015; Jauhiainen et al., 2016) have mentioned using some pre-processing prior to the feature extraction for the DSL shared task. This often involves removing the distinction between upper- and lowercase characters, number simplification (reducing all digits to a single one) or removal of punctuation. In the previous VarDial edition, named entities were also replaced by a conventional string. Lastly, pre-processing has proved to be a useful strategy for several other classification tasks, including Author Profiling in social media texts (Gómez-Adorno et al., 2016a; Gómez-Adorno et al., 2016b), cross-genre Author Profiling (Markov et al., 2016), and similarity detection between programming languages (Sidorov et al., 2016). Though several experiments have been conducted using different pre-processing techniques, these failed to improve the results. Hence all pre-processing techniques have been dropped altogether, and those experiments are not reported here. Still, this can indicate that pre-processing removes features relevant to the DSL task.

The appropriate tuning of feature set size has proved to be important in other NLP tasks, such as Authorship Attribution (Stamatatos, 2013), and Author Profiling (Markov et al., 2016). In this work, an attempt was made to select the most appropriate frequency threshold based on a grid search. In more detail, the following frequency threshold (*frq*) values were examined: *frq* = 5, 10, 20, 50, and 100. Other experiments were also carried out by cutting out the most frequently occurring features in the training corpus, namely by discarding the 100 most frequent words. This strategy has proved to be helpful in other classification tasks, such as Author Profiling (Markov et al., 2016). However, in the DSL task discarding the most frequent features did not lead to improvements in accuracy. This result indicates that the most frequent words, which are stop-words for the most part, are important for DSL.

4 Experimental Results

Table 3 shows the final ranking of all the participating teams on the closed track of the DSL shared task. Except for the last system, results of all the participants are relatively similar, their accuracy ranging from 0.9274 (CECL) to 0.8894 (BAYESLINE), that is a difference of 0.038. The best submitted run (run 2) of the CIC_UALG team was ranked 6th among the 11 participants. However, the difference in accuracy from the 1th place is only 0.0128.

Next, the results of the three runs on the DSL 2017 test set are presented in Table 4. Firstly, the results of run 3 (single-step, 14 languages and no language group classification, using MNB) are slightly worse than those for runs 1 and 2 (0.0052 and 0.0077, respectively). This seems to confirm the validity of the two-step approach. Secondly,

Team	Rank	Accuracy
CECL	1	0.9274
MM_LCT	2	0.9254
XAC_BAYESLINE	3	0.9247
TUBASFS	4	0.9249
GAUGE	5	0.9165
CIC_UALG	**6**	**0.9146**
SUKI	7	0.9099
TIMEFLOW	8	0.9076
CITIUS_IXA_IMAXIN	9	0.9030
BAYESLINE	10	0.8894
DEEPCYBERNET	11	0.2046

Table 3: Final ranking for the closed track of the DSL shared task.

results of run 2 (two-step classification approach using SVM for groups and MNB for languages) slightly outperformed those of run 1 (similar setting to those of run 2, but using SVM or MNB depending on language group). This behavior was the opposite of the one seen in the experiments conducted on the development set, where the best results were achieved using an SVM classifier for both group and language classification. Since time constraints precluded repeating in run 1 test set (mixed SVM/MNB in the second step) exactly the experimental settings adopted for the development set (only SVM in both classification steps), it remains to be seen whether such scenario would change the results, and by how much.

Group classification is extremely important, since a model is unable to recover from mistakes made at the group prediction step. Table 5 shows the performance of run 2 for the language group classification. The overall results for all the language groups are very high and are in line with the experiments on the development set, where similar results were achieved.

As one can see from Table 6, the results for language classification are lower than those for group classification. The most challenging languages are the ones in groups A and F, where the average precision is 0.85 and 0.88, respectively. In group A, the Bosnian language showed a precision of 0.79, which makes it the most difficult language to identify when compared with Serbian and Croatian. Another interesting result emerges from the results concerning the Spanish language (group F), which also show a wide variation in the performance of the classifiers. This may be due to the (relatively)

Run	Accuracy	F1 (micro)	F1 (macro)	F1 (weighted)
run 1	0.9121	0.9121	0.9121	0.9121
run 2	**0.9146**	**0.9146**	**0.9146**	**0.9146**
run 3	0.9069	0.9069	0.9068	0.9068

Table 4: Results in terms of accuracy and F1 measures for the three submitted runs on the test set.

Language	Precision	Recall	F1-score
Group A	0.9980	0.9990	0.9985
Group B	0.9995	0.9975	0.9985
Group C	1.0000	0.9995	0.9997
Group D	0.9965	0.9995	0.9980
Group E	0.9940	0.9970	0.9955
Group F	0.9987	0.9953	0.9970

Table 5: Performance of run 2 per group of languages.

autonomous evolution of the American varieties not having followed the innovations of the Peninsular variety. Notice that, in comparison, the system shows a much more similar behavior when distinguishing the two Portuguese varieties, whose historic drift is also very evident.

Language	Precision	Recall	F1-score
hr	0.87	0.83	0.85
bs	0.79	0.79	0.79
sr	0.88	0.93	0.90
id	0.99	0.98	0.98
my	0.98	0.98	0.98
fa-af	0.97	0.94	0.95
fa-ir	0.94	0.97	0.96
fr-ca	0.95	0.93	0.94
fr-fr	0.92	0.95	0.94
pt-br	0.93	0.95	0.94
pt-pt	0.95	0.93	0.94
es-ar	0.87	0.86	0.86
es-es	0.85	0.88	0.87
es-pe	0.92	0.90	0.91

Table 6: Performance of run 2 per language.

The confusion matrix for our best run (run 2) in the closed DSL task is shown in Figure 1. The greatest confusion is in the Bosnian-Croatian-Serbian group, followed by the Spanish and Portuguese dialect groups. Bosnian is the most difficult language for identification among all the 14 classes.

5   Typed N-grams

A new type of features was introduced for the DSL task, typed character n-grams. Table 7 shows the different feature combinations experimented for the first step (language group) classification task, the number of features (N) considered in each experiment and the corresponding accuracy (Acc. (%)). For lack of space, only the experiments with typed 3-grams (and one experiment with 4-grams), using a frequency threshold of *frq*=20 and the SVM algorithm are shown here.

Words	Untyped 3-grams	Typed 3-grams	Untyped 4-grams	Typed 4-grams	Untyped 5-grams	Untyped 6-grams	N	Acc. (%)
✓							40,525	99.5607
	✓						36,626	99.7893
		✓					43,390	99.7929
	✓	✓					80,016	99.8071
✓	✓	✓					120,541	99.8214
✓	✓	✓	✓				240,322	99.8214
✓	✓	✓	✓		✓		**493,075**	**99.8250**
✓	✓	✓	✓		✓	✓	847,782	99.8250
✓	✓	✓	✓	✓	✓	✓	956,295	99.8071

Table 7: Results from different feature combinations on the language group classification step over the development set.

It is possible to observe that the basic bag-of-words approach (*Words*) already performs at a very reasonable level (99.5607%), but also that this result was always outperformed in all the other experiments where n-gram features were added.

Secondly, there is a slight increase (0.0036) in the performance when the typed 3-grams are used, instead of just the traditional, untyped 3-grams. The size of the feature set, however, also increases. Combining typed and untyped 3-grams improves the results further (0.142), while combining words and both kinds of n-grams provides an even better accuracy (99.8214%), a result 0.2607 above the simple, bag-of-words approach.

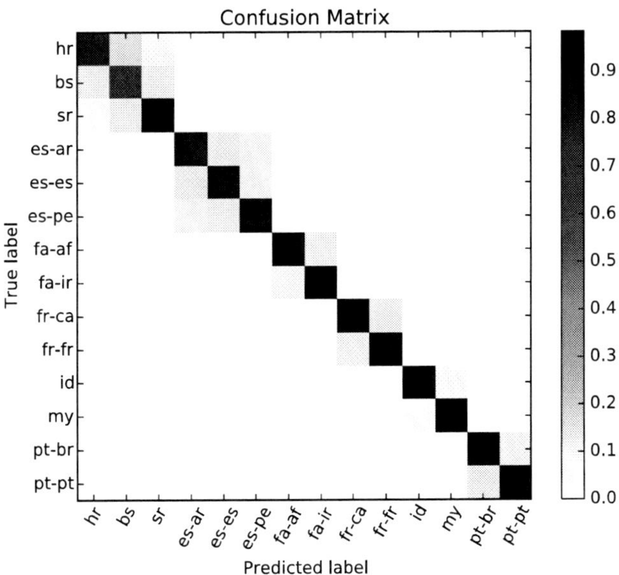

Figure 1: Confusion matrix of run 2.

In the next experiments, we successively added larger untyped n-grams to the feature set, with n from 4 to 6. Naturally, the size of the feature set increases significantly. Adding larger n-grams increased the results up to 99.8250% accuracy, but it is noteworthy that the untyped 6-grams did not improve the results above those already obtained with the untyped 5-grams, while the feature set increases 1.72 times.

Finally, a new set of typed 4-grams was added to the previous experimental settings. This, however, hindered the results, producing the same accuracy as just combining typed and untyped 3-grams. Notice that size of the feature set is approximately 12 times larger than that experiment.

As far as the language classification within language groups is concerned, experiments were carried out comparing the use of typed against untyped n-grams on the development set. Typed n-grams systematically outperformed the untyped ones. Moreover, different feature combinations were also tested for language classification; however, none of them was able to outperform the feature combination selected for the language group classification (typed 3-grams, untyped n-grams ($n = 3$–5), and words), and therefore, this combination was also selected for discriminating between the languages within the group.

6   Conclusions

This paper presented the description of the three runs submitted by the CIC_UALG team to the Discriminating between Similar Languages (DSL) shared task at the VarDial 2017 Workshop. The best performance was obtained by run 2, which achieved an accuracy of 0.9146 (6th place out of 11). This run implements a two-step classification approach, predicting first the group of languages and then discriminating the languages within the group.

Typed character n-grams was a new type of features that had been introduced in the DSL task for the first time. It was found during the preliminary experiments (on the development set) that these features improve the classification accuracy when used in combination with other types of features such as word unigrams and untyped n-grams. It was demonstrated that having increasingly larger typed or untyped n-grams can only improve results up to a certain point, and then performance deteriorates. A careful selection of feature combinations is thus required to obtain optimal results while controlling the increase in the size of the feature set, which can become computationally too costly.

One of the directions for future work would be to conduct experiments using doc2vec-based (distributed) feature representation, which has proved to provide good results for DSL (Franco-Salvador et al., 2015) and other NLP tasks, such as Authorship Attribution (Posadas-Durán et al., 2016) and Author Profiling (Markov et al., 2017), among others. Moreover, classifier ensembles will be examined, since it has been demonstrated that they are efficient for DSL (Malmasi and Dras, 2015), as well as for different real-word problems (Oza and Tumer, 2008).

Acknowledgments

This work was partially supported by the Mexican Government (Conacyt projects 240844 and 20161958, SIP-IPN 20151406, 20161947, 20161958, 20151589, 20162204, and 20162064, SNI, COFAA-IPN) and by the Portuguese Government, through Fundação para a Ciência e a Tecnologia (FCT) with reference UID/CEC/50021/2013.

References

Yonatan Belinkov and James Glass. 2016. A character-level convolutional neural network for distinguishing similar languages and dialects. In *Proceedings of the 3rd Workshop on NLP for Similar Languages, Varieties and Dialects*, VarDial '16, pages 145–150.

Victoria Bobicev. 2015. Discriminating between similar languages using PPM. In *Proceedings of the Joint Workshop on Language Technology for Closely Related Languages, Varieties and Dialects*, LT4VarDial '15, pages 59–65.

Çağrı Çöltekin and Taraka Rama. 2016. Discriminating similar languages: experiments with linear SVMs and neural networks. In *Proceedings of the 3rd Workshop on NLP for Similar Languages, Varieties and Dialects*, VarDial'16, pages 15–24.

Marc Franco-Salvador, Paolo Rosso, and Francisco Rangel. 2015. Distributed representations of words and documents for discriminating similar languages. In *Proceedings of the Joint Workshop on Language Technology for Closely Related Languages, Varieties and Dialects*, LT4VarDial '15, pages 11–16.

Helena Gómez-Adorno, Ilia Markov, Grigori Sidorov, Juan-Pablo Posadas-Durán, and Carolina Fócil-Arias. 2016a. Compilación de un lexicón de redes sociales para la identificación de perfiles de autor. *Research in Computing Science*, 115:19–27.

Helena Gómez-Adorno, Ilia Markov, Grigori Sidorov, Juan-Pablo Posadas-Durán, Miguel A. Sanchez-Perez, and Liliana Chanona-Hernandez. 2016b. Improving feature representation based on a neural network for author profiling in social media texts. *Computational Intelligence and Neuroscience*, 2016:13 pages.

Cyril Goutte, Serge Léger, and Marine Carpuat. 2014. The NRC system for discriminating similar languages. In *Proceedings of the Workshop on Applying NLP Tools to Similar Languages, Varieties and Dialects*, VarDial '14, pages 139–145.

Cyril Goutte, Serge Léger, and Marine Carpuat. 2015. Experiments in discriminating similar languages. In *Proceedings of the Joint Workshop on Language Technology for Closely Related Languages, Varieties and Dialects*, LT4VarDial '15, pages 78–84.

Cyril Goutte, Serge Léger, Shervin Malmasi, and Marcos Zampieri. 2016. Discriminating similar languages: Evaluations and explorations. In *Proceedings of the Language Resources and Evaluation (LREC)*, pages 1800–1807, Portoroz, Slovenia.

Radu Ionescu and Marius Popescu. 2016. UnibucKernel: An approach for Arabic dialect identification based on multiple string kernels. In *Proceedings of the 3rd Workshop on NLP for Similar Languages, Varieties and Dialects*, VarDial '16, pages 135–144.

Tommi Jauhiainen, Krister Lindén, and Heidi Jauhiainen. 2016. HeLI, a word-based backoff method for language identification. In *Proceedings of the 3rd Workshop on NLP for Similar Languages, Varieties and Dialects*, VarDial'16, pages 153–162.

Ashraf M. Kibriya, Eibe Frank, Bernhard Pfahringer, and Geoffrey Holmes. 2005. Multinomial naive Bayes for text categorization revisited. In *Proceedings of the 17th Australian joint conference on Advances in Artificial Intelligence*, AI '04, pages 488–499.

Marco Lui and Timothy Baldwin. 2011. Cross-domain feature selection for language identification. In *Proceedings of 5th International Joint Conference on Natural Language Processing*, IJCBLP '17, pages 553–561.

Suraj Maharjan and Thamar Solorio. 2015. Using wide range of features for author profiling. In *CLEF (Working Notes)*, volume 1391.

Shervin Malmasi and Mark Dras. 2015. Language identification using classifier ensembles. In *Proceedings of the Joint Workshop on Language Technology for Closely Related Languages, Varieties and Dialects*, LT4VarDial'15, pages 35–43.

Shervin Malmasi, Marcos Zampieri, Nikola Ljubešić, Preslav Nakov, Ahmed Ali, and Jörg Tiedemann. 2016. Discriminating between similar languages and arabic dialect identification: A report on the third DSL shared task. In *Proceedings of the*

3rd *Workshop on Language Technology for Closely Related Languages, Varieties and Dialects*, VarDial '16, pages 1–14.

Ilia Markov, Helena Gómez-Adorno, Grigori Sidorov, and Alexander Gelbukh. 2016. Adapting cross-genre author profiling to language and corpus. In *Working Notes Papers of the CLEF 2016 Evaluation Labs*, volume 1609 of *CEUR Workshop Proceedings*, pages 947–955. CLEF and CEUR-WS.org.

Ilia Markov, Helena Gómez-Adorno, Juan-Pablo Posadas-Durán, Grigori Sidorov, and Alexander Gelbukh. 2017. Author profiling with doc2vec neural network-based document embeddings. In *Proceedings of the 15th Mexican International Conference on Artificial Intelligence*, volume 10062 of *MICAI '16*. LNAI, Springer.

Nikunj Oza and Kagan Tumer. 2008. Classifier ensembles: Select real-world applications. *Information Fusion*, 9(1):4–20.

Juan-Pablo Posadas-Durán, Helena Gómez-Adorno, Grigori Sidorov, Ildar Batyrshin, David Pinto, and Liliana Chanona-Hernández. 2016. Application of the distributed document representation in the authorship attribution task for small corpora. *Soft Computing*, 21:627–639.

Upendra Sapkota, Steven Bethard, Manuel Montes-y-Gómez, and Thamar Solorio. 2015. Not all character n-grams are created equal: A study in authorship attribution. In *Proceedings of the 2015 Annual Conference of the North American Chapter of the ACL: Human Language Technologies*, NAACL-HLT '15, pages 93–102.

Grigori Sidorov, Martín Ibarra Romero, Ilia Markov, Rafael Guzman-Cabrera, Liliana Chanona-Hernández, and Francisco Velásquez. 2016. Detección automática de similitud entre programas del lenguaje de programación Karel basada en técnicas de procesamiento de lenguaje natural. *Computación y Sistemas*, 20(2):279–288.

Thamar Solorio, Elizabeth Blair, Suraj Maharjan, Steven Bethard, Mona Diab, Mahmoud Gohneim, Abdelati Hawwari, Fahad AlGhamdi, Julia Hirschberg, Alison Chang, et al. 2014. Overview for the first shared task on language identification in code-switched data. In *Proceedings of the 1th Workshop on Computational Approaches to Code Switching*, pages 62–72.

Efstathios Stamatatos. 2013. On the robustness of authorship attribution based on character n-gram features. *Journal of Law & Policy*, 21(2):427–439.

Liling Tan, Marcos Zampieri, Nikola Ljubešic, and Jörg Tiedemann. 2014. Merging comparable data sources for the discrimination of similar languages: The dsl corpus collection. In *Proceedings of the 7th Workshop on Building and Using Comparable Corpora*, BUCC '14, pages 11–15.

Ian H. Witten, Eibe Frank, Mark A. Hall, and Christopher J. Pal. 2016. *Data Mining: Practical machine learning tools and techniques*. Morgan Kaufmann, 4th edition.

Marcos Zampieri, Liling Tan, Nikola Ljubešic, and Jörg Tiedemann. 2014. A report on the DSL shared task 2014. In *Proceedings of the Workshop on Applying NLP Tools to Similar Languages, Varieties and Dialects*, VarDial '14, pages 58–67.

Marcos Zampieri, Liling Tan, Nikola Ljubešić, Jörg Tiedemann, and Preslav Nakov. 2015. Overview of the DSL shared task 2015. In *Proceedings of the Joint Workshop on Language Technology for Closely Related Languages, Varieties and Dialects*, LT4VarDial '15, pages 1–9.

Marcos Zampieri, Shervin Malmasi, Nikola Ljubešić, Preslav Nakov, Ahmed Ali, Jörg Tiedemann, Yves Scherrer, and Noëmi Aepli. 2017. Findings of the vardial evaluation campaign 2017. In *Proceedings of the 4th Workshop on NLP for Similar Languages, Varieties and Dialects*, VarDial '17.

Ayah Zirikly, Bart Desmet, and Mona Diab. 2016. The GW/LT3 VarDial 2016 shared task system for dialects and similar languages detection. In *Proceedings of the 3rd Workshop on NLP for Similar Languages, Varieties and Dialects*, VarDial '16, pages 33–41.

Tübingen system in VarDial 2017 shared task:
experiments with language identification and cross-lingual parsing

Çağrı Çöltekin
Department of Linguistics
University of Tübingen, Germany
`ccoltekin`
`@sfs.uni-tuebingen.de`

Taraka Rama
Department of Linguistics
University of Tübingen, Germany
`taraka-rama.kasicheyanula`
`@uni-tuebingen.de`

Abstract

This paper describes our systems and results on VarDial 2017 shared tasks. Besides three language/dialect discrimination tasks, we also participated in the cross-lingual dependency parsing (CLP) task using a simple methodology which we also briefly describe in this paper. For all the discrimination tasks, we used linear SVMs with character and word features. The system achieves competitive results among other systems in the shared task. We also report additional experiments with neural network models. The performance of neural network models was close but always below the corresponding SVM classifiers in the discrimination tasks.

For the cross-lingual parsing task, we experimented with an approach based on automatically translating the source treebank to the target language, and training a parser on the translated treebank. We used off-the-shelf tools for both translation and parsing. Despite achieving better-than-baseline results, our scores in CLP tasks were substantially lower than the scores of the other participants.

1 Introduction

In this paper, we describe our efforts in two rather different tasks during our participation in VarDial 2017 shared tasks (Zampieri et al., 2017). The first task, which we collectively call *language identification* task, aims to identify closely related languages or dialects. VarDial 2017 hosted three related language identification tasks: *Discriminating between similar languages* (DSL) shared task which includes closely related languages in six groups, *Arabic dialect identification* (ADI), and *German dialect identification* (GDI). The second task, *cross-lingual parsing* (CLP), aims to exploit resources available for a related source language for parsing a target language for which no syntactically annotated corpora (treebank) is available. This paper focuses on the language identification, while providing a brief summary of our methods and results for the CLP task as well.

Although language identification is a mostly solved problem, closely related languages and dialects still pose a challenge for the language identification systems (Tiedemann and Ljubešić, 2012; Zampieri et al., 2014; Zampieri et al., 2015; Zampieri et al., 2017). For this task, we experimented with two different families of models: linear support vector machines (SVM), and (deep) neural network models. For both models we used combination of character and word (n-gram) features. Similar to our earlier experiments in Var-Dial 2016 shared task (Çöltekin and Rama, 2016), the linear models performed better than the neural network models in all language identification tasks. We describe both families of models, and compare the results obtained. In the VarDial 2017 shared task campaign, the DSL and ADI shared tasks had both open and closed track submissions, while GDI had only closed tracks. For all the tasks, we only participate in the closed track.

While discriminating closely related languages is a challenge for the language identification task, the similarities can be useful in other tasks. By using information or resources available for a related (source) language one can build or improve natural language tools for a (target) language. This is particularly useful for low-resource languages, and tasks that require difficult-to-build language-specific tools or resources. Parsing fits into this category well, since treebanks, the primary resources used for parsing, require considerable time

Proceedings of the Fourth Workshop on NLP for Similar Languages, Varieties and Dialects, pages 146–155,
Valencia, Spain, April 3, 2017. ©2017 Association for Computational Linguistics

and effort to create. Hence, transferring knowledge from one or more (not necessarily related) languages is studied extensively in some recent work and found to be useful (Yarowsky et al., 2001; Hwa et al., 2005; Zeman and Resnik, 2008; McDonald et al., 2011; Tiedemann et al., 2014a, just to name a few). Particularly, it has been shown that these approaches tend to perform better than purely unsupervised methods, which can be another natural choice for parsing a language without a treebank.

There are two common approaches for transfer parsing. The first one is often called *model transfer*, which typically involves training a delexicalized parser on the source language treebank, and using it on the target language, with further adaptation or lexicalization with the help of additional monolingual or parallel corpora (McDonald et al., 2011; Naseem et al., 2012). The second method is *annotation transfer*, which utilizes parallel resources to map the existing annotations for the source language to the target language (Yarowsky et al., 2001; Hwa et al., 2005; Tiedemann, 2014). In this work, we use a straightforward annotation-transfer method using freely available tools. Similar to the language identification, we only participated in the closed track of the CLP task.

The remainder of the paper is organized as follows. The next section provides brief descriptions of the tasks and the data sets. Section 3 describes the methods and the systems we used for both tasks, Section 4 presents our results and we conclude in Section 5 after a brief discussion.

2 Task description

In this section, we provide a brief description of the tasks, and the data sets. Detailed description of the task and data can be found in Zampieri et al. (2017).

2.1 Language identification

VarDial 2017 shared task included three language identification challenges.

- *Discriminating between similar languages* (DSL) shared task includes closely related languages in six groups:
    - Bosnian (bs), Croatian (hr) and Serbian (sr)
    - Malay (my) and Indonesian (id)
    - Persian (fa-ir) and Dari (fa-af)

variety	characters		tokens	
	mean	sd	mean	sd
bs	196.53	90.80	30.86	14.18
hr	236.91	102.32	36.56	15.59
sr	209.13	97.47	33.64	15.45
es-ar	253.61	96.73	41.48	15.75
es-es	262.58	94.16	43.90	15.62
es-pe	148.48	79.66	25.33	13.26
fa-af	139.24	60.34	27.83	12.12
fa-ir	187.30	72.42	36.61	14.35
fr-ca	174.37	53.82	28.30	8.40
fr-fr	207.95	98.67	33.76	15.82
id	236.53	93.61	33.00	13.03
my	180.28	69.49	25.20	9.72
pt-br	235.51	96.82	38.63	15.66
pt-pt	217.59	90.21	35.46	14.58

Table 1: Average characters and space-separated tokens in the DSL data (training and development set combined).

- Canadian (fr-ca) and Hexagonal French (fr-fr)
- Brazilian (pt-br) and European Portuguese (pt-pt)
- Argentine (es-ar), Peninsular (es-es), and Peruvian Spanish (es-pe)

- *Arabic dialect identification* task involves discriminating between five Arabic varieties:
    - Egyptian (egy)
    - Gulf (glf)
    - Levantine (lav)
    - North-African (nor)
    - Modern Standard Arabic (msa)

- *German dialect identification* (GDI) tasks involves identifying four Swiss German dialects from the following areas.
    - Basel (bs)
    - Bern (be)
    - Lucerne (lu)
    - Zurich (zh)

The organizers provided separate training and development sets for the DSL task. The training set consists of 18 000 documents and the development set consists of 2 000 documents for each

variety	characters		tokens		docs
	mean	sd	mean	sd	
egy	141.50	200.63	25.74	35.78	3 415
glf	125.47	237.55	22.66	42.50	3 008
lav	105.48	145.35	19.37	26.03	3 308
msa	191.67	203.67	33.17	34.91	2 488
nor	80.30	121.13	14.41	21.06	3 305

Table 2: Average characters and space-separated tokens in the ADI data (training and development set combined).

variety	characters		tokens		docs
	mean	sd	mean	sd	
be	36.74	19.40	7.34	3.99	3 889
bs	44.75	26.38	8.41	4.97	3 411
lu	45.55	23.66	8.91	4.65	3 214
zh	39.11	21.57	7.24	3.96	3 964

Table 3: Average characters and space-separated tokens in the GDI data (only training set, no development set was porovided).

language variety. Although the data is balanced with respect to the number of documents, there is a slight variation with respect to the number of characters and tokens among different language varieties as presented in Table 1. These differences may explain some of the biases towards certain varieties within groups. Further details about the task and the data can be found in Goutte et al. (2016).

The ADI data includes transcriptions of speech from five different Arabic varieties. Besides the transcribed words, the ADI data also includes i-vectors, fixed-length vectors representing some acoustic properties of whole utterances. The ADI data shows slightly more class imbalance than the DSL data, as shown in Table 2. The lengths of the documents in the ADI data is also more varied. More information on the data and the task can be found in Malmasi et al. (2015).

The GDI task includes data from four Swiss German dialects. This data set includes much shorter documents compared to the DSL and ADI data sets. The GDI data statistics are also presented in Table 3.

2.2 Cross-lingual parsing

The cross lingual parsing tasks involved using one or more source language treebanks along with parallel texts to parse the target languages. The source–target language pairs for this task are,

- Target language: Croatian, Source language: Slovenian

- Target language: Slovak, Source language: Czech

- Target language: Norwegian, Source languages: Danish and Swedish

The source language treebanks are part of the Universal Dependencies (UD) version 1.4 (Nivre et al., 2016). The parallel texts are subtitles from the OPUS corpora collection (Tiedemann, 2012).

3 System descriptions

3.1 Language identification with SVMs

Similar to our past year's participation, we submitted results using a multi-class (one-vs-one) support vector machine (SVM) model. Unlike our last year's submissions (Çöltekin and Rama, 2016) where we used only character n-grams as features, we used a combination of both character and word n-grams. Both character and word n-gram features are weighted using sub-linear tf-idf scaling (Jurafsky and Martin, 2009, p.805). We did not apply any filtering (e.g., case normalization), except for removing features that occur in only a single document.

The ADI data set also included fixed-length numeric features, i-vectors, for each document. We concatenated these vectors with the tf-idf features in our best performing model for the ADI task. In all SVM models we combine the features in a flat manner and predict the varieties directly without using a two-stage or hierarchical approach. We also tuned the number of character and word n-grams, as well as the SVM margin parameter 'C' for each task separately. The SVMs were not very sensitive to the changes in these parameters. Table 4 lists the configurations of the SVM models in our main submission. We present further results on the effects of these parameters in Section 4. In all of our experiments, we combined the development and training sets for the DSL and ADI tasks and used 10-fold cross validation for tuning. We also used 10-fold cross validation for tuning the parameters of the system for the GDI task for which no designated development data was provided.

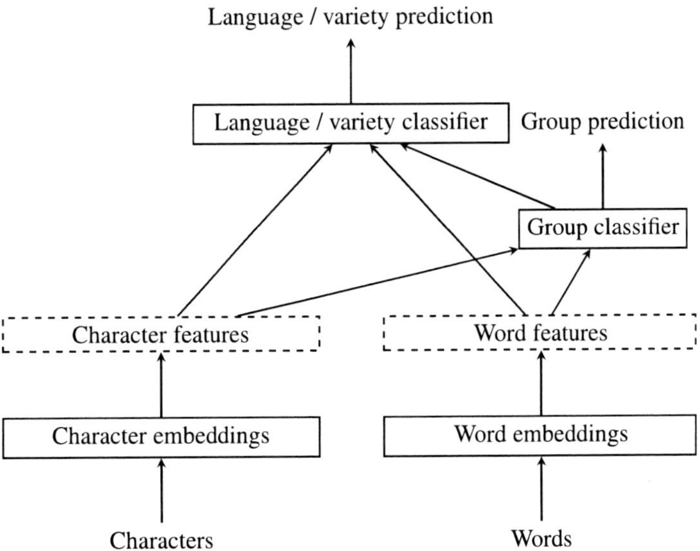

Figure 1: The schematic representation of our neural network architecture.

Task	word	char	C
DSL	3	7	1.8
ADI	3	10	0.5
GDI	2	7	0.7

Table 4: Maximum word and character n-grams, and the SVM margin parameter, C, used for each language identification task, for our main submission. We use all n-grams starting unigrams up to the indicated maximum n-gram value.

We also experimented with logistic regression, using both one-vs-rest and one-vs-one multi-class strategies. Like the previous year, the SVM models always performed slightly better than logistic regression models. In this paper, we only describe the SVM models and discuss the results obtained using them.

All linear models were implemented with scikit-learn (Pedregosa et al., 2011) and trained and tested using Liblinear backend (Fan et al., 2008).

3.2 Language identification with neural networks

The general architecture used for our hierarchical network model is presented in Figure 1. This is virtually identical to the general architecture described in Çöltekin and Rama (2016).

In this study, we use both task-specific character and word embeddings to train our model. They are trained during learning to discriminate the languages varieties. As opposed to general-purpose embeddings, they are expected to capture the input features (characters words) that are indicative of a particular language variety rather than words that are semantically similar.

The presented architecture is an instance of multi-label classification. During training, model parameters are optimized to guess both the group and the specific language variety correctly. Furthermore, we feed the model's prediction of the group to the classifier predicting the specific language variety. For instance, we would use the information that *fr-fr* and *fr-ca* labels belong to the French group. The intuition behind this model is that it will use the highly accurate group prediction during test time to tune into features that are useful within a particular language group for predicting individual varieties. For ADI, and GDI tasks, we do not use the group prediction since these data set contain only as single language group.

In principle, the boxes 'Group classifier' and 'Language / variety classifier' in Figure 1 may include multiple layers for allowing the classifier to generalize based on non-linear combinations in its input features. However, in the experiments reported in this paper, we did not use multiple layers in both the classifiers, since, it did not improve the results.

The dashed boxes in Figure 1 turn the sequence of word and character embeddings into fixed-size feature vectors. Any network layer/model that extracts useful features from a sequence of embeddings are useful here. The convolutional and recurrent neural networks are typical choices for this step. We have experimented with both methods, as well as simple averaging of embeddings.

In the experiments reported below, the documents are padded or truncated to 512 characters for the character embedding input, and they are padded or truncated to 128 tokens for the word embeddings input. For both embedding layers, we used dropout with rate 0.40. Both classifiers in the figure were single layer networks (with softmax activation function), predicting one-hot representations of groups and varieties. The network was trained using categorical cross-entropy loss function for both outputs using Adam optimization algorithm. To prevent overfitting, the training was stopped when validation set accuracy stopped improving after two iterations. All neural network experiments are realized using Keras (Chollet, 2015) with Tensorflow backend (Abadi et al., 2015).

3.3 Cross-lingual parsing

We adopted the *word-based MT* approach of Tiedemann et al. (2014b) for translating the source language dependency treebank(s) to target languages. In the first step, we used the *efmaral* system (Östling and Tiedemann, 2016) to word-align the OPUS parallel corpus of a source-target language pair. We word-aligned the parallel corpus from both source to target and target to source; and, then proceeded to symmetrize the alignments using *grow-diag-final-and* method. Then, we supplied the symmetric alignments to Moses (Koehn et al., 2007) and constrained the Moses system to train using phrase translations of length 1. Finally, we used the Moses decoder with the default settings to translate the source language treebank to target language. The intuition behind this approach is that word based translations do not require heuristics to correct the trees that result from the default phrase-based translation settings of Moses. We used this approach to create treebanks for Norwegian, Croatian, and Slovak languages.

Task	Run	Accuracy	F1 (micro)	F1 (weighted)
ADI	1	69.71	69.71	69.75
ADI	2	57.44	57.44	56.90
DSL	1	92.49	92.49	92.45
GDI	1	65.28	65.28	62.64

Table 5: Main results of language identification tasks on the test set as calculated by the organizers.

4 Results

4.1 Language identification

In the language identification subtasks, our best performing models were SVM models with the parameters listed in Table 4. We have participated in the shared task using only these models. For the ADI task, we submitted two runs, the first one using both the transcriptions and the i-vectors, and the second one using only the transcriptions. The scores of our systems in each task on the test set is presented in Table 5.

According to rankings based on absolute F1 scores, our results indicate that the systems are in mid-range in all tasks. More precisely, we get 4th, 3th, 6th, positions in DSL, ADI, and GDI tasks, respectively. However, for the DSL task, the difference from the best score is rather small. Our accuracy scores are behind the top scores in each task by $0.25\,\%$, $6.57\,\%$ and $2.78\,\%$ for DSL, ADI, and GDI respectively. We also present the confusion matrices for each task. For the DSL task, as shown in Table 6, almost all confusions occur within the groups. Within the groups, there seems to be a slight tendency for the members of the group with shorter documents on average to be confused more. Looking at inter-language group confusions on the development set more closely reveals that all such confusions are difficult to classify correctly without further context. Table 9 lists a few of the documents that were assigned a label from another language group by the classifier. The confused documents mainly consist of named entities, addresses, numbers or other symbols.

The confusion tables for ADI and GDI tasks are presented in Table 7 and Table 8 respectively. Since these represent a single group of varieties, the confusions are common in both tables. We do not observe any clear patterns in the mistakes made by the classifier in ADI task. Similarly, the confusion matrix of the GDI task does not indicate very clear patterns, except the Lucerne variety seems to be very difficult to identify for our system. The documents from the Lucerne area are more often recognized as from Basel or Zurich than Lucerne itself.

In our last year's participation, we only used character n-grams as features. Intuitively, the character n-grams are useful since they can capture parts of the morphology of languages. This helps generalizing over suffixes or prefixes that were possibly not observed in the training data. Larger character n-grams also include words, and also fragments from word sequences. However, very large character n-grams do not provide much help since they suffer from data sparsity. In our experiments, we often found improvements in language discrimination up to 7-grams. This may not be able to capture most variety-specific word bigrams or trigrams. As a result, we expect word n-grams to be also useful, despite the fact the information from (large) character n-grams and word n-grams will overlap considerably. To investigate the relative merits of combining character and word ngrams, we present the best average accuracies scores obtained with 10-fold cross validation experiments on the DSL training and development set combination in Table 10. Increasing the maximum length of the character n-grams helps in for all cases up to character n-gram length of 7. Increasing maximum word n-grams length also has a positive effect in all cases, although, the effect diminishes after bigrams.

As in the previous year, the accuracy of the neural network model was close to the SVM model, but despite additional efforts of tuning, the neural models did not perform better than the SVM model in any of the tasks. We performed a random search involving the type of feature extractors for characters and words, the length of embeddings for characters and words, the width of the convolutional filter (in case one of the feature extractors were convolutional networks), length of the embedding representations (number of convolutions, or length of RNN representations), and the amount of dropout used in various parts of the network.

In the case of the DSL development set, the best accuracy score obtained by the neural network was 90.72 as opposed 92.58 from our best performing SVM model in the same setting. In general, the performance of the model was relatively stable across 200 different random configurations of hyperparameters listed above, all lying within

the range 0.88–0.91. Convolutional networks performed well over characters, but they yielded bad scores over the words, likely due to large number of filters over words that would be needed in the multilingual corpus processing. Recurrent neural network flavors (GRUs and LSTMs) were among the better options for obtaining better document representations from the word embeddings. However, simple averaging of the embedding vectors performed similarly. On character features, recurrent networks were impractical in our computing environment due to longer input sequence (512 characters).

4.2 Cross-lingual parsing

We used UDpipe (Straka et al., 2016) to train our parsers on the translated treebanks. We report both the Labeled Attachment Scores (LAS) and the Unlabeled Attachment Scores (UAS) in Table 11. In the case of Norwegian, we trained our system on both individual and combined treebanks from Swedish and Danish. In the case of Norwegian, we obtained the best results (9 points more than the baseline) when we trained the dependency parser on Norwegian treebank which is translated from Swedish. We obtained slightly better results than the baseline in the case of Croatian. In the case of Slovak, we obtained an improvement of 10 points over the baseline. In all the cases, our results are behind the other two participants by a margin of 5 points in Croatian and Norwegian; and, 14 points in the case of Slovak.

5 Discussion and conclusions

In this paper we described our systems participating in the VarDial 2017 shared tasks. We participated in all the four tasks offered during this shared task campaign. Although our main focus has been language identification tasks, we have also participated in the cross-lingual parsing shared task with a simple approach, and reported results in this paper.

Our participation in the language discrimination tasks, namely *Discriminating between similar languages* (DSL), *Arabic dialect identification* (ADI), and *German dialect identification* (GDI), is similar to to our previous year's participation (Çöltekin and Rama, 2016). We experimented with both SVMs and (deep) neural network models. Similar to our last year's experience, SVMs performed better than neural networks. This is inline with

	hr	bs	sr	es-ar	es-es	es-pe	fa-af	fa-ir	fr-ca	fr-fr	id	my	pt-br	pt-pt
hr	873	112	13	0	0	0	0	0	0	1	0	0	1	0
bs	112	783	103	0	1	0	0	0	0	1	0	0	0	0
sr	8	64	927	0	0	0	0	0	0	1	0	0	0	0
es-ar	0	0	0	836	62	93	0	0	0	3	0	0	4	2
es-es	0	0	0	72	879	45	0	0	0	0	0	0	2	2
es-pe	0	0	0	18	28	953	0	0	0	1	0	0	0	0
fa-af	0	0	0	0	0	0	969	31	0	0	0	0	0	0
fa-ir	0	0	0	0	0	0	31	968	0	0	0	0	1	0
fr-ca	0	0	0	0	0	0	0	0	951	49	0	0	0	0
fr-fr	0	0	0	0	0	0	0	0	61	939	0	0	0	0
id	0	0	0	0	2	0	0	0	0	1	983	14	0	0
my	0	0	0	0	0	0	0	0	0	2	10	88	0	0
pt-br	0	0	0	0	0	0	0	0	0	2	0	0	950	48
pt-pt	0	0	0	0	1	0	0	0	0	1	0	0	49	949

Table 6: Confusion matrix for the DSL task.

	egy	glf	lav	msa	nor
egy	210	18	37	17	20
glf	15	165	45	13	12
lav	36	40	218	17	23
msa	10	16	10	212	14
nor	36	22	36	15	235

Table 7: Confusion matrix for the ADI task.

	be	bs	lu	zh
be	634	57	24	191
bs	69	679	41	150
lu	181	263	244	228
zh	21	27	11	818

Table 8: Confusion matrix for the GDI task.

gold std.	predicted	text
hr	fr-FR	2. 27/4 vrt 118 27/2 149,60
fr-FR	hr	Nadal (Esp) { Cilic (Cro): 6-2, 6-4, 6-3
bs	fr-FR	- 17.30 Galatasaray - Jadran (Split)
pt-BR	fr-FR	Shangri-La: 10 Avenue d'Iéna, 16ème arrondissement, Paris. Tel. (33 1) 5367-1998.
id	pt-BR	Kiper: Julio Cesar (Inter Milan), Victor (Gremio), Jefferson (Botafogo), Fabio (Cruzeiro)

Table 9: Examples of inter-group confusions from the DSL task.

		Max word n-gram length		
		0	**1**	**2**	**3**
	0		90.47	91.48	91.53
	1	84.25	90.84	91.63	91.84
	2	84.25	91.68	92.07	92.22
Max char n-gram length	3	90.16	91.83	92.23	92.24
	4	91.69	92.12	92.38	92.40
	5	92.17	92.37	92.49	92.53
	6	92.34	92.48	92.55	92.55
	7	92.39	92.50	92.56	92.58
	8	92.37	92.48	92.52	92.54

Table 10: Best accuracy scores obtained on the DSL data by combinations of character and word n-grams of varying sizes.

target (source)	Baseline		Translation	
	LAS	UAS	LAS	UAS
no (sv)	56.63	66.24	65.62	74.61
no (da)	54.91	64.53	58.55	67.48
no (sv+da)	59.95	69.02	64.91	73.50
hr (sl)	53.35	63.94	55.20	66.75
sk (cz)	53.72	65.70	64.05	73.16

Table 11: Labeled (LAS) and unlabeled (UAS) attachment scores obtained by the translation model in comparison to the baseline provided by the organizers.

the results of VarDial 2016 shared task, where linear models (Jauhiainen et al., 2016; Zirikly et al., 2016; Goutte and Léger, 2016; Herman et al., 2016; Cianflone and Kosseim, 2016; Barbaresi, 2016; Adouane et al., 2016; McNamee, 2016; Nisioi et al., 2016; Gamallo et al., 2016; Malmasi and Zampieri, 2016; Ionescu and Popescu, 2016; Eldesouki et al., 2016, for example), performed better than the neural network models (Bjerva, 2016; Belinkov and Glass, 2016). Our current experiments also follow the same trend. As in the last year, our SVM models performed better than neural network models, and our main results only include scores obtained by SVM classifiers.

Unlike last year, where we only used character n-grams, this year we used a combination of character and word n-grams as features, and tuned the maximum number of n-grams included for each task. We obtained scores competitive with the scores of the other participating teams. In general, all scores are slightly higher for the DSL task compared to the last year. Besides the results on the shared task, we presented some results from the additional experiments that we performed in Section 4. The combination of character and word n-grams seem to have made a small but consistent difference in the experiments performed on the development data.

For the cross-lingual parsing task, we followed a simple method by automatically translating the source treebank and training an off-the-shelf parser on the translated treebank. We did not perform any further adaptation or pre-trained word representations which may have been helpful in this task. Although we obtained results that are consistently better than the baseline, our results have been substantially lower than the scores of the other two participating systems.

Acknowledgments

The authors thank the reviewers for the comments which helped improve the paper. The second author is supported by the ERC Advanced Grant 324246 EVOLAEMP, which is gratefully acknowledged.

References

Martín Abadi, Ashish Agarwal, Paul Barham, Eugene Brevdo, Zhifeng Chen, Craig Citro, Greg S. Corrado, Andy Davis, Jeffrey Dean, Matthieu Devin, Sanjay Ghemawat, Ian Goodfellow, Andrew Harp, Geoffrey Irving, Michael Isard, Yangqing Jia, Rafal Jozefowicz, Lukasz Kaiser, Manjunath Kudlur, Josh Levenberg, Dan Mané, Rajat Monga, Sherry Moore, Derek Murray, Chris Olah, Mike Schuster, Jonathon Shlens, Benoit Steiner, Ilya Sutskever, Kunal Talwar, Paul Tucker, Vincent Vanhoucke, Vijay Vasudevan, Fernanda Viégas, Oriol Vinyals, Pete Warden, Martin Wattenberg, Martin Wicke, Yuan Yu, and Xiaoqiang Zheng. 2015. TensorFlow: Large-scale machine learning on heterogeneous systems. Software available from tensorflow.org.

Wafia Adouane, Nasredine Semmar, and Richard Johansson. 2016. ASIREM Participation at the Discriminating Similar Languages Shared Task 2016. In *Proceedings of the Third Workshop on NLP for Similar Languages, Varieties and Dialects (VarDial3)*, pages 163–169, Osaka, Japan.

Adrien Barbaresi. 2016. An Unsupervised Morphological Criterion for Discriminating Similar Languages. In *Proceedings of the Third Workshop on NLP for Similar Languages, Varieties and Dialects (VarDial3)*, pages 212–220, Osaka, Japan.

Yonatan Belinkov and James Glass. 2016. A Character-level Convolutional Neural Network for Distinguishing Similar Languages and Dialects. In *Proceedings of the Third Workshop on NLP for Similar Languages, Varieties and Dialects (VarDial3)*, pages 145–152, Osaka, Japan.

Johannes Bjerva. 2016. Byte-based Language Identification with Deep Convolutional Networks. In *Proceedings of the Third Workshop on NLP for Similar Languages, Varieties and Dialects (VarDial3)*, pages 119–125, Osaka, Japan.

Çağri Çöltekin and Taraka Rama. 2016. Discriminating Similar Languages with Linear SVMs and Neural Networks. In *Proceedings of the Third Workshop on NLP for Similar Languages, Varieties and Dialects (VarDial3)*, pages 15–24, Osaka, Japan.

François Chollet. 2015. Keras. `https://github.com/fchollet/keras`.

Andre Cianflone and Leila Kosseim. 2016. N-gram and Neural Language Models for Discriminating Similar Languages. In *Proceedings of the Third Workshop on NLP for Similar Languages, Varieties and Dialects (VarDial3)*, pages 243–250, Osaka, Japan.

Mohamed Eldesouki, Fahim Dalvi, Hassan Sajjad, and Kareem Darwish. 2016. QCRI @ DSL 2016: Spoken Arabic Dialect Identification Using Textual Features. In *Proceedings of the Third Workshop on NLP for Similar Languages, Varieties and Dialects (VarDial3)*, pages 221–226, Osaka, Japan.

Rong-En Fan, Kai-Wei Chang, Cho-Jui Hsieh, Xiang-Rui Wang, and Chih-Jen Lin. 2008. LIBLINEAR: A library for large linear classification. *Journal of Machine Learning Research*, 9:1871–1874.

Pablo Gamallo, Iñaki Alegria, José Ramom Pichel, and Manex Agirrezabal. 2016. Comparing Two Basic Methods for Discriminating Between Similar Languages and Varieties. In *Proceedings of the Third Workshop on NLP for Similar Languages, Varieties and Dialects (VarDial3)*, pages 170–177, Osaka, Japan.

Cyril Goutte and Serge Léger. 2016. Advances in Ngram-based Discrimination of Similar Languages. In *Proceedings of the Third Workshop on NLP for Similar Languages, Varieties and Dialects (VarDial3)*, pages 178–184, Osaka, Japan.

Cyril Goutte, Serge Léger, Shervin Malmasi, and Marcos Zampieri. 2016. Discriminating Similar Languages: Evaluations and Explorations.

Ondřej Herman, Vít Suchomel, Vít Baisa, and Pavel Rychlý. 2016. DSL Shared Task 2016: Perfect Is The Enemy of Good Language Discrimination Through Expectation–Maximization and Chunk-based Language Model. In *Proceedings of the Third Workshop on NLP for Similar Languages, Varieties and Dialects (VarDial3)*, pages 114–118, Osaka, Japan.

Rebecca Hwa, Philip Resnik, Amy Weinberg, Clara Cabezas, and Okan Kolak. 2005. Bootstrapping parsers via syntactic projection across parallel texts. 11(3):311–325.

Radu Tudor Ionescu and Marius Popescu. 2016. UnibucKernel: An Approach for Arabic Dialect Identification Based on Multiple String Kernels. In *Proceedings of the Third Workshop on NLP for Similar Languages, Varieties and Dialects (VarDial3)*, pages 135–144, Osaka, Japan.

Tommi Jauhiainen, Krister Lindén, and Heidi Jauhiainen. 2016. HeLI, a Word-Based Backoff Method for Language Identification. In *Proceedings of the Third Workshop on NLP for Similar Languages, Varieties and Dialects (VarDial3)*, pages 153–162, Osaka, Japan.

Daniel Jurafsky and James H. Martin. 2009. *Speech and Language Processing: An Introduction to Natural Language Processing, Computational Linguistics, and Speech Recognition*. Pearson Prentice Hall, second edition.

Philipp Koehn, Hieu Hoang, Alexandra Birch, Chris Callison-Burch, Marcello Federico, Nicola Bertoldi, Brooke Cowan, Wade Shen, Christine Moran, Richard Zens, et al. 2007. Moses: Open source toolkit for statistical machine translation. In *Proceedings of the 45th annual meeting of the ACL on interactive poster and demonstration sessions*, pages 177–180. Association for Computational Linguistics.

Shervin Malmasi and Marcos Zampieri. 2016. Arabic Dialect Identification in Speech Transcripts. In *Proceedings of the Third Workshop on NLP for Similar Languages, Varieties and Dialects (VarDial3)*, pages 106–113, Osaka, Japan.

Shervin Malmasi, Eshrag Refaee, and Mark Dras. 2015. Arabic Dialect Identification using a Parallel Multidialectal Corpus. In *Proceedings of the 14th Conference of the Pacific Association for Computational Linguistics (PACLING 2015)*, pages 209–217, Bali, Indonesia, May.

Ryan McDonald, Slav Petrov, and Keith Hall. 2011. Multi-source transfer of delexicalized dependency parsers. In *Proceedings of the 2011 Conference on Empirical Methods in Natural Language Processing*, pages 62–72. Association for Computational Linguistics, July.

Paul McNamee. 2016. Language and Dialect Discrimination Using Compression-Inspired Language Models. In *Proceedings of the Third Workshop on NLP for Similar Languages, Varieties and Dialects (VarDial3)*, pages 195–203, Osaka, Japan.

Tahira Naseem, Regina Barzilay, and Amir Globerson. 2012. Selective sharing for multilingual dependency parsing. In *Proceedings of the 50th Annual Meeting of the Association for Computational Linguistics*

(Volume 1: Long Papers), pages 629–637. Association for Computational Linguistics, July.

Sergiu Nisioi, Alina Maria Ciobanu, and Liviu P. Dinu. 2016. Vanilla Classifiers for Distinguishing between Similar Languages. In *Proceedings of the Third Workshop on NLP for Similar Languages, Varieties and Dialects (VarDial3)*, pages 235–242, Osaka, Japan.

Joakim Nivre, Marie-Catherine de Marneffe, Filip Ginter, Yoav Goldberg, Jan Hajič, Christopher Manning, Ryan McDonald, Slav Petrov, Sampo Pyysalo, Natalia Silveira, Reut Tsarfaty, and Daniel Zeman. 2016. Universal dependencies v1: A multilingual treebank collection. In *Proceedings of the Tenth International Conference on Language Resources and Evaluation (LREC'16)*, pages 23–28.

Robert Östling and Jörg Tiedemann. 2016. Efficient word alignment with Markov Chain Monte Carlo. *Prague Bulletin of Mathematical Linguistics*, 106:125–146, October.

F. Pedregosa, G. Varoquaux, A. Gramfort, V. Michel, B. Thirion, O. Grisel, M. Blondel, P. Prettenhofer, R. Weiss, V. Dubourg, J. Vanderplas, A. Passos, D. Cournapeau, M. Brucher, M. Perrot, and E. Duchesnay. 2011. Scikit-learn: Machine learning in Python. *Journal of Machine Learning Research*, 12:2825–2830.

Milan Straka, Jan Hajic, and Jana Straková. 2016. Ud-pipe: Trainable pipeline for processing conll-u files performing tokenization, morphological analysis, pos tagging and parsing. In *Proceedings of the Tenth International Conference on Language Resources and Evaluation (LREC 2016)*.

Jörg Tiedemann and Nikola Ljubešić, Ljubešić. 2012. Efficient discrimination between closely related languages. In *Proceedings of COLING 2012*, pages 2619–2634.

Jörg Tiedemann, Željko Agić, and Joakim Nivre. 2014a. Treebank translation for cross-lingual parser induction. In *Proceedings of the Eighteenth Conference on Computational Natural Language Learning*, pages 130–140. Association for Computational Linguistics, June.

Jörg Tiedemann, Željko Agić, and Joakim Nivre. 2014b. Treebank translation for cross-lingual parser induction. In *Eighteenth Conference on Computational Natural Language Learning (CoNLL 2014)*.

Jörg Tiedemann. 2012. Parallel data, tools and interfaces in opus. In *Proceedings of the Eight International Conference on Language Resources and Evaluation (LREC'12)*, Istanbul, Turkey.

Jörg Tiedemann. 2014. Rediscovering annotation projection for cross-lingual parser induction. In *Proceedings of COLING 2014, the 25th International Conference on Computational Linguistics: Technical Papers*, pages 1854–1864. Dublin City University and Association for Computational Linguistics, August.

David Yarowsky, Grace Ngai, and Richard Wicentowski. 2001. Inducing multilingual text analysis tools via robust projection across aligned corpora. In *Proceedings of the first international conference on Human language technology research*, pages 1–8. Association for Computational Linguistics.

Marcos Zampieri, Liling Tan, Nikola Ljubešić, and Jörg Tiedemann. 2014. A report on the dsl shared task 2014. In *Proceedings of the First Workshop on Applying NLP Tools to Similar Languages, Varieties and Dialects*, pages 58–67.

Marcos Zampieri, Liling Tan, Nikola Ljubešic, Jörg Tiedemann, and Preslav Nakov. 2015. Overview of the dsl shared task 2015. In *Joint Workshop on Language Technology for Closely Related Languages, Varieties and Dialects*, pages 1–9.

Marcos Zampieri, Shervin Malmasi, Nikola Ljubešić, Preslav Nakov, Ahmed Ali, Jörg Tiedemann, Yves Scherrer, and Noëmi Aepli. 2017. Findings of the VarDial Evaluation Campaign 2017. In *Proceedings of the Fourth Workshop on NLP for Similar Languages, Varieties and Dialects (VarDial)*, Valencia, Spain.

Daniel Zeman and Philip Resnik. 2008. Cross-language parser adaptation between related languages. In *Proceedings of the IJCNLP-08 Workshop on NLP for Less Privileged Languages*, pages 35–42.

Ayah Zirikly, Bart Desmet, and Mona Diab. 2016. The GW/LT3 VarDial 2016 Shared Task System for Dialects and Similar Languages Detection. In *Proceedings of the Third Workshop on NLP for Similar Languages, Varieties and Dialects (VarDial3)*, pages 33–41, Osaka, Japan.

When Sparse Traditional Models Outperform Dense Neural Networks: the Curious Case of Discriminating between Similar Languages

Maria Medvedeva[♡]   **Martin Kroon**[◇]   **Barbara Plank**[◇]

[♡]Dept. of Computational Linguistics, Saarland University, Saarbrücken, Germany
[◇]Center for Language and Cognition Groningen, University of Groningen, The Netherlands
`mariam@coli.uni-saarland.de,martinkroon06@gmail.com,b.plank@rug.nl`

Abstract

We present the results of our participation in the VarDial 4 shared task on discriminating closely related languages. Our submission includes simple traditional models using linear support vector machines (SVMs) and a neural network (NN). The main idea was to leverage language group information. We did so with a two-layer approach in the traditional model and a multi-task objective in the neural network. Our results confirm earlier findings: simple traditional models outperform neural networks consistently for this task, at least given the amount of systems we could examine in the available time. Our two-layer linear SVM ranked 2nd in the shared task.

1 Introduction

The problem of automatic language identification has been a popular task for at least the last 25 years. From early on, different solutions showed very high results (Cavnar et al., 1994; Dunning, 1994), while the more recent models achieve near-perfect accuracies.

Distinguishing closely-related languages, however, still remains a challenge. The *Discriminating between similar languages* (DSL) shared task (Zampieri et al., 2017) is aimed at solving this problem. For this year's task our team (mm_lct) built a model that discriminates between 14 languages or language varieties across 6 language groups (which had two or three languages or language varieties in them).[1]

The most popular of the more recent systems, such as `langid.py` (Lui and Baldwin, 2012) and CLD/CLD2[2] produce very good results based on

---

[1]The term *language* shall henceforth be used for both 'language' and 'language variety'.

[2]`https://github.com/CLD2Owners/cld2`

datasets containing fewer than 100 languages, but even a model trained on as many as 131 languages (Kocmi and Bojar, 2017) and whatlang (Brown, 2013) with trained on 184 and 1100 languages, are not able to distinguish closely-related (and therefore very similar) languages and dialects to a satisfying degree, at least not to the extent of the data available.

As part of the DSL 2017 shared task we chose to further explore traditional linear approaches, as well as deep learning methods. In the next Section we shortly discuss previous approaches to the task of discriminating between similar languages. Then in Section 3 we describe our systems and the data, followed by the results in Section 4, which are discussed in Section 5. We conclude in Section 6.

2 Related Work

Even though a number of researches in dialect identification have been conducted, (Tiedemann and Ljubešić, 2012; Lui and Cook, 2013; Maier and Gómez-Rodriguez, 2014; Ljubešić and Kranjcic, 2015, among many others), they mostly deal with particular language groups or language variations. We saw as our goal to create a language identifier that is able to produce comparable results for languages within all provided groups with the same set of features for every language group, so that it can be expanded outside those languages provided by the DSL shared task without any changes other than to the training corpus – as to make the system as language-independent and universal as possible.

Most of the language identifiers that use linear classifiers rely on character n-gram models (Carter et al., 2011; Ng and Selamat, 2011; Zampieri and Gebre, 2012) and combinations of character and word n-grams (Milne et al., 2012;

Proceedings of the Fourth Workshop on NLP for Similar Languages, Varieties and Dialects, pages 156–163,
Valencia, Spain, April 3, 2017. ©2017 Association for Computational Linguistics

Vogel and Tresner-Kirsch, 2012; Goldszmidt et al., 2013), also including top systems from previous DSL shared tasks (Goutte and Léger, 2015; Malmasi and Dras, 2015; Çöltekin and Rama, 2016).

The overviews of the previous DSL shared tasks (Zampieri et al., 2014; Zampieri et al., 2015; Goutte et al., 2016) showed that SVMs always produce some of the top results in this task, especially when tested on same-domain datasets (Çöltekin and Rama, 2016). Thus, we chose to put our efforts into improving upon SVM approaches, but still decided to experiment with an neural network to see if we could get comparable results, while using fewer features and reducing the chance of overfitting.

The popularity of using NNs for NLP tasks is growing. A few neural language identifiers already exist as well (Tian and Suontausta, 2003; Takçi and Ekinci, 2012; Simões et al., 2014, among others), however on average traditional systems still seem to outperform them. The results of the DSL 2016 shared task also show the same tendency overall (Bjerva, 2016; Cianflone and Kosseim, 2016; Çöltekin and Rama, 2016; Malmasi et al., 2016).

3 Methodology and Data

In this section, we first describe the datasets that were provided for the DSL 2017 shared task. Then we describe the three systems we used to tackle the problem: first a two-layer SVM that uses language-group classification, then a single-layer SVM that does not use grouping and finally an neural network-based approach.

3.1 Data

This year's data is a new version of the DSL *Corpus Collection* (DSLCC) (Tan et al., 2014), with again 18,000 instances for training and 2,000 instances for development. The test data consists of 1,000 instances per language and contains the same languages as the training and development data. The test data is furthermore very similar to the development data, as supported by the results – during-development performance was almost the same as the performance on the test set. All instances come from short newspaper texts.

However whereas last year's version of the DSLCC contained Mexican Spanish, this year's version has Peruvian Spanish (es-PE). Another

new addition is the Farsi language group, with the two variations Persian (fa-IR) and Dari (fa-AF). Thus, this year's version contains 14 languages belonging to 6 groups:

- BCS: containing Bosnian, Croatian and Serbian;

- Spanish: containing Argentine, Peninsular and Peruvian varieties;

- Farsi: containing Afghan Farsi (or Dari) and Iranian Farsi (or Persian);

- French: containing Canadian and Hexagonal varieties;

- Indonesian and Malay; and

- Portuguese: containing Brazilian and European varieties.

An overview of the data is given in Table 1, which includes the number of instances as well as the number of tokens for each language in the training and development data.

In the final submissions we performed no preprocessing on the data. During development we explored the usefulness of replacing all characters for lower case, having placeholders for numbers and removing punctuation, but we found that it decreased performance of the system.

Finally, for the final submission we have had all our runs trained on the combination of both training and development datasets, as has been shown to be effective by last year's winning team (Çöltekin and Rama, 2016).

3.2 Run 1 – SVM with grouping

As our first, most promising run we have developed and submitted a two-layer classifier, which first predicts for all instances which language group it belongs to, and then classifies the specific languages within the guessed language groups. This method has been used by DSL participants before (Franco-Salvador et al., 2015; Nisioi et al., 2016), and has shown to have a positive impact on the performance. Adopting this method, we have built a combination of SVMs with linear kernels.

The first SVM is for deciding on the language group to which the language belongs. As features it uses character-based uni- to 6-grams (including whitespace and punctuation characters) weighted

Language	Code	Training		Dev.	
		Instances	Tokens	Instances	Tokens
Croatian	hr	18,000	658,492	2,000	72,731
Bosnian	bs	18,000	555,680	2,000	61,574
Serbian	sr	18,000	606,403	2,000	66,494
Argentine Spanish	es-AR	18,000	746,531	2,000	83,090
Peninsular Spanish	es-ES	18,000	789,870	2,000	88,116
Peruvian Spanish	es-PE	18,000	455,630	2,000	51,021
Dari	fa-AF	18,000	501,157	2,000	55,249
Persian	fa-IR	18,000	659,040	2,000	72,894
Canadian French	fr-CA	18,000	510,134	2,000	55,934
Hexagonal French	fr-FR	18,000	746,531	2,000	68,136
Indonesian	id	18,000	595,187	2,000	64,749
Malay	my	18,000	453,326	2,000	50,692
Brazilian Portuguese	pt-BR	18,000	695,826	2,000	76,694
European Portuguese	pt-PT	18,000	638,124	2,000	71,153

Table 1: The number of instances and number of tokens for all languages in the training data and the development data.

by tf-idf.[3] While testing it on the development set it appeared to be very reliable, as all misclassified instances on the group level contained only names and digits and were, therefore, impossible to be classified by a human either.

The second SVM predicts the specific languages within each group (with the same feature parameters for every group), using word-based uni- and bigrams, in combination with character-based n-grams up to 6 characters weighted by tf-idf, as well.

Figure 1a shows that when trained on a subset of 100,000 randomly selected instances (while keeping the language distribution the same) of the training data, the best accuracy is achieved when using character n-grams from 1 to 6 characters and no word n-grams. However, when we trained and tested it on the DSL 2016 data, it scored lower than the winning team (for the in-domain test set). We therefore chose a different set of features by adding word unigrams and bigrams that gave us a slight advantage over last year's task's results. It did, though, reduce the performance on this

year's development, but the reduction was so minimal that we deemed it unlikely to be significant (accuracies of 0.90296 without word n-grams vs. 0.90206 with word uni- and bigrams), especially when considering that the difference between the accuracies becomes smaller the more training data is available.

Fine-tuning the second SVM for particular language groups seemed to defeat the goal of developing a language-independent classifier – retraining on other languages would have not been possible, without largely adjusting the system.

3.3 Run 2 – SVM without grouping

As the second run we submitted a single system, a linear kernel SVM that does not use language-group classification first but classifies languages straight away. When exploring different combinations of word and character n-grams we trained the system on the 100,000 same instances and found that the highest results were achieved with a combination of word uni- and bigrams and character uni- to 6-grams (see Figure 1b). Thus, for this run we have the same parameters as the *within-groups* classifier of run 1.

When trained on this year's full training set and tested on the development set, this system performs slightly better than the two-layer system

---

[3]The formula used to compute tf-idf is as follows, as defined by `scikit-learn` Python package: $\text{tf-idf}(d, t) = \text{tf}(t) * \text{idf}(d, t)$ where $\text{idf}(d, t) = \log(n/\text{df}(d, t)) + 1$ where n is the total number of documents and $\text{df}(d, t)$ is the document frequency; the document frequency is the number of documents d that contain term t (Pedregosa et al., 2011).

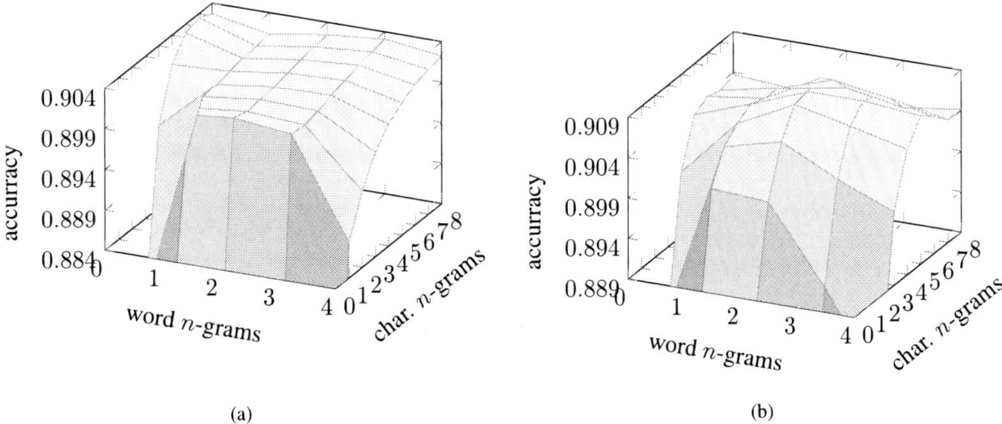

Figure 1: Visualisation of the differences in accuracy with changing maximum lengths of word and character n-grams trained on 100,000 instances of training data and tested on the development dataset. Where n-grams are 0, n-grams were turned off; the left lower corner, therefore, is the random baseline. (a) shows the accuracies for the SVM with grouping, (b) for the SVM without grouping.

3.4 Run 3 – CBOW multi-task NN

We also experimented with NNs, in particular, an NN with a multi-task objective. The idea was to take advantage of language group information to guide learning. This represents a complimentary approach to run 1.

Our preliminary experiments confirmed earlier findings that NN-based approaches are outperformed by more simple linear models for language identification (Çöltekin and Rama, 2016; Gamallo et al., 2016). We compared recurrent NNs to simpler models based on continuous bag of word (CBOW) representations (Mikolov et al., 2013), which are similar to feedforward NNs and simply take the mean vector of the input embeddings as input representation. CBOW was not only quicker to train, it also outperformed their RNN/LSTM counterparts, thus resulting in our final submission.

In particular, run 3 is a simple CBOW NN with two output layers: the first predicting the actual language identifier, the second predicting the language group. The CBOW multi-task NN training objective is to minimise the cross-entropy loss on language identity (L_1) and language group identification (L_2), weighted by λ set on the development set and trained on a subset of 10,000 in-stances. The joined training objective was:

$$L = (1 - \lambda)L_1 + \lambda L_2, \quad \text{where} \quad \lambda = 0.1$$

As input features it uses embeddings on character uni- to 5-grams, which outperforms simple word input alone. We observed that the multi-task objective sped up learning, although ultimately the difference between an MTL and a non-MTL counterpart was minor. We submitted the MTL model as final run. It was trained on the joined training and development data without any preprocessing, as to make it more comparable to our SVM submissions.

Note that due to time constraints we did not fully explore many directions here, like feature space, hyperparameters or alternative models, but overall NN seemed less promising for this task.

4 Results

Based on absolute scores, our first system (SVM with grouping) performed second best in the DSL shared task (Zampieri et al., 2017) with an accuracy of 0.9254. Both our other systems also performed substantially higher than the random baseline of 0.0714: accuracies of 0.9236 and 0.8997 for the SVM without grouping and the NN, respectively. See Table 2 for an overview of the accuracies and F_1-scores of our three systems.

Table 3 presents the confusion matrix for the SVM with grouping. Out-of-group confusions – which are very rare in general, in all three runs –

Run	Accuracy	F_1 (micro)	F_1 (macro)	F_1 (weighted)
Random baseline	0.0714			
SVM with grouping	0.9254	0.9254	0.9250	0.9250
SVM without grouping	0.9226	0.9226	0.9221	0.9221
CBOW NN	0.8997	0.8997	0.9001	0.9001

Table 2: Accuracies and F_1-scores (micro, macro and weighted) for the three systems, along with the random baseline.

	hr	bs	sr	es-AR	es-ES	es-PE	fa-AF	fa-IR	fr-CA	fr-FR	id	my	pt-BR	pt-PT
hr	894	92	13	0	0	0	0	0	0	1	0	0	0	0
bs	120	760	119	0	1	0	0	0	0	0	0	0	0	0
sr	11	71	918	0	0	0	0	0	0	0	0	0	0	0
es-AR	0	0	0	846	69	80	0	0	0	1	0	0	3	1
es-ES	0	0	0	62	893	42	0	0	0	1	0	0	1	1
es-PE	0	0	0	20	29	951	0	0	0	0	0	0	0	0
fa-AF	0	0	0	0	0	0	968	32	0	0	0	0	0	0
fa-IR	0	0	0	0	0	0	27	972	0	1	0	0	0	0
fr-CA	0	0	0	0	0	0	0	0	948	52	0	0	0	0
fr-FR	1	0	1	0	0	0	0	0	61	937	0	0	0	0
id	0	0	0	0	2	0	0	0	0	1	987	10	0	0
my	0	0	0	0	0	0	0	0	0	2	14	984	0	0
pt-BR	0	0	0	0	0	0	0	0	0	2	0	0	943	55
pt-PT	0	0	0	1	1	0	0	0	0	1	0	0	43	954

Table 3: Confusion matrix for the SVM with grouping.

occur notably less often with the SVM with grouping (only 2.2% of the confusions it makes are out-of-group confusions) than with the other runs. This is to be expected as the SVM with grouping is designed to group instances of the same language group together and then to discriminating between the particular language variations within the groups. Within-group confusions also occur relatively less often with the SVM with grouping (in all groups, except for French, the accuracy is higher for the SVM with grouping than the SVM without grouping; the NN has notably lower accuracies for all groups: see Table 4).

Overall, fewest within-group confusions occurred in the Indonesian-Malay group. The most mistakes were made in the BSC group. This is also supported by the accuracies. The values, though, do not necessarily support claims that Bosnian, Serbian and Croatian must then be more alike

	SVM-1	SVM-2	NN
hr-bs-sr	0.8579	0.8518	0.8295
es	0.8991	0.8986	0.8657
fa	0.9705	0.9680	0.9505
fr	0.9434	0.9449	0.9340
id-my	0.9880	0.9840	0.9659
pt	0.9509	0.9498	0.9256

Table 4: Accuracies for all language groups for the first SVM (with grouping), the second SVM (without grouping) and the NN.

than, e.g., Indonesian and Malay are: differences in the amount of training data or the quality of the data may cause incomparable results. Also the language groups that contain three languages perform, as expected, overall worse than the groups with two languages.

Another striking aspect of the confusion matrix is that, in the BSC group, Bosnian seems to be confused more than Croatian or Serbian. Serbian and Croatian are rarely confused with each other. This suggests that in a gradual transition between Croatian and Serbian, Bosnian is somewhere in the middle. A similar gradual transition does not seem to exist for the Spanish varieties (as supported by the confusion matrix).

This is also supported by the fact that Bosnian, of all 14 languages, performs the worst in terms of both precision and recall ($F_1 = 0.79$). Indonesian and Malay both perform the best, both with an almost perfect $F_1 = 0.99$. A full report of language-specific performances for the SVM with grouping can be found in Table 5.

	Precision	Recall	F_1-score
hr	0.87	0.89	0.88
bs	0.82	0.76	0.79
sr	0.87	0.92	0.90
es-AR	0.91	0.85	0.88
es-ES	0.90	0.89	0.90
es-PE	0.89	0.95	0.92
fa-AF	0.97	0.97	0.97
fa-IR	0.97	0.97	0.97
fr-CA	0.94	0.95	0.94
fr-FR	0.94	0.94	0.94
id	0.99	0.99	0.99
my	0.99	0.98	0.99
pt-BR	0.95	0.94	0.95
pt-PT	0.94	0.95	0.95

Table 5: Language-specific performance measures for the SVM with grouping.

5   Discussion

We presented our approaches to tackling the problem of discriminating between similar languages and dialects. The SVM which first groups instances based on language group using word uni- and bigrams and character unigrams to 6-grams as features works best by a very small margin – in the DSL shared task it performed second in absolute F_1-scores, but also by a small margin.

The margin between our two SVMs, though, is so small that it might not even be statistically sig-

nificant.[4] However, although grouping does not really improve the performance of the system, it does make the model noticeably faster. This is because, when grouping, the system requires less memory at once, as it fits the data for only one language group at a time, which is only about a sixth of the total data (in this dataset), depending on the group. It only processes the total amount of the data once – when grouping the instances in language groups, but then it uses fewer features.

As expected, the SVMs do perform notably better than the deep-learning approach we tried. However, our NN uses simple CBOW and still places itself rather well among other systems.

Figure 1a suggests that the two-layer SVM approach might perform slightly better when using no word n-grams altogether. Although we decided against such a system, it will be interesting to see what the impact of removing word n-grams for the two-layer SVM feature set will have on the performance of said approach. It would also be interesting to see if having only longer n-grams (i.e. only 3-5 character n-grams) or only combinations of particular lengths would improve the results.

6   Conclusions

Discriminating between similar languages is still not a fully solved problem – no known system reaches perfect performance. The models presented in this paper once again confirm that traditional models, such as SVMs, perform better on this task than deep learning techniques. We also showed that a two-layer approach in which languages are first classified based on language groups barely improves performance – yet, in our experience, it speeds up the system significantly.

References

Johannes Bjerva. 2016. Byte-based Language Identification with Deep Convolutional Networks. In *Proceedings of the Third Workshop on NLP for Similar Languages, Varieties and Dialects (VarDial3)*, pages 119–125, Osaka, Japan.

Ralf D. Brown. 2013. Selecting and weighting n-grams to identify 1100 languages. In *International Conference on Text, Speech and Dialogue*, pages 475–483. Springer.

---

[4]In fact, on the development dataset, the SVM with grouping performed slightly worse than the one that does not group – contrary to the performance on the test data.

Simon Carter, Manos Tsagkias, and Wouter Weerkamp. 2011. Semi-supervised priors for microblog language identification. In *Proceedings of the 11th Dutch-Belgian Information Retrieval Workshop (DIR 2011)*, pages 12–15.

William B. Cavnar, John M. Trenkle, et al. 1994. N-gram-based text categorization. *Ann Arbor MI*, 48113(2):161–175.

Çağri Çöltekin and Taraka Rama. 2016. Discriminating Similar Languages with Linear SVMs and Neural Networks. In *Proceedings of the Third Workshop on NLP for Similar Languages, Varieties and Dialects (VarDial3)*, pages 15–24, Osaka, Japan.

Andre Cianflone and Leila Kosseim. 2016. N-gram and Neural Language Models for Discriminating Similar Languages. In *Proceedings of the Third Workshop on NLP for Similar Languages, Varieties and Dialects (VarDial3)*, pages 243–250, Osaka, Japan.

Ted Dunning. 1994. *Statistical identification of language*. Computing Research Laboratory, New Mexico State University.

Marc Franco-Salvador, Paolo Rosso, and Francisco Rangel. 2015. Distributed representations of words and documents for discriminating similar languages. In *Proceedings of the Joint Workshop on Language Technology for Closely Related Languages, Varieties and Dialects (LT4VarDial)*, pages 11–16, Hissar, Bulgaria.

Pablo Gamallo, Iñaki Alegria, José Ramom Pichel, and Manex Agirrezabal. 2016. Comparing Two Basic Methods for Discriminating Between Similar Languages and Varieties. In *Proceedings of the Third Workshop on NLP for Similar Languages, Varieties and Dialects (VarDial3)*, pages 170–177, Osaka, Japan.

Moises Goldszmidt, Marc Najork, and Stelios Paparizos. 2013. Boot-strapping language identifiers for short colloquial postings. In *Joint European Conference on Machine Learning and Knowledge Discovery in Databases*, pages 95–111. Springer.

Cyril Goutte and Serge Léger. 2015. Experiments in discriminating similar languages. In *Proceedings of the Joint Workshop on Language Technology for Closely Related Languages, Varieties and Dialects (LT4VarDial)*, pages 78–84, Hissar, Bulgaria.

Cyril Goutte, Serge Léger, Shervin Malmasi, and Marcos Zampieri. 2016. Discriminating Similar Languages: Evaluations and Explorations. In *Proceedings of the Language Resources and Evaluation (LREC)*, pages 1800–1807, Portoroz, Slovenia.

Tom Kocmi and Ondřej Bojar. 2017. Lanidenn: Multilingual language identification on character window. *arXiv preprint arXiv:1701.03338*.

Nikola Ljubešić and Denis Kranjcic. 2015. Discriminating between closely related languages on twitter. *Informatica*, 39(1):1.

Marco Lui and Timothy Baldwin. 2012. langid.py: An off-the-shelf language identification tool. In *Proceedings of the ACL 2012 system demonstrations*, pages 25–30. Association for Computational Linguistics.

Marco Lui and Paul Cook. 2013. Classifying English documents by national dialect. In *Proceedings of the Australasian Language Technology Association Workshop*, pages 5–15. Citeseer.

Wolfgang Maier and Carlos Gómez-Rodriguez. 2014. Language variety identification in Spanish tweets. In *Proceedings of the EMNLP2014 Workshop on Language Technology for Closely Related Languages and Language Variants*, pages 25–35.

Shervin Malmasi and Mark Dras. 2015. Language identification using classifier ensembles. In *Proceedings of the Joint Workshop on Language Technology for Closely Related Languages, Varieties and Dialects (LT4VarDial)*, pages 35–43, Hissar, Bulgaria.

Shervin Malmasi, Marcos Zampieri, Nikola Ljubešić, Preslav Nakov, Ahmed Ali, and Jörg Tiedemann. 2016. Discriminating between similar languages and Arabic dialect identification: A report on the third DSL shared task. In *Proceedings of the 3rd Workshop on Language Technology for Closely Related Languages, Varieties and Dialects (VarDial)*, Osaka, Japan.

Tomas Mikolov, Kai Chen, Greg Corrado, and Jeffrey Dean. 2013. Efficient estimation of word representations in vector space. *arXiv preprint arXiv:1301.3781*.

Rachel Mary Milne, Richard A. O'Keefe, and Andrew Trotman. 2012. A study in language identification. In *Proceedings of the Seventeenth Australasian Document Computing Symposium*, pages 88–95. ACM.

Choon-Ching Ng and Ali Selamat. 2011. Improving language identification of web page using optimum profile. In *International Conference on Software Engineering and Computer Systems*, pages 157–166. Springer.

Sergiu Nisioi, Alina Maria Ciobanu, and Liviu P. Dinu. 2016. Vanilla Classifiers for Distinguishing between Similar Languages. In *Proceedings of the Third Workshop on NLP for Similar Languages, Varieties and Dialects (VarDial3)*, pages 235–242, Osaka, Japan.

Fabian Pedregosa, Gaël Varoquaux, Alexandre Gramfort, Vincent Michel, Bertrand Thirion, Olivier Grisel, Mathieu Blondel, Peter Prettenhofer, Ron Weiss, Vincent Dubourg, Jake VanderPlas, Alexandre Passos, David Cournapeau, Matthieu Brucher, Matthieu Perrot, and Edouard Duchesnay. 2011.

Scikit-learn: Machine learning in Python. *Journal of Machine Learning Research*, 12:2825–2830.

Alberto Simões, José João Almeida, and Simon D. Byers. 2014. Language identification: a neural network approach. In *OASIcs-OpenAccess Series in Informatics*, volume 38. Schloss Dagstuhl-Leibniz-Zentrum fuer Informatik.

Hidayet Takçi and Ekin Ekinci. 2012. Minimal feature set in language identification and finding suitable classification method with it. *Procedia Technology*, 1:444–448.

Liling Tan, Marcos Zampieri, Nikola Ljubešić, and Jörg Tiedemann. 2014. Merging Comparable Data Sources for the Discrimination of Similar Languages: The DSL Corpus Collection. In *Proceedings of the 7th Workshop on Building and Using Comparable Corpora (BUCC)*, pages 11–15, Reykjavik, Iceland.

Jilei Tian and Janne Suontausta. 2003. Scalable neural network based language identification from written text. In *Acoustics, Speech, and Signal Processing, 2003. Proceedings.(ICASSP'03). 2003 IEEE International Conference on*, volume 1, pages I–48. IEEE.

Jrg Tiedemann and Nikola Ljubešić. 2012. Efficient discrimination between closely related languages. In *Proceedings of COLING 2012*, pages 2619–2634, Mumbai, India, December. The COLING 2012 Organizing Committee.

John Vogel and David Tresner-Kirsch. 2012. Robust language identification in short, noisy texts: Improvements to liga. In *Proceedings of the Third International Workshop on Mining Ubiquitous and Social Environments (MUSE 2012)*, pages 43–50.

Marcos Zampieri and Binyam Gebrekidan Gebre. 2012. Automatic identification of language varieties: The case of Portuguese. In *KONVENS2012-The 11th Conference on Natural Language Processing*, pages 233–237. Österreichischen Gesellschaft für Artificial Intelligende (ÖGAI).

Marcos Zampieri, Liling Tan, Nikola Ljubešić, and Jörg Tiedemann. 2014. A Report on the DSL Shared Task 2014. In *Proceedings of the First Workshop on Applying NLP Tools to Similar Languages, Varieties and Dialects (VarDial)*, pages 58–67, Dublin, Ireland.

Marcos Zampieri, Liling Tan, Nikola Ljubešić, Jörg Tiedemann, and Preslav Nakov. 2015. Overview of the DSL Shared Task 2015. In *Proceedings of the Joint Workshop on Language Technology for Closely Related Languages, Varieties and Dialects (LT4VarDial)*, pages 1–9, Hissar, Bulgaria.

Marcos Zampieri, Shervin Malmasi, Nikola Ljubešić, Preslav Nakov, Ahmed Ali, Jörg Tiedemann, Yves Scherrer, and Noëmi Aepli. 2017. Findings of the VarDial Evaluation Campaign 2017. In *Proceedings of the Fourth Workshop on NLP for Similar Languages, Varieties and Dialects (VarDial)*, Valencia, Spain.

German Dialect Identification in Interview Transcriptions

Shervin Malmasi
Harvard Medical School, USA
Macquarie University, Australia
`shervin.malmasi@mq.edu.au`

Marcos Zampieri
University of Cologne
Germany
`mzampie2@uni-koeln.de`

Abstract

This paper presents three systems submitted to the German Dialect Identification (GDI) task at the VarDial Evaluation Campaign 2017. The task consists of training models to identify the dialect of Swiss-German speech transcripts. The dialects included in the GDI dataset are Basel, Bern, Lucerne, and Zurich. The three systems we submitted are based on: a plurality ensemble, a mean probability ensemble, and a meta-classifier trained on character and word n-grams. The best results were obtained by the meta-classifier achieving 68.1% accuracy and 66.2% F1-score, ranking first among the 10 teams which participated in the GDI shared task.

1 Introduction

German is well-known for its intrinsic dialectal variation. Standard national varieties spoken in Germany, Austria, and Switzerland co-exist with a number of dialects spoken in everyday communication. The case of Switzerland is particular representative of this situation because of the multitude and importance of dialects which are widely spoken throughout the country.

The German Dialect Identification (GDI) task, part of the VarDial Evaluation Campaign 2017 (Zampieri et al., 2017), addressed the problem of German dialectal variation by providing a dataset of transcripts from interviews with speakers of Swiss German dialects from Basel, Bern, Lucern, and Zurich recorded within the scope of the Archi-Mob[1] project (Samardžić et al., 2016). The goal of the GDI task is to evaluate how well computational methods can discriminate between these four Swiss German dialects.

[1] `http://archimob.ch/`

In this paper we present the entries submitted by the team MAZA to the GDI task 2017. We investigate different combinations of classifiers for the task, namely: a plurality ensemble method, a mean probability ensemble method, and a meta-classifier trained on character and word n-grams.

2 Related Work

Processing dialectal data is a challenge for NLP applications. When dealing with non-standard language, systems are trained to recognize spelling and syntactic variation for further processing in applications such as Machine Translation. In the case of German, a number of studies have been published on developing NLP tools and resources for processing non-standard language (Dipper et al., 2013), dealing with spelling variation on dialectal data and carrying out spelling normalization (Samardžić et al., 2015), and improving the performance of POS taggers for dialectal data (Hollenstein and Aepli, 2014).

The identification of Swiss German dialects, the topic of the GDI shared task, has been the focus of a few recent studies. Methods for German dialect identification have proved to be particularly important for the validation of methods applied to the compilation of German dialect corpora (Scherrer and Rambow, 2010a; Scherrer and Rambow, 2010b; Hollenstein and Aepli, 2015).

The work presented here also relates to studies on the discrimination between groups of similar languages, language varieties, and dialects such as South Slavic languages (Ljubešić et al., 2007), Portuguese varieties (Zampieri and Gebre, 2012), English varieties (Lui and Cook, 2013), Romanian dialects (Ciobanu and Dinu, 2016), Chinese varieties (Xu et al., 2016), and past editions of the DSL shared task (Zampieri et al., 2014; Zampieri et al., 2015; Malmasi et al., 2016c).

Proceedings of the Fourth Workshop on NLP for Similar Languages, Varieties and Dialects, pages 164–169,
Valencia, Spain, April 3, 2017. ©2017 Association for Computational Linguistics

3 Methods and Data

3.1 Data

The GDI training/test data was extracted from the aforementioned ArchiMob corpus (Samardžić et al., 2016) which contains transcriptions of 34 interviews with native speakers of various German dialects spoken in Switzerland. The subset used for GDI contains 18 interviews (14 for training and 4 for testing) from four Swiss German dialects: Basel, Bern, Lucerne, and Zurich. No acoustic data was released with the transcriptions.

According to the information provided by the task organizers, each interview was transcribed using the 'Schwyzertütschi Dialäktschrift' writing system (Dieth, 1986). The interviews were divided into utterances and each utterance was considered to be an instance to be classified by the systems. The training set contains a total of around 14,000 instances (114,000 tokens) and the test set contains a total of 3,638 instances (29,500 tokens).

We approach the text using ensemble classifiers and a meta-classifier. In the next sections we describe the features and algorithms used in the MAZA submissions in detail.

3.2 Features

We employ two lexical surface feature types for this task, as described below.

- **Character n-grams:** This is a sub-word feature that uses the constituent characters that make up the whole text. When used as n-grams, the features are n-character slices of the text. From a linguistic point of view, the substrings captured by this feature, depending on the length, can implicitly capture various sub-lexical features including single letters, phonemes, syllables, morphemes and suffixes. In this study we examine n-grams of order 1–6.

- **Word n-grams:** The surface forms of words can be used as a feature for classification. Each unique word may be used as a feature (i.e. unigrams), but the use of bigram distributions is also common. In this scenario, the n-grams are extracted along with their frequency distributions. For this study we evaluate unigram features.

We did not pre-process[2] the data prior to feature extraction. This was not needed as the data are human-generated transcripts.

3.3 Classifier

For our base classifier we use a linear Support Vector Machine (SVM). SVMs have proven to deliver very good performance in discriminating between language varieties and in other text classification problems,[3] SVMs achieved first place in both the 2015 (Malmasi and Dras, 2015a) and 2014 (Goutte et al., 2014) editions of the DSL shared task.[4]

3.4 Ensemble Classifiers

The best performing system in the 2015 edition of the DSL challenge (Malmasi and Dras, 2015a) used SVM ensembles evidencing the adequacy of this approach for the task of discriminating between similar languages and language varieties. In light of this, we decided to test two ensemble methods. Classifier ensembles have also proven to be an efficient and robust alternative in other text classification tasks such as grammatical error detection (Xiang et al., 2015), and complex word identification (Malmasi et al., 2016a).

We follow the methodology described by Malmasi and Dras (2015a): we extract a number of different feature types and train a single linear model using each feature type. Our ensemble was created using linear Support Vector Machine classifiers. We used the seven feature types listed in Section 3.2 to create our ensemble of classifiers.

Each classifier predicts every input and also assigns a continuous output to each of the possible labels. Using this information, we created the following two ensembles.

- **System 1 - Plurality Ensemble**
  In this system each classifier votes for a single class label. The votes are tallied and the label with the highest number[5] of votes wins. Ties are broken arbitrarily. This voting method is very simple and does not have any parameters to tune. An extensive analysis of this method and its theoretical underpinnings can be found in the work of (Kuncheva, 2004, p. 112). We submitted this system as run 1.

---

[2]For example, case folding or tokenization.

[3]For example, Native Language Identification is often performed using SVMs (Malmasi and Dras, 2015b)

[4]See Goutte et al. (2016) for a comprehensive evaluation.

[5]This differs with a *majority* voting combiner where a label must obtain over 50% of the votes to win. However, the names are sometimes used interchangeably.

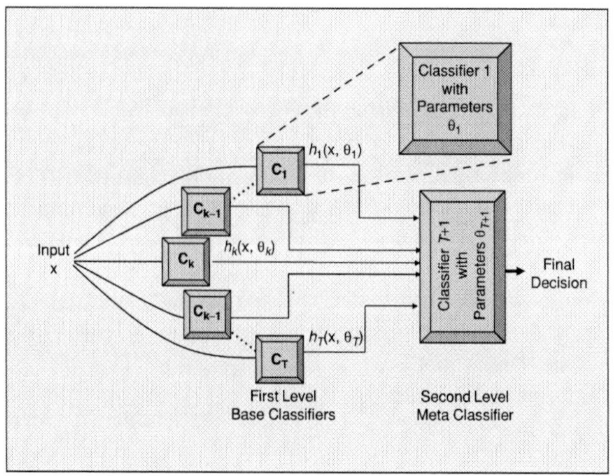

Figure 1: An illustration of a meta-classifier architecture. Image reproduced from Polikar (2006).

- **System 2 - Mean Probability Ensemble**
  The probability estimates for each class are added together and the class label with the highest average probability is the winner. An important aspect of using probability outputs in this way is that a classifier's support for the true class label is taken in to account, even when it is not the predicted label (*e.g.* it could have the second highest probability). This method has been shown to work well on a wide range of problems and, in general, it is considered to be simple, intuitive, stable (Kuncheva, 2014, p. 155) and resilient to estimation errors (Kittler et al., 1998) making it one of the most robust combiners discussed in the literature. We submitted this system as run 2.

3.5 Meta-classifier System

In addition to classifier ensembles, meta-classifier systems have proven to be very competitive for text classification tasks (Malmasi and Zampieri, 2016) and we decided to include a meta-classifier in our entry. Also referred to as classifier stacking. A meta-classifier architecture is generally composed of an ensemble of base classifiers that each make predictions for all of the input data. Their individual predictions, along with the gold labels are used to train a second-level meta-classifier that learns to predict the label for an input, given the decisions of the individual classifiers. This setup is illustrated in Figure 1. This meta-classifier attempts to learn from the collective knowledge represented by the ensemble of local classifiers.

The first step in such an architecture is to create the set of base classifiers that form the first layer. For this we used the same seven base classifiers as our ensemble.

- **System 3 - Meta-classifier**
  In this system we combined the probability outputs of our seven individual classifiers and used them to train a meta-classifier using 10-fold cross-validation. Following Malmasi et al. (2016b), we used a Random Forest as our meta-classification algorithm. We submitted this system as run 3.

4 Results

In this section we present results in two steps. First we comment on the performance obtained using each feature type and the results obtained by cross-validation on the training set. Secondly, we present the official results obtained by our system on the test set and we discuss the performance of our best method in identifying each dialect.

4.1 Cross-validation Results

We first report our cross-validation results on the training data. We began by testing individual feature types, characters n-grams (2-6) and word unigrams. Results are presented in Figure 2.

As expected we observe that character n-grams outperform word features. Character 3-grams, 4-grams, and 5-grams obtained higher results than

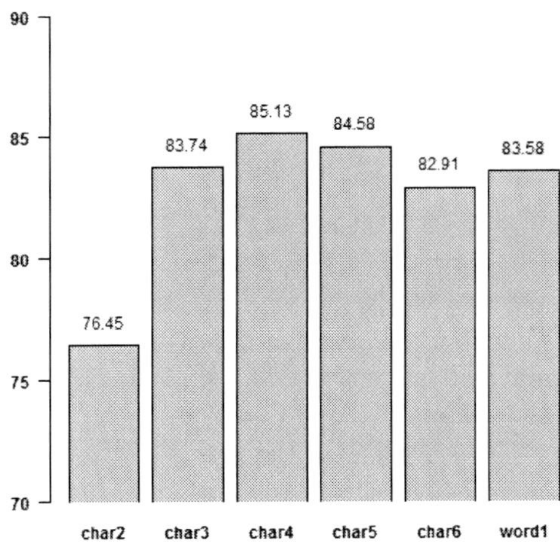

Figure 2: Cross-validation performance for each individual feature type (Y axis - Accuracy (%), X axis - Feature Type).

those obtained using word unigrams. The best results were obtained with character 4-grams achieving 85.13% accuracy. As transcriptions have been carried out using the same transcription method, character unigrams were not very informative features for the classifier achieving much lower performance than the other feature types, 52.02% accuracy. For this reason, character unigrams were not included in Figure 2

We next tested our ensemble and meta-classifier configurations on the training data. Accuracy results are shown in Table 1.

System	Accuracy
Majority Class Baseline	0.2738
Voting Ensemble (System 1)	0.8621
Probability Ensemble (System 2)	0.8674
Meta-Classifier (System 3)	**0.8725**

Table 1: Cross-validation results for the German training data.

We note that all of these methods outperform any individual feature type, with the meta-classifier achieving the best result of 87.2% accuracy and the two ensemble methods achieving comparable performance of 86.2% and 86.7% accuracy. With this information in hand we proceed to the test set evaluation.

4.2 Test Set Results

In this section we report the results of our three submissions generated from the unlabelled test data. The samples in the test set were slightly unbalanced with a majority class baseline of 25.8%.

The performance of all participants was evaluated by the shared task organizers and a more detailed description of the results is presented in the VarDial Evaluation Campaign report (Zampieri et al., 2017). Teams were ranked according to the weighted F1-score which provides a balance between precision and recall. We present the ranks with the best results for each team in Table 2.

MAZA achieved the best performance overall with 66.2% weighted F1-score. It is important to note that this rank is based on absolute scores. In the shared task report (Zampieri et al., 2017), organizers are likely to calculate ranks with statistical significance tests, which is a common practice in other shared tasks such as the DSL 2016 (Malmasi et al., 2016c) and the shared tasks from WMT (Bojar et al., 2016).

Rank	Team	F1 (weighted)
1	**MAZA**	**0.662**
2	CECL	0.661
3	CLUZH	0.653
4	qcri_mit	0.639
5	unibuckernel	0.637
6	tubasfs	0.626
7	ahaqst	0.614
8	Citius_Ixa_Imaxin	0.612
9	XAC_Bayesline	0.605
10	deepCybErNet	0.263

Table 2: GDI Closed Submission Results

Accuracy, along with macro- and micro-averaged F1-scores obtained by the three runs submitted by MAZA are presented in Table 3. We observe that the results follow the same relative pattern as the cross-validation results, with the meta-classifier achieving the best result and ranking first among the 10 teams that participated in the GDI task.

An important observation is that the test set results, for all teams, are much lower than the cross-validation results. It may have been the case that the test data was drawn from a different distribution as the training data, although this was not specified by the task organizers.

System	Accuracy	F1 (micro)	F1 (macro)	F1 (weighted)
Majority Class Baseline	0.258	—	—	—
Voting Ensemble (run1)	0.649	0.649	0.628	0.627
Probability Ensemble (run2)	0.669	0.669	0.648	0.647
Meta-classifier (run3)	**0.681**	0.681	0.663	**0.662**

Table 3: MAZA official results for the GDI task.

4.2.1 Accuracy per Dialect

Finally, we discuss the results obtained by our best method, the meta-classifier, in identifying each dialect in the test set. We present a confusion matrix with a column containing the total number of documents in each class and the performance for each dialect in Table 4.

The column 'Total' provides us an indication of the aforementioned imbalance between each dialect in the test set. The number of test instances varied from 939 instances from Basel to 877 from Zurich.

	be	bs	lu	zh	Total	Acc.
be	659	67	33	147	906	72.8%
bs	47	697	67	128	939	74.2%
lu	157	269	315	175	916	34.4%
zh	23	38	11	805	877	91.8%

Table 4: Confusion Matrix: Per Dialect Results

As expected, the four dialects are not equally difficult to be identified. The dialect from Lucern was the most difficult to be identified and the performance of the classifier was only slightly better than the 25.8% baseline.

An interesting outcome is that the dialect from Zurich, which was by far the easiest do be identified obtaining 91.8% accuracy, was also the one which generated most confusion with the other three dialects. This seems counter-intuitive on a first glance, but it might indicate that the algorithm achieves great performance for this dialect because it tries to label most of its predictions to Zurich to maximize performance. An error analysis of the misclassified instances can help understand this outcome.

5 Conclusion

In this paper we presented three systems submitted by the MAZA team to the GDI shared 2017. A meta-classifier system trained on word and character n-grams achieved 66.2% F1-score ranking first among the 10 teams that participated in the shared task. We showed that the meta-classifier outperforms two ensemble-based methods, namely plurality and mean probability, on both the training and test sets.

More than the NLP task itself, the GDI task provided participants with an interesting opportunity to study the differences between Swiss German dialects using computational methods. We observed that the dialect from Zurich is at the same time the easiest to be identified and also the one which causes the most confusion for the classifier. A linguistic analysis along with an error analysis of the misclassified instances is necessary to determine the reasons for this outcome.

Acknowledgement

We would like to thank the GDI task organizers, Noëmi Aepli and Yves Scherrer, for proposing and organizing this shared task.

References

Ondrej Bojar, Rajen Chatterjee, Christian Federmann, Yvette Graham, Barry Haddow, Matthias Huck, Antonio Jimeno Yepes, Philipp Koehn, Varvara Logacheva, Christof Monz, et al. 2016. Findings of the 2016 Conference on Machine Translation. In *Proceedings of WMT*.

Alina Maria Ciobanu and Liviu P. Dinu. 2016. A Computational Perspective on Romanian Dialects. In *Proceedings of LREC*.

Eugen Dieth. 1986. *Schwyzertütschi Dialäktschrift*. Sauerländer, Aarau, 2 edition.

Stefanie Dipper, Anke Lüdeling, and Marc Reznicek. 2013. NoSta-D: A corpus of German Non-standard Varieties. *Non-standard Data Sources in Corpus-based Research*.

Cyril Goutte, Serge Léger, and Marine Carpuat. 2014. The NRC System for Discriminating Similar Languages. In *Proceedings of the VarDial Workshop*.

Cyril Goutte, Serge Léger, Shervin Malmasi, and Marcos Zampieri. 2016. Discriminating Similar Languages: Evaluations and Explorations. In *Proceedings of LREC*.

Nora Hollenstein and Noëmi Aepli. 2014. Compilation of a Swiss German Dialect Corpus and its Application to POS Tagging. In *Proceedings of the VarDial Workshop*.

Nora Hollenstein and Noëmi Aepli. 2015. A Resource for Natural Language Processing of Swiss German Dialects. In *Proceedings of GSCL*.

Josef Kittler, Mohamad Hatef, Robert PW Duin, and Jiri Matas. 1998. On combining classifiers. *IEEE Transactions on Pattern Analysis and Machine Intelligence*, 20(3):226–239.

Ludmila I. Kuncheva. 2004. *Combining Pattern Classifiers: Methods and Algorithms*. John Wiley & Sons.

Ludmila I. Kuncheva. 2014. *Combining Pattern Classifiers: Methods and Algorithms*. Wiley, second edition.

Nikola Ljubešić, Nives Mikelic, and Damir Boras. 2007. Language Identification: How to Distinguish Similar Languages? In *Proceedings of ITI*.

Marco Lui and Paul Cook. 2013. Classifying English Documents by National Dialect. In *Proceedings of ALTW*.

Shervin Malmasi and Mark Dras. 2015a. Language Identification using Classifier Ensembles. In *Proceedings of the LT4VarDial Workshop*.

Shervin Malmasi and Mark Dras. 2015b. Multilingual Native Language Identification. In *Natural Language Engineering*.

Shervin Malmasi and Marcos Zampieri. 2016. Arabic Dialect Identification in Speech Transcripts. In *Proceedings of the VarDial Workshop*.

Shervin Malmasi, Mark Dras, and Marcos Zampieri. 2016a. LTG at SemEval-2016 Task 11: Complex Word Identification with Classifier Ensembles. In *Proceedings of SemEval*.

Shervin Malmasi, Marcos Zampieri, and Mark Dras. 2016b. Predicting Post Severity in Mental Health Forums. In *Proceedings of the CLPsych Workshop*.

Shervin Malmasi, Marcos Zampieri, Nikola Ljubešić, Preslav Nakov, Ahmed Ali, and Jörg Tiedemann. 2016c. Discriminating between Similar Languages and Arabic Dialect Identification: A Report on the Third DSL Shared Task. In *Proceedings of the VarDial Workshop*.

Robi Polikar. 2006. Ensemble based systems in decision making. *Circuits and Systems Magazine, IEEE*, 6(3):21–45.

Tanja Samardžić, Yves Scherrer, and Elvira Glaser. 2015. Normalising Orthographic and Dialectal Variants for the Automatic Processing of Swiss German. In *Proceedings of LTC*.

Tanja Samardžić, Yves Scherrer, and Elvira Glaser. 2016. ArchiMob–A corpus of spoken Swiss German. In *Proceedings of LREC*.

Yves Scherrer and Owen Rambow. 2010a. Natural Language Processing for the Swiss German Dialect Area. In *Proceedings of KONVENS*.

Yves Scherrer and Owen Rambow. 2010b. Word-based Dialect Identification with Georeferenced Rules. In *Proceedings of EMNLP*.

Yang Xiang, Xiaolong Wang, Wenying Han, and Qinghua Hong. 2015. Chinese Grammatical Error Diagnosis Using Ensemble Learning. In *Proceedings of the NLP-TEA Workshop*.

Fan Xu, Mingwen Wang, and Maoxi Li. 2016. Sentence-level Dialects Identification in the Greater China Region. *International Journal on Natural Language Computing (IJNLC)*, 5(6).

Marcos Zampieri and Binyam Gebrekidan Gebre. 2012. Automatic Identification of Language Varieties: The Case of Portuguese. In *Proceedings of KONVENS*.

Marcos Zampieri, Liling Tan, Nikola Ljubešić, and Jörg Tiedemann. 2014. A Report on the DSL Shared Task 2014. In *Proceedings of the VarDial Workshop*.

Marcos Zampieri, Liling Tan, Nikola Ljubešić, Jörg Tiedemann, and Preslav Nakov. 2015. Overview of the DSL Shared Task 2015. In *Proceedings of the LT4VarDial Workshop*.

Marcos Zampieri, Shervin Malmasi, Nikola Ljubešić, Preslav Nakov, Ahmed Ali, Jörg Tiedemann, Yves Scherrer, and Noëmi Aepli. 2017. Findings of the VarDial Evaluation Campaign 2017. In *Proceedings of the VarDial Workshop*.

CLUZH at VarDial GDI 2017: Testing a Variety of Machine Learning Tools for the Classification of Swiss German Dialects

Simon Clematide
Institute of Computational Linguistics
University of Zurich
`simon.clematide@cl.uzh.ch`

Peter Makarov
Institute of Computational Linguistics
University of Zurich
`makarov@cl.uzh.ch`

Abstract

Our submissions for the GDI 2017 Shared Task are the results from three different types of classifiers: Naïve Bayes, Conditional Random Fields (CRF), and Support Vector Machine (SVM). Our CRF-based run achieves a weighted F1 score of 65% (third rank) being beaten by the best system by 0.9%. Measured by classification accuracy, our ensemble run (Naïve Bayes, CRF, SVM) reaches 67% (second rank) being 1% lower than the best system. We also describe our experiments with Recurrent Neural Network (RNN) architectures. Since they performed worse than our non-neural approaches we did not include them in the submission.

1 Introduction

The goal of our participation in the newly introduced German Dialect Identification (GDI) Shared Task of the VarDial Workshop 2017 (Zampieri et al., 2017) was to quickly test how far we could get on this classification problem using standard machine learning techniques (as only closed runs were allowed for this task).

The task is to predict the correct Swiss German dialect for manually transcribed utterances (Samardzic et al., 2016).[1] The Dieth transcription (Dieth, 1986)—developed in the 1930s in Switzerland—is not a scholarly phonetic transcription system. It is designed to be applicable by laymen to all Swiss German dialects and uses the Standard German alphabet and a few optional diacritics.

In this task, the number of possible Swiss German dialects is limited to four main varieties: the dialects spoken in the cantons of Basel (BS), Bern (BE), Lucerne (LU), and Zurich (ZH).

The four approaches that we have worked on for this task are: i) a powerful baseline that uses an off-the-shelf Naïve Bayes classifier trained on bags of character n-gram features; ii) an unconventional yet effective application of a CRF classifier to sequence classification—the system performing best on the official test set among all our runs; iii) a majority-vote ensemble of the Naïve Bayes, CRF and SVM systems; and iv) an RNN character-sequence classifier trained on augmented data, which however has not been included in our final submission.[2]

2 Related Work

Scherrer and Rambow (2010) describe dialect identification approaches to written Swiss German. To distinguish among six dialects, they experiment with a word n-gram model. Additionally, they attempt word-based identification by turning Standard German words into their dialectal forms according to hand-written transfer rules. They discuss the linguistic aspects of the problem and difficulties in predicting for the multitude and continuum of Swiss German dialects.

Most of our final submission, except probably Run 2, is an application of well-established techniques for text classification (Sebastiani, 2002). We use regularized linear classifiers on a bag-of-character-n-grams representations of utterances. Despite its conceptual simplicity, this recipe produces state-of-the-art results on language identification tasks (Malmasi et al., 2016) and is particularly easy to implement given the wide variety of readily available tools for feature extraction and classification. Having this as a baseline, we

---

[1]Since the text segments are transcribed speech, with a slight abuse of terminology, we shall refer to them as utterances.

[2]Our code is available at `https://github.com/simon-clematide/GDI-task-2017`.

Proceedings of the Fourth Workshop on NLP for Similar Languages, Varieties and Dialects, pages 170–177,
Valencia, Spain, April 3, 2017. ©2017 Association for Computational Linguistics

	BE		BS		LU		ZH		Total
Training Set	3889	0.27	3411	0.24	3214	0.22	3964	0.27	14478
Test Set	906	0.25	939	0.26	916	0.25	877	0.24	3638
Difference		-2%		+2%		+3%		-3%	
Training 4+	3260	0.26	2974	0.24	2865	0.23	3327	0.27	12426

Table 1: Distribution of classes in the training and test sets of the GDI task. Row "Training 4+" shows the effect of removing sentences with less than 4 tokens on the training set composition.

Tokens	1	2	3	4	5	6	7	8	9	10+
Training	360	731	961	1244	1416	1491	1428	1317	1125	4405
Rel.	2%	5%	7%	9%	10%	10%	10%	9%	8%	30%
Test				495	530	465	450	368	320	1010
Rel.				14%	15%	13%	12%	10%	9%	28%

Table 2: Distribution of numbers of tokens per utterance in the training and test sets of the GDI task.

focus on experimenting with CRFs and character-sequence neural network classifiers. Zhang et al. (2015) achieve competitive results on character-level document classification tasks with Convolutional Neural Networks (CNNs). Word-level RNNs have been applied to a variety of text classification tasks (Carrier and Cho, 2014). Xiao and Cho (2016) present an efficient character-level RNN document classifier.

3 Data and Methodology

In this section, we first describe the training and test data sets. Second, we detail the methods that we apply in our runs as well as report the results of post-submission experiments using RNNs.

3.1 Properties of the Data

As Table 1 shows, the GDI training data set has roughly balanced classes (a maximum of ± 3 percentage points away from a uniform distribution). The official test set is slightly better balanced (a maximum of ± 1 percentage points away from a uniform distribution). However, the data sets do not have the same minority/majority classes.

Another noticeable difference between the training and test data is the presence of short utterances. The training set has 2,052 utterances (14%) which consist of only one, two or three words. This contrasts with the test set, whose utterances contain four or more words. Predicting the dialect of a short utterance is much harder than predicting the dialect of a long one. We systematically drop very short utterances from the training data in order to compensate for the differences between the

data sets[3] and to reduce the noise.

The data only contain lowercase characters. Due to the variability in the dialects, many of the 14,065 word types appear only once (9,372), twice (2,032), or three times (929). This extreme Zipfian distribution makes it hard to build reliable statistics for prediction.

3.2 Our Methods

All our methods except the RNNs use character n-gram features derived from separate words.

3.2.1 Run 1: Naïve Bayes

Run 1 is our baseline, which has proven hard to beat. For the final submission, we drop from the training set short noisy utterances and substitute character combinations for characters with complex diacritics (e.g. "ü2" for "ü") and single characters for the common digraph "ch" and trigraph "sch". All one-character words are dropped. We represent each utterance with a bag of character n-grams, ranging from bigrams to six-grams. This set-up produces the highest average validation ac-

---

[3]This violates the default assumption in machine learning scenarios "that training and test data are independently and identically (iid) drawn from the same distribution. When the distributions on training and test set do not match, we are facing sample selection bias or covariate shift" (Huang et al., 2007). Different unsupervised domain adaptation techniques have been developed in order to mitigate this problem, e.g. instance weighting (Jiang and Zhai, 2007). A very simple weighting schema consists in assigning a weight of zero to short utterances, i.e. removing them. Two reviewers had the opinion that it is a methodological problem to adapt the models to the evidence in the test set and that one is not supposed to look at the test set at all. Ultimately, it is a question of the task guidelines whether unsupervised domain adaptation is considered legitimate or not.

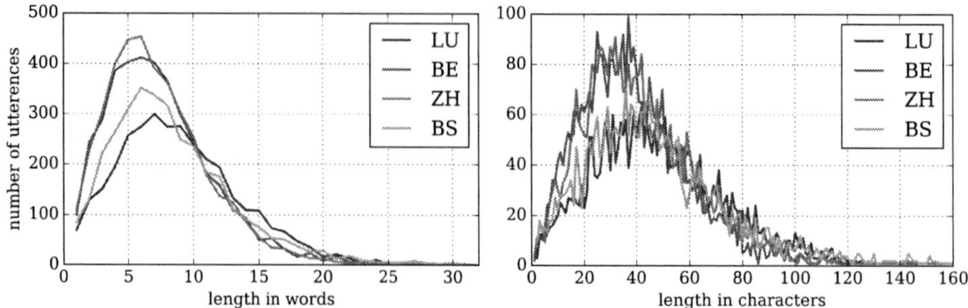

Figure 1: Per-dialect distribution of numbers of tokens and characters per utterance in the training set.

curacy among competing configurations (e.g. differing in n-gram ranges). We use the *scikit-learn* machine learning library (Pedregosa et al., 2011) to implement the entire pipeline. We fit a Naïve Bayes classifier with add-one smoothing.

3.2.2 Run 2: CRF

For Run 2, we use *wapiti* (Lavergne et al., 2010), an efficient off-the-shelf linear-chain CRF sequence classifier (Sutton and McCallum, 2012). Each word of an utterance is treated as a tagged item in a sequence and the utterance classification task is cast as a sequence classification of all items. For instance, the utterance "jaa ich han ja" with sequence label ZH is turned into a verticalized format corresponding to "jaa/ZH ich/ZH han/ZH ja/ZH".

The motivation behind this approach is that a single word is often ambiguous, however, we know a priori by the definition of the task that all words in an utterance must have the same class. Therefore, we rely on the machinery of CRFs to adjust the weights of the word features in the exponential model during training in such a way that sequences get optimally and homogeneously classified. Indeed, the predicted sequence of classification tags within one utterance is always consistent, and we take the class of the first word as the class of the whole utterance.

The features for the CRF are built from individual words. We experimented with different replacement rules for the diacritics, but in the end just applied two phonetically motivated replacements ("sch" and "ch") before feature extraction.

We use 4 types of features for the representation of a token:

WD The word form using our two replacements.

PS Concatenations of the prefix and suffix of each word (from 1 to 3 characters depending on the length of the word).

NG Character n-grams (from 1 to 6 characters). Before extracting the n-grams, we prefix each word with an "A" and suffix it with a "Z" in order to distinguish n-grams at word boundaries from n-grams within a word.

CV Word shapes selecting or mapping character classes for consonants and vowels. Specifically, feature types V and C contain all vowels and consonants of a word in the order of appearance. Feature types Cs and Vs contain the sets of all consonants and vowels, respectively. Feature types VV and CC contain the word shape where either all vowels or all consonants get masked with a "C" or a "V". Feature type CCVV masks all characters with a "C" or a "V".

b Each word also has a so-called bigram output feature that encodes the transition probability of class labels. This ensures that the system learns to predict sequences with only homogeneous class labels. The unigram output feature "u", which encodes the global distribution of class labels, was not useful, however.

CRF tools like wapiti allow each feature to be used as evidence only for the class of the current token (feature prefix "u:") or the class of the preceding and/or current token (feature prefix "*:").[4] For the GDI task, we only use "u:" features. Thus, for a word like "vernoo" (en: heard), the following features are extracted:

---

[4]See Lavergne et al. (2010) for technical details.

Length in words	Replaced with	Example
$10 \geq l > 15$	a) First 3/4 of words, and b) last 3/4	"a a de a der annere wand sis schwiizer welo" $\Rightarrow$ a) "a a de a der annere wand sis", b) "de a der annere wand sis schwiizer welo"
$l \geq 15$	a) First 2/3 of words, b) last 2/3, and c) 1/3 in the middle	"aber das händ dänn d schuurnalischten am prozss zum biischpil isch dä saz wider choo" $\Rightarrow$ a) "aber das händ dänn d schuurnalischten am prozäss zum biischpil", b) "schuurnalischten am prozäss zum biischpil isch dä saz wider choo", c) "händ dänn d schuurnalischten am prozäss zum biischpil isch dä saz"

Table 3: Data augmentation rules.

WD=vernoo b u:PS=vo u:PS=veoo u:NG=Av u:NG=Ave u:NG=v u:NG=ve u:NG=ver u:NG=e u:NG=er u:NG=ern u:NG=r u:NG=rn u:NG=rno u:NG=n u:NG=no u:NG=noo u:NG=o u:NG=oo u:NG=ooZ u:NG=o u:NG=oZ u:V=eoo u:C=vrn u:Cs=nrv u:Vs=eo u:VV=vVrnVV u:CC=CeCCoo u:CCVV=CVCCVV.

The CV word shape features add about one percentage point in accuracy.

A typical training fold (90% of the training data) results in about 540,000 different feature candidates. After thirty five training epochs using the Elastic Net regularization (Zou and Hastie, 2005), around 90,000 features are still active.

The only hyper-parameter that we need to adjust is the maximal number of training epochs of the L-BFGS optimizer (Liu and Nocedal, 1989). A maximum of thirty five training epochs guarantees optimal performance. We use a development set of 10% of the training set to control for overfitting and finding a reasonable number of epochs. Still, we find no clear and smooth convergence. Changing the default parameters for the Elastic Net regularization or any other hyper-parameter of wapiti does not result in systematic and consistent improvements.

3.2.3 Run 3: Ensemble of Naïve Bayes, CRF, and linear SVM

Run 3 is a majority-vote ensemble system built from the results of Run 1, Run 2, and predictions generated from a linear SVM over the same feature model as for Run 1. Whenever all classifiers disagree with one another, the ensemble falls back to the prediction by the Run 1 system. We used *scikit-learn*'s implementation of linear SVM trainable with the Stochastic Gradient Descent optimization algorithm and searched for the value of the regularization parameter with the highest average cross-validation accuracy.

3.2.4 Experiments with LSTMs

We have invested a considerable amount of effort in RNN models. We implement particularly simple Long Short-Term Memory (LSTM) networks (Hochreiter and Schmidhuber, 1997): with and without an initial character embedding layer, with a recurrent layer, and a softmax output layer. Like in the other runs, we experiment with single character and character group replacements. We fix the size of the character embedding layer to two thirds the input size, which therefore varies from model to model as a result of character replacements (twenty five or twenty nine units). The size of the LSTM layer is fixed to ninety hidden units. The softmax layer takes as input the values of the LSTM hidden units at the final character. All the models are rather small, with the leanest models having 41,760 parameters and the largest having 48,600 parameters. Adding a character embedding layer results in a 9% reduction in model parameters, on average. The reduction in the number of character types shrinks the model by another 4%, and the replacement of common di- and trigraphs shortens input sequences and further speeds up training. We discarded the idea of using bidirectional LSTMs (Graves and Schmidhuber, 2005): They are slower to train (the number of model parameters roughly doubles), which has been the main bottleneck for us since we have intended to experiment with multiple model set-ups.

One important theme in our neural network experiments has been data augmentation. Having examined the predictions of the baseline classifier, we observed that the longer the utterance the more likely it is to be classified correctly. We hypothesized that a simple trick of slicing long utterances into multiple shorter chunks and substituting those chunks for the original utterances in the training data would improve performance (Table 3). Like in the other runs, we drop short utterances com-

	Σ	Run 1				Run 2				Run 3			
		BE	BS	LU	ZH	BE	BS	LU	ZH	BE	BS	LU	ZH
BE	906	601	56	45	204	623	56	36	191	**660**	51	23	172
BS	939	48	621	75	195	65	**694**	58	122	58	683	57	141
LU	916	156	260	278	222	137	268	**315**	196	183	233	292	208
ZH	877	17	26	24	810	23	26	20	808	25	24	13	**815**
Precision		73	64	66	57	73	66	73	61	71	69	76	61
Recall		66	66	30	92	69	74	34	92	73	73	32	93
F1		70	65	42	70	71	70	47	74	72	71	45	74
P / R / F1		65 / 63 / 62				69 / 67 / 65				69 / 67 / 65			

Table 4: Confusion matrices and result breakdown for our official GDI runs. Rows are true labels, columns are predicted labels.

Run	Accuracy	F1 (macro)	F1 (weighted)
Baseline	25.80		
1	63.50	61.65	61.56
2	67.07	**65.38**	**65.31**
3	**67.34**	65.34	65.27

Table 5: Official results for the GDI task. The baseline predicts the majority class. For all classes, F1 (micro) is the same as accuracy.

pletely (in this case, one-word and two-word utterances). As a result of this data augmentation, the training data for the internal system evaluation have grown by almost a quarter (from 11,726 to 15,340 utterances).

All neural-network implementation is done using high-level structures of the *keras* neural networks library (Chollet, 2015). For training the models, we use the Root Mean Square Propagation (RMSProp) algorithm (Tieleman and Hinton, 2012), a variant of Stochastic Gradient Descent, with default hyper-parameters suggested by the library. We use Dropout (Srivastava et al., 2014) for regularization. We train for at least 100 epochs and at most 300 epochs.

4 Results

4.1 Official Results

Table 5 shows the official results of our submitted runs. Run 3 has the best accuracy among our runs, but is slightly worse on the macro-averaged F1 score and the weighted F1 score (see Zampieri et al. (2017) for further information on the evaluation metrics). The performance in absolute numbers is much lower than expected from cross-validation.

4.2 Internal Evaluation

Table 6 shows average validation scores of the systems featured in our submissions. We retrain the systems with the same hyper-parameter settings as in the submissions. The ensemble performs best followed closely by the baseline system of Run 1. To compare the systems with the best-performing LSTM from the post-submission experiments, we set aside a stratified sample of one tenth the size of the training data as an internal evaluation set. Again, we retrain the models on the remaining data with the same hyper-parameter settings. Since these hyper-parameter values have been found to produce the best performance on the entire training data, internal evaluation set results are potentially biased upward for all the systems but the LSTM.

	Cross-validation results			Internal evaluation set results		
Run	**Accuracy**	**F1 (macro)**	**F1 (weighted)**	**Accuracy**	**F1 (macro)**	**F1 (weighted)**
1	85.10 (0.82)	84.99 (0.82)	85.10 (0.82)	85.43	85.36	85.44
2	83.96 (0.68)	83.87 (0.70)	83.93 (0.69)	85.01	85.02	85.01
3	**85.70 (0.59)**	**85.57 (0.60)**	**85.68 (0.60)**	**85.50**	**85.42**	**85.50**
SVM	82.46 (0.59)	82.36 (0.64)	82.43 (0.61)	82.39	82.36	82.39
LSTM	-	-	-	83.49	83.30	83.46

Table 6: System comparison: Results for ten-fold stratified cross-validation and performance on an internal evaluation set. Cross validation results: We report mean scores across the folds and indicate standard deviations in parentheses. The SVM is a model from the ensemble of Run 3.

Model configuration			Development set results			Internal evaluation set results		
data aug.	**char. repl.**	**char. emb.**	**Accuracy**	**F1 (macro)**	**F1 (weighted)**	**Accuracy**	**F1 (macro)**	**F1 (weighted)**
-	-	-	81.75	81.57	81.65	81.15	80.79	80.99
-	-	+	81.52	81.35	81.51	81.98	81.90	81.96
-	+	-	82.75	82.50	82.69	82.39	82.23	82.34
-	+	+	80.83	80.60	80.74	79.90	79.71	79.84
+	-	-	81.60	81.42	81.53	83.22	83.08	83.18
+	-	+	**82.82**	**82.66**	**82.78**	82.60	82.52	82.59
+	+	-	82.52	82.35	82.52	**83.49**	**83.30**	**83.46**
+	+	+	82.59	82.43	82.56	82.04	81.91	82.00

Table 7: Comparison of RNN sequence classifiers.

5 Discussion

ZH clearly dominates in terms of recall in all our runs (Table 4). The recognition rates for ZH, BE, and BS are fine (around 70% F1) in our official runs. However, the F1 score for LU is much lower (around 45%) due to severe recall problems. The numbers show that the recognition of LU suffers from more frequent predictions in favor of ZH and BS. This behavior fits the empirical distribution of the classes from the training set (short sentences removed) as shown in Table 1 where 27% of all sequences are ZH, but only 23% LU. As the problem may also lie in the data, it would be interesting to see whether all the systems participating in the shared task exhibit this bias.

The results on the official test data (Table 5) are unexpectedly lower than our cross-validation estimates from the training data (67% accuracy instead of about 88% with short sequences removed). Clearly, the training and test sets have not been consistently sampled from the same distribution.

The Naïve Bayes classifier of Run 1 has been exceptionally strong on same-domain data. Interestingly, it suffers worse compared to other systems from differently sampled data.

According to our observation during training, CRFs seem to run a bit into convergence problems. Therefore, one might try to systematically build more varying models (for instance, by bootstrap sampling and randomly selected subsets of extracted features) in order to have a broader ensemble system. Another line of work that we could not complete due to time restrictions is the integration of a word prediction model into the CRF system based on character-level CNNs (Xiao and Cho, 2016). Our expectation would be that convolution filters might be better at learning relevant character-level representations for estimating the label probability for a given word.

We have struggled to produce strong results with RNNs. By the submission deadline, no model had performed on a par with our non-neural systems. Table 7 presents the results of our post-submission experiments. Data augmentation brings about impressive gains of 0.7% on a development set and 1.5% on the internal evaluation set, on average across the three metrics. Character replacements largely hurt performance: On average, we see a drop of 0.2% on the development set and 0.9% on the internal evaluation set. The effects of a character embedding layer cancel out across the development and internal evaluation sets (-0.2%

and +0.3%, respectively). On the other hand, models with a character embedding layer and/or character replacements are faster to reach higher accuracy levels. Just like with other models, short utterances pose the largest difficulty, and performance goes up with utterance length. Overall, using slow-to-train neural models on this task has not paid off: Blazingly fast linear classifiers achieve very strong results, and so time is better spent on looking for good features.

6 Conclusion

We show that a character n-gram-based Naïve Bayes approach gives a very strong baseline for the classification of transcribed Swiss German dialects, especially when test and training sets are drawn from the same distribution. The CRF-based approach works better for the official test set (ranked third by weighted F1 score among all the submitted GDI runs). The official test set is clearly sampled differently from the training set. Given a rather large performance difference of 4.5% between the Naïve Bayes and the CRF, we suspect that the CRF-based approach has generalized better than the Naïve Bayes. In terms of accuracy, an ensemble approach using Naïve Bayes, CRF, and linear SVM gives the best results of our runs and ranks second among all GDI runs.

7 Acknowledgement

We would like to thank three anonymous reviewers for their helpful comments. Peter Makarov is supported by European Research Council Grant No. 338875.

References

Pierre Luc Carrier and Kyunghyun Cho. 2014. LSTM networks for sentiment analysis. *Deep Learning Tutorials*.

François Chollet. 2015. Keras. `https://github.com/fchollet/keras`.

Eugen Dieth. 1986. *Schwyzertütschi Dialäktschrift: Dieth-Schreibung*. Lebendige Mundart. Sauerländer, Aarau etc. 2. Aufl. / bearb. und hrsg. von Christian Schmid-Cadalbert (1. Aufl. 1938).

Alex Graves and Jürgen Schmidhuber. 2005. Framewise phoneme classification with bidirectional LSTM and other neural network architectures. *Neural Networks*.

Sepp Hochreiter and Jürgen Schmidhuber. 1997. Long short-term memory. *Neural computation*.

J. Huang, A. Smola, A. Gretton, K. Borgwardt, and B. Schoelkopf. 2007. Correcting sample selection bias by unlabeled data. In B. Schoelkopf, J. Platt, and T. Hoffman, editors, *Advances in Neural Information Processing Systems 19*, pages 601–608. MIT Press, Cambridge, MA.

Jing Jiang and ChengXiang Zhai. 2007. Instance weighting for domain adaptation in NLP. In *Proceedings of the 45th Annual Meeting of the Association of Computational Linguistics*, pages 264–271. Association for Computational Linguistics.

Thomas Lavergne, Olivier Cappé, and François Yvon. 2010. Practical very large scale CRFs. In *Proceedings the 48th Annual Meeting of the Association for Computational Linguistics (ACL)*. Association for Computational Linguistics.

D. C. Liu and J. Nocedal. 1989. On the limited memory BFGS method for large scale optimization. *Math. Program.*

Shervin Malmasi, Marcos Zampieri, Nikola Ljubešić, Preslav Nakov, Ahmed Ali, and Jörg Tiedemann. 2016. Discriminating between similar languages and arabic dialect identification: A report on the third dsl shared task. In *Proceedings of the 3rd Workshop on Language Technology for Closely Related Languages, Varieties and Dialects (VarDial)*, Osaka, Japan.

F. Pedregosa, G. Varoquaux, A. Gramfort, V. Michel, B. Thirion, O. Grisel, M. Blondel, P. Prettenhofer, R. Weiss, V. Dubourg, J. Vanderplas, A. Passos, D. Cournapeau, M. Brucher, M. Perrot, and E. Duchesnay. 2011. Scikit-learn: Machine learning in Python. *Journal of Machine Learning Research*.

Tanja Samardzic, Yves Scherrer, and Elvira Glaser. 2016. ArchiMob – A corpus of spoken Swiss German. In *Proceedings of the Language Resources and Evaluation (LREC)*, pages 4061–4066, Portoroz, Slovenia).

Yves Scherrer and Owen Rambow. 2010. Word-based dialect identification with georeferenced rules. In *Proceedings of the 2010 Conference on Empirical Methods in Natural Language Processing*. Association for Computational Linguistics.

Fabrizio Sebastiani. 2002. Machine learning in automated text categorization. *ACM computing surveys (CSUR)*.

Nitish Srivastava, Geoffrey E Hinton, Alex Krizhevsky, Ilya Sutskever, and Ruslan Salakhutdinov. 2014. Dropout: a simple way to prevent neural networks from overfitting. *Journal of Machine Learning Research*.

Charles A. Sutton and Andrew McCallum. 2012. An introduction to conditional random fields. *Foundations and Trends in Machine Learning*.

Tijmen Tieleman and Geoffrey Hinton. 2012. Lecture 6.5-rmsprop: Divide the gradient by a running average of its recent magnitude.

Yijun Xiao and Kyunghyun Cho. 2016. Efficient character-level document classification by combining convolution and recurrent layers. *CoRR*.

Marcos Zampieri, Shervin Malmasi, Nikola Ljubešić, Preslav Nakov, Ahmed Ali, Jörg Tiedemann, Yves Scherrer, and Noëmi Aepli. 2017. Findings of the VarDial Evaluation Campaign 2017. In *Proceedings of the Fourth Workshop on NLP for Similar Languages, Varieties and Dialects (VarDial)*, Valencia, Spain.

Xiang Zhang, Junbo Zhao, and Yann LeCun. 2015. Character-level convolutional networks for text classification. In *Advances in neural information processing systems*.

Hui Zou and Trevor Hastie. 2005. Regularization and variable selection via the elastic net. *Journal of the Royal Statistical Society: Series B (Statistical Methodology)*.

Arabic Dialect Identification Using iVectors and ASR Transcripts

Shervin Malmasi
Harvard Medical School, USA
Macquarie University, Australia
`shervin.malmasi@mq.edu.au`

Marcos Zampieri
University of Cologne
Germany
`mzampie2@uni-koeln.de`

Abstract

This paper presents the systems submitted by the MAZA team to the Arabic Dialect Identification (ADI) shared task at the VarDial Evaluation Campaign 2017. The goal of the task is to evaluate computational models to identify the dialect of Arabic utterances using both audio and text transcriptions. The ADI shared task dataset included Modern Standard Arabic (MSA) and four Arabic dialects: Egyptian, Gulf, Levantine, and North-African. The three systems submitted by MAZA are based on combinations of multiple machine learning classifiers arranged as (1) voting ensemble; (2) mean probability ensemble; (3) meta-classifier. The best results were obtained by the meta-classifier achieving 71.7% accuracy, ranking second among the six teams which participated in the ADI shared task.

1 Introduction

The interest in Arabic natural language processing (NLP) has grown substantially in the last decades. This is evidenced by several publications on the topic and the dedicated series of workshops (WANLP) co-located with major international computational linguistics conferences.[1]

Several Arabic dialects are spoken in North Africa and in the Middle East co-existing with Modern Standard Arabic (MSA) in a diglossic situation. Arabic dialects are used in both spoken and written forms (*e.g.* user-generated content) and pose a number of challenges for NLP applications. Several studies on dialectal variation of Arabic have been published including corpus compilation for Arabic dialects (Al-Sabbagh and Girju, 2012; Cotterell and Callison-Burch, 2014), parsing (Chiang et al., 2006), machine translation of Arabic dialects (Zbib et al., 2012), and finally, the topic of the ADI shared task, Arabic dialect identification (Zaidan and Callison-Burch, 2014; Sadat et al., 2014; Malmasi et al., 2015).

In this paper we present the MAZA entries for the 2017 ADI shared task which was organized as part of the VarDial Evaluation Campaign 2017 (Zampieri et al., 2017). The ADI shared task dataset (Ali et al., 2016) included audio and transcripts from Modern Standard Arabic (MSA) and four Arabic dialects: Egyptian, Gulf, Levantine, and North-African.

2 Related Work

There have been several studies published on Arabic dialect identification applied to both speech and text.[2] Examples of Arabic dialect identification on speech data include the work by Biadsy et al. (2009), Biadsy (2011), Biadsy and Hirschberg (2009), and Bahari et al. (2014). Identifying Arabic dialects in text also became a popular research topic in recent years with several studies published about it (Zaidan and Callison-Burch, 2014; Sadat et al., 2014; Tillmann et al., 2014; Malmasi et al., 2015).

To our knowledge, however, the 2017 ADI is the first shared task to provide participants with the opportunity to carry out Arabic dialect identification using a dataset containing both audio and text (transcriptions). The first edition of the ADI shared task, organized in 2016 as a sub-task of the DSL shared task (Malmasi et al., 2016c), used a similar dataset to the ADI 2017 dataset, but included only transcriptions.

---

[1] `https://sites.google.com/a/nyu.edu/wanlp2017/`

[2] See Shoufan and Al-Ameri (2015) for a survey on NLP methods for processing Arabic dialects including a section on Arabic dialect identification.

Proceedings of the Fourth Workshop on NLP for Similar Languages, Varieties and Dialects, pages 178–183,
Valencia, Spain, April 3, 2017. ©2017 Association for Computational Linguistics

3 Methods and Data

We approach this task as a multi-class classification problem. For our base classifier we utilize a linear Support Vector Machine (SVM). SVMs have proven to deliver very good performance in discriminating between language varieties and in other text classification problems, SVMs achieved first place in both the 2015 (Malmasi and Dras, 2015a) and 2014 (Goutte et al., 2014) editions of the DSL shared task.[3]

3.1 Data

The data comes from the aforementioned Arabic dialect dataset by Ali et al. (2016) used in the 2016 edition of the ADI shared task. It contains audio and ASR transcripts of broadcast, debate, and discussion programs from videos by Al Jazeera in MSA and four Arabic dialects: Egyptian, Gulf, Levantine, and North-African. In 2016, the organizers released only the transcriptions of these videos and in 2017 transcriptions are combined with audio features providing participants with an interesting opportunity to test computational methods that can be used both for text and speech. We combined all the train/dev data (25,311 samples). The test set contained 1,492 instances.

3.2 Features

In this section we describe our features and evaluate their performance under cross-validation.

We employ two lexical surface feature types for this task, as described below. These are extracted from the transcriptions without any pre-processing (*e.g.* case folding or tokenization) on texts prior to feature extraction. Pre-processing was not needed as the data are computer-generated ASR transcripts. We also used the provided iVector features, as described below.

- **Character n-grams:** This sub-word feature uses the constituent characters that make up the whole text. When used as n-grams, the features are n-character slices of the text. Linguistically, these substrings, depending on the length, can implicitly capture various sub-lexical features including single letters, phonemes, syllables, morphemes & suffixes. Here we examine n-grams of size 1–8.

- **Word n-grams:** The surface forms of words can be used as a feature for classification. Each unique word may be used as a feature (i.e. unigrams), but the use of bigram distributions is also common. In this scenario, the n-grams are extracted along with their frequency distributions. For this study we evaluate unigram features.

- **iVector Audio Features:** Identity vectors or iVectors are a probabilistic compression process for dimensionality reduction. They have been used in speech processing for dialect and accent identification (Bahari et al., 2014), as well as for language identification systems (Dehak et al., 2011).

We now report our cross-validation results on the training data. We began by testing individual feature types, with results displayed in Figure 1.

We observe that many character n-grams outperform the word unigram features. Character 4-grams and above obtained higher results than those obtained using word unigrams. The best transcript-based results were obtained with character 6-grams achieving 76.2% accuracy. The audio-based iVector features, however, performed substantially better with 85.3% accuracy. This is a very large difference of almost 10% accuracy compared to the performance obtained using words and characters.

Having demonstrated that these features are useful for this task, we proceed to describe our systems in the next section.

3.3 Systems

We created three systems for our submission, as described below.

3.4 Voting Ensemble (System 1)

The best performing system in the 2015 edition of the DSL challenge (Malmasi and Dras, 2015a) used SVM ensembles evidencing the adequacy of this approach for the task of discriminating between similar languages and language varieties. In light of this, we decided to test two ensemble methods. Classifier ensembles have also proven to be an efficient and robust alternative in other text classification tasks such as language identification (Malmasi and Dras, 2015a), grammatical error detection (Xiang et al., 2015), and complex word identification (Malmasi et al., 2016a).

---

[3]See the 2014 and 2015 DSL shared task reports for more information (Zampieri et al., 2015; Zampieri et al., 2014) and Goutte et al. (2016) for a comprehensive evaluation on the first two DSL shared tasks.

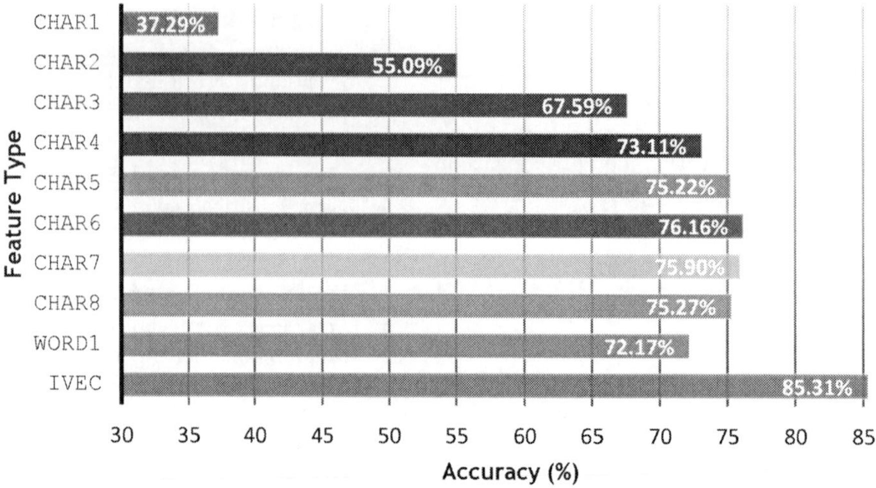

Figure 1: Cross-validation performance for each of our individual feature types.

We follow the methodology described by Malmasi and Dras (2015a): we extract a number of different feature types and train a single linear model using each feature type. Our ensemble was created using linear Support Vector Machine classifiers.[4] We used all of the feature types listed in Section 3.2 to create our ensemble of classifiers.

Each classifier predicts every input and also assigns a continuous output to each of the possible labels. Using this information, we created the following two ensembles.

In the first system each classifier votes for a single class label. The votes are tallied and the label with the highest number[5] of votes wins. Ties are broken arbitrarily. This voting method is very simple and does not have any parameters to tune. An extensive analysis of this method and its theoretical underpinnings can be found in the work of (Kuncheva, 2004, p. 112). We submitted this system as run 1.

3.5 Mean Probability Ensemble (System 2)

Our second system is similar to System 1 above, but with a different combination method. Instead of a single vote, the probability estimates for each class[6] are added together and the class label with the highest average probability is the winner. An important aspect of using probability outputs in this way is that a classifier's support for the true class label is taken in to account, even when it is not the predicted label (*e.g.* it could have the second highest probability). This method has been shown to work well on a wide range of problems and, in general, it is considered to be simple, intuitive, stable (Kuncheva, 2014, p. 155) and resilient to estimation errors (Kittler et al., 1998) making it one of the most robust combiners discussed in the literature. We submitted this system as run 2.

3.6 Meta-classifier (System 3)

In addition to classifier ensembles, meta-classifier systems have proven to be very competitive for text classification tasks (Malmasi and Zampieri, 2016) and we decided to include a meta-classifier in our entry. Also referred to as classifier stacking, a meta-classifier architecture is generally composed of an ensemble of base classifiers that each make predictions for all of the input data. Their individual predictions, along with the gold labels are used to train a second-level meta-classifier that learns to predict the label for an input, given the decisions of the individual classifiers. This setup is illustrated in Figure 2. This meta-classifier attempts to learn from the collective knowledge represented by the ensemble of local classifiers.

The first step in such an architecture is to create the set of base classifiers that form the first layer. For this we used the same base classifiers as our ensembles described above.

---

[4]Linear SVMs have proven effective for text classification tasks (Malmasi and Dras, 2014; Malmasi and Dras, 2015b).

[5]This differs with a *majority* voting combiner where a label must obtain over 50% of the votes to win. However, the names are sometimes used interchangeably.

[6]SVM results can be converted to per-class probability scores using Platt scaling.

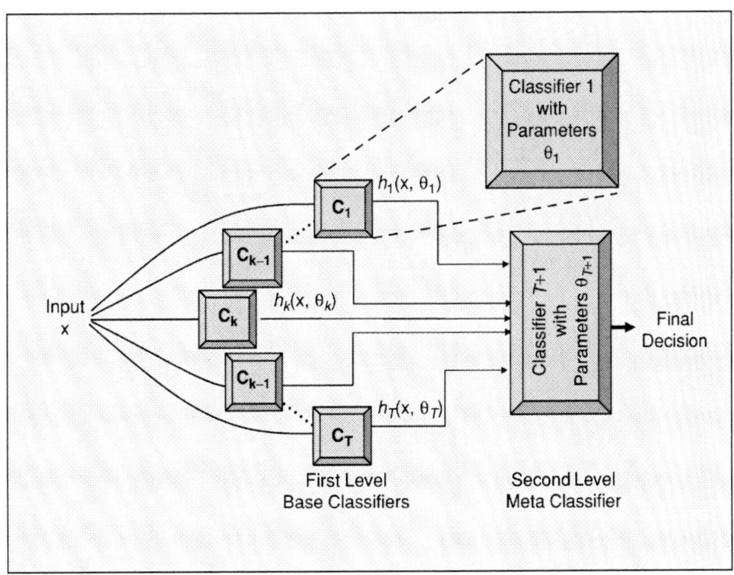

Figure 2: An illustration of a meta-classifier architecture. Image reproduced from Polikar (2006).

In this system we combined the probability outputs of our seven individual classifier and used them to train a meta-classifier via cross-validation. Following Malmasi et al. (2016b), we used a Random Forest as our meta-classification algorithm. We submitted this system as run 3.

4 Results

4.1 Cross-validation Results

We first report the cross-validation results of our three systems on the training data. Results are shown in Table 1.

System	Accuracy
Majority Class Baseline	0.219
Voting Ensemble (System 1)	0.854
Probability Ensemble (System 2)	0.950
Meta-Classifier (System 3)	**0.977**

Table 1: Cross-validation results for the Arabic training data.

We note that all of these methods outperform any individual feature type, with the meta-classifier achieving the best result of 97.7%. This is a very large increase over the weakest system, which is the voting ensemble with 85.4% accuracy. For the voting ensemble 1,165 of the 25,311 training samples (4.60%) were ties that were broken arbitrarily.

This is an issue that can occur when there are an even number of classifiers in a voting ensemble.

4.2 Test Set Results

Finally, in this section we report the results of our three submissions generated from the unlabelled test data. The samples in the test set were slightly unbalanced with a majority class baseline of 23.1%. Shared task performance was evaluated and teams ranked according to the weighted F1-score which provides a balance between precision and recall. Accuracy, along with macro- and micro-averaged F1-scores were also reported.

We observe that the meta-classifier achieved the best result among our three entries, following the same relative pattern as the cross-validation results. The meta-classifier system ranked second among the six teams participating in the ADI task.

In Figure 3 we present the confusion matrix heat map for the output of our best system, the meta-classifier. The confusion matrix confirms the assumption that not all classes presented in the dataset are equally difficult to identify. For example, the system is able to identify MSA utterances with substantially higher performance than the performance obtained when identifying any of the four Arabic dialects present in the dataset. We also observe a higher degree of confusion in discriminating between Gulf and Levantine Arabic compared to the other dialects and MSA.

System	Accuracy	F1 (micro)	F1 (macro)	F1 (weighted)
Majority Class Baseline	0.231	—	—	—
Voting Ensemble (run1)	0.6086	0.6086	0.6032	0.6073
Probability Ensemble (run2)	0.6689	0.6689	0.6671	0.6679
Meta-classifier (run3)	**0.7165**	**0.7165**	**0.7164**	**0.7170**

Table 2: MAZA Results for the ADI task.

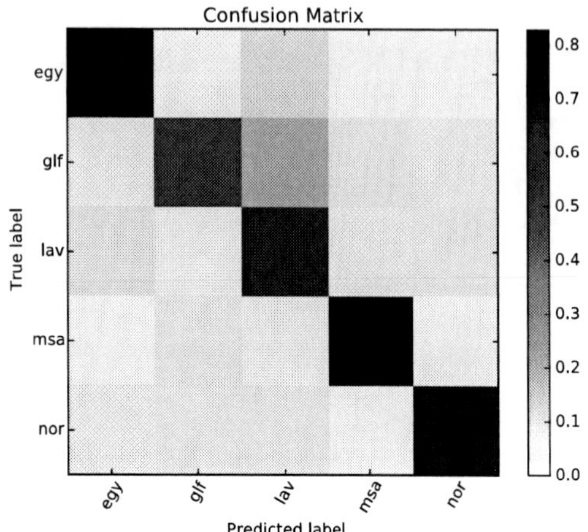

Figure 3: Confusion Matrix for Run 3.

Finally, another important observation is that the test set results are somewhat lower than the cross-validation results. Although this was not specified by the task organizers, it may have been the case that the test data was drawn from a different distribution as the training data. An analysis of the most informative features and the misclassified instances in both the training and test sets may provide an explanation for this difference.

5 Conclusion

We presented three systems trained to identified MSA and four Arabic dialects using iVectors and ASR transcripts. The best results were obtained by a meta-classifier achieving 71.7% accuracy and ranking second in the ADI shared task 2017. To the best of our knowledge, this was the first time that computational methods have been evaluated on Arabic dialect detection using audio and text.

An important insight is that combining text-based features from transcripts with audio-based features can substantially improve performance. Additionally, we also saw that a meta-classifier can provide a significant performance boost compared to a classifier ensemble approach.

Acknowledgements

We would like to thank Preslav Nakov and Ahmed Ali for proposing and organizing the ADI task. We also thank the VarDial workshop reviewers who provided us valuable feedback and suggestions to improve this manuscript.

References

Rania Al-Sabbagh and Roxana Girju. 2012. YADAC: Yet another Dialectal Arabic Corpus. In *Proceedings of LREC*.

Ahmed Ali, Najim Dehak, Patrick Cardinal, Sameer Khurana, Sree Harsha Yella, James Glass, Peter Bell, and Steve Renals. 2016. Automatic Dialect Detection in Arabic Broadcast Speech. In *Proceedings of INTERSPEECH*.

Mohamad Hasan Bahari, Najim Dehak, Lukas Burget, Ahmed M Ali, Jim Glass, et al. 2014. Non-negative Factor Analysis of Gaussian Mixture Model Weight Adaptation for Language and Dialect Recognition. *IEEE/ACM transactions on audio, speech, and language processing*, 22(7):1117–1129.

Fadi Biadsy and Julia Hirschberg. 2009. Using Prosody and Phonotactics in Arabic Dialect Identification. In *Proceedings of INTERSPEECH*.

Fadi Biadsy, Julia Hirschberg, and Nizar Habash. 2009. Spoken Arabic Dialect Identification using Phonotactic Modeling. In *Proceedings of the Workshop on Computational Approaches to Semitic Languages*.

Fadi Biadsy. 2011. *Automatic dialect and accent recognition and its application to speech recognition*. Ph.D. thesis, Columbia University.

David Chiang, Mona T Diab, Nizar Habash, Owen Rambow, and Safiullah Shareef. 2006. Parsing Arabic Dialects. In *Proceedings of EACL*.

Ryan Cotterell and Chris Callison-Burch. 2014. A Multi-dialect, Multi-genre Corpus of Informal Written Arabic. In *Proceedings LREC*.

Najim Dehak, Pedro A Torres-Carrasquillo, Douglas A Reynolds, and Reda Dehak. 2011. Language Recognition via i-vectors and Dimensionality Reduction. In *Proceedings of INTERSPEECH*.

Cyril Goutte, Serge Léger, and Marine Carpuat. 2014. The NRC System for Discriminating Similar Languages. In *Proceedings of the VarDial Workshop*.

Cyril Goutte, Serge Léger, Shervin Malmasi, and Marcos Zampieri. 2016. Discriminating Similar Languages: Evaluations and Explorations. In *Proceedings of LREC*.

Josef Kittler, Mohamad Hatef, Robert PW Duin, and Jiri Matas. 1998. On combining classifiers. *IEEE Transactions on Pattern Analysis and Machine Intelligence*, 20(3):226–239.

Ludmila I Kuncheva. 2004. *Combining Pattern Classifiers: Methods and Algorithms*. John Wiley & Sons.

Ludmila I Kuncheva. 2014. *Combining Pattern Classifiers: Methods and Algorithms*. Wiley, second edition.

Shervin Malmasi and Mark Dras. 2014. Chinese Native Language Identification. In *Proceedings of EACL*.

Shervin Malmasi and Mark Dras. 2015a. Language identification using classifier ensembles. In *Proceedings of the LT4VarDial Workshop*.

Shervin Malmasi and Mark Dras. 2015b. Multilingual Native Language Identification. *Natural Language Engineering*, pages 1–53.

Shervin Malmasi and Marcos Zampieri. 2016. Arabic Dialect Identification in Speech Transcripts. In *Proceedings of the VarDial Workshop*.

Shervin Malmasi, Eshrag Refaee, and Mark Dras. 2015. Arabic Dialect Identification using a Parallel Multidialectal Corpus. In *Proceedings of PACLING*.

Shervin Malmasi, Mark Dras, and Marcos Zampieri. 2016a. LTG at SemEval-2016 Task 11: Complex Word Identification with Classifier Ensembles. In *Proceedings of SemEval*.

Shervin Malmasi, Marcos Zampieri, and Mark Dras. 2016b. Predicting Post Severity in Mental Health Forums. In *Proceedings of the CLPsych Workshop*.

Shervin Malmasi, Marcos Zampieri, Nikola Ljubešić, Preslav Nakov, Ahmed Ali, and Jörg Tiedemann. 2016c. Discriminating between Similar Languages and Arabic Dialect Identification: A Report on the Third DSL Shared Task. In *Proceedings of the VarDial Workshop*.

Robi Polikar. 2006. Ensemble based systems in decision making. *Circuits and Systems Magazine, IEEE*, 6(3):21–45.

Fatiha Sadat, Farnazeh Kazemi, and Atefeh Farzindar. 2014. Automatic Identification of Arabic Language Varieties and Dialects in Social Media. In *Proceedings of the SocialNLP Workshop*.

Abdulhadi Shoufan and Sumaya Al-Ameri. 2015. Natural Language Processing for Dialectical Arabic: A Survey. In *Proceedings of the Arabic NLP Workshop*.

Christoph Tillmann, Saab Mansour, and Yaser Al-Onaizan. 2014. Improved Sentence-Level Arabic Dialect Classification. In *Proceedings of the VarDial Workshop*.

Yang Xiang, Xiaolong Wang, Wenying Han, and Qinghua Hong. 2015. Chinese grammatical error diagnosis using ensemble learning. In *Proceedings of the NLP-TEA Workshop*.

Omar F Zaidan and Chris Callison-Burch. 2014. Arabic Dialect Identification. *Computational Linguistics*.

Marcos Zampieri, Liling Tan, Nikola Ljubešić, and Jörg Tiedemann. 2014. A Report on the DSL Shared Task 2014. In *Proceedings of the VarDial Workshop*.

Marcos Zampieri, Liling Tan, Nikola Ljubešić, Jörg Tiedemann, and Preslav Nakov. 2015. Overview of the DSL Shared Task 2015. In *Proceedings of the LT4VarDial Workshop*.

Marcos Zampieri, Shervin Malmasi, Nikola Ljubešić, Preslav Nakov, Ahmed Ali, Jörg Tiedemann, Yves Scherrer, and Noëmi Aepli. 2017. Findings of the VarDial Evaluation Campaign 2017. In *Proceedings of the VarDial Workshop*.

Rabih Zbib, Erika Malchiodi, Jacob Devlin, David Stallard, Spyros Matsoukas, Richard Schwartz, John Makhoul, Omar F Zaidan, and Chris Callison-Burch. 2012. Machine translation of Arabic Dialects. In *Proceedings of NAACL-HLT*.

Discriminating between Similar Languages using Weighted Subword Features

Adrien Barbaresi
Austrian Academy of Sciences (ÖAW-AC), Vienna
Berlin-Brandenburg Academy of Sciences and Humanities (BBAW)
`adrien.barbaresi@oeaw.ac.at`

Abstract

The present contribution revolves around a contrastive subword n-gram model which has been tested in the *Discriminating between Similar Languages* shared task. I present and discuss the method used in this 14-way language identification task comprising varieties of 6 main language groups. It features the following characteristics: (1) the preprocessing and conversion of a collection of documents to sparse features; (2) weighted character n-gram profiles; (3) a multinomial Bayesian classifier. Meaningful bag-of-n-grams features can be used as a system in a straightforward way, my approach outperforms most of the systems used in the DSL shared task (3rd rank).

1 Introduction

Language identification is the task of predicting the language(s) that a given document is written in. It can be seen as a text categorization task in which documents are assigned to pre-existing categories. This research field has found renewed interest in the 1990s due to advances in statistical approaches, and it has been active ever since, particularly since the methods developed have also been deemed relevant for text categorization, native language identification, authorship attribution, text-based geolocation, and dialectal studies (Lui and Cook, 2013).

As of 2014 and the first Discriminating between Similar Languages (DSL) shared task (Zampieri et al., 2014), a unified dataset (Tan et al., 2014) comprising news texts of closely-related language varieties has been used to test and benchmark systems. The documents to be classified are quite short and may even be difficult to distinguish for human annotators, thus adding to the difficulty and the interest of the task. A second shared task took place in 2015 (Zampieri et al., 2015). An analysis of recent developments can be found in Goutte el al. (2016) as well as in the report on the third shared task (Malmasi et al., 2016).

The present study was conducted on the occasion of the fourth VarDial workshop (Zampieri et al., 2017). It focuses on submissions to the DSL task, a 14-way language identification task comprising varieties of six main language groups: Bosnian (bs), Croatian (hr), and Serbian (sr); Argentine (es-AR), Peruan (es-PE), and Peninsular Spanish (es-ES); Dari Persian (fa-AF) and Farsi/Iranian Persian (fa-IR); Québec French (fr-CA) and Hexagonal French (fr-FR); Malay (*Bahasa Melayu*, my) and Indonesian (*Bahasa Indonesia*, id); Brazilian Portuguese (pt-BR) and European Portuguese (pt-PT).

Not all varieties are to be considered equally since differences may stem from extra-linguistic factors. It is for instance assumed that Malay and Indonesian derive from a millenium-old *lingua franca*, so that shorter texts have been considered to be a problem for language identification (Bali, 2006). Besides, the Bosnian/Serbian language pair seems to be difficult to tell apart whereas Croatian distinguishes itself from the two other varieties mostly because of political motives (Ljubeši[Pleaseinsertintopreamble] et al., 2007; Tiedemann and Ljubešić, 2012).

The remainder of this paper is organized as follows: in section 2 the method is presented, it is then evaluated and discussed in section 3.

2 Method

2.1 Preprocessing

Preliminary tests have shown that adding a custom linguistic preprocessing step could slightly

Proceedings of the Fourth Workshop on NLP for Similar Languages, Varieties and Dialects, pages 184–189,
Valencia, Spain, April 3, 2017. ©2017 Association for Computational Linguistics

improve the results. As such, instances are tokenized using the *SoMaJo* tokenizer (Proisl and Uhrig, 2016), which achieves state-of-the-art accuracies on both web and CMC data for German. As it is rule-based, it is deemed efficient enough for the languages of the shared task. No stop words are used since relevant cues are expected to be found automatically as explained below. Additionnally, the text is converted to lowercase as it led to better results during development phase on 2016 data.

2.2 Bag of n-grams approach

Statistical indicators such as character- and token-based language models have proven to be efficient on short text samples, especially character n-gram frequency profiles from length 1 to 5, whose interest is (*inter alia*) to perform indirect word stemming (Cavnar and Trenkle, 1994). In the context of the shared task, a simple approach using n-gram features and discriminative classification achieved competitive results (Purver, 2014). Although features relying on the output of instruments may yield useful information such as POS-features (Zampieri et al., 2013), the diversity of the languages to classify as well as the prevalence of statistical methods call for low-resource methods that can be trained and applied easily.

In view of this I document work on a refined version of the *Bayesline* (Tan et al., 2014) which has been referenced in the last shared task (Barbaresi, 2016a) and which has now been used in official competition. After looking for linguistically relevant subword methods to overcome data sparsity (Barbaresi, 2016b), it became clear that taking frequency effects into consideration is paramount. As a consequence, the present method grounds on a bag-of-n-grams approach. It first proceeds by constructing a dictionary representation which is used to map words to indices. After turning the language samples into numerical feature vectors (a process also known as vectorization), the documents can be treated as a sparse matrix (one row per document, one column per n-gram).

Higher-order n-grams mentioned in the development tests below use feature hashing, also known as the "hashing trick" (Weinberger et al., 2009), where words are directly mapped to indices with a hashing function, thus sparing memory. The upper bound on the number of features has been fixed to 2^{24} in the experiments below.

2.3 Term-weighting

The next step resides in counting and normalizing, which implies to weight with diminishing importance tokens that occur in the majority of samples. The concept of term-weighting originates from the field of information retrieval (Luhn, 1957; Sparck Jones, 1972). The whole operation is performed using existing implementations by the *scikit-learn* toolkit (Pedregosa et al., 2011), which features an adapted version of the *tf-idf* (term-frequency/inverse document-frequency) term-weighting formula.[1] Smooth *idf* weights are obtained by systematically adding one to document frequencies, as if an extra document was seen containing every term in the collection exactly once, which prevents zero divisions.

2.4 Naive Bayes classifier

The classifier used entails a conditional probability model where events represent the occurrence of an n-gram in a single document. In this context, a multinomial Bayesian classifier assigns a probability to each target language during test phase. It has been shown that Naive Bayes classifiers were not only to be used as baselines for text classification tasks. They can compete with state-of-the-art classification algorithms such as support vector machines, especially when using approriate preprocessing concerning the distribution of event frequencies (Rennie et al., 2003); additionally they are robust enough for the task at hand, as their decisions may be correct even if their probability estimates are inaccurate (Rish, 2001).

2.5 "Bayesline" formula

The *Bayesline* formula used in the shared task grounds on existing code (Tan et al., 2014)[2] and takes advantage of a comparable feature extraction technique and of a similar Bayesian classifier. The improvements described here concern the preprocessing phase, the vector representation, and the parameters of classification. Character n-grams from length 2 to 7 are taken into account.[3]

---

[1] http://scikit-learn.org/stable/modules/feature_extraction.html

[2] https://github.com/alvations/bayesline

[3] `TfidfVectorizer(analyzer='char', ngram_range=(2,7), strip_accents=None, lowercase=True)` followed by `MultinomialNB(alpha=0.005)`, adapted from https://web.archive.org/web/20161215142013/http://scikit-learn.org/stable/auto_examples/text/document_classification_20-newsgroups.html

N-gram length	2	3	4	5	6	7	8*	9*
1	.690	.794	.852	.882	.894	**.902**	.895	.895
2	.705	.798	.854	.883	.895	**.902**	.899	.899
3		.808	.859	.884	.896	**.902**	.901	.901

Table 1: Benchmark by F1-weighted of a common range of n-gram length combinations on 2016 DSL data (*=hashed features)

3 Evaluation

3.1 Data from the third edition

In order to justify the choice of the formula, experiments have been conducted on data from the third edition of the DSL shared task (Malmasi et al., 2016); training and development sets have been combined as training data, and gold data used for evaluation. The method described above has been tested with several n-gram ranges; the results are summarized in Table 1. The best combinations were found with a minimum n-gram length of 1 to 3 and a maximum n-gram length of 6 to 8. Accordingly, an *aurea mediocritas* from 2 to 7 has been chosen.

Table 2 shows the extraction, training, and testing times for n-gram lengths with a mininum of 2. One can conclude that the method is computationnally efficient on the shared task data. Execution with feature hashing is necessary for higher-order n-grams due to memory constraints; it effectively improves scalability but it also seems to be a trade-off between computational efficiency and accuracy, probably due to the upper bound on used features and/or hash collisions.

Range	Extraction	Training	Testing
2,2	19	0.3	0.0
2,3	41	1.0	0.0
2,4	72	2.0	0.1
2,5	136	4.4	0.3
2,6	230	8.6	0.5
2,7	387	14.0	0.9
2,8*	179	15.4	0.9
2,9*	208	18.2	1.1

Table 2: Evolution of execution time (in seconds) with respect to n-gram length (*=hashed features)

Table 3 documents the efficiency and accuracy of several algorithms on the classification task, without extensive parameter selection. The Ridge (Rifkin and Lippert, 2007) and Naive Bayes classifiers would have outperformed the best submission of the 2016 competition (0.894) with scores of respectively 0.895 and 0.902, while the Passive-Aggressive (Crammer et al., 2006) and Linear Support Vector (Fan et al., 2008) classifiers would have been ranked second with a score of 0.892. It is noteworthy that the Naive Bayes classifier would still have performed best without taking the development data into consideration (accuracy of 0.898).

3.2 Data from the fourth edition

As expected, the method performed well on the fourth shared task, as it reached the 3rd place out of 11 teams (with an accuracy of 0.925 and a weighted F1 of 0.925). In terms of statistical significance, it was ranked first (among others) by the organizers. The official baseline/Bayesline used a comparable algorithm with lower results (accuracy and weighted F1 of 0.889).

The confusion matrix in Figure 1 details the results. Three-way classifications between the variants of Spanish and within the Bosnian-Croatian-Serbian complex still leave room for improvement, although Peruvian Spanish does not seem to be as noisy as the Mexican Spanish data from the last edition. The F-score on variants of Persian is fairly high (0.960) which proves that the method can be applied to a wide range of alphabets.

The same method has been tested without pre-processing on new data consisting in the identification of Swiss German dialects (GDI shared task). The low result (second to last with an accuracy of 0.627 and a weighted F1 of 0.606) can be explained by the lack of adaptation, most notably to the presence of much shorter instances. The classification of the Lucerne variant is particularly problematic, it calls for tailored solutions.

4 Conclusion

The present contribution revolves around a contrastive subword n-gram model which has been tested in the *Discriminating between Similar Languages* shared task. It features the following char-

Type	Training (s)	Accuracy	F1-weighted
Naive Bayes	14	.902	.902
Bernoulli NB	16	.882	.883
Nearest Centroid/Rocchio	33	.759	.760
Stochastic Gradient Descent	464	.813	.813
Perceptron	764	.884	.884
Passive-Aggressive	947	.892	.892
Linear Support Vector Classifier	1269	.892	.892
Ridge Classifier	1364	.895	.895

Table 3: Comparison of several classifier types on the extracted feature vectors, ordered by ascending training time (in seconds) on data from 2016. Classifiers used without extensive parameter tuning, linear SVC and SGD with L2 penalty.

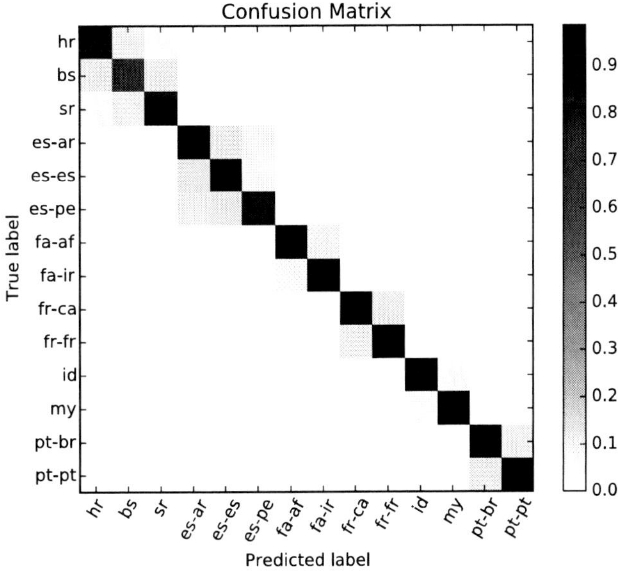

Figure 1: Confusion matrix for DSL task (closed training, 2017 data)

acteristics: (1) the conversion of a collection of preprocessed documents to a matrix of sparse *tf-idf* features; (2) weighted character n-gram profiles; (3) a multinomial Bayesian classifier, hence the name "Bayesline". Meaningful bag-of-n-grams features can be used as a system in a straightforward way. In fact my method outperforms most of the systems used in the DSL shared task.

Thus, I propose a new baseline and make the necessary components available under an open source licence.[4] The *Bayesline* efficiency as well as the difficulty to reach higher scores in open training could be explained by artificial regular-

ities in the test data. For instance, the results for the Dari/Iranian Persian and Malay/Indonesian pairs are striking, these clear distinctions do not reflect the known commonalities between these language varieties. This could be an artifact of the data, which feature standard language of a different nature than the continuum "on the field", that is between two countries as well as within a single country. The conflict between in-vitro and real-world language identification has already been emphasized in the past (Baldwin and Lui, 2010); it calls for the inclusion of web texts (Barbaresi, 2016c) into the existing task reference.

---

[4]https://github.com/adbar/vardial-experiments

Acknowledgments

Thanks to the anonymous reviewers for their comments.

References

Timothy Baldwin and Marco Lui. 2010. Language Identification: The Long and the Short of the Matter. In *Human Language Technologies: The 2010 Annual Conference of the North American Chapter of the Association for Computational Linguistics*, pages 229–237. Association for Computational Linguistics.

Ranaivo-Malançon Bali. 2006. Automatic Identification of Close Languages–Case Study: Malay and Indonesian. *ECTI Transaction on Computer and Information Technology*, 2(2):126–133.

Adrien Barbaresi. 2016a. An Unsupervised Morphological Criterion for Discriminating Similar Languages. In *Proceedings of the Third Workshop on NLP for Similar Languages, Varieties and Dialects (VarDial3)*, pages 212–220. The COLING 2016 Organizing Committee.

Adrien Barbaresi. 2016b. Bootstrapped OCR error detection for a less-resourced language variant. In Stefanie Dipper, Friedrich Neubarth, and Heike Zinsmeister, editors, *Proceedings of the 13th Conference on Natural Language Processing (KONVENS 2016)*, pages 21–26. University of Bochum.

Adrien Barbaresi. 2016c. Efficient construction of metadata-enhanced web corpora. In *Proceedings of the 10th Web as Corpus Workshop*, pages 7–16. Association for Computational Linguistics.

William B. Cavnar and John M. Trenkle. 1994. N-Gram-Based Text Categorization. In *Proceedings of the 3rd Annual Symposium on Document Analysis and Information Retrieval*, pages 161–175.

Koby Crammer, Ofer Dekel, Joseph Keshet, Shai Shalev-Shwartz, and Yoram Singer. 2006. Online Passive-Aggressive Algorithms. *Journal of Machine Learning Research*, 7:551–585.

Rong-En Fan, Kai-Wei Chang, Cho-Jui Hsieh, Xiang-Rui Wang, and Chih-Jen Lin. 2008. LIBLINEAR: A Library for Large Linear Classification. *Journal of Machine Learning Research*, 9:1871–1874.

Cyril Goutte, Serge Léger, Shervin Malmasi, and Marcos Zampieri. 2016. Discriminating Similar Languages: Evaluations and Explorations. In *Proceedings of the 10th International Conference on Language Resources and Evaluation (LREC 2016)*, pages 1800–1807. European Language Resources Association (ELRA).

Nikola Ljubešić, Nives Mikelić, and Damir Boras. 2007. Language identification: how to distinguish similar languages? In *29th International Conference on Information Technology Interfaces*, pages 541–546. IEEE.

Hans Peter Luhn. 1957. A Statistical Approach to Mechanized Encoding and Searching of Literary Information. *IBM Journal of research and development*, 1(4):309–317.

Marco Lui and Paul Cook. 2013. Classifying English Documents by National Dialect. In *Proceedings of the Australasian Language Technology Association Workshop*, pages 5–15.

Shervin Malmasi, Marcos Zampieri, Nikola Ljubešić, Preslav Nakov, Ahmed Ali, and Jörg Tiedemann. 2016. Discriminating between Similar Languages and Arabic Dialect Identification: A Report on the Third DSL Shared Task. In *Proceedings of the 3rd Workshop on Language Technology for Closely Related Languages, Varieties and Dialects (VarDial)*.

F. Pedregosa, G. Varoquaux, A. Gramfort, V. Michel, B. Thirion, O. Grisel, M. Blondel, P. Prettenhofer, R. Weiss, V. Dubourg, J. Vanderplas, A. Passos, D. Cournapeau, M. Brucher, M. Perrot, and E. Duchesnay. 2011. Scikit-learn: Machine learning in Python. *Journal of Machine Learning Research*, 12:2825–2830.

Thomas Proisl and Peter Uhrig. 2016. SoMaJo: State-of-the-art tokenization for German web and social media texts. In *Proceedings of the 10th Web as Corpus Workshop*, pages 57–62. Association for Computational Linguistics.

Matthew Purver. 2014. A Simple Baseline for Discriminating Similar Languages. In *Proceedings of the First Workshop on Applying NLP Tools to Similar Languages, Varieties and Dialects*, pages 155–160.

Jason D. Rennie, Lawrence Shih, Jaime Teevan, and David R. Karger. 2003. Tackling the Poor Assumptions of Naive Bayes Text Classifiers. In *Proceedings of the Twentieth International Conference on Machine Learning*, pages 616–623. ACM.

Ryan M. Rifkin and Ross A. Lippert. 2007. Notes on Regularized Least Squares. Technical report, MIT-CSAIL.

Irina Rish. 2001. An Empirical Study of the Naive Bayes Classifier. In *IJCAI 2001 workshop on empirical methods in artificial intelligence*, pages 41–46. IBM New York.

Karen Sparck Jones. 1972. A Statistical Interpretation of Term Specificity and its Application in Retrieval. *Journal of Documentation*, 28(1):11–21.

Liling Tan, Marcos Zampieri, Nikola Ljubešić, and Jörg Tiedemann. 2014. Merging Comparable Data Sources for the Discrimination of Similar Languages: The DSL Corpus Collection. In *Proceedings of the 7th Workshop on Building and Using Comparable Corpora*, pages 11–15.

Jörg Tiedemann and Nikola Ljubešić. 2012. Efficient discrimination between closely related languages. In *Proceedings of COLING*, pages 2619–2633.

Kilian Weinberger, Anirban Dasgupta, John Langford, Alex Smola, and Josh Attenberg. 2009. Feature Hashing for Large Scale Multitask Learning. In *Proceedings of the 26th Annual International Conference on Machine Learning*, pages 1113–1120. ACM.

Marcos Zampieri, Binyam Gebrekidan Gebre, and Sascha Diwersy. 2013. N-gram language models and POS distribution for the identification of Spanish varieties. In *Proceedings of TALN 2013*, pages 580–587.

Marcos Zampieri, Liling Tan, Nikola Ljubešić, and Jörg Tiedemann. 2014. A Report on the DSL Shared Task 2014. In *Proceedings of the First Workshop on Applying NLP Tools to Similar Languages, Varieties and Dialects*, pages 58–67.

Marcos Zampieri, Liling Tan, Nikola Ljubešić, Jörg Tiedemann, and Preslav Nakov. 2015. Overview of the DSL Shared Task 2015. In *Proceedings of the Joint Workshop on Language Technology for Closely Related Languages, Varieties and Dialects*, pages 1–9.

Marcos Zampieri, Shervin Malmasi, Nikola Ljubešić, Preslav Nakov, Ahmed Ali, Jörg Tiedemann, Yves Scherrer, and Noëmi Aepli. 2017. Findings of the VarDial Evaluation Campaign 2017. In *Proceedings of the Fourth Workshop on NLP for Similar Languages, Varieties and Dialects (VarDial)*.

Exploring Lexical and Syntactic Features
for Language Variety Identification

Chris van der Lee
Dept. of Communication and Information Sciences
Tilburg University
Tilburg, The Netherlands
`c.vdrlee@tilburguniversity.edu`

Antal van den Bosch
Centre for Language Studies
Radboud University, Nijmegen, and
Meertens Institute, Amsterdam,
The Netherlands
`antal.van.den.bosch@meertens.knaw.nl`

Abstract

We present a method to discriminate between texts written in either the Netherlandic or the Flemish variant of the Dutch language. The method draws on a feature bundle representing text statistics, syntactic features, and word n-grams. Text statistics include average word length and sentence length, while syntactic features include ratios of function words and part-of-speech n-grams. The effectiveness of the classifier was measured by classifying Dutch subtitles developed for either Dutch or Flemish television. Several machine learning algorithms were compared as well as feature combination methods in order to find the optimal generalization performance. A machine-learning meta classifier based on AdaBoost attained the best F-score of 0.92.

1 Introduction

Language identification, the task of automatically determining the natural language used in a document, is considered to be an important first step for many applications. Automatically determining a document's language can be a fairly easy step in certain situations (McNamee, 2005). However, some bottlenecks have been identified which leaves language identification unsolved as yet. It has been argued and demonstrated that one of the main bottlenecks is distinguishing between similar languages (Tiedemann and Ljubešić, 2012). Languages that are closely related such as Croatian and Serbian or Indonesian and Malay are very similar in their spoken and their written forms, which makes it difficult for automated systems to accurately discriminate between them. Recently, some advances have been achieved in the automated distinction between closely related languages, largely due to the *Discriminating between Similar Languages* (DSL) shared task. In the DSL competitions accuracies of over 95% have been reported, mostly using character and word n-grams with various classification algorithms.

Despite the fact that the accuracy of systems discriminating between similar languages is increasing, there are still challenges when it comes to discriminating between varieties of the same language, e.g. Spanish from South America or Spain. It has been claimed that language variety identification is even more difficult than similar language identification (Goutte et al., 2016). Results in the DSL competitions support this claim: only one system was able to score slightly above the 50% baseline when distinguishing between British and American English (Zampieri et al., 2014).

This work is related to recent studies that applied text classification methods to discriminate between written texts in different language varieties or dialects (Lui and Cook, 2013; Maier and Gómez-Rodriguez, 2014; Malmasi and Dras, 2015; Malmasi et al., 2015; Zampieri et al., 2016). The aim of the current work is to explore lesser studied techniques and features that could be beneficial to the accuracy of language variety classifiers. As a case study, classifiers were built to discriminate between Netherlandic Dutch and Flemish Dutch subtitles.

2 Related work

2.1 Language varieties

Research on varieties of the same language is scarce and the existing body of research on the topic shows that discriminating between language varieties is an even bigger challenge compared to similar languages. Six systems were submitted

Proceedings of the Fourth Workshop on NLP for Similar Languages, Varieties and Dialects, pages 190–199,
Valencia, Spain, April 3, 2017. ©2017 Association for Computational Linguistics

in the 2014 DSL shared task to discriminate between British English and American English, and only one of those systems scored above the 50% baseline (Zampieri et al., 2014). However, it is possible that the poor results attained in the 2014 DSL shared task were due to problems in the data set. Some classifiers have been built outside of the DSL shared task with higher accuracy scores. Lui and Cook (2013) built a classifier to distinguish the British, Canadian, and Australian English language varieties and tested this classifier on various corpora. The obtained F-scores varied greatly between the corpora: an F-score of over .9 was obtained in the best case, but scores were below the baseline in the worst cases.

Not only English language varieties have been studied. Maier and Gómez-Rodriguez (2014) developed a classifier to discriminate between five Spanish languages with tweets (short messages posted on the Twitter.com social media platform) as input. They achieved an average F-score of 0.34, which is somewhat above baseline, though not particularly high. Furthermore, Malmasi and Dras (2015) distinguished Dari and Farsi news texts with an accuracy of 96%. Malmasi et al. (2015) developed a classifier for multiple Arabic dialects. They achieved accuracy scores as high as 94%, but the results were relatively worse when they classified more closely-related dialects such as Palestinian and Jordanian (76%). Similarly, Zampieri et al. (2016) ventured to classify Portuguese news articles published in Brazil, Macau, and Portugal with differing accuracy scores. Macau versus European Portuguese was somewhat difficult (74%), while classifying Brazilian versus Macau Portuguese and Brazilian versus European Portuguese turned out to be substantially easier (at accuracies of 90% and 88%, respectively).

Classifiers that distinguish Dutch language varieties have also been developed. Trieschnigg et al. (2012) developed a classifier to discriminate between folktales written in Middle Dutch (the predecessor of modern Dutch, used in the Netherlands between 1200 and 1500) and 17th century Dutch, 20th century Frisian, and a number of 20th century Dutch dialects using the Dutch folktale database as a corpus. The performance of the classifier varied greatly per language variety: near-perfect to very good identification was achieved for some varieties (e.g. Frisian was identified with an F-score of 0.99; Liemers 0.88; Gronings 0.83), while classification was very difficult for other varieties (e.g. Overijssels at an F-score of 0.09; Waterlands 0.16; Drents 0.31). Tulkens et al. (2016) used corpora containing texts from mixed media (newspapers, Wikipedia, internet, social media) to build a Dutch language variety classifier based on provinces, and attained a relatively high score on some language varieties (up to 85% accuracy for Brabantian as spoken in the Belgian province of Antwerp), but they also report scores of 0% for six language varieties and a very low score on two others.

2.2 Features

While some exceptions exist (Tulkens et al., 2016), most of the current research in similar languages and language varieties use the same types of features, namely n-gram-based features. The results of the DSL shared task have shown that these approaches generally perform the best. However, scholars have argued that adding certain underused feature types could help improve the accuracy of state-of-the-art classifiers (Cimino et al., 2013). With the present study we investigate this claim by using two types of features in addition to word n-grams, namely text statistics (e.g. average word length, ratio of long/short words) and syntactic features (grammar-level features, e.g. PoS-tags).

Syntactic features have been used previously, though scarcely, in the context of language identification. Lui and Cook (2013) and Lui et al. (2014) used PoS n-grams as features for a classifier to make a distinction between English language varieties, while Zampieri et al. (2013) used PoS n-grams to classify Spanish language varieties. All three studies report that using POS n-grams leads to above-baseline results. This lends support to the notion that systematic differences between language varieties can be found using syntactic features.

The usage of text statistics for the identification of languages is even more uncommon compared to syntactic features. However, text statistics have been successfully used for similar research domains. One of these domains is native language identification (Jarvis et al., 2013; Cimino et al., 2013).

The successful implementation of text statistics features in this research domain implies that there

Language variant	Documents	Tokens
Netherlandic Dutch	77,430 (70%)	100,527,052 (68%)
Flemish Dutch	32,848 (30%)	47,888,260 (32%)
Total	110.278	148.415.312

Table 1: Document and token counts per language variety.

are systematic differences in stylistic choices between languages. A study by Windisch and Csink (2005) is one of the few studies using text statistics features for language identification. The authors found that these features can indeed be used for language identification. However, it should be noted that they studied dissimilar languages. The effectiveness of text statistics features for similar languages, or language variety identification remains an understudied subject.

2.3 Current work

The current study will explore lesser used techniques in the domain of language variety identification to see whether the current state-of-the art accuracy can be improved upon. This is done by using commonly used word n-grams together with the more uncommon lexical and syntactic features. Various approaches for combining these different feature types will be explored to investigate the added benefit of an ensemble classifier.

The current study focuses on the discrimination of Netherlandic Dutch (i.e. Dutch as spoken and written in the Netherlands) vs. Flemish Dutch (i.e. Dutch as spoken and written in the Dutch-speaking regions of Belgium). Speakers of Netherlandic Dutch and Flemish Dutch adhere to the same standard language, but, even so, linguists have stated that there are differences between Netherlandic and Flemish Dutch on every linguistic level, among which the lexical and syntactical level (De Caluwe, 2002). These differences tend to be subtle. Some examples of differences found between the two language varieties are word choice preference (e.g. *orange* in Netherlandic Dutch: *sinaasappel*, Flemish Dutch: *appelsien*), plural preference (e.g. *teachers* in Netherlandic Dutch: *leraren*, Flemish Dutch: *leraars*), and the order in which a particle and finite verb are preferably used (e.g. *I don't believe he* **has come** in Netherlandic Dutch: *Ik geloof niet dat hij* **is gekomen**, Flemish Dutch: *Ik geloof niet dat hij* **gekomen is**) (Schuurman et al., 2003).

Dutch language varieties have thus far remained a scarcely studied topic of research, although researchers have shown an interest in it. A limitation to the study of these varieties has always been the lack of available data (Zampieri et al., 2014). However, the recent introduction of the SUBTIEL corpus offers a usable corpus for such research. The feasibility of using this corpus is further explored in this work.

3 Method

3.1 Collection of the corpus

The SUBTIEL corpus contains over 500,000 subtitles in Dutch and English. These subtitles were produced by a professional studio operating in several countries, among which The Netherlands and Belgium. The procedure for these countries is mostly the same: a single translator provides the subtitles for a series episode or a movie. The main focus of the studio are movies and television shows, and to a smaller degree documentaries.

After filtering out the English subtitles and the Dutch subtitles without information on whether they were intended for Dutch or Flemish television, 110.278 documents remain; cf. Table 1. A document in this context is the subtitles for one movie, or one episode of a television show. For the subtitles used in this study, a distinction is made between subtitles that were shown on a Dutch or a Flemish television network. In comparison to similar work (Trieschnigg et al., 2012; Tulkens et al., 2016), the number of documents and tokens that is used in the current study is relatively large.

Using an automated mining tool, the subtitles in the corpus were scanned for a match in the Internet Movie Database (IMDb)[1], which provides additional information about the show or movie (e.g. genre, year, actors). The main interest was genre, since a vastly different genre distribution per language variety could have an impact on classification accuracy. An IMDb match was found for roughly half of the subtitles. The genre distribution for these matches did show minor dif-

---

[1] http://www.imdb.com

Genre	Netherlandic Dutch	Flemish Dutch
Drama	21.14%	25.11%
Comedy	14.51%	17.96%
Reality-TV	11.31%	5.63%
Crime	7.11%	9.40%
Action	5.52%	5.94%
Mystery	5.40%	4.95%
Documentary	5.88%	2.80%
Romance	5.56%	2.80%
Adventure	3.44%	3.33%
Family	2.87%	3.66%
Subtotal	83.15%	81.16%

Table 2: Distribution of the ten most frequent genres in the SUBTIEL corpus.

ferences between the language varieties, as can be seen in Table 2 For instance, the Netherlandic Dutch part of the corpus contained more subtitles for Reality-TV, Documentaries and Romance, while the Flemish Dutch part of the corpus contained more Drama and Comedy. Overall, the distribution of genres can be said to be reasonably similar.

Various types of information from the text were extracted as features to feed machine learning classifiers; cf. Table 3. Features were adopted based on previous work by Abbasi and Chen (2008) and Huang et al. (2010). The extracted features can be clustered into three groups: text statistics, syntactic features, and content-specific features. Text statistics features are based on counts at various levels (e.g. sentence/word length and word length distributions); syntactic features represent aspects of the syntactic patterns present in the data (e.g. the number of function words, punctuation and part-of-speech tag n-grams); content-specific features are any characters, character n-grams, words, or word n-grams that may be indicative of one particular language variant.

3.2 Classification methods

The five machine learning algorithms used in this study are AdaBoost with a decision tree core, C4.5, Naive Bayes, Random Forest Classifier, and Linear-kernel SVM. These types of algorithms have been used frequently for Language Identification tasks. SVM algorithms (Goutte et al., 2014; Malmasi and Dras, 2015; Jauhiainen et al., 2016) and Naive Bayes (King et al., 2014; Franco-Penya and Sanchez, 2016) are amongst the most popular algorithms. Decision tree approaches, which C4.5, AdaBoost, and Random Forest Classifier are examples of, have been used as well, but less frequently (Zampieri, 2013; Malmasi et al., 2016). The machine learning algorithms were deployed using the scikit-learn library (Pedregosa et al., 2011).

One of the challenges in the current study is to find an effective method of selecting the best combination of feature categories. One study on language variety classification has shown that an effective feature combination approach could increase classification accuracy (Malmasi et al., 2015). Three combination approaches are tested in the current study, namely the super-vector approach, two rule-based meta-classifiers, and one algorithm-based meta-classifier:

Super-vector All features, regardless of feature category, are merged into a single vector to predict the language variety.

Sum-rule meta-classifier The probabilistic outputs of the most accurate text statistics, syntactic, and content-specific classifier are summed, and the language variety with the highest sum is chosen.

Product-rule meta-classifier The product is calculated for the probabilistic outputs of the most accurate lexical, syntactic and content-specific classifier, and the language variety with the highest product is chosen.

Algorithm-based meta-classifier The probabilistic outputs of the most accurate lexical, syntactic and content-specific classifier are

Group	Category	Description	Number
Lexical	Average words per minute		1
	Average characters per minute		1
	Average word length		1
	Average sentence length in terms of words		1
	Average sentence length in terms of characters		1
	Type/token ratio	Ratio of different words to the total number of words	1
	Hapax legomena ratio	Ratio of once-occurring words to the total number of words	1
	Dis legomena ratio	Ratio of twice-occurring words to the total number of words	1
	Short words ratio	Words < 4 characters to the total number of words	1
	Long words ratio	Words > 6 characters to the total number of words	1
	Word-length distribution	Ratio of words in length of 1–20	20
Syntactic	Function words ratio	Ratio of function words (e.g. *dat, de, ik*) to the total number of words	1
	Descriptive words to nominal words ratio	Adjectives and adverbs to the total number of nouns	1
	Personal pronouns ratio	Ratio of personal pronouns (e.g. *ik, jou, mij*) to the total number of words	1
	Question words ratio	Proportion of wh-determiners, wh-pronouns, and wh-adverbs (e.g. *wie, wat, waar*) to the total number of words	1
	Question mark ratio	Proportion of question marks to the total number of end of sentence punctuation	1
	Exclamation mark ratio	Proportion of exclamation marks to the total number of end of sentence punctuation	1
	Part-of-speech tag n-grams	Part-of-speech tag n-grams (e.g. NP, VP)	Varies
Content-specific	Word n-grams	Bag-of-word n-grams (e.g. *lat, erg hoog*)	Varies

Table 3: Features adopted in our experiments.

used to train a higher level classifier, which is subsequently used to predict the language variety.

The algorithms tested as algorithm-based meta-classifier are the same algorithms that are used for the individual feature categories (AdaBoost, C4.5, Naive Bayes, Random Forest Classifier, and Linear SVM).

3.3 Processing and performance increases

Several preprocessing steps were undertaken. The goal for the content-specific classifier was to decrease the number of features, thus increasing processing speed, while retaining the most useful information. This was done by removing stop words, number strings and punctuation from the corpus: tokens that appear frequently, while carrying little meaning. Furthermore, words were normalized using lemmatization[2] to decrease the number of types for the content-specific features. Finally, words that did not appear more than 10 times in the corpus were removed.

To get the syntactic information necessary for the syntactic features, Pattern (Smedt and Daelemans, 2012) was applied to the texts, obtaining the part-of-speech tags. Part-of-speech tag n-grams that appeared less than 10 times in the corpus were removed.

After the frequency-based thresholding selection, another feature selection step was performed based on the chi-square weights of all features. Ranking the features and starting from the features with the largest weight, the subset of features was selected at which a saturation point was reached in performance on held-out data. No more than 10% of the features in the syntactic and content-free category turned out to be selected.

Besides steps to increase processing speed, steps to increase classification accuracy were also undertaken: hyperparameter optimization was applied to the algorithms. The optimal parameters were found by using 30-step Bayesian optimization on a random sample of 10% of the corpus.

---

[2]Lemmatization was performed with Frog, https://languagemachines.github.io/frog/

Method	Algorithm	# of features	Precision	Recall	F-score	Accuracy
Lexical only	AdaBoost	5	0.73	0.98	0.83	0.73
Syntactic only	AdaBoost	392	0.83	0.92	0.87	0.81
Content-specific only	Linear SVM	30,514	0.87	0.95	0.91	0.87
Lexical/Syntactic	AdaBoost	407	0.83	0.92	0.87	0.81
Lexical/Content-specific	AdaBoost	76.288	0.87	0.95	0.91	0.87
Syntactic/Content-specific	AdaBoost	76.325	0.87	0.95	0.91	0.86
Supervector	AdaBoost	76,325	0.86	0.94	0.90	0.86
Meta classifier (add)	-	-	0.87	**0.96**	0.91	0.87
Meta classifier (product)	-	-	0.87	**0.96**	0.91	0.87
Meta classifier (ML)	AdaBoost	6	**0.88**	**0.96**	**0.92**	**0.88**

Table 4: Classification performance.

4 Results

Table 4 lists the results obtained when classifying the Netherlandic Dutch and Flemish Dutch language varieties. Evaluation was done using 10-fold cross-validation and with precision, recall, F-score (with $\beta = 1$) and accuracy as metrics. Results range from a 73% accuracy score using lexical features only to 88% accuracy using an algorithm-based meta classifier. Thus, similar to Malmasi et al. (2015), the results of this study show that the best results are obtained when combining different types of features, using an algorithm-based meta-classifier.

AdaBoost appeared to be the most effective algorithm for most feature categories, except for the content-specific feature type, where the Linear-kernel SVM algorithm was the most accurate algorithm. This is in line with most DSL Shared Task entries, where the most common and accurate classifiers are SVM classifiers with content-specific features.

The recall values turn out to be particularly high, most of them above 0.95, while the precision scores are slightly lower: most of the classifiers obtained a score of around 0.85 for precision. This is further illustrated in Table 5, where a confusion matrix for the algorithm-based meta-classifier is shown: the classifier that obtained the highest performance.

The confusion matrix shows that Flemish Dutch documents were markedly harder to classify compared to Netherlandic Dutch documents. Nearly one third, 10,474 of the 32,848 Flemish documents, were incorrectly classified as Netherlandic Dutch, while a substantially smaller proportion of Netherlandic Dutch documents were incorrectly

Document language	Language variant	
	Flemish	Netherlandic
Flemish	22,374	10,474
Netherlandic	3208	74,222

Table 5: Confusion matrix for the algorithm-based meta-classifier.

classified as Flemish Dutch (3208 out of 77,430). This may be partly explained by the fact that the number of Flemish Dutch documents is about half the number of Netherlandic Dutch documents in the SUBTIEL corpus.

4.1 Important features

The most important features per feature category are presented in Table 6. These features could be an indication of fundamental differences between the Netherlandic Dutch and Flemish Dutch language varieties and may therefore be useful from a linguistic perspective. The selection of feature importance is based on Random Forest Classification.

At the text statistics level, it can be observed that the ratio of words, especially shorter words, highlights important differences between Netherlandic Dutch and Flemish Dutch. There is a higher ratio of 1-, 2- and 5-letter words in the Flemish subtitles, while an average Netherlandic Dutch document contains more 3-letter words compared to Flemish Dutch documents, surprisingly. Additionally, sentences in Netherlandic Dutch subtitles contain more characters and words on average, and the ratio of words and characters per minute is higher in Netherlandic Dutch.

At the syntactic level, singular proper nouns (NNP) seem to be an important part-of-speech

Lexical		syntactic	Content-specific
Ratio of 1-letter words		NNP NN	nou
Ratio of 3-letter words		NNP PRP$	zandloper
Ratio of 5-letter words		NN FW	plots
Average amount of sentences in terms of words		, NNP	jij
Average amount of sentences in terms of characters	Personal pronouns ratio		hen
Ratio of 2-letter words		. PRP$	amuseren
Long words ratio		CD	orde
Words per minute		VB	vinden
Characters per minute	Function words ratio		lief helpen
Short words ratio		,	't

Table 6: Top 10 most important features per feature category.

category to discriminate Netherlandic Dutch from Flemish Dutch subtitles. Flemish subtitles have a higher ratio of sequences of singular proper nouns and singular nouns (NNP NN), singular proper nouns and possessive pronouns (NNP PRP$), and commas and singular proper nouns (, NNP). Furthermore, Flemish subtitles seem to contain a higher degree of singular nouns and foreign words (NN FW), periods and possessive pronouns (. PRP$), and commas (,), while Netherlandic Dutch subtitles contain more personal pronouns, cardinal numbers, and function words.

Some of the most important content-specific features indicate typical lexical differences between language varieties. For instance, *nou* has been previously noted to be a word that is not used as much in Flemish as compared to Netherlandic Dutch,[3] and *plots* is noted to be a word used more in Flemish.[4] No such categorical status is known for the other important content-specific features, although *amuseren* and *lief helpen* may arguably be associated more with Flemish Dutch. *Zandloper*, *jij*, *hen*, and *orde* also appeared more frequently in Flemish subtitles compared to Netherlandic Dutch, while *vinden* and *'t* appeared more in Netherlandic Dutch subtitles. The relative importance of some of these features in the current task could be due to hidden artifacts of the corpus.

5 Conclusion and future work

In this paper we presented language identification experiments carried out with five machine learning

techniques (AdaBoost, C4.5, Naive Bayes, Random Forest Classifier, and Linear SVM), and three feature categories (text statistics, syntactic features, and content-specific features) focusing on the Netherlandic and Flemish variants of Dutch. Subtitles collected in the SUBTIEL corpus were used to train and test the classifiers on. With the exception of a few studies (Lui and Cook, 2013; Lui et al., 2014; Windisch and Csink, 2005; Zampieri et al., 2013), text statistics and syntactic features have rarely been explored in language identification tasks. Additionally, there are not many classification studies focusing on Dutch language varieties, exceptions being Trieschnigg et al. (2012) and Tulkens et al. (2016).

The highest accuracy score was obtained when using a meta-classifier approach with a machine-learning algorithm, AdaBoost. In this approach the probabilistic scores obtained from classifiers trained exclusively on text statistics features, syntactic features, and content-free classifiers respectively were used as input for training a higher-level classifier. This result is in agreement with the findings of Malmasi et al. (2015), where the best results were also obtained using a meta classifier. This result suggests that a meta-classifier approach is a viable approach to language (variety) identification, and also supports the claim by Cimino et al. (2013) that underused feature types such as text statistics and syntactic features could improve classification accuracy. Furthermore, most of the classifiers performed best using an AdaBoost algorithm with decision tree core.

The accuracy, precision, recall and F-measure scores obtained with the algorithm-based meta-classifier are substantially higher than scores obtained with previous Dutch language variety clas-

---

[3] http://www.taaltelefoon.be/standaardtaal-verschillen-tussen-belgie-en-nederland

[4] http://taaladvies.net/taal/advies/vraag/665/plotsklaps_eensklaps_plots_plotseling/

sifiers. Trieschnigg et al. (2012) obtained an F-score of 0.80 versus the F-score of 0.92 in this study, and Tulkens et al. (2016) achieved an average accuracy of around 15% versus 88% in this study. Furthermore, the results seem to be on par with state-of-the-art methods: Zampieri et al. (2016) obtained accuracy scores between 74% and 90% in the binary classification of newspaper texts in variants of Portuguese, and Malmasi et al. (2015) obtained accuracy scores between 76% and 94% for binary classification of Arabic language varieties.

However, it is important to note that direct comparison between the current work and previous language variety identification studies is likely to be misleading. In this study, the classification of language varieties was based on the country the subtitle was developed for. It was not based on the country the subtitle writer was originally from, since this information was not known. Furthermore, Zampieri et al. (2016) and Malmasi et al. (2015) have shown that classification accuracy could be markedly different depending on how closely related the language varieties are, Lui and Cook (2013) have shown that different corpora could result in different accuracy scores, and the amount of language varieties that a classifier discriminates between has an effect on the accuracy as well. Thus, the difference between this study and the studies of Trieschnigg et al. (2012) and Tulkens et al. (2016) could be a matter of different corpora, corpus size, and the fact that the classifier in this study discriminated between two language varieties while the classifiers of Trieschnigg et al. (2012) and Tulkens et al. (2016) between sixteen and ten varieties, respectively.

Therefore, it would be interesting to see how the current approach competes against other approaches using the same corpus. When competing in such a task, it would be interesting to test whether the performance of the current approach could be further increased, for instance by including character-level features in the lexical and content-specific feature categories, since all the features in the current work reside at the word-level. Windisch and Csink (2005) have shown that character-level lexical features (word endings, character ratios, consonant congregations) are useful features for the classification of different languages, and character n-grams are one of the most popular features for language classifica-

tion (Zampieri, 2013). Furthermore, partial replication of the current study could be interesting with modifications to the current corpus and algorithms. Accuracy scores could change if the Netherlandic Dutch and Flemish Dutch data are balanced and if proper names are removed from the corpus (Zampieri et al., 2015). There are also different types of meta-classifiers (e.g. a voting-based meta-classifier) and algorithms (e.g. XG-Boost, Multilayer Perceptron) that were not tested in the current study and that might improve classification accuracy, which is worth further exploration.

The ranked list of most useful features found in this work could be a basis for future linguistic research on differences between Netherlandic Dutch (as spoken mainly in the Netherlands) and Flemish Dutch (as spoken mainly in Flanders). The findings for the lexical features suggest a difference in text difficulty between Netherlandic Dutch and Flemish Dutch texts: Flemish subtitles contain a higher ratio of short words, shorter sentences and generally less text. We would like to stress that these results could be do to differences in the SUBTIEL corpus. More research would be necessary to investigate whether such a stylistic difference between Netherlandic Dutch and Flemish Dutch exists outside of the SUBTIEL corpus.

References

Ahmed Abbasi and Hsinchun Chen. 2008. Writeprints: A stylometric approach to identity-level identification and similarity detection in cyberspace. *ACM Transactions on Information Systems*, 26(2):1–29.

Andrea Cimino, Felice Dell'Orletta, Giulia Venturi, and Simonetta Montemagni. 2013. Linguistic profiling based on general-purpose features and native language identification. In *Proceedings of the Eighth Workshop on Innovative Use of NLP for Building Educational Applications*, pages 207–215, Stroudsburg, PA, June. Association for Computational Linguistics.

Johan De Caluwe. 2002. In *Taalvariatie en taalbeleid : bijdragen aan het taalbeleid in Nederland en Vlaanderen*. Garant.

Hector-Hugo Franco-Penya and Liliana Mamani Sanchez. 2016. Tuning Bayes Baseline for dialect detection. In Preslav Nakov, Marcos Zampieri, Liling Tan, Nikola Ljubešić, Jörg Tiedemann, and Shervin Malmasi, editors, *Proceedings of the Third Workshop on NLP for Similar Languages, Varieties and Dialects*, pages 227–234, Stroudsburg, PA, December. Association for Computational Linguistics.

Cyril Goutte, Serge Léger, and Marine Carpuat. 2014. The NRC system for discriminating similar languages. In Marcos Zampieri, Liling Tan, Nikola Ljubešić, and Jörg Tiedemann, editors, *Proceedings of the First Workshop on Applying NLP Tools to Similar Languages, Varieties and Dialects*, pages 139–145, Stroudsburg, PA, August. Association for Computational Linguistics.

Cyril Goutte, Serge Léger, Shervin Malmasi, and Marcos Zampieri. 2016. Discriminating similar languages: Evaluations and explorations. In Nicoletta Calzolari, Khalid Choukri, Thierry Declerck, Sara Goggi, Marko Grobelnik, Bente Maegaard, Joseph Mariani, Hélène Mazo, Asunción Moreno, Jan Odijk, and Stelios Piperidis, editors, *Proceedings of the Tenth International Conference on Language Resources and Evaluation*, pages 1800–1807, Paris, France, May. European Language Resources Association.

Chunneng Huang, Tianjun Fu, and Hsinchun Chen. 2010. Text-based video content classification for online video-sharing sites. *Journal of the American Society for Information Science and Technology*, 61(5):891–906.

Scott Jarvis, Yves Bestgen, and Steve Pepper. 2013. Maximizing classification accuracy in native language identification. In *Proceedings of The 8th Workshop on Innovative Use of NLP for Building Educational Applications*, pages 111–118, Stroudsburg, PA, June. Association for Computational Linguistics.

Tommi Jauhiainen, Krister Lindén, and Heidi Jauhiainen. 2016. HeLI, a word-based backoff method for language identification. In Preslav Nakov, Marcos Zampieri, Liling Tan, Nikola Ljubešić, Jörg Tiedemann, and Shervin Malmasi, editors, *Proceedings of the Third Workshop on NLP for Similar Languages, Varieties and Dialects*, pages 153–162, Stroudsburg, PA, December. Association for Computational Linguistics.

Ben King, Dragomir Radev, and Steven Abney. 2014. Experiments in sentence language identification with groups of similar languages. In Marcos Zampieri, Liling Tan, Nikola Ljubešić, and Jörg Tiedemann, editors, *Proceedings of the First Workshop on Applying NLP Tools to Similar Languages, Varieties and Dialects*, pages 146–154, Stroudsburg, PA, August. Association for Computational Linguistics.

Marco Lui and Paul Cook. 2013. Classifying English documents by national dialect. In Sarvnaz Karimi and Karin Verspoor, editors, *Proceedings of the Australasian Language Technology Association Workshop 2013*, pages 5–15, Stroudsburg, PA, December. Association for Computational Linguistics.

Marco Lui, Ned Letcher, Oliver Adams, Long Duong, Paul Cook, and Timothy Baldwin. 2014. Exploring methods and resources for discriminating similar languages. In Marcos Zampieri, Liling Tan, Nikola Ljubešić, and Jörg Tiedemann, editors, *Proceedings of the First Workshop on Applying NLP Tools to Similar Languages, Varieties and Dialects*, pages 129–138, Stroudsburg, PA, August. Association for Computational Linguistics.

Wolfgang Maier and Carlos Gómez-Rodriguez. 2014. Language variety identification in Spanish tweets. In *Proceedings of the EMNLP'2014 Workshop on Language Technology for Closely Related Languages and Language Variants*, pages 25–35, Stroudsburg, PA, October. Association for Computational Linguistics.

Shervin Malmasi and Mark Dras. 2015. Large-scale native language identification with cross-corpus evaluation. In *Proceedings of the 2015 Conference of the North American Chapter of the Association for Computational Linguistics: Human Language Technologies*, pages 1403–1409, Stroudsburg, PA, June. Association for Computational Linguistics.

Shervin Malmasi, Eshrag Refaee, and Mark Dras. 2015. Arabic dialect identification using a parallel multidialectal corpus. In Kôiti Hasida and Ayu Purwarianti, editors, *Proceedings of the Fourteenth International Conference of the Pacific Association for Computational Linguistics*, pages 35–53, Singapore, May. Springer.

Shervin Malmasi, Marcos Zampieri, Nikola Ljubešić, Preslav Nakov, Ahmed Ali, and Jörg Tiedemann. 2016. Discriminating between similar languages and Arabic dialect identification: A report on the third DSL shared task. In Preslav Nakov, Marcos Zampieri, Liling Tan, Nikola Ljubešić, Jörg Tiedemann, and Shervin Malmasi, editors, *Proceedings of the Third Workshop on NLP for Similar Languages, Varieties and Dialects*, pages 1–14, Stroudsburg, PA, December. Association for Computational Linguistics.

Paul McNamee. 2005. Language identification: a solved problem suitable for undergraduate instruction. *Journal of Computing Sciences in Colleges*, 20(3):94–101.

Fabian Pedregosa, Gaël Varoquaux, Alexandre Gramfort, Vincent Michel, Bertrand Thirion, Olivier Grisel, Mathieu Blondel, Peter Prettenhofer, Ron Weiss, Vincent Dubourg, Jake Vanderplas, Alexandre Passos, David Cournapeau, Matthieu Brucher, Matthieu Perrot, and Édouard Duchesnay. 2011. Scikit-learn: Machine learning in Python. *Journal of Machine Learning Research*, 12:2825–2830.

Ineke Schuurman, Machteld Schouppe, Heleen Hoekstra, and Ton Van der Wouden. 2003. CGN, an annotated corpus of spoken Dutch. In *Proceedings of 4th International Workshop on Language Resources and Evaluation*, pages 340–347.

Tom de Smedt and Walter Daelemans. 2012. Pattern for Python. *Journal of Machine Learning Research*, 13(Jun):2063–2067.

Jörg Tiedemann and Nikola Ljubešić. 2012. Efficient discrimination between closely related languages. In Martin Kay, editor, *Proceedings of the 24th International Conference on Computational Linguistics*, pages 2619–2634, Stroudsburg, PA, May. Association for Computational Linguistics.

Dolf Trieschnigg, Djoerd Hiemstra, Mariët Theune, Franciska de Jong, and Theo Meder. 2012. An exploration of language identification techniques for the Dutch folktale database. In Petya Osenova, Stelios Piperidis, Milena Slavcheva, and Cristina Vertan, editors, *Proceedings of the Workshop on Adaptation of Language Resources and Tools for Processing Cultural Heritage*, pages 47–51, May.

Stéphan Tulkens, Chris Emmery, and Walter Daelemans. 2016. Evaluating unsupervised Dutch word embeddings as a linguistic resource. In Nicoletta Calzolari, Khalid Choukri, Thierry Declerck, Sara Goggi, Marko Grobelnik, Bente Maegaard, Joseph Mariani, Hélène Mazo, Asunción Moreno, Jan Odijk, and Stelios Piperidis, editors, *Proceedings of the Tenth International Conference on Language Resources and Evaluation*, pages 4130–4136, Paris, France, May. European Language Resources Association.

Gergely Windisch and László Csink. 2005. Language identification using global statistics of natural languages. In *Proceedings of the Second Romanian-Hungarian Joint Symposium on Applied Computational Intelligence*, pages 243–255, May.

Marcos Zampieri, Binyam Gebrekidan Gebre, and Sascha Diwersy. 2013. N-gram language models and POS distribution for the identification of Spanish varieties. In *Proceedings of the Confrence sur le Traitement Automatique des Langues Naturelles 2013*, pages 580–587, Stroudsburg, PA, June. Association for Computational Linguistics.

Marcos Zampieri, Liling Tan, Nikola Ljubešić, and Jörg Tiedemann. 2014. A report on the DSL shared task 2014. In Marcos Zampieri, Liling Tan, Nikola Ljubešić, and Jörg Tiedemann, editors, *Proceedings of the First Workshop on Applying NLP Tools to Similar Languages, Varieties and Dialects*, pages 58–67, Stroudsburg, PA, August. Association for Computational Linguistics.

Marcos Gebre Zampieri, Binyam Gebrekidan, Hernani Costa, and Josef van Genabith. 2015. Comparing approaches to the identification of similar languages. In Preslav Nakov, Marcos Zampieri, Petya Osenova, Liling Tan, Cristina Vertan, Nikola Ljubešić, and Jörg Tiedemann, editors, *Proceedings of the Second Workshop on NLP for Similar Languages, Varieties and Dialects*, pages 66–72, Stroudsburg, PA, September. Association for Computational Linguistics.

Marcos Zampieri, Shervin Malmasi, Octavia-Maria Şulea, and Liviu P. Dinu. 2016. A computational approach to the study of Portuguese newspapers published in Macau. In Larry Birnbaum, Octavian Popescu, and Carlo Strapparava, editors, *Proceedings of the Workshop on Natural Language Processing Meets Journalism*, pages 47–51, Stroudsburg, PA, July. Association for Computational Linguistics.

Marcos Zampieri. 2013. Using bag-of-words to distinguish similar languages: How efficient are they? In *Proceedings of the Fourteenth Symposium on Computational Intelligence and Informatics*, pages 37–41, New York, NY, November. Institute of Electrical and Electronics Engineers.

Learning to Identify Arabic and German Dialects using Multiple Kernels

Radu Tudor Ionescu and **Andrei M. Butnaru**

University of Bucharest
Department of Computer Science
14 Academiei, Bucharest, Romania
raducu.ionescu@gmail.com
butnaruandreimadalin@gmail.com

Abstract

We present a machine learning approach for the Arabic Dialect Identification (ADI) and the German Dialect Identification (GDI) Closed Shared Tasks of the DSL 2017 Challenge. The proposed approach combines several kernels using multiple kernel learning. While most of our kernels are based on character p-grams (also known as n-grams) extracted from speech transcripts, we also use a kernel based on i-vectors, a low-dimensional representation of audio recordings, provided only for the Arabic data. In the learning stage, we independently employ Kernel Discriminant Analysis (KDA) and Kernel Ridge Regression (KRR). Our approach is shallow and simple, but the empirical results obtained in the shared tasks prove that it achieves very good results. Indeed, we ranked on the first place in the ADI Shared Task with a weighted F_1 score of 76.32% (4.62% above the second place) and on the fifth place in the GDI Shared Task with a weighted F_1 score of 63.67% (2.57% below the first place).

1   Introduction

The recent 2016 Challenge on Discriminating between Similar Languages (DSL) (Malmasi et al., 2016) shows that dialect identification is a challenging NLP task, actively studied by researchers in nowadays. For example, a state-of-the-art Arabic dialect identification system achieves just over 50% (Ionescu and Popescu, 2016b; Malmasi and Zampieri, 2016), in a 5-way classification setting. In this context, we present a method based on learning with multiple kernels, that we designed for the Arabic Dialect Identification (ADI) and

the German Dialect Identification (GDI) Shared Tasks of the DSL 2017 Challenge (Zampieri et al., 2017). In the ADI Shared Task, the participants had to discriminate between Modern Standard Arabic (MSA) and four Arabic dialects, in a 5-way classification setting. A number of 6 teams have submitted their results on the test set, and our team (UnibucKernel) ranked on the first place with an accuracy of 76.27% and a weighted F_1 score of 76.32%. In the GDI Shared Task, the participants had to discriminate between four German dialects, in a 4-way classification setting. A number of 10 teams have submitted their results, and our team ranked on the fifth place with an accuracy of 66.36% and a weighted F_1 score of 63.67%.

Our best scoring system in both shared tasks combines several kernels using multiple kernel learning. The first kernel that we considered is the p-grams presence bits kernel[1], which takes into account only the presence of p-grams instead of their frequency. The second kernel is the (histogram) intersection string kernel[2], which was first used in a text mining task by Ionescu et al. (2014). The third kernel is derrived from Local Rank Distance (LRD)[3], a distance measure that was first introduced in computational biology (Ionescu, 2013; Dinu et al., 2014), but it has also shown its application in NLP (Popescu and Ionescu, 2013; Ionescu, 2015). All these string kernels have been previously used for Arabic dialect identification by Ionescu and Popescu (2016b), and they obtained very good results, taking the second place in the ADI Shared Task of the DSL 2016 Challenge (Malmasi et al., 2016). While

---

[1]We computed the p-grams presence bits kernel using the code available at http://string-kernels.herokuapp.com.

[2]We computed the intersection string kernel using the code available at http://string-kernels.herokuapp.com.

[3]We computed the Local Rank Distance using the code available at http://lrd.herokuapp.com.

Proceedings of the Fourth Workshop on NLP for Similar Languages, Varieties and Dialects, pages 200–209,
Valencia, Spain, April 3, 2017. ©2017 Association for Computational Linguistics

three of our kernels are based on character p-grams from speech transcrips, we also use an RBF kernel (Shawe-Taylor and Cristianini, 2004) based on i-vectors (Ali et al., 2016), a low-dimensional representation of audio recordings, available only for the Arabic data. To the best of our knowledge, none of the string kernels have been previously combined with a kernel based on i-vectors or used for German dialect identification.

We considered two kernel classifiers (Shawe-Taylor and Cristianini, 2004) for the learning task, namely Kernel Ridge Regression (KRR) and Kernel Discriminant Analysis (KDA). In a set of preliminary experiments performed on the GDI training set, we found that KDA gives slightly better results than KRR. On the other hand, KRR seems to yield a better performance on the ADI training and development sets. In the end, we decided to submit results using both classifiers. However, our best scoring system in both shared tasks employs Kernel Ridge Regression (KRR) in the learning stage. Before submitting our results, we have also tuned our string kernels for the task. First of all, we tried out p-grams of various lengths, including blended variants of string kernels as well. Second of all, we have evaluated the individual kernels and various kernel combinations. The empirical results indicate that combining kernels can help to improve the accuracy by at least 1%. When we added the kernel base on i-vectors into the mix, we found that it can further improve the performance, by nearly 5%. All these choices played a significant role in obtaining the first place in the final ranking of the ADI Shared Task.

The paper is organized as follows. Work related to Arabic and German dialect identification and to methods based on string kernels is presented in Section 2. Section 3 presents the kernels that we used in our approach. The learning methods used in the experiments are described in Section 4. Details about the experiments on Arabic and German dialect identification are provided in Sections 5 and 6, respectively. Finally, we draw our conclusion in Section 7.

2 Related Work

2.1 Arabic Dialect Identification

Arabic dialect identification is a relatively new NLP task with only a handful of works to address it (Biadsy et al., 2009; Zaidan and Callison-Burch, 2011; Elfardy and Diab, 2013; Darwish et al., 2014; Zaidan and Callison-Burch, 2014; Malmasi et al., 2015). Although it did not received too much attention, the task is very important for Arabic NLP tools, as most of these tools have only been design for Modern Standard Arabic. Biadsy et al. (2009) describe a phonotactic approach that automatically identifies the Arabic dialect of a speaker given a sample of speech. While Biadsy et al. (2009) focus on spoken Arabic dialect identification, others have tried to identify the Arabic dialect of given texts (Zaidan and Callison-Burch, 2011; Elfardy and Diab, 2013; Darwish et al., 2014; Malmasi et al., 2015). Zaidan and Callison-Burch (2011) introduce the Arabic Online Commentary (AOC) data set of 108K labeled sentences, 41% of them having dialectal content. They employ a language model for automatic dialect identification on their collected data. A supervised approach for sentence-level dialect identification between Egyptian and MSA is proposed by Elfardy and Diab (2013). Their system outperforms the approach presented by Zaidan and Callison-Burch (2011) on the same data set. Zaidan and Callison-Burch (2014) extend their previous work (Zaidan and Callison-Burch, 2011) and conduct several ADI experiments using word and character p-grams. Different from most of the previous work, Darwish et al. (2014) have found that word unigram models do not generalize well to unseen topics. They suggest that lexical, morphological and phonological features can capture more relevant information for discriminating dialects. As the AOC corpus is not controlled for topic bias, Malmasi et al. (2015) also state that the models trained on this corpus may not generalize to other data as they implicitly capture topical cues. They perform ADI experiments on the Multidialectal Parallel Corpus of Arabic (MPCA) (Bouamor et al., 2014) using various word and character p-grams models in order to assess the influence of topic bias. Interestingly, Malmasi et al. (2015) find that character p-grams are "in most scenarios the best single feature for this task", even in a cross-corpus setting. Their findings are consistent with the results of Ionescu and Popescu (2016b) in the ADI Shared Task of the DSL 2016 Challenge (Malmasi et al., 2016), as they ranked on the second place using solely character p-grams from Automatic Speech Recognition (ASR) transcripts. However, the 2017 ADI Shared Task data set (Ali et al., 2016) contains the original audio files and some low-level audio features, called i-vectors, along with the ASR transcripts of Arabic speech collected from the Broadcast News domain. Our experiments indicate that the audio features produce a much better performance, probably because there are many ASR errors (perhaps more in the dialectal speech segments) that make Arabic dialect identification from ASR transcripts much more difficult.

2.2 German Dialect Identification

German dialect identification is even less studied than Arabic dialect identification. Scherrer and Rambow (2010) describe a system for written dialect identification based on an automatically generated Swiss German lexicon that associates word forms with their geographical extensions. At test time, they split a sentence into words and look up their geographical extensions in the lexicon. Hollenstein and Aepli (2015) present a Swiss German dialect identification system based on character trigrams. They train a trigram language model for each dialect and score each test sentence against every model. The predicted dialect is chosen based on the lowest perplexity. Although Samardzic et al. (2016) present a corpus that can be used for GDI, they do not deal with this task in their paper. Nonetheless, their corpus was used to evaluate the participants in the GDI Shared Task of the DSL 2017 Challenge.

2.3 String Kernels

In recent years, methods of handling text at the character level have demonstrated impressive performance levels in various text analysis tasks (Lodhi et al., 2002; Sanderson and Guenter, 2006; Kate and Mooney, 2006; Grozea et al., 2009; Popescu, 2011; Escalante et al., 2011; Popescu and Grozea, 2012; Ionescu et al., 2014; Ionescu et al., 2016). String kernels are a common form of using information at the character level. They are a particular case of the more general convolution kernels (Haussler, 1999). Lodhi et al. (2002) used string kernels for document categorization with very good results. String kernels were also successfully used in authorship identification (Sanderson and Guenter, 2006; Popescu and Grozea, 2012). For example, the system described by Popescu and Grozea (2012) ranked first in most problems and overall in the PAN 2012 Traditional Authorship Attribution tasks. More recently, various blended string kernels reached

state-of-the-art accuracy rates for native language identification (Ionescu et al., 2016) and Arabic dialect identification (Ionescu and Popescu, 2016b).

3 Kernels for Dialect Identification

3.1 String Kernels

The kernel function captures the intuitive notion of similarity between objects in a specific domain and can be any function defined on the respective domain that is symmetric and positive definite. For strings, many such kernel functions exist with various applications in computational biology and computational linguistics (Shawe-Taylor and Cristianini, 2004). String kernels embed the texts in a very large feature space, given by all the substrings of length p, and leave it to the learning algorithm to select important features for the specific task, by highly weighting these features.

Perhaps one of the most natural ways to measure the similarity of two strings is to count how many substrings of length p the two strings have in common. This gives rise to the p-spectrum kernel. Formally, for two strings over an alphabet Σ, $s, t \in \Sigma^*$, the p-spectrum kernel is defined as:

$$k_p(s, t) = \sum_{v \in \Sigma^p} \text{num}_v(s) \cdot \text{num}_v(t),$$

where $\text{num}_v(s)$ is the number of occurrences of string v as a substring in s.[4] The feature map defined by this kernel associates to each string a vector of dimension $|\Sigma|^p$ containing the histogram of frequencies of all its substrings of length p (p-grams). A variant of this kernel can be obtained if the embedding feature map is modified to associate to each string a vector of dimension $|\Sigma|^p$ containing the presence bits (instead of frequencies) of all its substrings of length p. Thus, the character p-grams presence bits kernel is obtained:

$$k_p^{0/1}(s, t) = \sum_{v \in \Sigma^p} \text{in}_v(s) \cdot \text{in}_v(t),$$

where $\text{in}_v(s)$ is 1 if string v occurs as a substring in s, and 0 otherwise.

In computer vision, the (histogram) intersection kernel has successfully been used for object class recognition from images (Maji et al., 2008; Vedaldi and Zisserman, 2010). Ionescu et

---

[4]The notion of substring requires contiguity. Shawe-Taylor and Cristianini (2004) discuss the ambiguity between the terms *substring* and *subsequence* across different domains: biology, computer science.

al. (2014) have used the intersection kernel as a kernel for strings. The intersection string kernel is defined as follows:

$$k_p^{\cap}(s, t) = \sum_{v \in \Sigma^p} \min\{\text{num}_v(s), \text{num}_v(t)\},$$

where $\text{num}_v(s)$ is the number of occurrences of string v as a substring in s.

For the p-spectrum kernel, the frequency of a p-gram has a very significant contribution to the kernel, since it considers the product of such frequencies. On the other hand, the frequency of a p-gram is completely disregarded in the p-grams presence bits kernel. The intersection kernel lies somewhere in the middle between the p-grams presence bits kernel and p-spectrum kernel, in the sense that the frequency of a p-gram has a moderate contribution to the intersection kernel. In other words, the intersection kernel assigns a high score to a p-gram only if it has a high frequency in both strings, since it considers the minimum of the two frequencies. The p-spectrum kernel assigns a high score even when the p-gram has a high frequency in only one of the two strings. Thus, the intersection kernel captures something more about the correlation between the p-gram frequencies in the two strings. Based on these comments, we decided to use only the p-grams presence bits kernel and the intersection string kernel for ADI and GDI.

Data normalization helps to improve machine learning performance for various applications. Since the value range of raw data can have large variation, classifier objective functions will not work properly without normalization. After normalization, each feature has an approximately equal contribution to the similarity between two samples. To obtain a normalized kernel matrix of pairwise similarities between samples, each component is divided by the square root of the product of the two corresponding diagonal components:

$$\hat{K}_{ij} = \frac{K_{ij}}{\sqrt{K_{ii} \cdot K_{jj}}}.$$

To ensure a fair comparison of strings of different lengths, normalized versions of the p-grams presence bits kernel and the intersection kernel are being used. Taking into account p-grams of different lengths and summing up the corresponding kernels, new kernels, termed *blended spectrum kernels*, can be obtained. We have used various blended spectrum kernels in the experiments in order to find the best combination.

3.2 Kernel based on Local Rank Distance

Local Rank Distance (Ionescu, 2013) is a recently introduced distance that measures the non-alingment score between two strings. It has already shown promising results in computational biology (Ionescu, 2013; Dinu et al., 2014) and native language identification (Popescu and Ionescu, 2013; Ionescu, 2015).

In order to describe LRD, we use the following notations. Given a string x over an alphabet Σ, the length of x is denoted by $|x|$. Strings are considered to be indexed starting from position 1, that is $x = x[1]x[2] \cdots x[|x|]$. Moreover, $x[i : j]$ denotes its substring $x[i]x[i + 1] \cdots x[j - 1]$. Given a fixed integer $p \geq 1$, a threshold $m \geq 1$, and two strings x and y over Σ, the *Local Rank Distance* between x and y, denoted by $\Delta_{LRD}(x, y)$, is defined through the following algorithmic process. For each position i in x ($1 \leq i \leq |x| - p + 1$), the algorithm searches for that position j in y ($1 \leq j \leq |y| - p + 1$) such that $x[i : i + p] = y[j : j + p]$ and $|i - j|$ is minimized. If j exists and $|i - j| < m$, then the offset $|i - j|$ is added to the Local Rank Distance. Otherwise, the maximal offset m is added to the Local Rank Distance. LRD is focused on the local phenomenon, and tries to pair identical p-grams at a minimum offset. To ensure that LRD is a (symmetric) distance function, the algorithm also has to sum up the offsets obtained from the above process by exchanging x and y. LRD is formally defined in (Ionescu, 2013; Dinu et al., 2014; Ionescu and Popescu, 2016a).

The search for matching p-grams is limited within a window of fixed size. The size of this window is determined by the maximum offset parameter m. We set $m = 300$ in our experiments, which is larger than the maximum length of the transcripts provided in both training sets. In the experiments, the efficient algorithm of Ionescu (2015) is used to compute LRD. However, LRD needs to be used as a kernel function. We use the RBF kernel (Shawe-Taylor and Cristianini, 2004) to transform LRD into a similarity measure:

$$\hat{k}_p^{LRD}(s, t) = exp\left(-\frac{\Delta_{LRD}(s, t)}{2\sigma^2}\right),$$

where s and t are two strings and p is the p-grams length. The parameter σ is usually chosen so that values of $\hat{k}(s, t)$ are well scaled. We have tuned σ in a set of preliminary experiments. In the above equation, Δ_{LRD} is already normalized to a value in the $[0, 1]$ interval to ensure a fair comparison of strings of different length. The resulted similarity matrix is then squared to ensure that it becomes a symmetric and positive definite kernel matrix.

3.3 Kernel based on Audio Features

For the ADI Shared Task, we also build a kernel from the i-vectors provided with the data set (Ali et al., 2016). The i-vector approach is a powerful speech modeling technique that comprises all the updates happening during the adaptation of a Gaussian mixture model (GMM) mean components to a given utterance. The provided i-vectors have 400 dimensions. In order to build a kernel from the i-vectors, we first compute the euclidean distance between each pair of i-vectors. We then employ the RBF kernel to transform the distance into a similarity measure:

$$\hat{k}^{i\text{-}vec}(x, y) = exp\left(-\frac{\sqrt{\sum_{m}^{j=1}(x_j - y_j)^2}}{2\sigma^2}\right),$$

where x and y are two i-vectors and m represents the size of the two i-vectors, 400 in our case. For optimal results, we have tuned the parameter σ in a set of preliminary experiments. As for the LRD kernel, the similarity matrix is squared to ensure its symmetry and positive definiteness.

4 Learning Methods

Kernel-based learning algorithms work by embedding the data into a Hilbert feature space and by searching for linear relations in that space. The embedding is performed implicitly, by specifying the inner product between each pair of points rather than by giving their coordinates explicitly. More precisely, a kernel matrix that contains the pairwise similarities between every pair of training samples is used in the learning stage to assign a vector of weights to the training samples. Let α denote this weight vector. In the test stage, the pairwise similarities between a test sample x and all the training samples are computed. Then, the following binary classification function assigns a positive or a negative label to the test sample:

$$g(x) = \sum_{i=1}^{n} \alpha_i \cdot k(x, x_i),$$

where x is the test sample, n is the number of training samples, $X = \{x_1, x_2, ..., x_n\}$ is the set of training samples, k is a kernel function, and α_i is the weight assigned to the training sample x_i.

The advantage of using the dual representation induced by the kernel function becomes clear if the dimension of the feature space m is taken into consideration. Since string kernels are based on character p-grams, the feature space is indeed very high. For instance, using 5-grams based only on the 28 letters of the basic Arabic alphabet will result in a feature space of $28^5 = 17,210,368$ features. However, our best models are based on a feature space that includes 3-grams, 4-grams, 5-grams, 6-grams and 7-grams. As long as the number of samples n is much lower than the number of features m, it can be more efficient to use the dual representation given by the kernel matrix. This fact is also known as the *kernel trick* (Shawe-Taylor and Cristianini, 2004).

Various kernel methods differ in the way they learn to separate the samples. In the case of binary classification problems, kernel-based learning algorithms look for a discriminant function, a function that assigns $+1$ to examples belonging to one class and -1 to examples belonging to the other class. In the ADI and GDI experiments, we used the Kernel Ridge Regression (KRR) binary classifier. Kernel Ridge Regression selects the vector of weights that simultaneously has small empirical error and small norm in the Reproducing Kernel Hilbert Space generated by the kernel function. KRR is a binary classifier, but dialect identification is usually a multi-class classification problem. There are many approaches for combining binary classifiers to solve multi-class problems. Typically, the multi-class problem is broken down into multiple binary classification problems using common decomposition schemes such as: one-versus-all and one-versus-one. We considered the one-versus-all scheme for our dialect classification tasks. There are also kernel methods that take the multi-class nature of the problem directly into account, for instance Kernel Discriminant Analysis. The KDA classifier is sometimes able to improve accuracy by avoiding the masking problem (Hastie and Tibshirani, 2003). More details about KRR and KDA are given in (Shawe-Taylor and Cristianini, 2004).

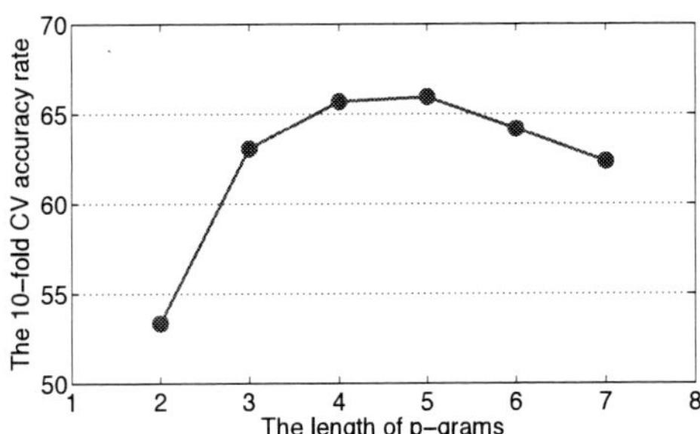

Figure 1: Accuracy rates of the KRR based on the intersection kernel with p-grams in the range 2-7. The results are obtained in a 10-fold cross-validation procedure carried out on the ADI training set.

5 Experiments on Arabic Dialects

5.1 Data Set

The ADI Shared Task data set (Ali et al., 2016) contains audio recordings and ASR transcripts of Arabic speech collected from the Broadcast News domain. The task is to discriminate between Modern Standard Arabic (MSA) and four Arabic dialects, namely Egyptian (EGY), Gulf (GLF), Levantine (LAV), and North-African or Maghrebi (NOR). As the samples are not very evenly distributed, an accuracy of 23.10% can be obtained with a majority class baseline on the test set. It is worth mentioning that the test set from the 2016 ADI Shared Task was included as a development set in this year's task.

5.2 Parameter and System Choices

In our approach, we treat ASR transcripts as strings. Because the approach works at the character level, there is no need to split the texts into words, or to do any NLP-specific processing before computing the string kernels. The only editing done to the transcripts was the replacing of sequences of consecutive space characters (space, tab, and so on) with a single space character. This normalization was needed in order to prevent the artificial increase or decrease of the similarity between texts, as a result of different spacing.

For tuning the parameters, we fixed 10 folds in order to evaluate each option in a 10-fold cross-validation (CV) procedure on the training set. We first carried out a set of preliminary experiments to determine the optimal range of p-grams for each kernel using the 10-fold CV procedure. We fixed the learning method to KRR based on the inter-section kernel and we evaluated all the p-grams in the range 2-7. The results are illustrated in Figure 1. Interestingly, the best accuracy (65.93%) is obtained with 5-grams. Furthermore, experiments with different blended kernels were conducted to see whether combining p-grams of different lengths could improve the accuracy. More precisely, we evaluated combinations of p-grams in five ranges: 3-5, 3-6, 4-6, 4-7 and 3-7. For the intersection kernel and the LRD kernel, the best accuracy rates were obtained when all the p-grams with the length in the range 3-7 were combined. For the presence bits kernel, we obtained better results with p-grams in the range 3-5. Further experiments were also conducted to establish what type of kernel works better, namely the blended p-grams presence bits kernel ($\hat{k}_{3-5}^{0/1}$), the blended p-grams intersection kernel ($\hat{k}_{3-7}^{\cap}$), the kernel based on LRD ($\hat{k}_{3-7}^{LRD}$), or the kernel based on i-vectors ($\hat{k}^{i\text{-}vec}$). Since these different kernel representations are obtained either from ASR transcripts or from low-level audio features, a good approach for improving the performance is combining the kernels. When multiple kernels are combined, the features are actually embedded in a higher-dimensional space. As a consequence, the search space of linear patterns grows, which helps the classifier to select a better discriminant function. The most natural way of combining two or more kernels is to sum them up. Summing up kernels or kernel matrices is equivalent to feature vector concatenation. The kernels were evaluated alone and in various combinations, by employing either KRR or KDA for the learning task. This time, we used the development set to evaluate the kernel combinations and compare them with the top two systems from the last year's ADI Shared Task (Ionescu and Popescu, 2016b; Malmasi and Zampieri, 2016) and the state-of-the-art system of Ali et al. (2016). All the results obtained on the development set are given in Table 1.

The empirical results presented in Table 1 reveal several interesting patterns of the proposed methods. The difference in terms of accuracy between KRR and KDA is almost always less than 1%, and there is no reason to chose one in favor of the other. Regarding the individual kernels, the results are fairly similar among the string kernels, but the kernel based on i-vectors definitely stands out. Indeed, the best individual kernel is the kernel based on i-vectors with an accuracy of 59.84%

Method	Accuracy	
Ionescu and Popescu (2016b)	51.82%	
Malmasi and Zampieri (2016)	51.17%	
Ali et al. (2016)	60.20%	
Kernel	**KRR**	**KDA**
$\hat{k}_{3-5}^{0/1}$	52.36%	51.18%
$\hat{k}_{3-7}^{\cap}$	51.64%	52.17%
$\hat{k}_{3-7}^{LRD}$	51.77%	52.55%
$\hat{k}_{3-5}^{0/1} + \hat{k}_{3-7}^{\cap}$	52.30%	52.49%
$\hat{k}_{3-5}^{0/1} + \hat{k}_{3-7}^{LRD}$	52.48%	52.42%
$\hat{k}_{3-7}^{\cap} + \hat{k}_{3-7}^{LRD}$	52.05%	52.66%
$\hat{k}_{3-5}^{0/1} + \hat{k}_{3-7}^{\cap} + \hat{k}_{3-7}^{LRD}$	52.63%	52.82%
$\hat{k}^{i\text{-}vec}$	59.84%	58.99%
$\hat{k}^{i\text{-}vec} + \hat{k}_{3-5}^{0/1} + \hat{k}_{3-7}^{\cap} + \hat{k}_{3-7}^{LRD}$	**64.17%**	**63.85%**

Table 1: Accuracy rates of various kernels combined with either KRR or KDA versus several state-of-the-art methods. The results are obtained on the ADI development set. The submitted systems are highlighted in bold.

Run	Accuracy	F_1 (macro)	F_1 (weighted)
1	76.27%	76.40%	76.32%
2	75.54%	75.94%	75.81%

Table 2: Results on the test set of the ADI Shared Task (closed training) of KRR (run 1) and KDA (run 2) based on a combination of three string kernels and a kernel based on i-vectors.

when it is combined with KRR, and an accuracy of 58.99% when it is combined with KDA. By contrast, the best individual string kernel yields an accuracy of 52.55%. Thus, we may conclude that the i-vector representation extracted from audio recordings is much more suitable for the task than the character p-grams extracted from ASR transcripts. This is consistent with the findings of Ali et al. (2016). Interestingly, the best accuracy is actually obtained when all four kernels are combined together. Indeed, KRR reaches an accuracy of 64.17% when the blended p-grams presence bits kernel, the blended intersection kernel, the blended LRD kernel and the kernel based on i-vectors are summed up. With the same kernel combination, KDA yields an accuracy of 63.85%. In the end, we decided to submit two models for the test set. The first submission (run 1) is the KRR classifier based on the sum of $\hat{k}^{i\text{-}vec}$, $\hat{k}_{3-5}^{0/1}$, $\hat{k}_{3-7}^{\cap}$, and $\hat{k}_{3-7}^{LRD}$. The second submission (run 2) is the KDA classifier based on the sum of the same four kernels. For a better generalization, the submitted models are trained on both the provided training and development sets.

Dialects	EGY	GLF	LAV	NOR	MSA
EGY	244	12	29	6	11
GLF	14	177	43	8	8
LAV	36	26	231	23	18
NOR	10	13	10	222	7
MSA	24	16	31	9	264

Table 3: Confusion matrix (on the test set) of KRR based on the sum of three string kernels and a kernel based on i-vectors (run 1).

5.3 Results

Table 2 presents our results for the Arabic Dialect Identification Closed Shared Task of the DSL 2017 Challenge. Among the two classifiers, the best performance is obtained by KRR (run 1). The submitted systems were ranked by their weighted F_1 score, and among the 6 participants, our best model obtained the first place with a weighted F_1 score of 76.32%. As the development and the test sets are from the same source (distribution), we obtained better performance on the test set by including the development set in the training. The confusion matrix for our best model is presented in Table 3. The confusion matrix reveals that our system has some difficulties in distinguishing the Levantine dialect from the Egyptian dialect on one hand, and the Levantine dialect from the Gulf dialect on the other hand. Overall, the results look good, as the main diagonal scores dominate the other matrix components. Remarkably, both of our submitted systems are more than 4% better than the system ranked on the second place.

6 Experiments on German Dialects

6.1 Data Set

The GDI Shared Task data set (Samardzic et al., 2016) contains manually annotated transcripts of Swiss German speech. The task is to discriminate between Swiss German dialects from four different areas: Basel (BS), Bern (BE), Lucerne (LU), Zurich (ZH). As the samples are almost evenly distributed, an accuracy of 25.80% can be obtained with a majority class baseline on the test set.

6.2 Parameter and System Choices

As for the ADI task, we edit the transcripts by replacing the sequences of consecutive space characters with a single space character. For tuning the parameters and deciding what kernel learning method works best, we fixed 5 folds in order to evaluate each option in a 5-fold CV procedure on the training set. We first carried out a set of prelim-

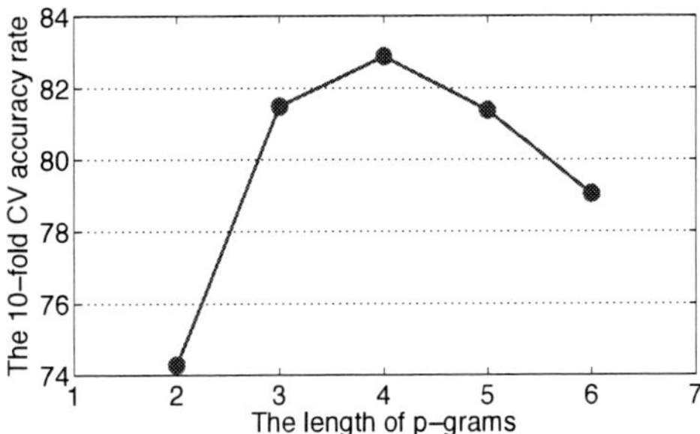

Figure 2: Accuracy rates of the KRR based on the intersection kernel with p-grams in the range 2-6. The results are obtained in a 5-fold CV procedure carried out on the GDI training set.

Kernel	KRR	KDA
$\hat{k}_{3-6}^{0/1}$	83.99%	84.10%
$\hat{k}_{3-6}^{\cap}$	83.96%	84.09%
$\hat{k}_{3-5}^{LRD}$	83.85%	84.25%
$\hat{k}_{3-6}^{0/1} + \hat{k}_{3-6}^{\cap}$	84.03%	**84.15%**
$\hat{k}_{3-6}^{0/1} + \hat{k}_{3-5}^{LRD}$	84.25%	84.33%
$\hat{k}_{3-6}^{\cap} + \hat{k}_{3-5}^{LRD}$	84.22%	84.35%
$\hat{k}_{3-6}^{0/1} + \hat{k}_{3-6}^{\cap} + \hat{k}_{3-5}^{LRD}$	**84.39%**	**84.49%**

Table 4: Accuracy rates of various kernels combined with either KRR or KDA. The results are obtained using 5-fold CV on the GDI training set. The submitted systems are highlighted in bold.

inary experiments to determine the optimal range of p-grams for each kernel. We fixed the learning method to KRR based on the intersection kernel and we evaluated all the p-grams in the range 2-6. The results are illustrated in Figure 2. We obtained the best accuracy (82.87%) by using 4-grams. We next evaluated combinations of p-grams in three ranges: 3-5, 3-6, 4-6. For the intersection and the presence bits kernels, the best accuracy rates were obtained when all the p-grams with the length in the range 3-6 were combined. For the LRD kernel, we obtained better results with p-grams in the range 3-5. Further experiments were also performed to establish what type of kernel works better, namely the blended p-grams presence bits kernel, the blended p-grams intersection kernel or the kernel based on LRD. The kernels were evaluated alone and in various combinations, by employing either KRR or KDA for the learning task. All the results obtained in the 5-fold CV carried out on the training set are given in Table 4. As in the ADI experiments, the empirical results presented in Table 4 show that there are no significant differences between KRR and KDA. The individual kernels yield fairly similar results. The best in-

Run	Accuracy	F$_1$ (macro)	F$_1$ (weighted)
1	66.36%	63.76%	63.67%
2	65.81%	63.63%	63.54%
3	65.64%	63.44%	63.36%

Table 5: Results on the test set of the GDI Shared Task (closed training) of KRR (run 1) and KDA (run 2 and 3) based on various combinations of string kernels.

Dialects	BE	BS	LU	ZH
BE	662	53	19	172
BS	76	676	38	149
LU	185	260	249	222
ZH	14	29	7	827

Table 6: Confusion matrix (on the test set) of KRR based on the sum of three string kernels (run 1).

dividual kernel is the kernel based on LRD with an accuracy of 84.25% when it is combined with KDA. Each and every kernel combination yields better results than each of its individual components alone. The best accuracy rates, 84.39% for KRR and 84.49% for KDA, are indeed obtained when all three kernels are combined together. In the end, we submitted the following models. The first submission (run 1) is the KRR based on the three kernels sum. Our second submission (run 2) is the KDA based on the sum of $\hat{k}_{3-6}^{0/1}$ and $\hat{k}_{3-6}^{\cap}$. Our third submission (run 3) is the KDA based on the combination of all three kernels.

6.3 Results

Table 5 presents our results for the German Dialect Identification Closed Shared Task of the DSL 2017 Challenge. Among the three systems, the best performance is obtained by KRR (run 1). Among the 10 participants, our best model obtained the fifth place with a weighted F_1 score of 63.67%. However, our best performance is only 2.57% below the performance achieved by the system ranked on the first place. The confusion matrix presented in Table 6 indicates that our model is hardly able to distinguish the Lucerne dialect from the others.

7 Conclusion

We have presented an approach based on learning with multiple kernels for the ADI and the GDI Shared Tasks of the DSL 2017 Challenge (Zampieri et al., 2017). Our approach attained very good results, as our team (UnibucKernel) ranked on the first place in the ADI Shared Task and on the fifth place in the GDI Shared Task.

References

Ahmed Ali, Najim Dehak, Patrick Cardinal, Sameer Khurana, Sree Harsha Yella, James Glass, Peter Bell, and Steve Renals. 2016. Automatic dialect detection in arabic broadcast speech. *Proceedings of Interspeech*, pages 2934–2938.

Fadi Biadsy, Julia Hirschberg, and Nizar Habash. 2009. Spoken Arabic Dialect Identification Using Phonotactic Modeling. *Proceedings of the EACL 2009 Workshop on Computational Approaches to Semitic Languages*, pages 53–61.

Houda Bouamor, Nizar Habash, and Kemal Oflazer. 2014. A Multidialectal Parallel Corpus of Arabic. *Proceedings of LREC*, pages 1240–1245, may.

Kareem Darwish, Hassan Sajjad, and Hamdy Mubarak. 2014. Verifiably Effective Arabic Dialect Identification. *Proceedings of EMNLP*, pages 1465–1468.

Liviu P. Dinu, Radu Tudor Ionescu, and Alexandru I. Tomescu. 2014. A rank-based sequence aligner with applications in phylogenetic analysis. *PLoS ONE*, 9(8):e104006, 08.

Heba Elfardy and Mona T. Diab. 2013. Sentence Level Dialect Identification in Arabic. *Proceedings of ACL*, pages 456–461.

Hugo Jair Escalante, Thamar Solorio, and Manuel Montes-y-Gómez. 2011. Local histograms of character n-grams for authorship attribution. *Proceedings of ACL: HLT*, 1:288–298.

Cristian Grozea, Christian Gehl, and Marius Popescu. 2009. ENCOPLOT: Pairwise Sequence Matching in Linear Time Applied to Plagiarism Detection. *Proceedings of 3rd PAN WORKSHOP*, page 10.

Trevor Hastie and Robert Tibshirani. 2003. *The Elements of Statistical Learning*. Springer, corrected edition, July.

David Haussler. 1999. Convolution Kernels on Discrete Structures. Technical Report UCS-CRL-99-10, University of California at Santa Cruz, Santa Cruz, CA, USA.

Nora Hollenstein and Noëmi Aepli. 2015. A Resource for Natural Language Processing of Swiss German Dialects. *Proceedings of GSCL*, pages 108–109.

Radu Tudor Ionescu and Marius Popescu. 2016a. *Knowledge Transfer between Computer Vision and Text Mining*. Advances in Computer Vision and Pattern Recognition. Springer International Publishing.

Radu Tudor Ionescu and Marius Popescu. 2016b. UnibucKernel: An Approach for Arabic Dialect Identification based on Multiple String Kernels. *Proceedings of VarDial Workshop of COLING*, pages 135–144.

Radu Tudor Ionescu, Marius Popescu, and Aoife Cahill. 2014. Can characters reveal your native language? A language-independent approach to native language identification. *Proceedings of EMNLP*, pages 1363–1373, October.

Radu Tudor Ionescu, Marius Popescu, and Aoife Cahill. 2016. String kernels for native language identification: Insights from behind the curtains. *Computational Linguistics*, 42(3):491–525.

Radu Tudor Ionescu. 2013. Local Rank Distance. *Proceedings of SYNASC*, pages 221–228.

Radu Tudor Ionescu. 2015. A Fast Algorithm for Local Rank Distance: Application to Arabic Native Language Identification. *Proceedings of ICONIP*, 9490:390–400.

Rohit J. Kate and Raymond J. Mooney. 2006. Using String-kernels for Learning Semantic Parsers. *Proceedings of ACL*, pages 913–920.

Huma Lodhi, Craig Saunders, John Shawe-Taylor, Nello Cristianini, and Christopher J. C. H. Watkins. 2002. Text Classification using String Kernels. *Journal of Machine Learning Research*, 2:419–444.

Subhransu Maji, Alexander C. Berg, and Jitendra Malik. 2008. Classification using intersection kernel support vector machines is efficient. *Proceedings of CVPR*.

Shervin Malmasi and Marcos Zampieri. 2016. Arabic Dialect Identification in Speech Transcripts. *Proceedings of VarDial Workshop of COLING*, pages 106–113.

Shervin Malmasi, Eshrag Refaee, and Mark Dras. 2015. Arabic Dialect Identification using a Parallel Multidialectal Corpus. *Proceedings of PACLING*, pages 209–217, May.

Shervin Malmasi, Marcos Zampieri, Nikola Ljubešić, Preslav Nakov, Ahmed Ali, and Jörg Tiedemann. 2016. Discriminating between similar languages and arabic dialect identification: A report on the third dsl shared task. *Proceedings of the 3rd Workshop on Language Technology for Closely Related Languages, Varieties and Dialects (VarDial)*.

Marius Popescu and Cristian Grozea. 2012. Kernel methods and string kernels for authorship analysis. *CLEF (Online Working Notes/Labs/Workshop)*, September.

Marius Popescu and Radu Tudor Ionescu. 2013. The Story of the Characters, the DNA and the Native Language. *Proceedings of the Eighth Workshop on Innovative Use of NLP for Building Educational Applications*, pages 270–278, June.

Marius Popescu. 2011. Studying translationese at the character level. *Proceedings of RANLP*, pages 634–639, September.

Tanja Samardzic, Yves Scherrer, and Elvira Glaser. 2016. ArchiMob–A corpus of spoken Swiss German. *Proceedings of LREC*, pages 4061–4066.

Conrad Sanderson and Simon Guenter. 2006. Short text authorship attribution via sequence kernels, markov chains and author unmasking: An investigation. *Proceedings of the 2006 Conference on Empirical Methods in Natural Language Processing*, pages 482–491, July.

Yves Scherrer and Owen Rambow. 2010. Word-based dialect identification with georeferenced rules. *Proceedings of EMNLP*, pages 1151–1161.

John Shawe-Taylor and Nello Cristianini. 2004. *Kernel Methods for Pattern Analysis*. Cambridge University Press.

Andrea Vedaldi and Andrew Zisserman. 2010. Efficient additive kernels via explicit feature maps. *Proceedings of CVPR*, pages 3539–3546.

Omar F. Zaidan and Chris Callison-Burch. 2011. The Arabic Online Commentary Dataset: An Annotated Dataset of Informal Arabic with High Dialectal Content. *Proceedings of ACL: HLT*, 2:37–41.

Omar F. Zaidan and Chris Callison-Burch. 2014. Arabic dialect identification. *Computational Linguistics*, 40(1):171–202.

Marcos Zampieri, Shervin Malmasi, Nikola Ljubešić, Preslav Nakov, Ahmed Ali, Jörg Tiedemann, Yves Scherrer, and Noëmi Aepli. 2017. Findings of the VarDial Evaluation Campaign 2017. *Proceedings of VarDial Workshop of EACL*.

Slavic Forest, Norwegian Wood

Rudolf Rosa and **Daniel Zeman** and **David Mareček** and **Zdeněk Žabokrtský**
Charles University, Faculty of Mathematics and Physics
Institute of Formal and Applied Linguistics
Malostranské náměstí 25, Prague, Czech Republic
{rosa, zeman, marecek, zabokrtsky}@ufal.mff.cuni.cz

Abstract

[D]We once had a corp,

or should we say,[C]it once had[D]us

[D]They showed us its tags,

isn't it great,[C]unified[D]tags

[Dmi]They asked us to parse

and they told us to use[G]everything

[Dmi]So we looked around

and we noticed there was near[Em]nothing[AA7]

We took other langs,

bitext aligned: words one-to-one

We played for two weeks,

and then they said, here is the test

The parser kept training till morning,

just until deadline

So we had to wait and hope what we get

would be just fine

And, when we awoke,

the results were done, we saw we'd won

So, we wrote this paper,

isn't it good, Norwegian wood.

1 Introduction

This paper describes the winning submission to the Cross-lingual Dependency Parsing shared task at VarDial 2017 (Zampieri et al., 2017).

The goal was to devise a labeled dependency parser for a target language with no treebank available, utilizing treebanks of other very close source languages, and plaintext sentence-aligned source-target parallel data. The task is simulated on target languages for which treebanks do exists, but are not provided to the participants.

As the focus of the task is on parsing per se, a supervised part-of-speech (*POS*) tagger for each target language is provided. Moreover, all of the treebanks come from the Universal Dependencies (*UD*) collection v 1.4 (Nivre et al., 2016), which means that their syntactic and morphological an-

notation – tree topology, dependency relation labels (*deprels*), universal POS tags (*UPOS*), and morphological features (*morpho feats*) – follows the universal cross-lingual UD scheme.[1]

Consonantly with the focus of the VarDial workshop on similar languages, the source and target languages are very close to each other, with very similar grammars and a nearly one-to-one correspondence on the level of individual words. Therefore, we decided to mostly disregard systematic structural heterogeneity between the languages, and focus primarily on lexical differences.

Our method relies on a context-independent word-by-word machine translation (*MT*) of the source treebank into the target language, based on a one-to-one word alignment provided by a heuristic aligner for similar languages. This switch from a cross-lingual to a pseudo-monolingual setting allows us to easily apply source-trained taggers and parsers to the target data and vice versa.

We also employ several homogenization techniques, mostly to overcome systematic differences in treebank annotations. Specifically, we normalize the deprels in the source treebanks to better correspond to the target deprels, and we subselect only cross-lingually consistent morpho feats.

2 Related Work

The notorious fact that there are several thousand languages used around the globe makes it necessary to search for NLP methods that could be applicable to a wider range of languages, ideally without too much effort invested into building language-specific resources for new languages again and again. This is by far not specific to dependency parsing, for which—like for most other "traditional" NLP tasks—various approaches have

---

[1]See http://universaldependencies.org/ docsv1 for a description of the UD scheme.

Proceedings of the Fourth Workshop on NLP for Similar Languages, Varieties and Dialects, pages 210–219,
Valencia, Spain, April 3, 2017. ©2017 Association for Computational Linguistics

been developed, ranging from fully unsupervised methods (whose performance seems to be limited) to supervised methods with radically economy-driven annotation management.

We limit the scope of the following overview only to cross-lingual transfer of dependency parsers from a resource-rich source language(s) to a resource-poor target language. In addition, this paper does not touch the discussions whether a tree (and what kind of tree) is a reasonable representation for a sentence structure, and whether all languages do really share their structural properties to such an extent that a single type of representation is viable for all of them. Though such issues deserve intensive attention, and perhaps even more so now when UD have gained such a fascinating momentum, we take the two assumptions simply for granted. Neither do we present the genesis of the current UD collection, preceded by HamleDT treebank collection by Zeman et al. (2014), going back to the CoNLL 2006 and 2007 tasks (Buchholz and Marsi, 2006; Nivre et al., 2007), and to earlier POS standardization efforts. In this overview, we limit ourselves to the scope outlined by the VarDial shared task, whose goal is to develop a parser for a (virtually) under-resourced language closely related to a resource-rich language.[2]

We believe that most of the published approaches could be classified into two broad families which we call *tree-transfer-based* methods and *common-abstraction-based* methods. The former project individual dependency trees across the language boundary prior to training a target parser. The latter methods transfer a parser model trained directly on the source treebank, but limited only to abstract features shared by both languages.

2.1 Tree-transfer-based approaches

In the tree-transfer-based approaches, a synthetic pseudo-target treebank is created by some sort of projection of individual source trees into the target language. Then a standard monolingual parser can be trained using the pseudo-target treebank in a more or less standard way. As it is quite unlikely that a manually annotated source treebank

with high-quality human-made target translations and high-quality alignment exists, one or more of the necessary components must be approximated. And even if all these data components existed, the task of dependency tree projection would inevitably lead to collisions that have to be resolved heuristically, especially in the case of many-to-one or many-to-many alignments, as investigated e.g. by Hwa et al. (2005) and more recently by Tiedemann (2014) or Ramasamy et al. (2014).

This family embraces the following approaches:

- using a *parallel corpus* and projecting the trees through word-alignment links, with authentic texts in both languages but an automatically parsed source side,
- using a *machine-translated parallel corpus*, with only one side containing authentic texts and the other being created by MT; both translation directions have pros and cons:
  - source-to-target MT allows for using a gold treebank on the source side,
  - target-to-source MT allows the parser to learn to work with real texts in the target language, for which, in addition, a gold POS labeling might be available.

Obviously there are certain trade-offs related to this family of tree transfer approaches. For example, using MT to create a synthetic parallel corpus often results in a considerably lower text quality, but provides more reliable alignment links. In addition, such alignment typically has a higher amount of one-to-one word alignments, which facilitates tree projection; in case of extremely close languages, as in this paper, the MT system can be constrained to produce only 1:1 translations.

There are two additional advantages of the tree-transfer-based approach:

- the feature set used by the target language parser is independent of the features that are applicable to the source language,
- we can easily use only sentence pairs (or tree fragments) with a reasonably high correspondence between source and target structures, as done by Rasooli and Collins (2015).

2.2 Common-abstraction-based approaches

By using a "common abstraction" we mean using features that have the same or very similar "meaning" both in the source and target language. Obviously, word forms cannot be easily used directly, as there are various spelling and morpho-

---

[2]Crosslingual transfer is not used only in truly under-resourced scenarios, but also in situations in which it is hoped that features explicitly manifested in one language (such as morphological agreement) could boost parsing performance in some other language in which they are less overt. Such bilingually informed parsing scenarios are studied e.g. by Haulrich (2012).

logical differences even between very close languages. Using such shared features allows a parser that was trained on a source treebank to be used directly on target texts; i.e. the source-target "transfer" of the parser is trivial, compared to a source-target transfer of the treebank as described in §2.1.

The common abstraction features used by the parser can be linguistically motivated, or induced by mathematical methods such as clustering and vector space representation:

- Unified POS tags: a POS tagset simplified and unified to the extent that it was usable for both source and target languages was behind one of the first experiments with delexicalized parsing by Zeman and Resnik (2008). The advantage of such approaches lies in their linguistic interpretability. On the other hand, in spite of the substantial progress in tagset harmonization since the work of Zeman (2008), this approach can end up in a very limited intersection of morphological categories in case of more distant languages.
- Word clusters have been successfully applied in many NLP fields, with the clusters of Brown et al. (1992) being probably the most prominent representative. Täckström et al. (2012) showed that cross-lingually induced clusters can serve as the common abstract features for cross-lingual parsing.
- Word embeddings, if induced with some cross-lingual constraints and mapped into a shared low-dimensional space, can also be used, as shown e.g. by Duong et al. (2015).

An obvious trade-off that appears with this family of methods is associated with the specificity/generality of the shared abstract representation of words. For example, in the case of delexicalization by a common POS tagset, the question arises what is the best granularity of shared tags. The more simplified tags, the more language-universal information is captured, but the more information is lost at the same time. Moreover, even if two languages share a particular morphological category, e.g. pronoun reflexivity, it is hard to predict whether adding this distinction into the shared tagset helps the resulting parser or not.

A variation that appers with this family of methods is the usage of "relexicalization". The base parser resulting from the transfer is applied on (unseen) target data, and a new parser is self-trained on this data; a successful application of this approach is documented by Täckström et al. (2013).

2.3 Other variations

Aufrant et al. (2016) combines both main strategies described above by adapting the word order in source sentences to be more similar to that of the target language, e.g. by swapping the order of an attribute and its nominal head; the information about these configurations was extracted from the WALS World Atlas of Language Structures (Dryer and Haspelmath, 2013). Such processing of source language trees fits to the first family of approaches, as it resembles a (very limited) MT preprocessing; but after this step, a POS-delexicalized parser transfer is used, which fits the second family.

When processing more than a few under-resourced languages, choosing the best source language should be ideally automatized too. One could rely on language phylogenetic trees or on linguistic information available e.g. in WALS, or on more mechanized measures, such as Kullback-Leibler divergence of POS trigram distributions (Rosa and Žabokrtský, 2015).

In addition, we might want to combine information from more source languages, like in the case of multi-source transfer introduced by McDonald et al. (2011). Choosing source language weights to be used as mixing coefficients becomes quite intricate then as we face a trade-off between similarity of the source languages to the target language and the size of resources available for them.

3 Task and Data

The task was to perform labeled dependency parsing of each of the three target languages, Slovak (*SK*), Croatian (*HR*), and Norwegian (*NO*), without using target treebanks. In the constrained track of the task, we were only allowed to use provided source treebanks and source-target parallel data for source languages closely related to the target languages: Czech (*CS*) as a source for SK, Slovenian (*SL*) for HR, and Danish (*DA*) and Swedish (*SV*) for NO. Because of reported good performance in the baselines, we use the DA and SV data concatenated into "Dano-Swedish" (*DS*).

For development testing of our systems, small target *dev treebanks* were provided, with golden syntactic annotation, and morphological annotation (UPOS and morpho feats) predicted by supervised taggers; the taggers were also provided. Final test treebanks were annotated in the same way.

For an exact description of the task, the datasets, models, baselines and upper-bounds, please refer to (Zampieri et al., 2017) and the task webpage.[3]

The task specifies Labeled Attachment Score (LAS) as the primary metric, and Unlabeled Attachment Score (UAS) as a secondary one.

4 Components

In §4.1 we describe the baseline setup, which we further enrich by the components described in the following sections; the final setups used for each of the target languages are specified in §5.

The development and employment of the components was guided by continual evaluation on the dev treebanks. We evaluated several variations of each component, and selected the best performing variant separately for each target language.[4] Hyperparameter tuning was performed neither for the tagger and parser nor for any of the components, as this was forbidden by the shared task rules.[5]

4.1 Baseline

As our starting point, we took the task baseline. It consists of a UDPipe tagger and parser (Straka et al., 2016),[6] trained on the source treebank with the default settings, except:

- the parser is trained without using the morpho feats (i.e. only using word form and UPOS)[7]
- the tagger is trained to only produce UPOS.[8]

We train the tagger and parser together, which means that UDPipe trains the tagger, applies it to the treebank, and trains the parser using morphological annotation predicted by the tagger. We have found this setup to perform better than training on gold annotation by +1.6 LAS on average.

4.2 Annotation Normalization

Unlike some older work in this area, we work with multi-lingual data that is harmonized across lan-

guages, i.e. all languages should be syntactically and morphologically annotated according to the same UD guidelines. However, the current level of harmonization is still far from perfect. Certain deprels occur in the source treebanks but not in the target treebank (or vice versa), but not due to differences in the treebank languages or domains – it is just because of differences in annotation, despite the intention of UD to annotate the same things in the same way. We obviously cannot modify the test data in any way, but we can make the source data as similar to the target annotation as possible. By doing so, we simulate a likely real-world scenario: when people want to parse a resource-poor language, they supposedly know what kind of deprels they want in the output.

For example, CS contains a language-specific `nummod:gov` deprel, which never occurs in SK. We do not want the parser to learn to assign that deprel, because we are not going to score on such relations. Hence, we replace all occurrences of `nummod:gov` in the source treebank by the more general `nummod` deprel, which is also used in SK.

Similarly, one may want to modify the UPOSes and morpho feats, which the parser gets as input and can use them to improve syntactic analysis. It seems reasonable to adjust or hide tags unavailable in the target data; e.g., the SK treebank does not distinguish `SCONJ` from `CONJ`, and `DET` from `PRON`; or, the Scandinavian treebanks disagree on when participles are `VERB` and when `ADJ`.

Finally, we tried to normalize several rather randomly spotted phenomena whose analysis systematically differs across languages. The most prominent example is the Scandinavian word *både* in *både A och/og B* "both A and B". In SV, the word is tagged `CONJ` and attached via the `advmod` deprel, in DA it is `ADV`/`advmod`, and in NO it is `CONJ`/`cc`. Normalizing instances of *både* alone increased LAS on NO by almost 1 point!

Our normalization is based on manual error analyses of parser outputs on the dev treebanks.

4.3 Word-by-Word Machine Translation

The core of our approach is a move from a cross-lingual to a pseudo-monolingual setting by translating the word forms in the source treebank into the target language. It has three steps: word-alignment of the parallel data, extraction of a translation table from the aligned data, and the treebank translation itself.

---

[3] `https://bitbucket.org/tiedemann/vardial2017`

[4] We evaluated 114 different setups: 63 were evaluated for all 3 target languages, 12 for 2, and 39 for 1 target language; in total, 252 LAS scores were computed on the dev treebanks.

[5] Following the UDPipe manual, we deviated from the default tagger hyperparameters in case of CS (due to its huge treebank), setting them to: `guesser_suffix_rules=6; guesser_enrich_dictionary=4`

[6] Version `3e65d69` from 3rd Jan 2017, obtained from `https://github.com/ufal/udpipe`

[7] Parameter: `embedding_feats=0`

[8] Parameters: `use_lemma=0;provide_lemma=0; use_xpostag=0;provide_xpostag=0; use_feats=1;provide_feats=1`

We employ a simple word-based MT approach, which we tried as a first attempt but found it good enough for our purpose; we have yet to evaluate how it compares to more sophisticated methods.

4.3.1 Word-alignment

Since the source and target languages in our task are very close to each other, we decided to use the heuristic Monolingual Greedy Aligner (*MGA*) of Rosa et al. (2012),[9] rather than e.g. the usual Giza++ (Och and Ney, 2003) – most standard word aligners ignore word similarity, which we believe to be useful and important in our setting.

MGA utilizes the word, lemma, and tag similarity based on Jaro-Winkler distance (Winkler, 1990), and the similarity of relative positions in the sentences, to devise a score for each potential alignment link as a linear combination of these, weighted by pre-set weights. The iterative alignment process then greedily chooses the currently highest scoring pair of words to align in each step; each word can only be aligned once. The process stops when one of the sides is fully aligned, or when the scores of the remaining potential links fall below a pre-set threshold.

We used MGA as is, with the default values of the hyperparameters and with no adaptation to the UD annotation style or the specific languages of the task. Even though MGA was originally designed for aligning same-language sentences (especially Czech), we found it to perform well enough in our setting, and therefore left potential tuning and adaptations for future work.

Before aligning, we preprocess the parallel data by the Treex tokenizer, the provided target tagger, and a source tagger trained on the source treebank.

4.3.2 Translation table extraction

For our methods to be easily applicable, we require a one-to-one translation, which we can afford due to the high similarity of the languages. Therefore, we extract a translation *word* table rather than the more usual phrase table from the aligned data. Moreover, due to the simplicity of the subsequent translation step, it is sufficient for us to only store the best (most frequent) translation for each word; we use Jaro-Winkler similarity of the source and target word forms as a tie breaker.

Identical source word forms with differing UPOS or morpho feats annotations are treated as distinct words, serving as a basic source-side disambiguation; we rely on these source annotations being available at inference for selecting the translation. To reduce the OOV rate, two backoff layers are also stored, the first disregarding the morpho feats, and the second also disregarding the UPOS.

An option that we leave for future research is to use the alignment scores provided by the MGA when constructing the translation table.

For simplicity, we create only one joint translation table for translating DS into NO.

4.3.3 Treebank translation

We translate each source treebank into the target language word-by-word, independent of any source or target context. We use the golden annotation of UPOS and morpho feats for source-side disambiguation; a backoff layer is used if the translation table does not contain the source word form with the given annotations. OOVs are left untranslated. This results in a pseudo-target treebank, with golden annotations from the source treebank and word forms in the target language.

In preliminary experiments, the opposite target-to-source translation led to worse results (by -1.3 LAS on average), possibly because the parser relies more on the correctness of the source, making it less robust when applied to the machine-translated target. Moreover, in case of DS-NO, the target-to-source translation is not straightforward.

4.4 Pre-training Word Embeddings

Because UDPipe uses a neural network parser, all input features have to be converted to vectors. By default, it trains embeddings of each input feature on the pseudo-target treebank jointly with training the parser. As larger data can provide better embeddings, we pretrain word form embeddings on the target side of the parallel data, pretokenized by the Treex tokenizer (Popel and Žabokrtský, 2010),[10] and provide them to UDPipe. We use word2vec (Mikolov et al., 2013), with the parameters suggested in the UDPipe manual.[11]

---

[9]`https://github.com/ufal/treex/blob/master/lib/Treex/Tool/Align/MonolingualGreedy.pm`

[10]`https://github.com/ufal/treex/blob/master/lib/Treex/Block/W2A/Tokenize.pm`

[11]`-cbow 0 -size 50 -window 10 -negative 5 -hs 0 -sample 1e-1 -binary 0 -iter 15 -min-count 2 -threads 12`

4.5 Morphological Features Subselection

We found out that in the default setting, not using the morphological features leads to better LAS than using them. This is probably caused by the fact that UDPipe treats the morpho feats string as a single unit and is not able to split it and assign different importance to individual features. We therefore try to find an effective subsection of the morphological features.

4.5.1 Keep useful

Collins et al. (1999) showed that *Case* was the most valuable feature for parsing Czech; indeed, when we discard all features but *Case*, we observe better accuracy for all target languages.

One other feature they use with words that do not have *Case* is called *SubPOS* and is specific to the tagset of their corpus. In UD, there are several features with similar function, e.g. *PronType* subcategorizing pronouns or *NumType* subcategorizing numerals. Unfortunately, we found neither of them to help in our setting.

4.5.2 Keep shared

Another possibility is to keep only those features that are highly consistent cross-lingually. For each feature-value pair in the tagged and aligned parallel data, we count the number of times it appears on both sides of an alignment pair. The consistency c of feature-value pair f is computed as:

$$c(f) = \frac{1}{2}\left(\frac{\#(f \in s, f \in t)}{\#(f \in s)} + \frac{\#(f \in s, f \in t)}{\#(f \in t)}\right)$$

where $\#()$ indicates the number of times the feature is present in the source (s), target (t), or both aligned words. We only keep feature-value pairs with consistency higher than a threshold, which we set to 0.7 after having evaluated the values of 0.6, 0.7, and 0.8. We also tried to condition the consistency scores on UPOS, which did not improve LAS.

The two described feature selection mechanisms can also be combined, e.g. by providing the *Case* feature in the morhpo feats field, and the other shared features in the XPOS field, thus enabling the parser to treat them separately.

4.6 Cross-Tagging

There is a considerable body of work on projecting POS taggers across aligned corpora, dating back to (Yarowsky and Ngai, 2001). In combination with cross-language parsing, such techniques are used to provide the parser with target-side POS tags. Our task is specific in that a supervised target POS tagger is available; however, there are still several possibilities of combining tagger and parser models in order to make the parsed data as similar as possible to what the parser was trained on.

- **Baseline.** Train a parser on the source treebank. Tag the target data by a supervised target tagger and parse it by the trained parser, hoping that the tags produced by the target tagger are similar enough to the source tags.
- **Source data cross-tagging (*source-xtag*).** Translate source treebank into the target language, tag it by a supervised target tagger and train a parser on it. Tag the target data by the supervised target tagger and parse it by the trained parser.
- **Target data cross-tagging (*target-xtag*).** Translate the source treebank into the target language and train a tagger and parser on in. Tag the target data by the trained tagger and then parse it by the trained parser.

In addition, we always train the parser jointly with a tagger, so that the parser is trained on monolingually predicted tags, as explained in §4.1.

We have found source-xtag to work well for heterogeneous source data, such as the DS mixture.

Conversely, target-xtag proved useful for SK, where the source treebank is much larger than the target data used to train the target tagger. A tagger trained on the large source treebank provides much better tags, which in turn boosts the parsing accuracy, despite the noise from MT and xtag.

Note that if no target tagger is available, we must either use target-xtag, or we may project a tagger across the parallel data in the style of Yarowsky and Ngai (2001) and use the resulting tagger in our baseline or source-xtag scenarios.[12]

We also experimented with cross-tagging of only the UPOS or only the morpho feats, with different setups being useful for different languages.

Although the UDPipe tagger can also be trained to perform lemmatization, we have not found any way to obtain and utilize lemmas that would improve the cross-lingual parsing.[13]

---

[12]Our approach still needs a target tagger to perform the word alignment, but we believe that for very close languages, the word forms alone might be sufficient to obtain a good-enough alignment; or, a different word aligner could be used.

[13]We tried to translate the lemmas, as well as to perform simple stemming, such as cropping or devowelling.

Component	SK	HR	NO
§4.2 Normalize source annotations	✓	✓	✓
§4.3 Translate word forms	✓	✓	✓
§4.4 Pre-train form embeddings	✓	✓	✓
§4.6 Source-xtag of UPOS	×	×	✓
§4.5 Add *Case* morpho feat	✓	✓	✓
§4.5 Add shared morpho feats	✓	×	×
§4.6 Target-xtag of morpho feats	✓	×	✓
§4.6 Target-xtag of UPOS	✓	×	×

Table 1: Components used for the various languages, listed in the order in which they are applied. The *Case* feature was used in the best (after-deadline) SK setup, but not in the submitted setup.

5 Individual Language Setups

In our final setup, we enrich the baseline (§4.1) by various components (§4), as listed in Table 1:

1. Normalize source treebank annotations
2. Translate source treebank to target language
3. Pre-train target word form embeddings
4. *For NO:* Cross-tag UPOS in source treebank
5. Prune source treebank morphological features, keeping only *Case*
6. *For SK:* Put frequently shared morpho feats into the "XPOS" field in source treebank
7. Train a tagger on source treebank, tagging UPOS and *Case* (for SK also "XPOS")
8. Retag source treebank by the trained tagger
9. Train a parser on source treebank, using the pre-trained word form embeddings, UPOS, and *Case* (for SK also "XPOS")
10. *For HR:* Prune target morphological features, keeping only *Case*
11. *For NO and SK:* Cross-tag *Case* in target
12. *For SK:* Cross-tag UPOS and morphological features in target
13. Parse target corpus by the trained parser

We believe that the utility of the language-specific components owes to the following:

- For NO, there are two different source languages. Translating them both to NO and re-tagging them with the NO tagger makes the training data more homogeneous.[14]
- SK and CS seem to be the closest languages in the shared task, both being morphologically very rich, which explains the usefulness of employing additional shared morpho feats.
- The CS treebank is extremely large, leading to the fact that a pseudo-SK tagger, trained on

---

[14]However, it is better to use the original morphological features in source treebank and cross-tag them on target treebank, presumably because annotation of *Case* in SV is much richer than in NO.

	SK	HR	NO
Setup	LAS on test		
Baseline	53.72	53.35	59.95
Our	**78.12**	60.70	70.21
Supervised	69.14	**68.51**	**78.23**
Reaching supervised	158%	48%	56%
Setup	LAS on dev		
Baseline	55.97	55.88	59.31
Our	77.49	64.32	69.99
Supervised	70.27	74.27	78.10
Reaching supervised	145%	48%	56%

Table 2: Evaluation using LAS. *Reaching supervised* is how far we got on the scale between the baseline and the supervised setup.

the CS treebank translated to SK, performs far better than the original SK tagger.

6 Results

The results we achieved on the dev and test treebanks are listed in Table 2. For SK, we got an even better result of 79.37% LAS (78.63% on dev) just 6 minutes after the deadline by combining shared morphological features and *Case*, while the submitted setup only contained the shared features without *Case*. The baseline and supervised LAS are shown as reported by organizers.

We can see that for both HR and NO, we achieve a score that is approximately half the way from the baseline to the supervised setup. The fact the CS and SK are very close, and that the CS treebank is huge, leads to amazing results for SK, leaving the supervised "upper-bound" far behind.

Table 3 shows our results in comparison to the second-best system of (Tiedemann, 2017). When evaluating with LAS, our system clearly outperforms them by a large margin for all three languages; however, the score difference practically disappears for NO and HR and is greatly diminished for SK when UAS is used for evaluation instead. We hypothesize that most of these additional gains in LAS are due to the deprel normalization, which (Tiedemann, 2017) might not have employed, and which is bound to have negligible effect on UAS. This belief is also strongly supported by the estimated improvement brought by the normalization component according to the ablation analysis (see next paragraph), which very tightly corresponds to the amount of lead we lose when going from LAS to UAS evaluation.

Table 4 reports the ablation analysis performed on the dev treebanks to estimate the effect of individual components. We report the deterioration

System	SK	HR	NO
LAS			
Our	78.12	60.70	70.21
Tiedemann	73.14	57.98	68.60
UAS			
Our	84.92	69.73	77.13
Tiedemann	82.87	69.57	76.77

Table 3: Comparison of LAS and UAS scores of our system and the second-best system.

Component	SK	HR	NO
Normalize source annotations	2.50	3.11	1.67
Translate word forms	7.04	**5.02**	**6.66**
Pre-train form embeddings	2.83	3.88	5.28
Cross-tag	**11.36**	—	2.92
Add morphological features	2.09	1.70	1.43

Table 4: Ablation analysis: reduction of LAS score when removing various components.

in LAS versus our best setup[15] that occurs when a given component is removed.[16] This serves as an indication of the improvement brought by the component; it is not exact due to some interplay of the components and overlapping of their effects. The "Cross-tag" component refers to the joint effect of any cross-tagging steps used for the respective languages. Similarly, "Add morphological features" refers to adding only the *Case* feature for HR and NO, but adding both *Case* and shared morphological features for SK.

Overall, the most important component seems to be the translation of word forms, leading to improvements of +5 to +7 LAS. This seems to confirm our initial hypothesis that for very close languages, much of the gap between the baseline and the supervised parser can be bridged by appropriate lexicalization. However, the single largest improvement (+11.36 LAS) is achieved by target-xtag of SK, probably because the CS treebank is enormous and because CS and SK are extremely close languages. Other components also brought very nice improvements, amounting to +2.7 LAS on average per component and language.

7 Discussion and Future Work

Overall, our setup has achieved very good results. It surpassed all other submissions to the shared task on each language in both LAS and UAS, halv-

ing the gap between the baseline and the supervised parser for two of the languages and even far exceeding supervised for the third. The result for CS-SK shows that for pairs of very similar languages, the usefulness of cross-lingual methods can go beyond the realm of under-resourced languages, improving even upon respectable supervised setups; even better results could probably be obtained by a combination of both.

As we use many of the components in the same way for all of the languages with no need of manual adaptation or evaluation on target data, our approach could also be easily applied to other languages; we plan to do that in the near future.

Other components are unfortunately not applicable to new data in a straightforward manner. We employed cross-tagging in a different way for each of the languages, and although we offered possible explanations of why particular setups work best for particular languages, it is an open question whether these explanations can also be used to guide setting up a system for a new language pair. Furthermore, the annotation normalization has to be devised manually for each of the source and target languages.[17]

Although we found that the translation is the most important component of our pipeline, we have yet to evaluate it properly and identify potential ways to improve its performance.

We also believe that further increases in accuracy may be obtained by substituting UDPipe with a brand new tagger and/or parser that would feature current improvements in the field.

To allow other researchers to examine and/or apply our approach, we have freely released the source codes[18] and models.[19]

Acknowledgments

The work was supported by the grant 15-10472S of the Czech Science Foundation, SVV grant of Charles University, and by the EU project H2020-ICT-2014-1-644402. This work has been using language resources and tools developed, stored and distributed by the LINDAT/CLARIN project of the Ministry of Education, Youth and Sports of the Czech Republic (project LM2015071).

---

[15]For SK, we use the post-deadline setup which combines *Case* and shared morphological features.

[16]For MT, we take the best setup without cross-tagging as the basis, since the performance of the cross-tagger without MT is low and would obscure the effect of the MT itself.

[17]Or rather for the respective treebanks than languages, since the annotation differences do not necessarily correspond to real differences between the languages.

[18]http://hdl.handle.net/11234/1-1970

[19]http://hdl.handle.net/11234/1-1971

References

Lauriane Aufrant, Guillaume Wisniewski, and François Yvon. 2016. Zero-resource dependency parsing: Boosting delexicalized cross-lingual transfer with linguistic knowledge. In *Proceedings of COLING 2016, the 26th International Conference on Computational Linguistics: Technical Papers*, pages 119–130, Osaka, Japan, December. The COLING 2016 Organizing Committee.

Peter F. Brown, Peter V. Desouza, Robert L. Mercer, Vincent J. Della Pietra, and Jenifer C. Lai. 1992. Class-based n-gram models of natural language. *Computational linguistics*, 18(4):467–479.

Sabine Buchholz and Erwin Marsi. 2006. CoNLL-X shared task on multilingual dependency parsing. In *Proceedings of the Tenth Conference on Computational Natural Language Learning*, CoNLL-X '06, pages 149–164, Stroudsburg, PA, USA. Association for Computational Linguistics.

Michael Collins, Lance Ramshaw, Jan Hajič, and Christoph Tillmann. 1999. A statistical parser for Czech. In *Proceedings of the 37th Annual Meeting of the Association for Computational Linguistics on Computational Linguistics*, ACL '99, pages 505–512, Stroudsburg, PA, USA. Association for Computational Linguistics.

Matthew S. Dryer and Martin Haspelmath, editors. 2013. *WALS Online*. Max Planck Institute for Evolutionary Anthropology, Leipzig.

Long Duong, Trevor Cohn, Steven Bird, and Paul Cook. 2015. Cross-lingual transfer for unsupervised dependency parsing without parallel data. In *CoNLL*, pages 113–122.

Martin Wittorff Haulrich. 2012. *Data-driven bitext dependency parsing and alignment*. Copenhagen Business School, Department of International Business Communication.

Rebecca Hwa, Philip Resnik, Amy Weinberg, Clara Cabezas, and Okan Kolak. 2005. Bootstrapping parsers via syntactic projection across parallel texts. *Natural Language Engineering*, 11:11–311.

Ryan McDonald, Slav Petrov, and Keith Hall. 2011. Multi-source transfer of delexicalized dependency parsers. In *Proceedings of Empirical Methods in Natural Language Processing (EMNLP)*.

Tomas Mikolov, Ilya Sutskever, Kai Chen, Gregory S. Corrado, and Jeffrey Dean. 2013. Distributed representations of words and phrases and their compositionality. In *Advances in Neural Information Processing Systems 26: 27th Annual Conference on Neural Information Processing Systems 2013. Proceedings of a meeting held December 5-8, 2013, Lake Tahoe, Nevada, United States.*, pages 3111–3119.

Joakim Nivre, Johan Hall, Sandra Kübler, Ryan McDonald, Jens Nilsson, Sebastian Riedel, and Deniz Yuret. 2007. The CoNLL 2007 shared task on dependency parsing. In *Proceedings of the CoNLL Shared Task Session of EMNLP-CoNLL 2007*, pages 915–932, Prague, Czech Republic, June. Association for Computational Linguistics.

Joakim Nivre, Marie-Catherine de Marneffe, Filip Ginter, Yoav Goldberg, Jan Hajič, Christopher Manning, Ryan McDonald, Slav Petrov, Sampo Pyysalo, Natalia Silveira, Reut Tsarfaty, and Daniel Zeman. 2016. Universal dependencies v1: A multilingual treebank collection. In *Proceedings of the 10th International Conference on Language Resources and Evaluation (LREC 2016)*, pages 1659–1666, Portorož, Slovenia.

Franz Josef Och and Hermann Ney. 2003. A systematic comparison of various statistical alignment models. *Computational Linguistics*, 29(1):19–51.

Martin Popel and Zdeněk Žabokrtský. 2010. TectoMT: Modular NLP framework. In *Proceedings of IceTAL, 7th International Conference on Natural Language Processing, Reykjavík, Iceland, August 17, 2010*, pages 293–304. Springer.

Loganathan Ramasamy, David Mareček, and Zdeněk Žabokrtský. 2014. Multilingual dependency parsing: Using machine translated texts instead of parallel corpora. *The Prague Bulletin of Mathematical Linguistics*, 102:93–104.

Mohammad Sadegh Rasooli and Michael Collins. 2015. Density-driven cross-lingual transfer of dependency parsers. In *EMNLP*, pages 328–338.

Rudolf Rosa and Zdeněk Žabokrtský. 2015. KL_{cpos^3} – a language similarity measure for delexicalized parser transfer. In *ACL (2)*, pages 243–249.

Rudolf Rosa, Ondřej Dušek, David Mareček, and Martin Popel. 2012. Using parallel features in parsing of machine-translated sentences for correction of grammatical errors. In *Proceedings of the Sixth Workshop on Syntax, Semantics and Structure in Statistical Translation*, SSST-6 '12, pages 39–48, Stroudsburg, PA, USA. Association for Computational Linguistics.

Milan Straka, Jan Hajič, and Jana Straková. 2016. UDPipe: trainable pipeline for processing CoNLL-U files performing tokenization, morphological analysis, POS tagging and parsing. In *Proceedings of the Tenth International Conference on Language Resources and Evaluation (LREC'16)*, Paris, France, May. European Language Resources Association (ELRA).

Oscar Täckström, Ryan McDonald, and Jakob Uszkoreit. 2012. Cross-lingual word clusters for direct transfer of linguistic structure. In *Proceedings of the 2012 Conference of the North American Chapter of the Association for Computational Linguistics:*

Human Language Technologies, NAACL HLT '12, pages 477–487, Stroudsburg, PA, USA. Association for Computational Linguistics.

Oscar Täckström, Ryan T. McDonald, and Joakim Nivre. 2013. Target language adaptation of discriminative transfer parsers. In Lucy Vanderwende, Hal Daumé III, and Katrin Kirchhoff, editors, *Human Language Technologies: Conference of the North American Chapter of the Association of Computational Linguistics, Proceedings, June 9-14, 2013, Westin Peachtree Plaza Hotel, Atlanta, Georgia, USA*, pages 1061–1071. The Association for Computational Linguistics.

Jörg Tiedemann. 2014. Rediscovering annotation projection for cross-lingual parser induction. In *Proceedings of COLING 2014, the 25th International Conference on Computational Linguistics: Technical Papers*, pages 1854–1864, August.

Jörg Tiedemann. 2017. Cross-lingual dependency parsing for closely related languages – Helsinki's submission to VarDial 2017. In *Proceedings of the Fourth Workshop on NLP for Similar Languages, Varieties and Dialects (VarDial)*, Valencia, Spain.

William E. Winkler. 1990. String comparator metrics and enhanced decision rules in the Fellegi-Sunter model of record linkage. In *Proceedings of the Section on Survey Research*, pages 354–359.

David Yarowsky and Grace Ngai. 2001. Inducing multilingual POS taggers and NP bracketers via robust projection across aligned corpora. In *Proceedings of the Second Meeting of the North American Chapter of the Association for Computational Linguistics*, Pittsburgh, Pennsylvania. Association for Computational Linguistics.

Marcos Zampieri, Shervin Malmasi, Nikola Ljubešić, Preslav Nakov, Ahmed Ali, Jörg Tiedemann, Yves Scherrer, and Noëmi Aepli. 2017. Findings of the VarDial evaluation campaign 2017. In *Proceedings of the Fourth Workshop on NLP for Similar Languages, Varieties and Dialects (VarDial)*, Valencia, Spain.

Daniel Zeman and Philip Resnik. 2008. Cross-language parser adaptation between related languages. In *Workshop on NLP for Less-Privileged Languages, IJCNLP*, Hyderabad, India.

Daniel Zeman, Ondřej Dušek, David Mareček, Martin Popel, Loganathan Ramasamy, Jan Štěpánek, Zdeněk Žabokrtský, and Jan Hajič. 2014. HamleDT: Harmonized multi-language dependency treebank. *Language Resources and Evaluation*, 48(4):601–637.

Daniel Zeman. 2008. Reusable tagset conversion using tagset drivers. In *Proceedings of the 6th International Conference on Language Resources and Evaluation (LREC 2008)*, pages 213–218, Marrakech, Morocco. European Language Resources Association.

Author Index